Wealth, Land, and Property in Angola

Exploring the multifaceted history of dispossession, consumption, and inequality in West Central Africa, Mariana P. Candido presents a revisionist history of Angola from the sixteenth century until the Berlin Conference of 1884–85. Synthesizing disparate strands of scholarship, including the histories of slavery, land tenure, and gender in West Central Africa, Candido makes a significant contribution to ongoing historical debates. She demonstrates how ideas about dominion and land rights informed the appropriation and enslavement of free people and their labor. By centering the experiences of West Central Africans, and especially African women, this book challenges dominant historical narratives and shows that securing property was a gendered process. Drawing attention to how archives obscure African forms of knowledge and normalize conquest, Candido interrogates simplistic interpretations of ownership and pushes for the decolonization of African history.

Mariana P. Candido is Associate Professor at Emory University and a specialist on West Central African history, 1500–1880. Her publications include *An African Slaving Port and the Atlantic World* (2013), *African Women in the Atlantic World* (co-edited 2019), and *Crossing Memories* (co-edited 2011).

T0382464

African Studies Series

The African Studies series, founded in 1968, is a prestigious series of monographs, general surveys, and textbooks on Africa covering history, political science, anthropology, economics, and ecological and environmental issues. The series seeks to publish work by senior scholars as well as the best new research.

Editorial Board:
David Anderson, *The University of Warwick*
Carolyn Brown, *Rutgers University, New Jersey*
Christopher Clapham, *University of Cambridge*
Richard Roberts, *Stanford University, California*
Leonardo A. Villalón, *University of Florida*

Other titles in the series are listed at the back of the book.

Wealth, Land, and Property in Angola

A History of Dispossession, Slavery, and Inequality

Mariana P. Candido

Emory University

CAMBRIDGE
UNIVERSITY PRESS

Shaftesbury Road, Cambridge CB2 8EA, United Kingdom

One Liberty Plaza, 20th Floor, New York, NY 10006, USA

477 Williamstown Road, Port Melbourne, VIC 3207, Australia

314–321, 3rd Floor, Plot 3, Splendor Forum, Jasola District Centre, New Delhi – 110025, India

103 Penang Road, #05-06/07, Visioncrest Commercial, Singapore 238467

Cambridge University Press is part of Cambridge University Press & Assessment, a department of the University of Cambridge.

We share the University's mission to contribute to society through the pursuit of education, learning and research at the highest international levels of excellence.

www.cambridge.org
Information on this title: www.cambridge.org/9781316511503

DOI: 10.1017/9781009052986

First published 2022

A catalogue record for this publication is available from the British Library.

Library of Congress Cataloging-in-Publication Data
Names: Candido, Mariana P. (Mariana Pinho), 1975– author.
Title: Wealth, land, and property in Angola : a history of dispossession, slavery, and inequality / Mariana P. Candido, Emory University.
Description: New York : Cambridge University Press, [2022] | Series: African studies series | Includes bibliographical references and index.
Identifiers: LCCN 2022025822 (print) | LCCN 2022025823 (ebook) | ISBN 9781316511503 (hardback) | ISBN 9781009055987 (paperback) | ISBN 9781009052986 (epub)
Subjects: LCSH: Wealth–Angola–History. | Land tenure–Angola–History. | Property–Angola–History. | Angola–Economic conditions. | Angola–Social conditions. | BISAC: HISTORY / Africa / General
Classification: LCC HC950 .C36 2022 (print) | LCC HC950 (ebook) | DDC 330.967/303–dc23/eng/20220616
LC record available at https://lccn.loc.gov/2022025822
LC ebook record available at https://lccn.loc.gov/2022025823

ISBN 978-1-316-51150-3 Hardback
ISBN 978-1-009-05598-7 Paperback

Contents

Maps and Plans

Illustrations

Tables and Graphs

Acknowledgments

Many people have helped me find my way while I have been writing this book, listening to my ideas and encouraging me during this long process. The research and writing for this book would not have been possible without the support of several institutions, friends, and family. I began the archival research while I was teaching at the University of Kansas, where I benefited from the feedback of generous scholars such as Elizabeth MacGonagle, Elizabeth Kuznesof, and Marta Vicente. The University of Notre Dame allowed me to travel to Angola and Portugal and do most of the archival research for this book. Several colleagues read my grant proposals and earlier drafts and shared with me their knowledge, perspectives, and careful feedback. At the University of Notre Dame, I benefited from an intellectual community of scholars interested in Africa, African diaspora, race, and gender issues, which includes Karen Graubart, Paul Ocobock, Richard Pierce, Vanesa Miseres, Dianne Pinderhughes, Mike Amezcua, Jaimie Bleck, Cat Bolten, Liang Cai, Ilenin Kondo, Nikhil Menon, Magdalena Lopez, Korey Garibaldi, Esteban Salas, Francisco Robles, Sophie White, Sarah Quesada, and Marcio Bahia. Karen Graubart has been a tireless reader and interlocutor, and I am grateful for her friendship. I am also very thankful for all the support the Kellogg Institute for International Studies, the Institute of Liberal Studies, and the department of history provided me over the years, making it possible to spend months reading legal cases in Benguela and colonial correspondence in Luanda as well as taking an academic leave to write the first draft of this book. An American Philosophical Society Research Grant allowed me to do research in Brazilian archives. An American Council of Learned Societies fellowship provided me teaching release, so I could focus on this project. The final revisions were done after I joined a supportive community of Africanists at Emory University in 2020 during the COVID-19 global pandemic.

Several undergraduate and graduate students at Notre Dame heard me talk about this book project or read drafts of chapters. I had the privilege of having incredible research assistants, Mita Ramani, Akua

Agyei-Boateng, and Victoria Erdel. Esteban Salas read drafts and helped me track down primary sources while doing his own dissertation research. I learned a lot from graduate students in my seminars, and my reading and writing were shaped by their insights and our class discussion. In addition, Estaban Salas, Catalina Ararat Ospina, Natália Bueno, Ashley Greene, Heather Stanfiel, Dylan LaBlanc, Anna Vicenzi, John Nelson, Alexa McCall, Ana Sanchez Ramirez, Dan Fischer, Emily Smith, Noe Pliego Campos, Catherine Perl, Heather Lane, Erica Hasting Snader, Lauren Hamblen, Jessica Brockmole, Ian Van Dyke, Grace Song, and James Breen became part of my broader community and Notre Dame. Since I joined Emory, Madelyn Stone, Georgia Brunner, Anjuli Webster, Ursula Rall, Sonia Wind, and Olivia Cocking have also enriched my analysis and I have learned a lot from their own work.

Archivists in Angola and Portugal made my life easier and shared with me the excitement of finding familiar names in different documents. I would not have been able to write this book without the patience and dedication of the staff of Arquivo Histórico Ultramarino, Arquivo Nacional da Torre do Tombo, Biblioteca da Sociedade de Geografia de Lisboa, and Biblioteca Nacional de Lisboa, in Portugal. I also need to stress the professionalism of archivists and librarians at the Instituto Histórico Geográfico Brasil, in particular Regina Wanderley. At the Arquivo Nacional de Angola, I am grateful for all the support I have received over the years. Alexandra Aparicio, Rosa Cruz e Silva, Honoré Mbunga, Edna Lucília Pereira Cruz, Dominga Rodrigues, and Paula Alexandra da Costa have hosted me several time at the archives. Over the years, Mateus Neto, the late Fernando Gamboa, and Januário Silva brought me too many boxes and códices of documents. The Arquivo Nacional de Angola is a special place due to the hard work of archivists, who shared my excitement about reading historical documents. In Luanda, João Lourenço, Aurora Ferreira, Vladimiro Fortuna, and Contança Ceita provided much needed guidance and intellectual support. Herminia Barbosa, Verena, and Massalo shared their Luanda with me, and I am grateful for their friendship and guidance over the years.

This book is possible because the Universidade Katyavala Bwila hosted me on several occasions and helped me get access to the documents stored at the Nossa Senhora do Pópulo church and the Tribunal da Comarca de Benguela. Albano Ferreira, Alberto Quitembo, Ermelinda Cardoso, Manuel Tuca, and Juelma Matos Ngala have been following this project for many years, helping me to navigate bureaucracy and last-minute changes. Cristóvão Kajibanga and Helena Benjamin, as directors of the Secretaria da Cultura and Museu de Antropologia, respectively, have also provided guidance and support while I was struggling to have access to the Tribunal da Comarca de Benguela. Helena Benjamin, Cristóvao Kajibanga, Paula Gomes, Juelma Matos, and Ana Duarte shared their stories, calulú, quizaka, kissangua, and laughers with me, making every trip to Benguela a special occasion. I am also grateful for all the exchanges with the ISCED/ Benguela faculty, as well as with colleagues in the Faculdade de Direito, particularly Manuel Tomás Tchakamba, Sónia dos Santos Silva, and Paulino Lukamba. At the Tribunal da Comarca de Benguela, Judge Catarina literally opened doors to me and showed me rooms filled with legal cases waiting for historians willing to spend time in Benguela. Obrigada do fundo do meu coração a todos em Luanda e Benguela que me apoiaram e que dividiram esse projeto comigo.

Mariana Armond Dias Paes and Juelma Matos became research partners and co-authors in the process of organizing, identifying, and reading legal cases, and I have learned a lot from them. I have benefited from their input, their patience, and their friendship, and I hope our ongoing collaborations will last many decades.

An incredible group of generous scholars read earlier drafts and heard unfinished thoughts of many of the findings I present here. Colleen Kriger, Lorelle Semley, Eugénia Rodrigues, Hilary Jones, Morgan Robinson, Walter Hawthorne, Adam Jones, Assan Sarr, Ademide Adelusi-Adeluyi, Roquinaldo Ferreira, Zack Kagan-Guthrie, Daniel Domingues da Silva, Kazuo Kobayashi, Pamela Scully, Monica Lima, Adriana Chira, Walter Rucker, Ana Catarina Teixeira, Tom Rogers, Yanna Yannakakis, and Benjamin Lawrance pushed me to go further. Beatrix Heintze, John Thornton, Vanessa Oliveira, and Crislayne Alfagali shared sources and their own research findings with me, answered email queries, and provided me valuable feedback.

Encouraging scholars read the entire manuscript and offered valuable criticism and insights. I am always amazed by the generosity of fellow historians who sent me detailed notes and suggestions, in particular Ana Lucia Araujo, Kristin Mann, Suzanne Schwarz, Kathleen Sheldon, Toby Green, Mariana Armond Dias Paes, and Clifton Crais. I also benefited from the comments and suggestions of two anonymous readers.

English is my third language, and a team of copy editors have helped me to produce this book. Kathleen Sheldon, Cyndy Brown, Kristy Johnson, and Katie Van Heest have read different versions of this book and provided much-needed help. I am also grateful to the Institute of Liberal Studies at the University of Notre Dame, particularly Ken Garcia, and Allison Adams, from the Center for Faculty Development and Excellence at Emory University, who provided the funds to cover copy editing expenses. In a moment when universities aim to be global while cutting support for faculty research support, it is a privilege to have received generous financial support. Joe Crespino, Chair of the History Department, Allison Adam, Associate Director of the Research and Scholarly Writing Center, and Deboleena Roy, Senior Associate Dean of Faculty, have provided invaluable support in my transition to Emory University during a global pandemic. Their understanding and assistance alleviated much of the stress related to finishing a book in a non-native language. Aharon deGrassi assisted me with mapmaking. Cambridge University Press editors and staff, especially Maria Marsh, Atifa Jiwa, Stephanie Taylor, and Hemalatha Subramanian, helped me make this book a reality.

My family has always supported me. My mother, Roseli Maria Valente Pinho, has always been an inspiration and a great listener. My mother, an unapologetic feminist, was an example of a woman forced to juggle with too many things. Unfortunately, she was unable to see the result of so many trips to Angola and Portugal. My mother was a tireless supporter, and she would be very happy to see this book in print. Like my mother, my father, Roberto José de Alagão e Candido, departed too soon. I miss them daily, while trying to maintain their tenacity and love for knowledge. I dedicate this book to them. My sisters Isabela, Fernanda, and Joana are the best cheering crowd, and they have kept me grounded. I grew up surrounded by strong women, and I hope this book does justice to all the love and support I have received from all of them. Although studying and jobs have taken me away from Rio de Janeiro and the proximity of my family, I am profoundly shaped by my grandparents and my parents and their never-ending search for a more inclusive society. Their dreams and fights for social justice shaped my daily decisions. My friends Gabriela Medina, Alessandra Carvalho, Adriana Trindade, Claudia Souza, Monica Lima, Susana Draper, and Ana Lucia Araujo encouraged and held me when I most needed. Yacine Daddi Addoun has followed this project from its inception and had heard more about land and property rights in Angola than he ever imagined or wanted to know. My intellectual debt to Yacine is unquantifiable, neither can I describe or measure the sacrifices he has made to join me on trips to Angola and Portugal or in our several relocations within the United States. Without his support, I would not have been able to finish this book.

A Note on Currency
and Price-Level Adjustments

The *mil réis* was a unit of account rather than a currency, and its value varied substantially between Portugal and its overseas colonies. The unit was the real (plural réis), and the sign $ was used to designate the thousands. This way, 1 real is written as $001, and 1,000 réis or mil reís (one thousand réis) is 1$000.

Metal coins circulated in Portugal and its colonies. The chief silver coins were tostão, equivalent to 100 réis; the crusado was $400 or 400 réis. Gold coins were available in the amounts of 4$800 or 4,800, 5$000 or 5,000, and 8$000 or 8,000 réis. For larger amounts, there was the conto, which designated one million. One conto de reis was represented as 1.000$000 (one million réis).

In 1865, Lisbon authorities established bank succursal (Banco Nacional Ultramarino) in the colonies and controlled a fifteen-year monopoly over banking and issuing of notes in Angola, among other colonial territories. The Banco Nacional Ultramarino also provided loans and urban mortgages. Despite any attempts to maintain parity between the metropolitan réis and the réis in Portuguese colonies, in Angola the use of the expression *réis fortes* (strong reis) and *réis fracos* to indicate the currency devaluation in comparison to the metropolitan counterpart was widespread. In 1872, colonial currencies went through a series of reforms to address fluctuations, although the problem persisted, with primary sources from the 1870s and 1880s making extensive reference to *réis fracos* and *réis fortes*. Metric weight measures were also introduced.[1]

After 1910, with the overthrow of the monarchy and the implementation of the Republic government, the escudo replaced the real, a currency associated with the monarchy. The main challenge for historians is to

---

[1] *Collecção da legislação novíssima do ultramar* (Lisbon: Imprensa Nacional, 1901), 1019–1029; *Encyclopaedia Britannica: Or, Dictionary of Arts, Sciences, and General Literature*, vol. 18, eighth edition (Boston, MA: Little, Brown, & Company, 1859), 398; W. G. Clarence-Smith, *The Third Portuguese Empire, 1825–1975: A Study in Economic Imperialism* (Manchester: Manchester University Press, 1985), 68–70, 72–73.

convert a specific amount to a general price level, considering the discrepancy and variation within the Portuguese empire.

According to Gervase Clarence Smith, the number of mil réis to the pound sterling was

Year	Pound sterling
1820	4.62
1830	5.58
1844	4.53
1853	4.50
1876	4.52
1880	4.48

Source: W. G. Clarence Smith, *The Third Portuguese Empire, 1825–1975: A Study in Economic Imperialism* (Manchester: Manchester University Press, 1985), 227.

Measuring the worth of nineteenth-century réis in terms of current values is complicated, and it does not consider the inflation of Portuguese réis in Angola. I have relied on the "Currency Converter: 1270–2017" database, available at the National Archives, United Kingdom, to calculate equivalency and purchasing power. As stated in the National Archives website, "the result of the calculation is intended to be a general guide to historical value, rather than a categorical statement of fact."[2] All currency conversion and its equivalency must be taken as approximations and not as a certain measurement of worth. I realize the conversion exercise is important but also fraught and subject to criticisms that will be made as soon as readers finish reading this sentence.

[2] www.nationalarchives.gov.uk/currency-converter/, consulted March 3, 2021. Also very useful to understand worth calculation is www.measuringworth.com/ (consulted March 3, 2021).

Introduction
A History of Ownership, Dispossession, and Inequality

The mechanisms whereby Africans managed and expressed wealth and rights, including over people, have been a central concern of Africanists for the past five decades. The idea is that the accumulation of dependents, known as wealth in people, was a key organizing principle in the lives of West Central Africans. If this argument is true, why did coastal populations as well as nearby rulers, called *sobas*, *dembos*, or *somas*, claim and register land in the seventeenth and eighteenth centuries? Rulers, commoners, and colonial settlers entered into a series of disputes over property in the nineteenth century. Why would purchased chairs, tea sets, and silk socks be valued as assets in postmortem wills of West Central Africans? The violent systems and structures of colonization produced problematic and simplified interpretations of the African past. Colonial officers, missionaries, anthropologists, jurists, and historians perpetuated images of African societies as isolated and excluded from global processes. However, by emphasizing the absence of landed property as a central feature of African societies, scholars have overlooked how vital land was in securing social belonging, obligation, and protection. More often than not, the perspectives of West Central Africans on wealth, accumulation, and rights became invisible or exoticized in the scholarship as primitive, backward, or simplistic.

Since the 1960s, Africanist historians have argued that there was a surplus of land in the continent, which meant that wealth was accumulated through lineages and dependents rather than land.[1] This, according to these historians, explained the existence of slavery in the continent, before the contact with Europeans on the Atlantic Coast, as a form

---

[1] The literature on this subject is vast. See, among others, Jack Goody, *Technology, Tradition, and the State in Africa* (London: Oxford University Press, 1971), 21–37; J. D. Fage, "Slaves and Society in Western Africa, c. 1445- c.1700," *Journal of African History* 21, no. 3 (1980): 289–310; Antony G. Hopkins, "Property Rights and Empire Building: Britain's Annexation of Lagos, 1861," *The Journal of Economic History* 40, no. 4 (1980): 777–98; Joseph C. Miller, *Way of Death: Merchant Capitalism and the Angolan Slave Trade, 1730-1830* (Madison, WI: University of Wisconsin Press, 1988), 42–53.

of wealth accumulation. But Ndembu (such as Caculo Cacahenda), Ndombes, and Kakondas, as well as other populations that inhabited West Central Africa north and south of the Kwanza River (see Map I.1), clashed over land use and rights. Land could not have been widely available, nor was it "empty" as colonial administrators claimed in the seventeenth, eighteenth, and nineteenth centuries, a trope scholars helped to perpetuate.[2] Theories of unoccupied land, or land surplus, were laid in the tomes of colonial officers and jurists, seeking to justify the expropriation of land, European conquest, and settlement, a process parallel to what happened in the Americas. These arguments dismissed the rights of transhumance and the social role of land, as burial sites inhabited by ancestors and their spirits.

It was accepted that the main goal of West Central African heads of lineages and rulers was to accumulate people and mobilize their labor and not necessarily to amass land, which was free and plentiful.[3] According to the concept of wealth in people, land was abundant in the region, and thus powerful rulers and heads of lineages accumulated dependents who could provide labor. These dependents could be wives, children, impoverished migrants, or enslaved individuals who were put to work in the fields and generated more patrimony, more prestige, and more capital to recruit even more dependents. Rights-in-persons has been viewed as "an integral part of the African system of kinship and marriage" that shaped all social relationships, creating bonds of rights, obligation, respect, and protection. Rights could "be manipulated to increase the number of people in one's kin group, to gather dependents and supporters, and to build up wealth and power."[4]

[2] Jack Goody, *Death, Property and the Ancestors* (Stanford, CA: Stanford University Press, 1962); A. G. Hopkins, *An Economic History of West Africa* (New York: Columbia University Press, 1973); Gareth Austin, *Labour, Land, and Capital in Ghana: From Slavery to Free Labour in Asante, 1807-1956* (Rochester, NY: University of Rochester Press, 2005); Susan M. Martin, *Palm Oil and Protest: An Economic History of the Ngwa Region, South-Eastern Nigeria, 1800-1980* (New York: Cambridge University Press, 2006).

[3] Jan Vansina, *Paths in the Rainforests: Toward a History of Political Tradition in Equatorial Africa* (Madison, WI: University of Wisconsin Press, 1990), 251; Miller, *Way of Death*, 43–52; Wyatt MacGaffey, *Kongo Political Culture: The Conceptual Challenge of the Particular* (Bloomington, IN: Indiana University Press, 2000), 215–16; John K. Thornton, *Africa and Africans in the Making of the Atlantic World, 1400-1800* (New York: Cambridge University Press, 1998), 87–95. For non-West Central African specialists, see Hopkins, *An Economic History of West Africa*; Antony G. Hopkins, "The New Economic History of Africa," *The Journal of African History* 50, no. 2 (2009): 155–77.

[4] Suzanne Miers and Igor Kopytoff, eds., *Slavery in Africa: Historical and Anthropological Perspectives* (University of Wisconsin Press, 1977), 7 and 9; Goody, *Death, Property and the Ancestors*.

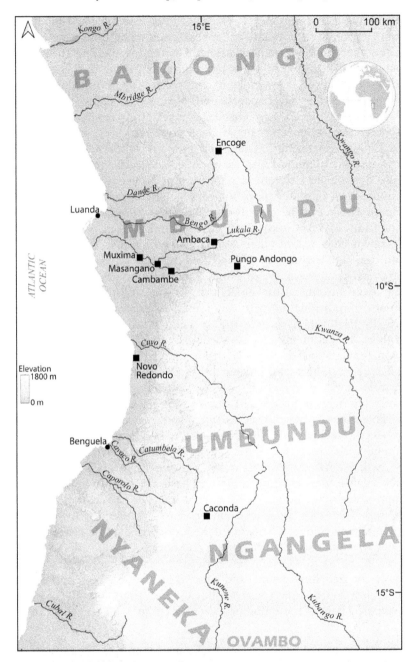

Map I.1 West Central Africa

Immovable and human property tend to be examined separately, but dispossession of African land and natural resources was intimately linked to the appropriation and enslavement of free people and their labor. Land ownership, property, gender, and law all relate to the Africanist historiography; let us extend this conversation to also include control over labor and enslaved people. On that argumentative foundation, *Wealth, Land, and Property* challenges a set of assumptions that views property and ownership rights as stable European ideas associated with the Enlightenment, civilization, and modernity, where African actors were unable to comprehend, or at least faced difficulty in exercising, rights due to their attachment to the accumulation of dependents.[5] As in Europe, West Central African societies had notions of rights and ownership systems, not necessarily homogeneous throughout the region. Mbundu, Ndombe, and other West Central African populations had clear ownership regimes that clashed with each other. The dispute over land use and rights was exacerbated by the arrival of Portuguese intruders, resulting in more disputes and adaptation, and adjusted to new ideas introduced by colonialism. In the early nineteenth century, notions of individual property were not stable or well defined, particularly in Portugal, as jurists and colonial officers portrayed in their writings. It was in the process of implementing such notions in their colonies that allowed the range of ideas regarding property systems to fully emerge and get consolidated in the books. Control over land plays a big role in this story; likewise, locals and foreigners clashed over the ownership rights of people and material objects as well.

The supremacy of the wealth in people concept has obscured the process through which Portuguese agents seized land from the Ndombe, Mbundu, Kakonda, Kilengues, and other groups that once inhabited the region north and south of the Kwanza River. This book pushes back against the historiographic emphasis on "rights in people" by emphasizing that land in West Central Africa was scarce, not abundant, and also valued by those who inhabited it. The singular focus on the accumulation of dependents has done a disservice to the history of this region, helping to justify colonialism and normalize population displacement in the past. West Central African specialists have embraced this notion of rights-in-persons and pushed it forward as a cornerstone to understanding the social, political, and economic life of local societies. Many of these findings were based on a close analysis of late

---

[5] For more on the long and complicated history of European rights and law, see Tamar Herzog, *A Short History of European Law: The Last Two and a Half Millennia* (Cambridge, MA: Harvard University Press, 2018).

nineteenth- and early twentieth-century jurists, such as Lopo Vaz de Sampaio de Melo and Caetano Gonçalves, who wrote authoritative texts on property rights over the indigenous population of Angola.[6] Portuguese jurists sided with colonialism, and indeed represented it, attesting that indigenous Africans did not have notions of possession rights or individual ownership.

In the context of colonialism and "effective occupation" that shaped the late nineteenth century, the emergence of theories that supported the lack of indigenous effective occupation of their territory favored the legitimization of Portuguese power. Effective occupation, according to administrators and jurists, was to make land productive, not for those who live in it, but according to those interested in acquiring agricultural crops from the tropical regions of the world, such as sugarcane, coffee, or cotton. The rights of pastoral populations, most of those who lived south of the Kwanza River were herders, were dismissed. To make the opposite assertion, or to recognize that African societies had such rights over land and their jurisdiction, was, in many ways, to challenge the legitimacy of colonialism. Colonialism was based on the expropriation of land and resources, in part because European elites claimed that non-European populations, in Africa, the Americas, or in Asia, were incapable of comprehending and protecting the basic concept of ownership. Ethnographers and jurists provided the evidence for colonial claims and ideologies with their cumbersome theories, feeding colonial bureaucrats the notion of vacant land, the legitimacy of Europeans occupying and colonizing the world, and ignoring how the indigenous population conceived land use and rights, occupation, and possession.[7] Many of these Portuguese jurists never visited the region, yet scholars often

---

[6] Lopo Vaz de Sampaio e Melo, *Política indígena* (Porto: Magalhães & Moniz, 1910); Lopo Vaz de Sampaio e Melo, *Regime da propriedade indígena, separata da "Revista Portugueza Colonial e Marítima"* (Lisbon: Ferin Editora, 1910); Caetano Gonçalves, "O regime das terras e as reservas indígenas na colonização portuguesa," *Boletim Geral das Colónias* 2, no. 13 (1926): 26–45.

[7] Martin Chanock, "Paradigms, Policies and Property: A Review of the Customary Law of Land Tenure," in *Law in Colonial Africa*, ed. Kristin Mann and Richard L. Roberts (Portsmouth, NH: Heinemann, 1991), 74–75; Peter Pels, "The Anthropology of Colonialism: Culture, History, and the Emergence of Western Governmentality," *Annual Review of Anthropology* 26 (1997): 173; Saliha Belmessous, "Introduction: The Problem of Indigenous Claim Making in Colonial History," in *Native Claims: Indigenous Law against Empire, 1500-1920*, ed. Saliha Belmessous (New York: Oxford University Press, 2012), 3–18; Anthony Pagden, "Law, Colonization, Legitimation, and the European Background," in *The Cambridge History of Law in America*, ed. Michael Grossberg et al. (Cambridge, MA: Cambridge University Press, 2008), 22–24; José Vicente Serrão, "Property, Land and Territory in the Making of Overseas Empires," in *Property Rights, Land and Territory in the European Overseas Empires*, ed. José Vicente Serrão et al. (Lisbon: CEHC-IUL, 2014), 8–9, http://hdl.handle.net/10071/2718.

embrace the ideas that they put forward and never question the links between Portuguese ethnographers, jurist treaties, colonialism, and land occupation and exclusion.

The rise of global liberalism in the nineteenth century was followed by land expropriation and dispossession. Consolidated practices and laws protected individual rights, usually those of Europeans and their descendants, at the expense of indigenous populations. This is not to say, however, that inequality was a nineteenth-century phenomenon. Slavery, displacement, and dependency predated the nineteenth century in West Central Africa. Societies were hierarchical; elite members enjoyed a series of privileges while commoners varied in their status, including people held in bondage.[8] Treaties, land charts, and written documents reveal diverse notions of jurisdiction and rights that existed in the region. The imposition of colonial notions of individual property was met with continuous challenges by local African rulers, from centralized states such as Kakonda or Caculo Cacahenda to more decentralized polities such as the Ndombe. West Central African rulers made claims with their own designs of occupation and possession, considered legitimate and valid until the early nineteenth century. *Wealth, Land, and Property* draws attention to the nature of archives that normalize conquest, occupation, and exclusion, and which ultimately obscure West Central African forms of knowledge, ownership, and legitimacy.[9]

West Central Africa and Land Rights

Africans have long been historical global actors who influenced and were affected by events and societies located far away.[10] For more than five

---

[8] Jan Vansina, "Ambaca Society and the Slave Trade c. 1760-1845," *The Journal of African History* 46, no. 1 (2005): 1–27; Joseph C. Miller, "Imbangala Lineage Slavery," in *Slavery in Africa: Historical and Anthropological Perspectives*, ed. Suzanne Miers and Igor Kopytoff (Madison, WI: University of Wisconsin Press, 1977), 205–33; Joseph C. Miller, "Central Africans during the Era of the Slave Trade, c. 1490s-1850s," in *Central Africans and Cultural Transformations in the American Diaspora* (Cambridge: Cambridge University Press, 2001); John Thornton, "The Slave Trade in Eighteenth Century Angola: Effects on Demographic Structures," *Canadian Journal of African Studies* 14, no. 3 (1980): 417–27; John K. Thornton, "Cannibals, Witches, and Slave Traders in the Atlantic World," *The William and Mary Quarterly* 60, no. 2, Third Series (2003): 273–94; Roquinaldo Ferreira, "Slaving and Resistance to Slaving in West Central Africa," in *The Cambridge World History of Slavery*, ed. David Eltis and Stanley L. Engerman, vol. 3 (Cambridge, MA: Cambridge University Press, 2011), 111–31; Linda M. Heywood, "Slavery and Its Transformation in the Kingdom of Kongo: 1491-1800," *The Journal of African History* 50, no. 1 (2009): 1–22.

[9] Boaventura de Sousa Santos, *Epistemologies of the South: Justice Against Epistemicide* (London: Routledge, 2014), 174.

[10] For more on the idea of Africans as actors connected to global economies, see Jeremy Prestholdt, *Domesticating the World: African Consumerism and the Genealogies of Globalization*

centuries, West Central African societies were connected to distant markets abroad and inland. After the 1600s, they influenced how European empires conceived of and regulated ownership, as well as how they engaged in struggles over possession, control, and rights. The social lives of societies and objects tell us why and how people accumulated things over time and the ways in which they expressed rights and wealth. At a time of economic transformation, new notions of rights emerged, and written forms of claiming ownership were consolidated. Based on historical documents available in Angolan, Portuguese, and Brazilian archives, this book examines the economic transformation, which was associated with the Portuguese conquest and occupation, the expansion of the transatlantic slave trade, the implementation of a plantation economy, and the land rush along the West Central African Coast from the sixteenth to the nineteenth century.

Evidence from Angolan archives reveals that West Central Africans owned land, material objects, and people before the twentieth century, but in most of the studies published in the past fifty years, only their ownership of dependents is recognized, as if the lands they occupied were devoid of legitimate occupants creating historical narratives that normalize displacement, removal, and violence.[11] The social inequalities of the last century in Angola relate to the past and are legacies of imposition of individual property rights over collective ones at a specific historical moment, the mid-nineteenth century. Liberal principles of land use, productivity, and ownership are also normalized in narratives that take for granted that European rights have always recognized individual property while multiple jurisdictions in West Central Africa did not, without interrogating the historicization of these processes. In the mid-nineteenth

---

(Berkeley, CA: University of California Press, 2008); Colleen E. Kriger, *Making Money: Life, Death, and Early Modern Trade on Africa's Guinea Coast* (Athens, OH: Ohio University Press, 2017); Jelmer Vos, "Coffee, Cash, and Consumption: Rethinking Commodity Production in the Global South," *Radical History Review* 2018, no. 131 (2018): 183–88; Toby Green, *A Fistful of Shells: West Africa from the Rise of the Slave Trade to the Age of Revolution* (Chicago, IL: Chicago University Press, 2019).

[11] Vansina, *Paths in the Rainforests*, 251; Miller, *Way of Death*, 43–52; MacGaffey, *Kongo Political Culture*, 215–16; Thornton, *Africa and Africans*, 87–95 and Catarina Madeira Santos, "Luanda: A Colonial City between Africa and the Atlantic, Seventeenth and Eighteenth Century," in *Portuguese Colonial Cities in the Early Modern World*, ed. Liam M. Brockey (New York, NY: Ashgate Publishing, 2008), 249–70. As Carola Lentz and Assan Sarr have discussed in their books, this problem is not restricted to West Central Africa. See Carola Lentz, *Land, Mobility, and Belonging in West Africa* (Bloomington, IN: Indiana University Press, 2013); Assan Sarr, *Islam, Power, and Dependency in the Gambia River Basin: The Politics of Land Control, 1790-1940* (Rochester, NY: University of Rochester Press, 2016). For an analysis on the political economy of land in South Africa, see Clifton Crais, *Poverty, War, and Violence in South Africa* (New York, NY: Cambridge University Press, 2011), 122–41.

century, the introduction of land registration in Angola was part of a colonial discourse of emancipation of enslaved bodies, agricultural productivity, and modernization. These liberal ideals implied new forms of administration and governance that directly affected subjected bodies in overseas colonies. Or, as Lisa Lowe states, "The abstract promises of abolition, emancipation, and the end of monopoly often obscure their embeddedness within colonial conditions of settlement, slavery, coerced labor, and imperial trades."[12]

West Central Africa has a long history of interaction with the outside world. Long-distance trade caravans connected coastal communities to those located inland, and Portuguese explorers arrived in the Kongo Kingdom by the late fifteenth century. For more than three hundred years, the Portuguese monarchy sent explorers, missionaries, traders, and colonial officers to identify mineral and natural resources and occupy the territories along the West Central African coast, with varying degrees of success. Centralized states and strong armies, such as Matamba, prevented Portuguese incursion into the interior for most of the seventeenth and eighteenth centuries, although important colonial centers such as Ambaca and Caconda did emerge in territories earlier chiefdoms or states had ruled. During most of the period before the nineteenth century, empire building's purpose was to control trade routes and exercise monopoly over commercial hubs. The Portuguese colonial state was able to tax and control trade in human beings, but it also claimed the regions north and south of the Kwanza River as colonial possessions, labeling them the Kingdom of Angola and the Kingdom of Benguela by the early seventeenth century. Despite the Portuguese monarchical names, there was no head of state identified as the king of Benguela, in the manner that the Manikongo was the ruler of the Kingdom of Kongo. Luanda became the capital of the so-called Kingdom of Angola, a vast territory that included many states, such as Matamba or Kasanje, and the region of Kisama, which was not under colonial control.

This patchwork did not prevent the European cartographers from elaborating maps that created the illusion of cohesive and clearly defined territories under Portuguese control (Map I.2). From the 1620s to 1779, a *capitão mor* ruled Benguela reporting directly to Lisbon authorities. In 1779, Benguela became subordinate to the governor of Angola, who resided in the colonial center of Luanda. Portuguese colonial rule claimed control of land and people since the early seventeenth century.

---

[12] Lisa Lowe, *The Intimacies of Four Continents* (Durham, NC: Duke University Press, 2015), 16. See also Vos, "Coffee, Cash, and Consumption."

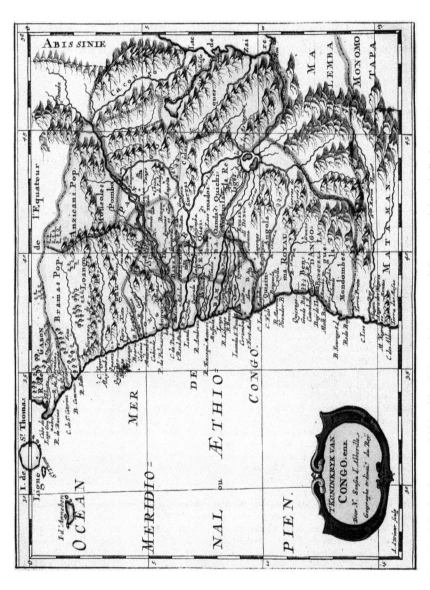

Map I.2 Nicolar Sanson d'Abbeville, "Map of the coast of Congo and Angola," circa 1650

9

Nonetheless, West Central Africans were classified as vassals or non-vassals; both groups exercised rights over their subjects and land, although vassals depended on Portuguese recognition.[13] By the nineteenth century, however, notions about rights and property recognition had begun to experience major transformations. The slow end of the transatlantic slave trade, officially banned in 1836 although it continued to operate until the mid-1860s, forced colonial authorities, settlers, and locals to reassess their economic options and priorities.

The label "West Central Africa" had varied meanings for the Portuguese, Dutch, English, and French at different historical moments. Historians, too, have defined the region in many ways.[14] *Wealth, Land, and Property* focuses mainly on the region that became known as "Reino de Benguela," or Kingdom of Benguela, after the Portuguese conquest and occupation of the territory south of the Kwanza River. It does, however, make several references to populations north of the Kwanza River, such as the Ndembo Caculo Cacahenda, who have produced a rich local archive documentation about their land rights. "West Central Africa" is vague and includes coastal and interior populations ranging

---

[13] For more on the early colonial encounter, see Beatrix Heintze, "Angola under Portuguese Rule: How It All Began," in *Africae Monumenta: a apropriação da escrita pelos africanos*, ed. Ana Paula Tavares and Catarina Madeira Santos, vol. 1 (Lisbon: IICT, 2002), 535–59; Catarina Madeira Santos, "Administrative Knowledge in a Colonial Context: Angola in the Eighteenth Century," *The British Journal for the History of Science* 43, no. 4 (2010): 539–56; John K Thornton, *A Cultural History of the Atlantic World, 1250-1820* (New York, NY: Cambridge University Press, 2012), 181–210; Mariana P. Candido, "Conquest, Occupation, Colonialism and Exclusion: Land Disputes in Angola," in *Property Rights, Land and Territory in the European Overseas Empires*, ed. José Vicente Serrão et al. (Lisbon: CEHC-IUL, 2014), 223–33, http://hdl .handle.net/10071/2718.

[14] For different definitions, see Miller, *Way of Death*, 7–8. Thornton, *Africa and Africans in the Making of the Atlantic World, 1400-1800*, 13, 19–20. Linda M. Heywood and John K. Thornton, *Central Africans, Atlantic Creoles, and the Making of the Foundation of the Americas, 1585-1660* (New York, NY: Cambridge University Press, 2007), 49. Phyllis Martin, *The External Trade of the Loango Coast, 1576-1870; the Effects of Changing Commercial Relations on the Vili Kingdom of Loango* (Oxford: Clarendon Press, 1972), 8–10; Phyllis M. Martin, "The Kingdom of Loango," in *Kongo Power and Majesty*, ed. Alisa Lagamma (New York and New Haven, CT: The Metropolitan Museum of Art and Yale University Press, 2015), 47–85; Johannes Postma, *The Dutch in the Atlantic Slave Trade* (New York, NY: Cambridge University Press, 1990), 60–61. Roquinaldo Ferreira, "The Suppression of the Slave Trade and Slave Departures from Angola, 1830-1860s," in *Extending the Frontiers: Essays on the New Transatlantic Slave Trade Database*, ed. David Eltis and David Richardson (New Haven, CT: Yale University Press, 2008), 313–15. Paul Tiyambe Zeleza, *The Study of Africa* (Dakar, Senegal: CODESRIA, 2006); Esperanza Brizuela-Garcia, "Towards a Critical Interdisciplinarity? African History and the Reconstruction of Universal Narratives," *Rethinking History* 12, no. 3 (2008): 299–316,; Roquinaldo Ferreira, "A institucionalização dos estudos Africanos nos Estados Unidos: advento, consolidação e transformações," *Revista Brasileira de História* 30, no. 59 (2010): 73–90.

from centralized states, chiefdoms, and stateless communities. African rulers controlled most of the territory, although parts of West Central Africa were under colonial control before the late nineteenth century. It includes Umbundu and Kimbundu speakers and important, and often neglected, non-Bantu populations.[15] Critically, there was no single centralized power south of the Kwanza River. Despite the lack of a centralized political unit, the Portuguese Crown went ahead and named the regions south of the Kwanza River as a kingdom – in part because they assumed the political organization would resemble the one they had encountered earlier in Kongo and north of the Kwanza River. Portuguese control of the territory was limited to coastal ports and certain inland locations rather than a continuous territorial occupation until the early twentieth century. Portuguese forces were small and weak and relied on political and commercial alliances with local rulers to survive. Yet their naming practices have survived and continue to influence how historians think and name territories, rulers, and people.[16]

Within the Portuguese empire, Luanda and Benguela operated with a bureaucracy and structure similar to that of Rio de Janeiro or Salvador da Bahia, although intimately connected to inland markets and states in West Central Africa. While Dutch, French, and English traders operated freely in the Loango coast ports, in part due to the decentralized nature of the Vili trading networks, the same was not true south of the Congo River. The Portuguese Crown established and defended their monopoly over the trade in human beings and natural resources such as ivory, wax, or copper from Luanda and Benguela since their foundation in 1575 and 1617, respectively.[17]

---

[15] For the non Bantu population, including the Kwandu groups, see Mariana P. Candido, *An African Slaving Port and the Atlantic World: Benguela and Its Hinterland* (New York, NY: Cambridge University Press, 2013), 46; R. P. Ch. Estermann, "Quelques observations sur les Bochimans !Kung de l'Angola Méridionale," *Anthropos* 41/44, no. 4/6 (July 1, 1946): 711–22.

[16] For more on this history, see Beatrix Heintze, "Ngonga a Mwiza: um sobado angolano sob domino português no século XVII.," *Revista Internacional de Estudos Africanos* 8–9 (1988): 221–34; Beatrix Heintze, "Luso-African Feudalism in Angola? The Vassal Treaties of the Sixteenth to the Eighteenth Century," *Separata da Revista Portuguesa de História* 18 (1980): 111–31; Candido, "Conquest, Occupation, Colonialism and Exclusion"; Mariana P. Candido, "Jagas e sobas no 'Reino de Benguela': vassalagem e criação de novas categorias políticas e sociais no contexto da expansão portuguesa na África durante ps séculos XVI e XVII," in *África: Históricas conectadas*, ed. Alexandre Vieira Ribeiro, Alexsander Lemos de Almeida Gebara, and Marina Berther (Niterói: PPGHISTÓRIA - UFF, 2014), 39–76.

[17] Ferreira, "Suppression of the Slave Trade," 315–16; Candido, *An African Slaving Port and the Atlantic World*, 154–64.

Since the seventeenth century, foreign travelers and colonial officers made extensive efforts to portray West Central Africans as dangerous people who threatened economic progress and production, as will be detailed in Chapters 1 and 2. Consequently, local political leaders in West Central Africa experienced external encroachment over their territories and subjects since the early contact with Portuguese merchants and colonial officers. In some instances, political leaders and their subjects migrated due to growing pressures and territorial disputes. Several were removed from power and replaced with political opponents more aligned with Portuguese interests. Yet we still know very little about how most sobas and other rulers slowly watched their power diminish or their views on the process of eventually losing control over their land and their people. Some, however, such as the Ndembu rulers, have produced rich documents since the seventeenth century that recorded how leaders and commoners understood their own land tenure and notions of ownership and accumulation (see Chapters 1 and 3). The Caculo Cacahenda ruling elite, for example, set up their own state archive and other Ndembu archives exist.[18] The existence of these sobados' archives, alongside treaties and charts available in the colonial documents, allows us to identify the nuances of the transformation of land tenure regimes.

Conceptually, rights in persons or wealth in people could explain the widespread warfare in the region, as conflict produced captives for sale. The idea of valuing wealth in people also explains why many more male captives were sold into the transatlantic slave trade in this era while women remained in local communities. Following this argument, women were incorporated into lineages and reproduced, naturally recuperating the lost population and preventing major demographic decline. The abundance of land and the scarcity of labor, as this argument goes, prevented the consolidation of ownership rights over land. However, land was not easily accessible in West Central Africa. Raids, warfare, and political instability made people vulnerable to slave raiders and threatened societies and the efforts to settle in unoccupied areas.

---

[18] In an article published in 2009, Catarina Madeira Santos refer to the existence of four sobados archives removed from Angolan chiefs in the 1930s and placed in the custody of the Instituto de Investigação Científica Tropical in Lisbon, now under the Arquivo Histórido Ultramarino management. According to Madeira Santos, besides the Caculo Cacuenda archive, there were also the Dembo Mufuque Aquitupa, the Dembo Ndala Cabassa, and the Dembo Pango Aluquem, covering documents from the eighteenth to the nineteenth century. Only recently these documents became available for consultation. See Catarina Madeira Santos, "Entre deux droits: les Lumières en Angola (1750-v. 1800)," *Annales. Histoire, Sciences Sociales* 60, no. 4 (2007): 772.

Besides, warfare was also intended to expand the territory, indicating that land control mattered. In many instances, land was vacant because it had been recently raided, indicating the vulnerability of the settlement. Several cases of people enslaved in the eighteenth and nineteenth centuries reveal that fetching water, selling goods, visiting distant markets, and farming had become dangerous activities with the expanded activity of Atlantic slavers.[19] And the spirits occupying and protecting forests and territories in West Central African societies made them unsuitable for settlement.[20]

Once the early nineteenth century rolled around, this region and its societies had experienced profound changes over more than two hundred years of interaction, clashes, and disputes with external forces associated with the pressures of the transatlantic slave trade. Raids, kidnappings, and warfare rationalized the transatlantic slave trade, slavery, and dispossession. The violence associated with the slave trade and colonialism was not restricted to the warfare and the enslavement of millions of people around Luanda and Benguela, but also occurred in the consolidation of a historical narrative that naturalized conquest and territorial occupation in the name of European expansion, rights, and progress.

By midcentury, it was considered legitimate and justifiable to remove West Central Africans from their lands, based on the arbitrary idea that locals did not recognize forms of individual property. These ideas might seem odd, but they are still prevalent and taught in law schools.[21]

[19] José C. Curto, "Experiences of Enslavement in West Central Africa," *Histoire Sociale/Social History* 41, no. 82 (2008): 381–415; Ferreira, "Slaving and Resistance to Slaving in West Central Africa"; Mariana P. Candido, "African Freedom Suits and Portuguese Vassal Status: Legal Mechanisms for Fighting Enslavement in Benguela, Angola, 1800–1830," *Slavery & Abolition* 32, no. 3 (2011): 447–59; Mariana P. Candido, "O limite tênue entre a liberdade e escravidão em Benguela durante a era do comércio transatlântico," *Afro-Ásia* 47 (2013): 239–68; Mariana P. Candido, "The Transatlantic Slave Trade and the Vulnerability of Free Blacks in Benguela, Angola, 1780-1830," in *Atlantic Biographies: Individuals and Peoples in the Atlantic World*, ed. Mark Meuwese and Jeffrey A. Fortin (Leiden: Brill, 2013), 193–210.

[20] Sarr, *Islam, Power, and Dependency*, 85–95; Sousa Santos, *Epistemologies of the South*. For studies that focus on religious forces, migration, and settlement in West Central Africa, see Wyatt MacGaffey, "Crossing the River. Myth and Movement in Central Africa," in *Angola on the Move. Transport Routes, Communications and History*, ed. Beatrix Heintze and Achim von Oppen (Frankfurt am Main: Verlag Otto Lembeck, 2008), 221–38; Robert Harms, *Games Against Nature: An Eco-Cultural History of the Nunu of Equatorial Africa* (Cambridge , MA: Cambridge University Press, 1999).

[21] See, among many other examples, Francisco Liberal Fernandes, "O direito de propriedade em Angola: aspectos gerais da Lei de Terras," *Boletim de Ciências Econômicas* 57, no. 2 (2014), 1463-78; Adilson das Necessidades Ricardo Rodrigues, "Reflexões sobre a influência do direito costumeiro no direito administrativo angolano à luz da constituição da República de Angola de 2010" (M.A. dissertation, Faculdade de Direito do Porto, Portugal, 2018), 41.

The Portuguese Crown claimed the right to grant land access in colonial centers such as Luanda and Benguela and to tax and redistribute plots of land, the argument being that foreign settlers could work it more productively. The existence of land registrations, titles, and property claims in the archives of the colonial period has been normalized as part of the political changes associated with the expansion of the so-called legitimate trade, which required land and labor to generate profit. These historical documents also normalize imperial political history as *history* written large at the expense of other units, narratives, or understandings. The evidence in the writing of colonial officers, European jurists, and missionaries who tried to understand local notions of ownership and property rights constantly portrayed Africans as incapable of comprehending these abstract concepts, as if land deeds or sales contracts had been inherently European since the beginning of time. Located in Europe and without any effort to understand local notions of wealth or mobilizing power, European jurists wrote extensive legal treatises about West Central African wealth accumulation and exchange. These jurists unanimously asserted the absence of individual property and notions of private ownership among Africans as an indication of economic primitivism, creating the legal framework to consolidate expropriation and seizure of possession.[22]

Portuguese colonial administrators compiled information about African land-tenure regimes, such as the publication of *usos e costumes*, the legal studies on customary law in the late nineteenth and early twentieth centuries. The assumption was, however, that Africans could not de facto have rights and that individual property had always existed in Europe. By the early twentieth century, recorded customary law, *usos e costumes*, no longer derived from a pre-colonial past but was the result of centuries of conflict between West Central African elites and Portuguese occupation and colonialism. The colonialism, dating to the late sixteenth century north of the Kwanza River and the early seventeenth century south of Kwanza River, resulted in dispossession and the creation of new elites, rulers, and rights.[23] The emergence of individual property rights is

---

[22] See Melo, *Política indígena*; Melo, *Regime da propriedade indígena*; Gonçalves, "Regime das terras."

[23] There is a vast scholarship on the problematic nature of customary law recorded by the late nineteenth century and the early twentieth century. See, for example, Sara Berry, *Chiefs Know Their Boundaries: Essays on Property, Power, and the Past in Asante, 1896-1996* (Porstmouth, NH: Heinemann, 2001); Sara Berry, *No Condition Is Permanent. The Social Dynamics of Agrarian Change in Sub-Saharan Africa* (Madison, WI: University of Wisconsin Press, 1993); Kristin Mann and Richard L. Roberts, eds., *Law in Colonial Africa* (Portsmouth, NH: Heinemann, 1991); Martin Chanock, *Law, Custom, and Social*

treated as an ahistorical idea having always existed in Europe, while they
are the result of the consolidation of liberal ideas among European ruling
elites in the early nineteenth century. The state imposition of individual
property rights in Portugal and Angola celebrated individual rights over
collective ones and normalized land occupation, population removal,
and colonialism (see Chapters 2, 3, and 6).

Given this scarcity of available land, and thus the high value placed
on it, by the mid-nineteenth century West Central Africans, including
several women, accumulated wealth not just in people but also in land
and material objects. This fact forces a reconsideration of the notion that
women were historically excluded from land rights except through
kinship connections that were tied to men. According to this view, women
could access land but not own it. They could cultivate the land, make
decisions about the crops planted, and even have input concerning the
terms of trade, but not contribute regarding how land was transferred or
transmitted.[24] The exception was in Muslim Africa, where several studies
have revealed that women enjoyed property rights.[25] Africanists have
emphasized that women, particularly single women, were excluded from
the control of land and cattle that offered men advantages in accumulating
wealth.[26] Yet African women owned land in different locations, including

Order: The Colonial Experience in Malawi and Zambia (New York, NY: Cambridge
University Press, 1985); Sean Hawkins, Writing and Colonialism in Northern Ghana:
The Encounter Between the LoDagaa and "the World on Paper" (Toronto, Canada:
University of Toronto Press, 2002); Lentz, Land, Mobility, and Belonging in West
Africa; Sarr, Islam, Power, and Dependency; Naaborko Sackeyfio-Lenoch, The Politics of
Chieftaincy. Authority and Property in Colonial Ghana, 1920-1950 (Rochester, NY:
University of Rochester Press, 2014); Lauren Honig, "Selecting the State or Choosing
the Chief? The Political Determinants of Smallholder Land Titling," World Development
100, no. Supplement C (2017): 94–107.

[24] Margaret Kinsman, "'Beasts of Burden': The Subordination of Southern Tswana
Women, ca. 1800–1840," Journal of Southern African Studies 10, no. 1 (1983): 42–43;
Miriam Goheen, Men Own the Fields, Women Own the Crops: Gender and Power in the
Cameroon Grassfields (Madison, WI: University of Wisconsin Press, 1996), 108–14;
Beverly L. Peters and John E. Peters, "Women and Land Tenure Dynamics in Pre-
Colonial, Colonial, and Post-Colonial Zimbabwe.," Journal of Public and International
Affairs 9, no. Spring (1998): 183–203.

[25] Paul E. Lovejoy and Jan S Hogendorn, Slow Death for Slavery: The Course of Abolition in
Northern Nigeria, 1897-1936 (Cambridge, MA: Cambridge University Press, 1993),
123–42; Randall Lee Pouwels, Horn and Crescent: Cultural Change and Traditional Islam
on the East African Coast, 800-1900 (New York, NY: Cambridge University Press, 1987),
193–94; Ghislaine Lydon, Trans-Saharan Trails: Islamic Law, Trade Networks, and Cross-
Cultural Exchange in Nineteenth-Century Western Africa (Cambridge, New York:
Cambridge University Press, 2009), 233–36; Elke Stockreiter, Islamic Law, Gender,
and Social Change in Post-Abolition Zanzibar (New York, NY: Cambridge University
Press, 2015), 109–202.

[26] Ester Boserup, Woman's Role in Economic Development (London: Allen & Unwin, 1970);
Claire C. Robertson and Iris Berger, Women and Class in Africa (New York, NY:

Luanda, Catumbela, Ambaca, Caconda, and Benguela and were able to transfer it in ways connected to individual ownership rights.

Dispossession

In recent decades, several studies have stressed the cultural and social importance of land for populations in West Africa.[27] Land value went beyond its materiality and defined rights, obligations that linked rulers and their subjects. In sum, land was central to the political economy that sustained relationships and sovereignty. The same is true for populations in West Central Africa, including Mbundu, Umbundu, and Kwanyama and other non-Bantu populations that understood land not simply as a space of food production but also a space of belonging and maintaining contact with previous generations. Occupation of territory, and its use, defined rights over access and use, including over rivers and small lagoons. These ideas, however, were challenged by the arrival of European powers during the Modern Era, who expropriated land and justified it, a context that I examine in this study.

Possession of territory and control of its inhabitants and natural resources were the ultimate goals of expansionist Iberian powers. Since the fifteenth century, Portuguese and Spanish monarchies aimed to exercise control of newly encountered territories, debating whether indigenous populations did or did not have a right to land and jurisdiction over territories and peoples.[28] Before the nineteenth century in Portugal,

Africana, 1986), 10; Sandra E. Greene, "Family Concerns: Gender and Ethnicity in Pre-Colonial West Africa," *International Review of Social History* 44 (1999): 15–31.

[27] Berry, *No Condition Is Permanent*; Kristin Mann, "Women, Landed Property, and the Accumulation of Wealth in Early Colonial Lagos," *Signs* 16, no. 4 (1991): 682–706; Nwando Achebe, *The Female King of Colonial Nigeria: Ahebi Ugbabe* (Bloomington, IN: Indiana University Press, 2011); Assan Sarr, "Women, Land, and Power in the Lower Gambia River Region," in *African Women in the Atlantic World. Property, Vulnerability and Mobility, 1660-1880*, ed. Mariana P. Candido and Adam Jones (Woodbridge: James Currey, 2019), 38–53; Sackeyfio-Lenoch, *Politics of Chieftaincy*; Muey Saeteurn, *Cultivating Their Own: Agriculture in Western Kenya during the "Development" Era* (Rochester, NY: University of Rochester Press, 2020).

[28] Ilídio do Amaral, *O consulado de Paulo Dias de Novais: Angola no último quartel do século XVI e primeiro do século XVII* (Lisbon: Ministério da Ciências e da Tecnologia/Instituto de Investigação Científica Tropical, 2000); Heintze, *Angola nos séculos XVI e XVII*; Lauren A. Benton, "The Legal Regime of the South Atlantic World, 1400-1750: Jurisdictional Complexity as Institutional Order," *Journal of World History* 11, no. 1 (2000): 27–56; Lauren Benton, "Possessing Empire. Iberian Claims and Interpolity Law," in *Native Claims: Indigenous Law against Empire, 1500-1920*, ed. Saliha Belmessous (New York, NL: Oxford University Press, 2012), 19–40; Tamar Herzog, "Colonial Law and 'Native Customs': Indigenous Land Rights in Colonial Spanish America," *The Americas* 69, no. 3 (2013): 303–21; Saliha Belmessous, ed., *Native Claims: Indigenous Law against Empire, 1500–1920* (Oxford ; New York: Oxford

or in most of Europe, however, there was no such a thing as a consolidated idea that land belonged to individuals and fixed law that legislated over it.[29] By the 1800s, when the Portuguese state became interested in legislating property laws in Angola, it was in the context of ongoing European debate regarding land enclosure, communal use of land, and unproductive land influenced by Enlightenment and liberal ideas regarding progress, modernity, and productivity. By the second decade of the nineteenth century, however, the state began to encroach on communal land in Portugal, seen as an obstacle to the progress of capitalist agricultural practices that privileged private investment at the expense of collective gains. In this perspective of liberal progress, communal land where people grazed sheep or cattle or collected water was understood as a sign of Portuguese economic shortfall; to achieve prosperity, the state had to distribute community land to individuals who would make their plots productive, addressing the market demands for specific crops.[30] The debate over property rights in Portugal was directly linked to the existence of overseas colonies and the need to justify its occupation. In Angola, legislating ownership normalized possession and occupation of the territory, but also the status of its inhabitants as colonial subjects with limited rights. Legislation implemented in nineteenth-century Angola to protect individual property rights over things, land, and people reflected and consolidated governance and legitimacy. Notably, those laws made use of a language and a technology, based on the dominance of a paper culture, that determined colonized populations as being outside of history, lacking the cultural practice and economic sophistication to rule themselves. The consolidation of legislation and colonial courts made expropriation easier and normalized conquest, occupation, and inequality.[31]

West Central African populations understandably also valued land and pushed back attempts of colonial officers to seize territory in different

University Press, 2012); Karen B. Graubart, "Shifting Landscape. Heterogenous Conceptions of Land Use and Tenure in the Lima Valley," *Colonial Latin American Review* 26, no. 1 (2017): 62–84.

[29] Although commodification of land was not a fact in Portugal, in England individuals started leasing and owning land earlier, with the enclosure movement. I am grateful for Suzanne Schwartz for pushing me to stress differences in Europe. For more on private property and law in Europe, see Herzog, *Short History of European Law*.

[30] Manuel Rodrigues, *Os Baldios* (Lisbon: Caminho, 1987), 38–39.

[31] For more on this, see Ann Laura Stoler, "'In Cold Blood': Hierarchies of Credibility and the Politics of Colonial Narratives," *Representations*, no. 37 (1992): 151–89; Clifton Crais, "Chiefs and Bureaucrats in the Making of Empire: A Drama from the Transkei, South Africa, October 1880," *American Historical Review* 108, no. 4 (2003): 1034–56; Amrita Malhi, "Making Spaces, Making Subjects: Land, Enclosure and Islam in Colonial Malaya," *The Journal of Peasant Studies* 38, no. 4 (2011): 727–46; Brenna

ways, most not necessarily effective from a long-term perspective. Rulers and commoners embraced techniques, such as written records, that allowed them to have their occupation rights recognized by others since the seventeenth century. In few instances, however, historians have access to these records – and this is the case of the surviving records of the Caculo Cacahenda's archives, which documented lineage history and migration, land tenure, and territorial limits since 1677. These documents became regalia of power in part because they described political and economic events, but, more importantly, control over these written papers legitimized political rule, the state, and its relationship with the colonial administration.[32] The existence of local state archives, such as the Caculo Cacahenda, as well as Umbundu records analyzed by Éva Sebestyén, indicates how the West Central African population embraced written technology to produce the evidence that could serve as proof for their land tenure claims.[33] Missing from these records, however, are gendered dynamics of land claims and use, which are prevalent in colonial historical documents.

West Central African rulers appropriated written records when they realized that paper evidence, not possession and occupation, achieved the role of land tenure proof. This change was linked to the advance of Enlightenment thought, new forms of governance, and the ensuing discourse of modernity and civilization at the turn of the nineteenth century. It led to the imposition of a new technique – writing – and to bureaucracy, altering everyday practices and governability. Manufactured evidence was privileged, in most cases, by omitting local populations' claims that supported counternarratives of ancestral rights. Writing was also linked to legislation, rights, and ownership, legitimizing one form of power over others and displacing multiple legal orders in favor of a single narrative that privileged the colonial experience as central. Written evidence and property law were crucial in philosophical and political narratives of development that privileged individual rights as modernity in opposition to West Central Africans who supposedly lacked regulations, written culture, and private ownership laws.

Bhandar, *Colonial Lives of Property: Law, Land, and Racial Regimes of Ownership* (Durham: Duke University Press Books, 2018); Sousa Santos, *Epistemologies of the South.*

[32] The Caculo Cacahenda political elites maintain a rich archive from 1718 to 1872, which have been published. Alongside the land charter collected by Eve Sebastyen, these documents provide a much-needed counternarrative to the colonial documents. See Madeira Santos and Sebastyen.

[33] Sebestyén. Similar processes of document production happened elsewhere. For more, see Bhavani Raman, *Document Raj: Writing and Scribes in Early Colonial South India* (Chicago, IL: University of Chicago Press, 2012).

This argument can be easily dismissed by the existence of the Caculo Cacahenda archive, seized by a colonial officer in 1934, as well as the survival of other records.[34] As we will see, this was all part of an imperial discourse that denied rights despite clear evidence that West Central African societies had multiple jurisdictions, recognized possession and occupation rights, and registered them.[35] African rulers and commoners produced evidence that legitimized their ownership claims, but Europeans looted their symbols of power, including seats, divination baskets, and written documents carefully manufactured and held.

By the mid-nineteenth century, titling processes and the designation of land for individual and communal use radically transformed the use and access to land in West Central Africa. In many ways, the recognition of private ownership of land in nineteenth-century Angola was a mode of dispossession that continued in the twentieth century and later. It legitimized the capacity of an individual, including a foreigner, to usurp, appropriate, and claim ownership over locals who lived and depended on land resources. The colonial state that ruled on ownership of land and things recognized inequality. In many ways, the consolidation of individual property rights played a significant role in the narrative of progress and modernity employed by colonial administrators and jurists in Portugal and Angola. During the nineteenth century, rights shifted from the earlier use of occupation of sobas and their subjects toward a more-abstract form of individual property rights based on registration, titles, and written evidence that privileged colonial governance. Many African subjects, particularly women, were able to navigate and employ colonial law to advance their economic interests and agendas. This does

---

[34] The 210 documents available at the Caculo Cacahenda archive have been published; and only recently the manuscripts became available for consultation. Other Ndembu archives have been identified and digitized by the Arquivo Histórico Ultramarino staff. These documents are now available at the Arquivo Histórico Ultramarino website.

[35] Graubart, "Shifting Landscape." For more on written and legal culture, see Ana Paula Tavares and Catarina Madeira Santos, "Fontes escritas africanas para a história de Angola," in *Africae Monumenta: A apropriação da escrita pelos africanos*, vol. 1 (Lisbon: Instituto de Investigação Científica Tropical, 2002), 471–509; Beatrix Heintze, "Hidden Transfers: Luso-Africans as European Explorers' Experts in Nineteenth-Century West-Central Africa," in *The Power of Doubt: Essays in Honor of David Henige*, ed. Paul Landau (Madison, WI: Parallel Press, 2011), 19–40; Roquinaldo Ferreira, *Cross-Cultural Exchange in the Atlantic World: Angola and Brazil during the Era of the Slave Trade* (New York, NY: Cambridge University Press, 2012), 88–125; Catarina Madeira Santos, "Esclavage africain et traite atlantique confrontés: transactions langagières et juridiques (à propos du tribunal de mucanos dans l'Angola des xviie et xviiie siècles)," *Brésil (s). Sciences Humaines et Sociales* 1 (2012): 127–48.

not mean that their ability to employ legal spaces was successful or unchallenged by their peers.

Jurists and colonial officers misunderstood and mispresented West Central African land regimes, privileging private over collective holdings, and setting in stone, or on paper, norms and practices that were undergoing reformulations. The support of chiefs who facilitated the colonial agenda favored the consolidation of specific voices and versions of the past, and practices that excluded youths, women, and anyone seen as dissident or nonconformist.[36] The rush to register customary law and jurisdictions reinforced Western perspectives and notions of property, in the context of the expansion of colonialism and territorialization. Thus, it is not surprising that the little information on customary law recorded in early twentieth-century Angola stresses the absence of private ownership and women's exclusion. Written culture and legal forms of individual ownership and knowledge production in indigenous societies were articulated and realized in conjunction with one another, consolidating dispossession, colonialism, and inequalities.[37]

Colonialism, Slavery, and Inequality

West Central African inhabitants – indigenous as well as colonizers – rushed to protect individual property by the mid-nineteenth century, in the context of pressure to end the slave trade in the Atlantic world and expand colonial territories along the African coast. In many African coastal areas, bringing the slave trade to an end meant European conquest and territorial occupation.[38] In West Central Africa, however,

[36] Chanock, *Law, Custom, and Social Order*; Berry, *Chiefs Know Their Boundaries*; Mann and Roberts, eds., *Law in Colonial Africa*; and Rachel Jean-Baptiste, *Conjugal Rights: Marriage, Sexuality, and Urban Life in Colonial Libreville, Gabon* (Athens, OH: Ohio University Press, 2014).

[37] I draw on the work of several scholars, such as Mann, "Women, Land and Wealth"; Berry, *No Condition Is Permanent*; Heintze, *Angola nos séculos XVI e XVII*; Lauren A. Benton, *A Search for Sovereignty. Law and Geography in European Empires, 1400-1900* (New York, NY: Cambridge University Press, 2010); Aida Freudenthal, *Arimos e fazendas: a transição agrária em Angola, 1850-1880* (Luanda: Chá de Caxinde, 2005); Lentz, *Land, Mobility, and Belonging in West Africa*; Sarr, *Islam, Power, and Dependency*; Graubart, "Shifting Landscape"; Green, *A Fistful of Shells*.

[38] For more on this, see Paul E. Lovejoy and Jan S. Hogendorn, *Slow Death for Slavery: The Course of Abolition in Northern Nigeria, 1897-1936* (Cambridge, MA: Cambridge University Press, 1993); W. G. Clarence-Smith, "Runaway Slaves and Social Bandits in Southern Angola, 1875–1913," *Slavery & Abolition* 6, no. 3 (1985): 23–33; Sandra E. Greene, *Slave Owners of West Africa: Decision Making in the Age of Abolition* (Bloomington, IN: Indiana University Press, 2017); Trevor R. Getz, *Slavery and Reform in West Africa Toward Emancipation in Nineteenth-Century Senegal and the Gold Coast*, Western African Studies (Athens, OH: Ohio University Press, 2004); Samuël

control over slave exports and territorial occupation had been linked since the seventeenth century. *Wealth, Land, and Property* examines the expansion of control over human property and the legal efforts intended to make bondage last longer. The nineteenth century was a time of profound and contradictory transformation along the African coast, with the decline and abolition of slave exports as well as the expansion of slave labor in coastal and inland urban centers. Despite historiography that celebrates the nineteenth century as the age of emancipation, liberty, and democratic revolutions, this study explores how slavery expanded in West Central Africa during this period, similar to other African territories, such as the Sokoto Caliphate or Dahomey – where slavery did not decline but became even stronger as an institution in the era of "legitimate trade."[39] The eighteenth- and nineteenth-century liberal revolutions that swept the North Atlantic did not represent the end of African labor

Coghe, "The Problem of Freedom in a Mid-Nineteenth-Century Atlantic Slave Society: The Liberated Africans of the Anglo-Portuguese Mixed Commission in Luanda (1844–1870)," *Slavery & Abolition* 33, no. 3 (2012): 479–500; Jelmer Vos, "Work in Times of Slavery, Colonialism, and Civil War: Labor Relations in Angola from 1800 to 2000," *History in Africa* 41, no. 1 (2014): 363–85; Roquinaldo Amaral Ferreira, "Agricultural Enterprise and Unfree Labour in Nineteenth Century Angola," in *Commercial Agriculture, the Slave Trade and Slavery in Atlantic Africa*, eds. Robin Law, Suzanne Schwarz, and Silke Strickrodt (Woodbridge: James Currey, 2013), 225–42; Suzanne Schwarz, "'A Just and Honourable Commerce.' Abolitionist Experimentation in Sierra Leone in the Late Eighteenth and Early Nineteenth Centuries," *African Economic History* 45, no. 1 (2017): 1–45.

[39] For studies that celebrate the late eighteenth and early nineteenth centuries as the "Age of Revolution and Liberty," see Eric Hobsbawm, *Age of Revolution 1789-1848* (London: Orion, 2010); Robert Roswell Palmer, *The Age of the Democratic Revolution: The Challenge* (Princeton, NJ: Princeton University Press, 1969); Janet L. Polasky, *Revolutions without Borders: The Call to Liberty in the Atlantic World* (New Haven, CT: Yale University Press, 2015). The scholarship on the Portuguese empire, however, stresses that slavery not only continued to exist but also thrived during the nineteenth century. See, for example, Valentim Alexandre and Jill Dias, *O Império africano* (Lisbon: Estampa, 1998); Roquinaldo Ferreira, "Abolicionismo versus colonialismo: Rupturas e continuidades em Angola (Século XIX)," in *África. Brasileiros e Portugueses, séculos XVI-XIX*, ed. Roberto Guedes, 95–112 (Rio de Janeiro: Mauad, 2013); and Vanessa S. Oliveira, "Trabalho escravo e ocupações urbanas em Luanda na segunda metade do século XIX," in *Em torno de Angola: Narrativas, identidades e conexões atlânticas* (São Paulo: Intermeios, 2014), 265–67. For the Sokoto Caliphate see Sean Arnold Stilwell, *Paradoxes of Power: The Kano "Mamluks" and Male Royal Slavery in the Sokoto Caliphate, 1804-1903* (Portsmouth, NH: Heinemann, 2004); Mohammed Bashir Salau, *The West African Slave Plantation: A Case Study*, 1st ed. (Palgrave Macmillan, 2011); Paul E. Lovejoy, *Jihād in West Africa during the Age of Revolutions* (Athens, OH: Ohio University Press, 2016). For Dahomey, see Patrick Manning, *Slavery, Colonialism and Economic Growth in Dahomey, 1640-1960.* (Cambridge, MA: Cambridge University, 1982); Edna G. Bay, *Wives of the Leopard Gender, Politics, and Culture in the Kingdom of Dahomey* (Charlottesville, VA: University of Virginia Press, 1998).

exploitation or even of slavery in West Central Africa.[40] Regaining, acquiring, or consolidating freedom became even more difficult for those who remained in bondage there. Individuals who petitioned for their emancipation did not necessarily encounter supportive colonial officials or individuals who could help them in their quest for freedom.[41] In common with Brazil or the United States, urban slavery threatened individuals, and several reports indicate that free Africans were kidnapped, enslaved, and deported to the Americas while conducting business, visiting friends or relatives, or traveling alone through coastal towns.[42]

[40] Neither in the Caribbean nor in Brazil. Rebecca J. Scott, *Slave Emancipation in Cuba the Transition to Free Labor, 1860–1899* (Pittsburgh, PA: University of Pittsburgh Press, 2000); Keila Grinberg, "Re-escravização, direitos e justiças no Brasil do século XIX," in *Direitos e Justiças: Ensaios de história social,* ed. Silvia Hunold Lara and Joseli Maria Nunes Mendonça (Campinas, SP: Editora da Unicamp, 2006), 101–28; Mamigonian, "Conflicts over the Meanings of Freedom: The Liberated Africans' Struggle for Final Emancipation in Brazil, 1840-1860," in *Paths to Freedom: Manumission in the Atlantic World,* ed. Rosemary Brana-Shute and Randy J. Sparks (Columbia, SC: University of South Carolina Press, 2009), 235–63; Sidney Chalhoub, *Visões da liberdade: Uma história das últimas décadas da escravidão na Corte* (São Paulo: Companhia das Letras, 2011); Luciana da Cruz Brito, *Temores da África: segurança, legislação e população africana na Bahia oitocentista* (Salvador: UFBA, 2016).

[41] In many ways, this examination of the nineteenth century engages with the work of Jill Dias, who made important contributions on the Mbundu entrepreneurs north of the Kwanza River. Jill R. Dias, "Changing Patterns of Power in the Luanda Hinterland. The Impact of Trade and Colonisation on the Mbundu ca. 1845-1920," *Paideuma* 32 (1986): 285–318; Jill R. Dias, "Mudanças nos padrões de poder no 'hinterland' de Luanda. O impacto da colonização sobre os Mbundu (c. 1845-1920)," *Penélope* 14 (1994): 43–91. See, also, José C. Curto, "Un Butin illégitime: Razzias d'esclaves et relations luso-africaines dans la région des fleuves Kwanza et Kwango en 1805," in *Déraison, esclavage et droit: Les fondements idéologiques et juridiques de la traite négrière et de l'esclavage,* eds. Isabel de Castro Henriques and Louis Sala-Molins (Paris: Unesco, 2002), 315–27; Roquinaldo Ferreira, "Slaving and Resistance to Slaving in West Central Africa," in *The Cambridge World History of Slavery,* vol. 3, eds. David Eltis and Stanley L. Engerman, 111–131 (Cambridge, MA: Cambridge University Press, 2011); Mariana P. Candido, "African Freedom Suits and Portuguese Vassal Status: Legal Mechanisms for Fighting Enslavement in Benguela, Angola, 1800–1830," *Slavery & Abolition* 32, no. 3 (2011): 447–59; Mariana P. Candido, "O limite tênue entre a liberdade e escravidão em Benguela durante a era do comércio transatlântico," *Afro-Ásia* 47 (2013): 239–68.

[42] See Randy J. Sparks, *The Two Princes of Calabar: An Eighteenth-Century Atlantic Odyssey* (Cambridge, MA: Harvard University Press, 2004); Catarina Madeira Santos, "Esclavage africain et traite atlantique confrontés : transactions langagières et juridiques (à propos du tribunal de mucanos dans l'Angola des xviie et xviiie siècles)," *Brésil (s): Sciences Humaines et Sociales* 1 (2012): 127–48; Enrique Martino, "Panya: Economies of Deception and the Discontinuities of Indentured Labour Recruitment and the Slave Trade, Nigeria and Fernando Pó, 1890s–1940s," *African Economic History* 44, no. 1 (2016): 91–129; Mariana P. Candido, "The Transatlantic Slave Trade and the Vulnerability of Free Blacks in Benguela, Angola, 1780-1830," in *Atlantic Biographies: Individuals and Peoples in the Atlantic World,* eds. Mark Meuwese and Jeffrey A. Fortin, 193–210 (Leiden: Brill, 2013).

The Portuguese Empire abolished slave exports from West Central Africa in 1836. In this same period, in a cruel irony, the institution of slavery expanded in the region. Local merchants and recently arrived immigrants from Portugal and Brazil set up plantations in the interior of Luanda, around Benguela, and in Moçâmedes, making extensive use of unfree labor. Cotton and sugarcane plantations were established in order to meet international demand for raw materials in the context of industrialization. In Luanda and Benguela, slave labor expanded until slavery was abolished in 1869, and a system of apprenticeship was put in place that lasted until 1878.[43] Under a new legal terminology, coerced labor lasted until 1961 in Angola, a process known as "slow death" of slavery.[44]

Wealth, Land, and Property builds on the studies of scholars who have examined this transition in West Central Africa.[45] Evidence available in Angolan and Portuguese archives reveals patterns of life and consumption that suggest that individual wealth was accumulated in different ways and forms, along the coast and in the interior. Enslaved labor was central to wealth accumulation. Ownership of real estate, human beings, or commodities entailed asserting control over the property in question. Coastal and inland elites invested in enslaved people who freed them from some work and were exhibited as symbols of prestige. Enslavement and slavery were legal in the Portuguese empire dating back to the Papal

---

[43] José de Almada, *Apontamentos históricos sobre a escravatura e o trabalho indígena nas colónias portuguesas* (Lisboa: Imprensa Nacional, 1932), 39–41. For studies on the transformations of slavery into new forms of exploitation in West Central Africa, see Maria da Conceição Neto, "De escravos a serviçais, de serviçais a contratados: omissões, percepções e equívocos na história do trabalho africano na Angola colonial," *Cadernos de Estudos Africanos* no. 33 (2017): 107–29; Aida Freudenthal, "Os quilombos de Angola no século XIX: A recusa da escravidão," *Estudos Afro-Asiáticos* 32 (1997): 109–34; Jelmer Vos, "Child Slaves and Freemen at the Spiritan Mission in Soyo, 1880-1885," *Journal of Family History* 35, no. 1 (January 2010): 71–90; Vos, "Work in Times of Slavery, Colonialism, and Civil War"; Ferreira, "Agricultural Enterprise," Vanessa Oliveira, *Slave Trade and Abolition. Gender, Commerce, and Economic Transition in Luanda* (Madison, WI: University of Wisconsin Press, 2021).

[44] Lovejoy and Hogendorn, *Slow Death for Slavery*. See also Oliveira, *Slave Trade and Abolition*.

[45] W. G. Clarence-Smith, *Slaves, Peasants, and Capitalists in Southern Angola, 1840-1926* (New York, NY: Cambridge University Press, 1979); W. G. Clarence-Smith, "Capitalist Penetration among the Nyaneka of Southern Angola, 1760 to 1920s," *African Studies* 37, no. 2 (1978); Freudenthal, *Arimos e fazendas*; Linda M. Heywood, "Slavery and Forced Labor in the Changing Political Economy of Central Angola, 1850-1949," in *The End of Slavery in Africa*, ed. Suzanne Miers and Richard Roberts (Madison, WI: Wisconsin University Press, 1988), 415–35; Linda M. Heywood, "The Growth and Decline of African Agriculture in Central Angola, 1890-1950," *Journal of Southern African Studies* 13, no. 3 (1987): 355–71; Neto, "De escravos a serviçais"; Ferreira, "Abolicionismo versus colonialismo," 95–112; Madeira Santos, "Esclavage africain et traite atlantique confronté."

Bull *Dum Diversas* (1452), which sanctioned attacks led by the Catholic Portuguese kingdom against heathens, Saracens, and enemies of Christ. *Dum Diversas* and the later *Romanus Pontifex* (1455) recognized the right of the Portuguese Crown and its agents to enslave its enemies, seize their goods, and occupy their lands. All these textual artifacts allowed conquest and slavery to act hand in hand in West Central Africa. By the nineteenth century, these well-established endeavors were codified and legalized, making it almost impossible to dismantle and disassociate colonialism, slavery, and territory usurpation. Among the Mbundu and Umbundu states and chiefdoms, slavery was also sanctioned and tolerated, with elite and nonelite members securing unfree dependents who could increase production and prestige. It is not clear, though, how different slavery and enslavement operated from earlier centuries before the contact with Europeans and the disruptive effects of the transatlantic slave trade demand. There were many similarities and adaptations between the multiple juridical systems, which explains how the institution of slavery managed to adapt and survive despite efforts to bring it to an end by the second half of the nineteenth century.[46]

Social inequality persisted despite slavery abolition in the late nineteenth century, in part because there was no effort to transform how wealth was accumulated and transmitted. The idea of freedom and life lived as a free individual was often a misconstrued concept in many West Central African societies that valued affiliation to lineages as a source of social insertion and belonging, even as dependents or clients. Lineage heads continued to mobilize labor due to the nature of colonial labor's reliance on local chiefs in the early twentieth century. Social integration was difficult for the descendants of formerly enslaved people, who continued to serve and work in the houses and farms of former owners and their families. In moments of conflict, these individuals were reminded of their subjugated position in the recent past, as will be examined in Chapters 3 and 5.[47]

[46] On slavery in West Central Africa, see Beatriz Heintze, "Traite de 'pièces' en Angola: Ce qui n'est pas dit dans nos sources," in *De la traite à l'esclavage: Actes du Colloque international sur la traite des Noirs*, Nantes, 1985, ed. Serge Daget (Nantes: Centre de Recherce sur l'historier Graubart, "Shifting Landscape"; Roquinaldo Ferreira, "Slavery and the Social and Cultural Landscape of Luanda," in *The Black Urban Atlantic in the Age of the Slave Trade*, ed. Jorge Cañizares-Esguerra, Matt Childs, and James Sidbury (Philadelphia, PA: University of Pennsylvania Press, 2013), 185–205; Ferreira, "Slaving and Resistance to Slaving in West Central Africa"; Madeira Santos, "Esclavage africain et traite atlantique confronté"; Candido, "Limite tênue."
[47] Maria da Conceição Neto, "A República no seu estado Colonial: combater a escravatura, estabelecer o 'Indigenato,'" *Ler História* 59 (2010): 205–222; Neto, "De escravos a serviçais"; Marcia Schenck and Mariana P. Candido, "Uncomfortable Pasts:

The nineteenth-century history of inequality in Angola is linked with the global rise of liberalism in the context of colonial expansion in Africa and Asia, accompanied by land expropriation, dispossession, and racial regimes of ownership.[48] It led to the concentration of land resources into fewer hands, the acceleration of raw material exports, and the fact that people continued to be bought and sold despite the legal abolition of slavery in 1869. The violence survives in the archives, although there is a paucity of sources on how enslaved people reflected on the ongoing inequalities. Colonial authorities made constant efforts to erase the violence and the experience of those who were the most victimized, yet historians can glimpse their daily resistance and negotiations in the historical documents concerning the counting and assessing of their value. In fragmentary evidence that reveals violence but obscures their thoughts about the process, enslaved people are shown to have pushed back against colonial laws and a system that recognized human beings as property, in an attempt to reassert their historical presence.

Consumption and Tastes

Historical narratives continue to place African people primarily as providers of labor, as marginal actors in the processes of global exchanges. *Wealth, Land, and Property* focuses instead on African interests, recognizing the imbalances and inequalities in colonized territories, and in the sources, which have been used to write its history. The transatlantic slave trade, implementation of legitimate commerce, and imperialism did not benefit African societies, but this does not mean that rulers and commoners were passive actors. West Central African demands for goods have not been fully examined nor have the implications for their wider society been entirely explored, yet they reveal peoples' desires to acquire material objects. This desire had consequences, including affecting local manufacturing, the expansion of imported goods, and introducing new kinds of material wealth.[49]

Talking About Slavery in Angola," in *African Heritage and Memories of Slavery in Brazil and the South Atlantic World*, ed. Ana Lucia Araujo (Amherst, NY: Cambria Press, 2015), 213–52.

[48] I draw here on Bhandar, *Colonial Lives of Property*, and Lowe, *Intimacies of Four Continents*.

[49] For more on this, see Walter Rodney, *How Europe Underdeveloped Africa* (Pambazuka Press, 2012); Martin, *External Trade of the Loango Coast*; Edward A. Alpers, *Ivory and Slaves: Changing Pattern of International Trade in East Central Africa to the Later Nineteenth Century* (Berkeley, CA: University of California Press, 1975); J. E. Inikori, *Africans and the Industrial Revolution in England: A Study in International Trade and Economic Development* (Cambridge: Cambridge University Press, 2002); Charlotte Walker-Said

During the nineteenth century, enslaved West Central Africans culti-vated crops that interested European markets, such as coffee, cotton, and sugarcane. While some continued to be enslaved and sent to the Americans through the 1860s, many were mobilized to new plantations along the African Atlantic coast. People in bondage carried loads of wax, rubber, and orchil, a lichen with dyestuff properties, to the harbors to be exported to Europe and North America. European ships arrived with loads of textiles, furniture, paper, and other items expected by coastal and inland societies. West Central Africans were producers of global commodities, no doubt, but they were also consumers, inserted into the world economy under different conditions and levels of power. Although there is important scholarship on the role of African demand in the global economy, we still know very little about what commoners rather than rulers desired, bought, and transmitted in life.[50] The social history of material objects reveals exchanges and relationships that place African consumers at the center of interactions. In order to comprehend the complexity of economic and social relationships, it is important to examine the operation of trade routes and the circulation of objects, and to understand the value of objects acquired in specific contexts. Material culture reveals human relationships and the efforts to establish strategies of distinction and gives substance to group identity claims that separate people from their neighbors.[51]

and Andrea Felber Seligman, "Wealth in Pluralities: Intersections of Money, Gender, and Multiple Values across African Societies," *International Journal of African Historical Studies*, 48, no. 3 (2015), 387–388.

[50] Phyllis M. Martin, "Power, Cloth and Currency on the Loango Coast," *African Economic History*, no. 15 (1986): 1–12; Roquinaldo Ferreira, "dinâmica do comércio intracolonial: gerebitas, panos asiáticos e guerra no tráfico angolano de escravos, século XVIII," in *O Antigo Regime nos Trópicos: A Dinâmica imperial portuguesa, séculos XVI–XVIII*, ed. João Luís Ribe Fragoso, Maria de Fátima Gouvêa, and Maria Fernanda Bicalho (Rio de Janeiro: Civilização Brasileira, 2001), 339–78; Inikori, *Africans and the Industrial Revolution in England*; Colleen E. Kriger, *Cloth in West African History* (Rowman Altamira, 2006); Prestholdt, *Domesticating the World*; David Richardson, "Consuming Goods, Consuming People. Reflections on the Transatlantic Slave Trade," in *The Rise and Demise of Slavery and the Slave Trade in the Atlantic World*, ed. Philip Misevich and Kristin Mann (Rochester, NY: University of Rochester Press, 2016), 32–63; Daniel B. Domingues da Silva, *The Atlantic Slave Trade from West Central Africa, 1780–1867* (Cambridge: Cambridge University Press, 2017); Mariza de Carvalho Soares, "'Por conto e peso': o comércio de marfim no Congo e Loango, séculos XV–XVII," *Anais do Museu Paulista: História e Cultura Material* 25, no. 1 (2017): 59–86; Kazuo Kobayashi, "Indian Textiles and Gum Arabic in the Lower Senegal River: Global Significance of Local Trade and Consumers in the Early Nineteenth Century," *African Economic History* 45, no. 2 (2017): 27–53.

[51] Pierre Bourdieu, *Distinction: A Social Critique of the Judgement of Taste* (Cambridge, MA: Harvard University Press, 1984); Arjun Appadurai, ed., *The Social Life of Things:*

Whether residing on the coast or in the interior, women and men invested in jewelry and clothing. The income earned by women and men involved in long-distance trade allowed them to consume goods perceived as valuable in the African context, such as silk blouses, shawls, socks and shoes, bowls, textiles from India, and tea sets from China. West Central Africans established new, gendered market economies, indicating a transition from wealth in people to wealth in material goods. These patterns of consumption indicate that women far into the interior were fully integrated into a global economy, even though imports had to be transported over 200 kilometers inland from the coast. The dismantling of earlier ownership regimes transformed West Central Africans into destitute or consumers. The expansion of consumerism and accumulation moved together with the lack of recognition of communal ownership.

A Note on Sources and the Archives

Violence and appropriation pervade the histories of property, rights, consumption, and claims. This violence is nearly erased from the colonial documents and the scholarship arguing that individual property rights were a natural and foreordained development in history. In fact, primary sources, the supremacy of statistical substantiation, and legal treatises that claim that West Central Africans did not have a concept of ownership and land tenure need to be reevaluated. These claims, proposed by jurists and colonial officers and defended by anthropologists and historians, legitimized land seizure and the appropriation of African resources and wealth in the past and even presently.[52]

Primary sources available in the colonial archives are rich in detail about individuals. Unlike scholars who work in other parts of the globe,

---

Commodities in Cultural Perspective (New York, NY: Cambridge University Press, 1988); Jane I. Guyer, "Wealth in People, Wealth in Things – Introduction," *The Journal of African History* 36, no. 1 (2009): 83–90; Hilary Jones, *The Métis of Senegal: Urban Life and Politics in French West Africa* (Bloomington, IN: Indiana University Press, 2013); Prestholdt, *Domesticating the World*.

[52] For more on archives and erasures, see Arjun Appadurai, "Archive and Aspiration," in *Information Is Alive*, ed. Joke Brouwer, Arjen Mulder, and Susan Charlton (Rotterdam: V2/NAi Publishers, 2003), 14–25; Raman, *Document Raj*; Nupur Chaudhuri, Sherry J. Katz, and Mary Elizabeth Perry, *Contesting Archives: Finding Women in the Sources* (Urbana, IL: University of Illinois Press, 2010); Jennifer L. Morgan, "Archives and Histories of Racial Capitalism. An Afterword," *Social Text* 33, no. 4 (2015): 153–61; Saidiya Hartman, "Venus in Two Acts," *Small Axe* 12, no. 2 (2008): 1–14; Marisa J. Fuentes, *Dispossessed Lives: Enslaved Women, Violence, and the Archive* (Philadelphia, PA: University of Pennsylvania Press, 2016); Paul Basu and Ferdinand De Jong, "Utopian Archives, Decolonial Affordances," *Social Anthropology* 24, no. 1 (2016): 5–19.

I did not have to overcome silences.[53] In fact, I encountered too much information, too many details about regular folks, including enslaved individuals. The colonial archives I have consulted are not characterized by absences but filled with data, which have allowed historians to bring individuals to the forefront of their analysis.[54] Men such as colonial officers, slavers, and missionaries produced written documents because they occupied positions of power. Many of these men were locally born and could be classified as Black or mixed race and part of the colonial bureaucracy. Through their accounts and writings, it is clear how locally born women, particularly free women, were also active agents in the social and economic changes. Women, in fact, are everywhere in the documents I have read and transcribed. Despite their Portuguese names, every woman discussed in this book was born in West Central Africa. Some were daughters of Portuguese- or Brazilian-born men, and many were related to powerful African chiefs, but all were colonial subjects regardless of their economic and social position. Most of the women who lived in Benguela, Caconda, Luanda, and other places mentioned in this study were poor, depended on the protection of wealthy residents, and remained nameless in the colonial archives. The contact with Europeans or, more specifically, with Portuguese colonialism offered local societies new possibilities of lineage expansion and enhanced positions. Local men and women employed mechanisms to create advantages in the context in which they were clearly losing political and economic space. They could not anticipate that nineteenth-century events would lead to the Conference of Berlin and the imposition of a new form of colonialism where old elites were once again displaced in favor of new ones.

Local narratives about land rights and first settler claims do exist. West Central African rulers documented their lineage claims in oral accounts and written documents, such as the Caculo Cacahenda archive. The fact that scholars, and the descendants of Caculo Cacahenda's leader and subjects, do not have access to these documents reinforces European ideology that denies agency and ownership rights to Africans. The violence of conquest and colonialism is carefully protected by custodians of

---

[53] Fuentes, *Dispossessed Lives*; Jessica Marie Johnson, "Markup Bodies: Black [Life] Studies and Slavery [Death] Studies at the Digital Crossroads," *Social Text* 36, no. 4 (2018): 57–79.

[54] See, for example, John K. Thornton, *The Kongolese Saint Anthony: Dona Beatriz Kimpa Vita and the Antonian Movement, 1684–1706* (Cambridge: Cambridge University Press, 1998); Mariana Brack Fonseca, *Nzinga Mbandi e as guerras de resistência em Angola. Século XVII* (Belo Horizonte: Mazza Edições, 2015); Linda M. Heywood, *Njinga of Angola: Africa's Warrior Queen* (Cambridge, MA: Harvard University Press, 2017); Ferreira, *Cross-Cultural Exchange*; Charlotte de Castelnau L'Estoile, *Páscoa et ses deux maris: Une esclave entre Angola, Brésil et Portugal* (Paris: PUF, 2019).

documents, who are not interested in non-European actors challenging centuries-old ideologies of white supremacy that justify enslavement, colonialism, and dispossession. The evidence, clearly sought by historians, is extant. Few, however, can get access to it, without intermediaries who edit and select what can be seen. The archives created by African rulers, for example, need to be widely available to the public.

Colonial documents provide much evidence on the physical and social mobility of intermediaries and the chain of information that connected internal and coastal societies. The coastal trader and the colonial officer relied on the host societies for information. They depended on trustworthy information about the origin and quality of tropical products, the political and economic organization of internal societies, and basic knowledge about tastes, desires, and consumption. Merchants relied on informed intermediaries.[55] The physical and social mobility of African women made them key agents who navigated between lineage societies and colonial structures.

This book challenges the liberal idea of individual property as a natural right, innate to human beings.[56] Despite the evidence available, colonial bureaucrats and jurists in Lisbon, Luanda, and Benguela insisted that West Central Africans did not have notions of rights, supporting their argument with the lack of proof of ownership and dismissing local forms of knowledge and alternative ways to exercise control. In the process, colonialism was legitimized, and the long history of West Central African forms of ownership and rights disappeared from history books, replaced by the stereotyped image of a tribal society lacking organization and institutions that could be comprehended by outsiders. Africans in general, and Angolans in particular, became primitive in the eyes of Europeans, and colonialism and settler occupation were ubiquitous in their past.

---

[55] For more on this, see Heintze, "Hidden Transfers: Luso-Africans as European Explorers' Experts in Nineteenth-Century West-Central Africa"; Cátia Antunes, "Free Agents and Formal Institutions in the Portuguese Empire: Towards a Framework of Analysis," *Portuguese Studies* 28, no. 2 (2012): 173–85; Toby Green, *Brokers of Change: Atlantic Commerce and Cultures in Precolonial Western Africa* (Oxford: The British Academy/Oxford University Press, 2012); Philip J. Havik, *Silences and Soundbites: The Gendered Dynamics of Trade and Brokerage in the Pre-Colonial Guinea Bissau Region* (Munster: LIT Verlag Münster, 2004); Kazuo Kobayashi, *Indian Cotton Textile in West Africa: African Agency, Consumer Demand and the Making of the Global Economy, 1750-1850* (London: Palgrave, 2019)

[56] I draw here on Walter D. Mignolo, "Epistemic Disobedience, Independent Thought and Decolonial Freedom," *Theory, Culture & Society* 26, no. 7–8 (2009): 159–81; Achille Mbembe, *Critique of Black Reason* (Durham, NC: Duke University Press, 2017); Sousa Santos, *Epistemologies of the South*; Mariana Armond Dias Paes, "Terras em contenda: circulação e produção de normatividades em conflitos agrários no Brasil império," *Revista da Faculdade de Direito UFMG* 74 (2019): 379–406.

Chapter Overview

This book reflects on the social lives of societies at a time of economic transformation, when new forms of rights emerged to justify the commodification of human beings, colonialism, and dispossession. Chapter 1 examines the transformations of the concept of land use, occupation, and possession in West Central Africa from the late sixteenth to the early nineteenth centuries. While most of the historiography emphasizes the importance of the concept of wealth in people in the organization of African societies, I explore how people exercised land rights and control and displayed wealth. The dynamics of land occupation and use were complex and unstable and always subject to intense negotiations. In West Central Africa, as elsewhere in the continent, claims over land, people, and things were based on and shaped by notions of kinship, community membership, and the broader social context. The distinction between the public and the private was blurred. Recognition of claims and rights was the result of political and economic competition among rulers, subjects, and neighbors. All actors, some with more power than others, engaged in the definition of land use, rights, occupation, and inheritance, retaining control of goods and wealth that could be expressed in a variety of ways. With the arrival of Europeans in the late sixteenth and early seventeenth centuries, more actors engaged in the principle of territorial occupation and subjugation to make bold claims of sovereignty based on the idea that land was unused or unoccupied. Since different ideas of possession and jurisdiction were at the center of these interactions, Chapter 1 examines these clashes between conceptions of land use, access, and occupation.

If competition shaped the three centuries of negotiation between African rulers and Portuguese conquistadores, the nineteenth century was the point at which land was commodified and re-signified at the expense of the firstcomer occupants. Chapter 2 therefore focuses on the fixing and transformation of property rights during the nineteenth century. Possession claims and inheritance practices change over time, and in many ways the available historical evidence hid these changes, retro-jecting a nineteenth-century understanding of land regimes. The imposition of land titles and land charts crystallized processes that were fluid until then. Yet the long list of vassalage treaties, inventories, and disputes between African rulers, their neighbors, and the Portuguese analyzed in the chapter provides a clear example of how all actors engaged in a continued negotiation over possession, jurisdiction, rights, and claims. The Portuguese misunderstandings about land use and rights are examined in detail, exploring the consequences for African historiography.

The focus of Chapter 3 is on the strengthening of the bureaucracy and written culture that, by the early nineteenth century, created an ersatz historical proof and solidified territorial and political claims. After two centuries of conquest, by the turn of the nineteenth century new forms of official records, such as land registries, deeds, and inventories, and the expansion of surveys and reports led to an association between individual ownership, written registration, and property recognition. As in other colonial experiences, paper records represented authenticity and legitimation in the eyes of colonizers and also brought changes in the perceptions of governance. Ndombe, Kilengues, Kakondas, and Bienos embraced written evidence and paper power as providing proof of ownership. The existence of the paper created a new reality, that is, the idea that occupation and possession could be proven, that an individual was a landowner, a farmer, and a respectable resident of the colonial town. Not surprisingly, West Central Africans, whether living in coastal colonial centers or not, recognized the importance of the written document and started to organize their own archives to verify rights and debts with the goal of legitimizing later claims. Local people made use of multiple strategies to protect and pursue rights, involving customary rights and direct use with law and the colonial system of property recognition. The establishment of written records and venues for petition such as courts allowed colonial subjects to make use of the colonial law and bureaucracy to strategically survive the new legal order and claim rights.

Property in human beings, or wealth in people, is at the center of the analysis in Chapter 4. Despite an Atlanticist scholarship that celebrates the early 1800s as a period of freedom, the evidence reveals that for most of the century, half of the population of Benguela remained in captivity as dispossessed people. In fact, slavery remained legal in Portuguese overseas territories until 1878, with enslaved people performing most of the productive tasks in urban towns and new plantations installed along the coast and around Dombe Grande. Owners and masters separated skills and activities by gender. In urban settings, enslaved men acted as sailors, coopers, tanners, and tailors. Enslaved women also performed skilled labor such as selling food and comfort in the urban streets. They also had special knowledge in farming, sewing clothes, taking care of the sick, and acting as midwives and cooks. Outside of areas controlled by the Portuguese administration, African elites and nonelites invested in acquiring captives and putting them to work for their own benefit, enriching themselves through the dispossession of others. The ability to display a large number of dependents became a way to solidify social prestige in different societies. Enslaved laborers allowed freed people to enjoy comfort, leisure, and other advantages and to maintain social hierarchies based on those who owned people and those who did not. In an area of expanding bureaucracy and paper culture, enslaved lives and experiences were registered and controlled in ecclesiastical records, slave registers, licenses and passports, and judicial cases. Documents such as petitions, fugitive add, inventories, wills, and public complaints allowed slave owners to claim ownership over people and exert their rights.

Chapter 5 explores the legal challenges to human ownership during the nineteenth century by paying attention to the cases of liberated and freed individuals known as *libertos*. This category included people who had been manumitted by various means as well as individuals from ships involved in illegal slave trading who had been freed. Some of those freed people had served in bondage in urban centers or had been kidnapped and smuggled though they had not necessarily lived in captivity before. While slavery as an institution expanded during the nineteenth century, legal venues opened to question property rights over human beings and the use of forced labor to maintain dependency links. Administrators and jurists defended the prolongation of the freed status and forced labor to advance infrastructure and economic enterprises. With support from the colonial administration, freed individuals were obligated by law to continue working for former owners or were simply placed under "apprenticeship" to new masters. The chapter examines the lingering persistence of human ownership, stressing the lived experiences of freed people, their ambivalent legal status, and their efforts to disassociate themselves from slavery. In the end, despite their nominal freedom, freed individuals continued to be treated as property, even when they were able to acquire goods, land, and even enslaved people.

Chapter 6 traces the discussion about land ownership, examining legal changes and the centrality of paper culture for its commodification during the nineteenth century. The chapter begins by stressing the role of twentieth-century jurists and colonial officers in defending the idea that no notion of possession and individual ownership ever existed in Africa, while simultaneously creating the narrative that individual property had always existed in Europe. Despite earlier evidence that demonstrates a clear perception of occupation and jurisdiction rights among local rulers and West Central Africans, jurists, missionaries, and later, anthropologists and historians claimed that such rights did not exist, emphasizing the centrality of wealth in people, not in land, as forms of accumulation and wealth. In many ways, ethnographers, jurists, and scholars provided evidence to support colonial claims and ideologies that non-Europeans were incapable of apprehending and protecting the basic concept of ownership. This has had lasting consequences on the scholarship on wealth and accumulation in Africa. I argue that the refusal to recognize West Central African possession rights sustained colonialism and legitimated occupation and alienation of land and other resources. Primary sources available in Angolan archives show that conflicts over land predated the nineteenth century, and that until that moment the colonial state recognized the right of occupancy and jurisdiction of African rulers and their subjects. During the nineteenth century, legal changes related to the expansion of liberal ideas in Europe and the end of slave exports from West Central Africa altered the value of and the relationship with land. Land occupation recognition and rights were adjusted according to new political and economic situations in a dynamic process related to external and internal contexts. Ownership and transfer of land did not start in the nineteenth century, yet the novelty of writing land deeds, wills, and registers makes these transactions visible to historians. A surprising number of women were able to use the colonial courts to make individual ownership claims, transmit wealth, or petition for land. As has become clear in several case studies, land became commodified during the nineteenth century while local rulers experienced dispossession.

Finally, in Chapter 7, the focus shifts to the process that transformed West Central Africans from forced laborers and their societies from global property into consumers of products manufactured elsewhere. Although the accumulation of goods predated the nineteenth century, the expansion of the paper culture and the colonial bureaucracy allows us to examine the items West Central Africans collected during their lifetimes and the emotional and financial value associated with material culture. The records reveal that West Central Africa accumulated things rather than solely investing in wealth in people. Their consumption patterns make it possible to explore the movement of goods, the role of commercial centers, and the changes in taste and fashion. Rulers and commoners desired material things beyond their basic needs and aspired to buy and collect a variety of goods, ranging from farming tools to luxury items such as silk wraps and socks. They consumed items that connected them to societies around the world, from the Americas to Asian markets, but mainly to markets in the Global South, ranging from Indian textiles to Brazilian tobacco and alcohol. Inevitably, the desire of African men and women in the interior and along the coast for firearms, Indian textiles, Chinese teacups, hats and shoes, and Brazilian alcohol encouraged African political elites and warlords to engage in warfare and other strategies to enslave enemies, exacerbating violence, dispossession, and displacement. Africans imported items that favored European industries at the expense of their local production, a clear demonstration of how colonial power, dispossession, and dependency have a long history and predate the twentieth century. The expansion of the colonial bureaucracy reveals that African women not only acquired imported goods and transmitted them to loved ones but also made constant efforts to protect the assets they had accumulated during their lives.

This study cannot fully represent the violence of occupation and dispossession that West Central Africans experienced in the centuries that predate the Berlin Conference and what scholars traditionally consider to be the beginning of colonialism in Africa. As I have shown elsewhere, colonialism in West Central Africa dates to the sixteenth century.[57] Colonial dispossession led to displacements, enslavement, deaths, and traumas that are difficult to capture in the archives. Although a small group of West Central Africans, an economic and political elite, may have been able to navigate and negotiate rights through the colonial bureaucracy, most of the population experienced land alienation, forced labor, and exclusion. The primary focus of this study is to examine the process through which possession and rights were transformed, yet I also aim to address the articulations between ownership, dispossession, and gender. While anthropologists and missionaries have stressed how local notions of property may have excluded women from claiming rights, it is very clear that West Central African women made use of colonial legal rights and acquired land, people, and material culture. Colonial records reveal the repertoire of legal techniques that West Central Africans, including local rulers, their subjects, and free and unfree inhabitants living in the colonial centers, employed to exercise control over people and land. This study is an effort to interrogate teleological interpretations that see private and individual property and accumulation of goods as a sign of modernity, progress, and economic prosperity. My hope is that more inquiries into histories of inequality and dispossession will emerge, leading to further debates about the historicization of colonial knowledge, private property, and the dispossessions that Africans and their descendants have experienced for the past 400 years, both in Africa and around the globe.

---

[57] Candido, *An African Slaving Port*; and Candido, *Fronteras da escravidão: Escravatura, comércio e identidade em Benguela, 1780-1850* (Benguela: Ondjiri, 2018).

1   Who Owned What?

Early Debate over Land Rights and Dispossession

Land grabbing in West Central Africa has a long history. Since the late sixteenth century, different local actors have clashed over who has the right to use land and have claimed rights over occupancy. Control over land, resources, and people represented power in different contexts, and not every actor shared a common understanding about claims and rights. At the early contact between Europeans and African leaders on the coast of Africa in the sixteenth and seventeenth centuries, in some regions, such as Elmina, landlords authorized European settlement and establishment of trading posts. In these circumstances, African rulers charged rent to European traders, who recognized the authority and followed the negotiated rules over trade operation and construction of fortresses, for example.[1] This kind of agreement neither represented subjugation nor limited African rulers' control over their territory or subjects. However, in West Central Africa, Portuguese agents claimed that these agreements represented conquest or acquisition of territory, leading to the foundation of the towns of Luanda (1576) and Benguela (1617), and expanding dominium rights over territories and their inhabitants. For more than three centuries, the Portuguese empire employed different policies regarding land rights and access, in part due to the resistance of African authorities but also due to the limited knowledge possessed by the Portuguese Crown about the peoples who inhabited West Central Africa, their legal practices, and their political organization.[2]

---

[1] For description of early contact in Elmina, see Harvey M. Feinberg, *Africans and Europeans in West Africa: Elminans and Dutchmen on the Gold Coast during the Eighteenth Century* (Philadelphia: American Philosophical Society, 1989). For more on how European traders recognized African landlords, see Pernille Ipsen, *Daughters of the Trade: Atlantic Slavers and Interracial Marriage on the Gold Coast* (Philadelphia: University of Pennsylvania Press, 2015).

[2] For more on this, see Ilídio do Amaral, *O Reino do Congo, os Mbundu (ou Ambundos), o Reino dos "Ngola" (ou de Angola) e a presença portuguesa de finais do século XV a meados do século XVI* (Lisbon: Ministério da Ciência e da Tecnologia/ Instituto de Investigação Científica Tropical, 1996); Ilídio do Amaral, *O consulado de Paulo Dias de Novais: Angola no último quartel do século XVI e primeiro do século XVII* (Lisbon: Ministério da Ciências e da

This chapter examines that long history of land use and rights, from the late sixteenth century to the late eighteenth century, underscoring changes. Ndembu and Ndombe populations regarded first settlers' rights of occupation, usually understood as rights of possession. Other groups figure into the analysis as well, but Ndembu and Ndombe people are important since they inhabited the north and south of the Kwanza River, respectively, and nowadays their descendants are identified as Kimbundu and Umbundu speakers, respectively. The long shift observed here is therefore not limited to a single region or community of West Central Africa. As in other regions of the African continent, first settlers hosted the migrant population and provided them access to land, but later-comers did not enjoy ownership rights, such as harvesting tree crops or the ability to host other migrants. Clashes happened when migrants who were granted rights to use land sought to transform their temporary privileges into more permanent rights of ownership, or when strangers, including the Portuguese, acted as de facto landlords.

Between the sixteenth and eighteenth centuries, ideas about land use or occupation morphed into ownership rights. The events and changes that took place in this time period formed the basis for the eventual implementation of property rights in West Central Africa during the nineteenth century. The Portuguese presence and colonialism in this region date back to the late sixteenth century, so they existed alongside the West Central African notions of land occupation and sovereignty for hundreds of years before the nineteenth-century transformation. How rulers and commoners expressed ideas about wealth is also an important matter for understanding the economic history of this region and for placing West Central Africa in the growing scholarship on the dynamics of property and expropriation in the colonized world.[3] Contrary to

Tecnologia/ Instituto de Investigação Científica Tropical, 2000); Beatrix Heintze, *Angola nos séculos XVI e XVII. Estudo sobre fontes, métodos e história* (Luanda: Kilombelombe, 2007); Mariana P. Candido, "Conquest, Occupation, Colonialism and Exclusion: Land Disputes in Angola," in *Property Rights, Land and Territory in the European Overseas Empires,* ed. José Vicente Serrão et al. (Lisbon: CEHC-IUL, 2014), 223–33, http://hdl.handle.net/10071/271.
[3] Sara Berry, "Debating the Land Question in Africa," *Comparative Studies in Society and History* 44, no. 4 (2002): 638–68; Martin Chanock, "A Peculiar Sharpness: An Essay on Property in the History of Customary Law in Colonial Africa," *The Journal of African History* 32, no. 1 (1991): 65–88; Miriam Goheen, *Men Own the Fields, Women Own the Crops: Gender and Power in the Cameroon Grassfields* (Madison: University of Wisconsin Press, 1996); Christian Lund, *Local Politics and the Dynamics of Property in Africa* (New York: Cambridge University Press, 2008); Carola Lentz, *Land, Mobility, and Belonging in West Africa* (Bloomington: Indiana University Press, 2013); Assan Sarr, "Land, Power, and Dependency along the Gambia River, Late Eighteenth to Early Nineteenth Centuries," *African Studies Review* 57, no. 3 (2014): 101–21; Cheryl Doss, Ruth

conventional understanding expressed in the literature, West Central Africans grappled with debates about land tenure and rights well before the late nineteenth century. Documents record how some West Central African groups, particularly Kimbundu speakers such as Caculo Cacahenda and other Ndembu populations north of the Kwanza River, understood land rights. However, for other regions, particularly south of the Kwanza River, the dearth of detailed and dated evidence renders a clear reconstruction of property regimes a challenge. The fact that Ndombe or Kwanyama societies did not dispose of or sell land, or that land was not commodified, does not indicate the absence of an idea of use or occupation rights. Nor does it suggest that land use and occupation rights were static. Assuming that things belong to an individual reinforces the intrinsically violent aspect of asserting rights over people and resources and denies the community's shared commitment to common goals. Recognized rights over a plot of land come at the expense of someone else who cannot enjoy the privilege. If an individual belongs to a person, it is because the enslaved person's rights are denied. In different African societies, land rights are intimately connected to the ability to host people and rely on their labor, and West Central Africa is not an exception.[4] Thus, as I will examine in later chapters, there is a clear connection between asserting rights over people and land.

Meinzen-Dick, and Allan Bomuhangi, "Who Owns the Land? Perspectives from Rural Ugandans and Implications for Large-Scale Land Acquisitions," *Feminist Economics* 20, no. 1 (2014): 76–100; Aharon Grassi and Jesse Salah Ovadia, "Trajectories of Large-Scale Land Acquisition Dynamics in Angola: Diversity, Histories, and Implications for the Political Economy of Development in Africa," *Land Use Policy* 67 (2017): 115–25; Lauren Honig, "Selecting the State or Choosing the Chief? The Political Determinants of Smallholder Land Titling," *World Development* 100, no. Supplement C (2017): 94–107; Karen B. Graubart, "Shifting Landscape. Heterogenous Conceptions of Land Use and Tenure in the Lima Valley," *Colonial Latin American Review* 26, no. 1 (2017): 62–84; Tamar Herzog, *Frontiers of Possession. Spain, Portugal in Europe and the Americas* (Cambridge, MA: Harvard University Press, 2015); Brenna Bhandar, *Colonial Lives of Property: Law, Land, and Racial Regimes of Ownership* (Durham, NC: Duke University Press Books, 2018); Toby Green, *A Fistful of Shells: West Africa from the Rise of the Slave Trade to the Age of Revolution* (Chicago: Chicago University Press, 2019).

[4] Sara Berry, *Chiefs Know Their Boundaries: Essays on Property, Power, and the Past in Asante, 1896–1996* (Portsmouth, NH: Heinemann, 2001); Holly Elisabeth Hanson, *Landed Obligation: The Practice of Power in Buganda* (Portsmouth, NH: Heinemann, 2003); Benjamin N. Lawrance, "'En Proie à La Fièvre du Cacao': Land and Resource Conflict on an Ewe Frontier, 1922–1939," *African Economic History* 31 (2003): 135–81; Lentz, *Land, Mobility, and Belonging in West Africa*; Sarr, "Land, Power, and Dependency," 101–21; Suzanne Schwarz, "Adaptation in the Aftermath of Slavery: Women, Trade, and Property in Sierra Leone, c. 1790–1812," in *African Women in the Atlantic World: Property, Vulnerability and Mobility, 1660–1880*, ed. Mariana P. Candido and Adam Jones (Woodbridge: James Currey, 2019), 19–37.

While written documents and narratives of migration clearly indicate that the West Central African population exercised rights in land and had political and territorial authority, colonialism was based on possession of land and controlling people. Rights of possession or dispossession of land were not stable categories for any of the actors involved but were the result of intense disputes and conflicts among social groups and between elites and the lower classes. In the context of European invasion and conquest in West Central Africa by the late sixteenth century, local rulers, the sobas, and their subjects resisted land expropriation, though not necessarily in successful ways. "Violence against enclosure, for instance, reflected a variety of point of views – on positions, on intrusions, on trespass, indeed on property rights."[5] In many ways, the resistance was also against conquest more broadly and in opposition to the Portuguese's assumption that they could claim rights over the territories and people they occupied.[6] The reigning interpretation has obscured the evidence of a counterhistory, which recognizes West Central Africans grappling with land rights since the sixteenth century.

West Central African Notions of Land Use and Occupation Rights

One of the challenges for understanding local practices of land rights is the lack of any systematic recording of how the Bantu populations south and north of the Kwanza River, as well as non-Bantu groups such as the Nyaneka, !Kung, and Nkhumbi, dealt with jurisprudence, including ownership and transmission regime. By the time evidence about ownership rights began to be recorded in the early twentieth century, the issue of who enjoyed rights over land, people, and cattle had already caused dispute, dispossession, and contestation for centuries. Colonial officials systematically missed out registering Axiluanda or Ndombe interpretations and understanding of land occupation, which rendered them as lacking land tenure regimes. Fast forward 80 years, and then, by the

---

[5] Rosa Congost, "Property Rights and Historical Analysis: What Rights? What History?," *Past & Present*, no. 181 (2003): 94.

[6] For similar situations, see Anthony Pagden, "Law, Colonization, Legitimation, and the European Background," in *The Cambridge History of Law in America*, ed. Michael Grossberg et al. (Cambridge: Cambridge University Press, 2008), 1–31; José Vicente Serrão, "Property, Land and Territory in the Making of Overseas Empires," in *Property Rights, Land and Territory in the European Overseas Empires*, ed. José Vicente Serrão et al. (Lisbon: CEHC-IUL, 2014), 9, http://hdl.handle.net/10071/2718; Suzanne Schwarz, "'A Just and Hounorable Commerce': Abolitionist Experimentation in Sierra Leone in the Late Eighteenth and Early Nineteenth Centuries," *African Economic History* 45, no. 1 (2017): 25–26.

second half of the twentieth century, scholars helped spread the notion of precolonial societies characterized by the absence of land tenure regimes.[7] Early accounts paid attention to how West Central African rulers claimed dominium rights, but not necessarily how common people exercised or claimed rights, particularly in relation to land use and access. Dispersed accounts provide some clues and reveal how the local population related to land tenure regimes, but most of them were collected in the late nineteenth or early twentieth century. By then, the notion that land could be bought and sold was consolidated in Europe, and jurists, missionaries, and colonial officers assumed that individual property rights were superior to other forms of ownership, such as collective ones.

For the communities that inhabited West Central Africa and its interior, and probably most of western Africa, land rights had been based on the principle of first occupation: Land belonged to the groups who arrived first, occupied it, and used it for cultivation or animal husbandry. Military conquest could also establish rights over lands. Land rights were collective, and kinship guaranteed access to the land by living and deceased members. Rights of use and occupation were transmitted to following generations, resulting in competition and negotiation with neighboring populations. This practice justified, for example, the idea that the Ndombe people were the first occupants of what became known as the Cattle Bay, as well the Axiluanda as the first settlers of the Luanda coast and inland (see Map 1.1). Ancestors guaranteed rights over possession and use of the land, and the heads of lineages arbitrated claims for its use through a series of obligations and patron–client links.

This system was not so different from the Portuguese concept of land conquest and occupation that prevailed until the mid-nineteenth century. Individuals could use the land, but its ultimate dominion rested on the Crown, not on individuals. In the areas under Portuguese rule, land access in Angola was regulated through the *sesmaria* regimen put into effect in mainland Portugal and its empire until the nineteenth century.

---

[7] See, for example, Jack Goody, *Death, Property and the Ancestors* (Stanford: Stanford University Press, 1962); Jan Vansina, *Paths in the Rainforests: Toward a History of Political Tradition in Equatorial Africa* (Madison: University of Wisconsin Press, 1990); A. G. Hopkins, *An Economic History of West Africa* (New York: Columbia University Press, 1973); Jan Vansina, *How Societies Are Born: Governance in West Central Africa before 1600* (Charlottesville: University of Virginia Press, 2004); Wyatt MacGaffey, *Kongo Political Culture: The Conceptual Challenge of the Particular* (Bloomington: Indiana University Press, 2000). For similar criticism of misconceptions about property rights in African societies, see Lentz, *Land, Mobility, and Belonging in West Africa*, 9–12; Assan Sarr, *Islam, Power, and Dependency in the Gambia River Basin: The Politics of Land Control, 1790–1940* (Rochester, NY: University of Rochester Press, 2016), 59–83.

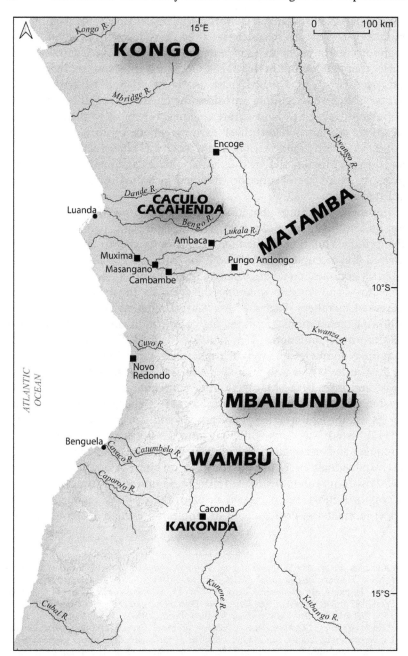

Map 1.1 Political Organizations of West Central Africa

According to the *sesmaria*, individuals could lease land for cultivation and assume the responsibilities related to its costs, thus freeing the state from investment. The land was not seen as owned but held, which allowed individuals to use it for cultivation or grazing, without having the right to dispose of it.[8] Thus, individual property rights over land did not exist in Portugal when *conquistadores* arrived in West Central Africa, putting the lie to narratives that individual ownership over land had always existed in Europe, a central argument used to justify land seizure and colonialism in the late nineteenth century. West Central African and Portuguese populations shared similar understandings about occupation and land rights.

Besides migration narratives that establish first settler claims among several West Central African groups, some chiefs appropriated the language and mechanisms of creating proof for their land claims, forming their own state archives to document their rights over land occupation. Éve Sebestyén, Ana Paula Tavares, and Catarina Madeira Santos have located written documents dating back to the seventeenth century that demonstrate that dynastic lineages kept records legitimizing their access to power and their privilege as the first settlers.[9] Most of these documents are written in Portuguese, but some are also in Kimbundu, showing chiefs appropriated writing and the paper culture to strengthen their political and territorial authorities. State archives, such as the Caculo Cacahenda archive, provide rich information that place Ndembu populations as legitimated landlords divided into different chiefdoms, as can be seen in Map 1.1 (an issue examined further in Chapter 3). These documents recorded migration, settlement, and the founding of villages to verify and validate traditions of land use and rights, probably an attempt to prevent Portuguese claims over Ndembu territory. They also describe in careful detail the boundaries of villages. It is not clear the intent of the Ndembu elite in creating the records and eventually the archive, but one can imagine their goal was to employ these documents as evidence for any possible land claims.

---

[8] Aida Freudenthal, *Arimos e fazendas: A transição agrária em Angola, 1850–1880* (Luanda: Chá de Caxinde, 2005), 137–39; Tuca Manuel, *Terra, a tradição e o poder. Contribuição ao estudo etno-histórico da Ganda* (Benguela: KAT – Aguedense, 2005); Dias Paes, "Escravos e terras."

[9] Éve Sebestyén, "Legitimation through Landcharters in Ambundo Villages, Angola," *Perspektiven afrikanistischer Forschung* , in eds. Thomas Bearth, Wilhelm Mohlig, Beat Sottas and Edgar Suter (Cologne, Germany: Rudiger Koppe Verlag, 1994), 363–78, and Ana Paula Tavares and Catarina Madeira Santos, *Africa Monumenta: A apropriação da escrita pelos africanos* (Lisbon: IICT, 2002).

In fact, for most of the seventeenth and eighteenth centuries, the colonial administration recognized sobas, *dembos*, and *mani* as lords of their lands in different colonial records and in some cases arbitrated land disputes between neighboring rulers. In 1739, the governor of Angola, João Jacques de Magalhães, wrote to the ruler of Caculo Cacahenda, Dembo Sebastião Francisco Xeque, recognizing him as the recently invested ruler with the support of his subjects and councilors (*macotas*) and tributary rulers (*sobas*). In this letter, Magalhães states,

Dom Sebastião Francisco Xeque is the lord of the lands of Caculo Cacahenda, able to enjoy all the honors, privileges, liberties, exceptions, and honesty, as his predecessors, with close relationship with the Majesty [of Portugal]. ... Dom Sebastião Francisco will enjoy the same conditions as those who preceded him in those lands and is obliged to [provide] the same service to me and those who will succeed me in the services of Your [Portuguese] Majesty.[10]

In oral traditions and written documents, ruling elites claimed rights of land occupancy based on narratives of migration and occupation of territories, which consolidated rights over resources such as land, rivers, lakes, and fauna and flora. In 1798, the soba of Humbe, identified as Nkumbi, argued that he had jurisdiction over his lands since "his ancestors had secured possession from time immemorial."[11] Firstcomer narratives settled disputes among several societies, mixing early settlement and ancestors' origins with access to land and full membership rights in their societies. Insiders were considered landlords, demonstrating that the argument claiming that land tenure regimes did not exist in African societies needs to be revisited.[12] In 1759, several sobas wrote to the governor of Angola to complain about the behavior of Jesuit priests who had "usurped the lands of their ancestors, with the evasion and cunning that were natural to them."[13] The residents along the Bengo River also complained about losing control over their land for more than

[10] Tavares and Madeira Santos, *Africa Monumenta*, doc. 3, "Carta de confirmação passada pelo Governador de Angola a Dom Sebastião Francisco Cheque," March 2, 1739, pp. 57–58.
[11] Instituto Histórico Geográfico Brasileiro (IHGB), DL81,02.31, "Comunicação para o Rei de Portugal," 1798.
[12] For similar suggestions, see Hanson, *Landed Obligation*, 41–52; Lentz, *Land, Mobility, and Belonging in West Africa*, 5–8 and 127–65; Sarr, "Land, Power, and Dependency," 104–5.
[13] Arquivo Histórico Ultramarino (AHU), caixa (cx.) 46, document (doc.) 4261, "Carta de António de Vasconcelos, governador de Angola, para o Conde de Oeiras. São Paulo de Assunção de Luanda," May 14, 1760. I am thankful to Crislayne Alfagali who shared her own transcription of this document with me.

Illustration 1.1 Portrait of the ruler of Caculo Cacahenda with his advisors, early twentieth century. The photograph reveals the different textiles worn as well as the variety of symbols of power, including shoes, hats, and scepter.
(*Source*: "O Dembo Caculo Cahenda e seus principais macotas," Arquivo Histórico Ultramarino.)

fifty years.[14] These cases from the eighteenth century reveal that Portuguese administrators recognized African sovereigns as the legitimate occupiers of the land despite the encroaching actions of the Jesuit priests.

[14] Maria Adelina Amorim, "A Real Fábrica de Ferro de Nova Oeiras. Angola, séc. XVIII," *CLIO – Revista do Centro de História da Universidade de Lisboa*, 9 (2003): 189–216 and Crislayne Alfagali, *Ferreiros e fundidores da Ilamba: Uma história social da fabricação do ferro e da Real Fábrica de Nova Oeiras (Angola, segunda metade do século XVIII)* (Luanda: Fundação Agostinho Neto, 2018), 113–14.

Struggles for power and land were closely related, and their records on paper created an interesting dynamic between local forms of knowledge, paper culture, and legitimization. A few years later, another conflict over occupation rights emerged. In 1768, the soba Muxixi, from the interior of Luanda, claimed to be the occupant of the lands of Ilamba, where the governor intended to establish a Royal Foundry to tap into steel resources.[15] The manager of the foundry notified Governor Inocêncio de Sousa Coutinho that the soba and the residents of the presidio de Massangano had different interpretations regarding land tenure. The residents of the colonial *presídio* claimed that they had bought the land from the soba, to which the governor replied that this purchase was illegal since sobas could not sell their land. Sousa Coutinho determined that any unoccupied land could be taken until the original owners could present ownership titles.[16] Written titles were unavailable, casting the firstcomers as outsiders in their own territory in a process that predated the European takeover of African lands in most of the African continent by 150 years.[17]

The issue of control over land also settled dynastic disputes. Rulers rushed to prove that their ancestors were the first to arrive and settle in disputed lands, in some cases creating paper trails that proved precedence over claims and questioned the presence of recently arrived groups in their lands. A new Caculo Cacahenda ruler came to power in the 1810s, and as the new sovereign, he requested the Portuguese a new charter (*carta patente*) that recognized his rise to power and his role as landlord. Despite the earlier correspondence between his predecessor and the colonial administration in 1739, the newly inaugurated Dembo Caculo Cacuhenda demanded written evidence of his power.

---

[15] For more on Nova Oeiras, see Alfagali, *Ferreiros e fundidores*, 140–74.

[16] IEB/USP, AL-083-003, "Carta de FISC para o coronel Antônio Anselmo Duarte de Siqueira, intendente geral da fábrica do ferro, ressaltando o zelo do intendente no cumprimento do seu ofício," February 3, 1768. I am very grateful to Cryslaine Alfagali who shared her transcription of this document. See also Alfagali, *Ferreiros e fundidores*, 114.

[17] While in Gorée, Cape Colony, Algiers, and Lagos, Africans were displaced from their land during the nineteenth century; in most of the continent, African rulers retained land control until the late nineteenth and early twentieth centuries. This was not the case in the coastal regions of West Central Africa. For more on this, see Marie-Hélène Knight, "Gorée au XVIIIe siècle du sol," *Revue française d'histoire d'outre-mer* 64, no. 234 (1977): 33–54; Sarr, "Land, Power, and Dependency"; Kristin Mann, "Women, Landed Property, and the Accumulation of Wealth in Early Colonial Lagos," *Signs* 16, no. 4 (1991): 682–706; Eugénia Rodrigues, "Women, Land, and Power in the Zambezi Valley of the Eighteenth Century," *African Economic History* 43, no. 1 (2015): 19–56. For regions where the twentieth century represented a major shift in land and property rights, see Lentz, *Land, Mobility, and Belonging in West Africa*.

The governor of Angola, José de Oliveira Barbosa, sent the charter stating that Dembo Sebastião Miguel Francisco Xeque was "the new Dembo and landlord of the Caculo Cacahenda lands, including all of his *macotas* and people, after the resignation of the previous Dembo, Sebastião Francisco Xeque." In 1812, the Angolan governor then confirmed "Dom Sebastião Miguel Franscisco Xeque in the role of Dembo, lord of his lands."[18] Other local rulers rushed to claim dynastic lineage rights and set territorial boundaries that could consolidate claims and inheritance rights for their descendants. In 1821, Chief Caputo Cazombo produced the following record:

I, Caputu CaCazombo, married to D. Macuca a Condo dia Ndala, ... had with her a daughter called Canhica CaCaputo, and I had a son called Caque CaCaputu with another woman, when they became [adults] I called my daughter Canhica's uncles: 1. Quitenda quia Caginga uá ginga or ngana Mundongo, 2. Ngola Uini Quitembe, and my father-in-law. About the lands: the co-inheritor, Caque, her brother, starts with the boundary of the land at the end of the river Caculo Cabaça, going up following the river Zenza to the island Nusimo Zenza, following Caputo CaCazumbo's boundary to the border with Ughi Amgombe, there making a circle and continuing along the bank of the river Caluategi to the entry of the Calucala into the Calutuegi, continuing to the source of the Ghonda, following to Quizanga quia Ngandu, continuing with Quianga, the boundary proceeds until the Camaluigi where there is the border with Dembo Quipete, coming down with the Camuluigi to Camienguica, where there is the site Quiebamba, from there to Ccazazala, where brother Caque's land boundary finishes. The other heir [mentioned] above I gave the regalia of the state with which she can govern the land which ends by the river Zenza. At the end I have divided everything between my heirs, except for the papers of the state which after my death I left in Caganga Camugila's possession in the quality of my paternal parent. Finishing, I recommend peace and harmony in order to defend each other as brothers. Banza Zanga do Quipungu, 12th of February 1821. Cross of declarante Caputo cá a Zombo dia nzunaga-diá-Ima-gon, subscribing on the declarant's request: Francisco Paulo da Cruz.[19]

---

[18] Tavares and Madeira Santos, *Africa Monumenta*, doc. 18, "Carta Patente de provimento e confirmação de Dom Sebastião Miguel Francisco Cheque no cargo de Dembo e senhoria das terras de Cacuclo Cacahenda," August 11, 1812, pp. 75–76. This appropriation of bureaucracy and paperwork regimes of the colonial order to support indigenous claims happened elsewhere as well. See, for example, Yanna Yannakakis, *The Art of Being In-between: Native Intermediaries, Indian Identity, and Local Rule in Colonial Oaxaca* (Durham, NC: Duke University Press, 2008); Bhavani Raman, "The Duplicity of Paper: Counterfeit, Discretion, and Bureaucratic Authority in Early Colonial Madras," *Comparative Studies in Society & History* 54, no. 2 (2012): 229–50; Karen B. Graubart, "Learning from the Qadi: The Jurisdiction of Local Rule in the Early Colonial Andes," *Hispanic American Historical Review* 95, no. 2 (2015): 195–228.

[19] "Manuscript from Cazombo," cited in Sebestyén, "Legitimation through Landcharters in Ambundo Villages," 372–73.

Firstcomer narratives justified inalienable land rights and are also very similar to oral narratives that legitimate claims elsewhere in Africa. An individual who could prove firstcomer rights based on clearing and occupying land was able to transmit these rights to heirs, in this specific case to Caputo CaCazombo's biological daughter and son. In addition, African rulers such as Caputo CaCazombo employed geographical and political markers to set the limits of their territories, such as rivers or the lands of neighboring chiefs. These accounts served as proofs for their subjects, neighboring rulers, and the colonial administrators of the land and ruling legitimacy to protect the interests of the lineage in the present and in the future. Political and territorial boundaries were not stable and subject to changes, as in the case of rivers changing courses or neighbors migrating to new territories.

Clashes over Land Use and Occupation Rights

The Portuguese Empire prioritized policies for fixing people to land and space. In the 1676 *Regimento do Governo de Angola*, the king of Portugal noted, "You will know about land and who has dominium over them. I have been informed that land grants were distributed to promote agriculture, although many have not been cultivated. The lands not occupied should be distributed to praiseworthy people (*pessoas beneméritas*), with the condition they will cultivate them within five years."[20] Local conceptions of land use and access were clashing with the European notion of control and dominium. The Portuguese administration expected land to be cultivated and its use to be limited to a specific person; it disregarded communal use or land reserved for religious purpose or occupied by spirits. These policies imposed the idea of permanent settlement and the notion that transhumant groups could not enjoy land use and rights, yet transhumance has remained part of Iberian life into the twenty-first century. Africanists have spent decades debating whether African societies had notions of individual ownership or land regime and how wealth was accumulated.[21] Communal use of land, for example, did

---

[20] "Regimento do Governo deste Reyno de Angolla, 12 de fevereiro de 1676" *Arquivos de Angola*, vol. I (n° 5–6) (1936), Chapter 4, no page number. For more on sedentarization as a colonial project, see Clifton Crais, "Chiefs and Bureaucrats in the Making of Empire: A Drama from the Transkei, South Africa, October 1880," *American Historical Review* 108, no. 4 (2003): 1045–52; James C. Scott, *Seeing like a State: How Certain Schemes to Improve the Human Condition Have Failed* (New Haven, CT: Yale University Press, 2005).

[21] There is a vast scholarship on this topic, see Max Gluckman, *The Ideas in Barotse Jurisprudence* (New Haven, CT: Yale University Press, 1965); Augusto Bastos, "Traços

not indicate general access to use of land since descendants of enslaved people and marginal members of society were excluded from decisions regarding land. Land access was political, and marginalized groups could till the soil but as dependents of more-powerful patrons or clients, very similar to feudal regimes in Europe.

West Central Africans also exercised rights of use and of disposal over movable goods, such as things and cattle, as well as over human beings, known in the historiography as wealth in people.[22] Men and women did not necessarily enjoy the same patterns of land rights and use; however, some historical documents reveal that both West Central African men and women owned cows, chickens, pigs, and sheep as part of their personal wealth, as well as accumulating material goods such as jewelry, baskets, pottery, and farming tools.[23] African rulers and commoners accumulated wealth in movable and immovable things that were considered individual property. Early travelers observed the desire of local rulers to acquire things that were infused with value, that expressed wealth, and that became instruments of power, such as the political elite of Kongo accumulating crucifixes carved in ivory, copper, and brass. They also purchased outfits to project power, mixing imported garments with locally produced clothes, as with the woven *mpu* cap that symbolized power in the Kongo court.[24] Reports from the sixteenth, seventeenth,

geraes sobre a ethnographia do districto de Benguella," *Boletim da Sociedade de Geografia de Lisboa* 26, no. 1 (1908): 5–15; 44–56; Goody, *Death, Property and the Ancestors*; Berry, "Debating the Land"; Sara Berry, *No Condition Is Permanent. The Social Dynamics of Agrarian Change in Sub-Saharan Africa* (Madison, WI: University of Wisconsin Press, 1993); Martin Chanock, *Law, Custom, and Social Order: The Colonial Experience in Malawi and Zambia* (New York: Cambridge University Press, 1985); Rhiannon Stephens, "'Wealth', 'Poverty' and the Question of Conceptual History in Oral Contexts: Uganda from c.1000 CE," in *Doing Conceptual History in Africa*, ed. Axel Fleisch and Rhiannon Stephens (New York: Berghahn, 2016), 21–48.

[22] For more on concept of wealth in people, see Suzanne Miers and Igor Kopytoff, eds., *Slavery in Africa: Historical and Anthropological Perspectives* (Madison, WI: University of Wisconsin Press, 1977), 7–9; Joseph C. Miller, *Way of Death: Merchant Capitalism and the Angolan Slave Trade, 1730-1830* (Madison, WI: University of Wisconsin Press, 1988), 43–52; Jane I. Guyer, "Wealth in People and Self-Realization in Equatorial Africa," *Man* 28, no. 2 (1993): 243–65, https://doi.org/10.2307/2803412; Jane I. Guyer and Samuel M. Eno Belinga, "Wealth in People as Wealth in Knowledge: Accumulation and Composition in Equatorial Africa," *Journal of African History* 36, no. 1 (1995): 91–120; Berry, *No Condition Is Permanent*, 15.

[23] Biblioteca Nacional do Rio de Janeiro (BNRJ), doc. I-28, 28, 29, "Notícias de São Filipe de Benguela e costumes dos gentios habitantes naquele sertão," 10 November 1797. Tribunal da Comarca de Benguela (TCB), "Inventário de Manuel Vidal Cesar," 16 August 1858; "Inventário de Florência Jose do Cadaval," 15 June. 1854

[24] Cécile Fromont, *The Art of Conversion: Christian Visual Culture in the Kingdom of Kongo* (Chapel Hill, NC: University of North Carolina Press, 2014), 99–100 and 109–38; and Green, *A Fistful of Shells*. For more on the demand on luxury items see Jeremy

and eighteenth centuries reveal several currencies operating in West Central Africa, such as *nzimbu*, a variety of clothes, salt, and copper *manillas* [a form of currency], as well as an intense trade in manufactured goods such as baskets and pottery.[25] Things were accumulated, individually owned, and bequeathed to heirs. They had market value and were exchanged for other commodities, allowing men and women to accumulate things over time.[26]

Supposedly, the accumulation of things was intimately related to the recruitment of dependents. The thinking goes like this: Goods created dependency and patron–client relationships, expanding debt and enslavement in what became known as wealth in people. Rulers and elites accumulated things due to their allure and the ability to attract dependents, consolidating a system based on holding the rights to another's labor and reproduction as the main organizing concept among West Central African societies.[27] According to John Thornton, wealth in people was "the preeminent form of private investment and manifestation of private wealth."[28] In the 1970s, Suzanne Miers and Igor Kopytoff proposed that rights-in-persons was "an integral part of African system of kinship and marriage"[29] and shaped all social relationships, creating bonds of rights, obligation, respect, and protection. Following this argument, rights could "be manipulated to increase the number of people in one's kin group, to gather dependents and supporters, and to build up wealth and power."[30] West Central African specialists embraced Miers and Kopytoff's notion of rights-in-persons and pushed it forward as a cornerstone to understanding the social, political, and economic lives of West Central African societies.

Prestholdt, *Domesticating the World: African Consumerism and the Genealogies of Globalization* (Berkeley, CA: University of California Press, 2008).

[25] See Eugenia W. Herbert, *Red Gold of Africa: Copper in Precolonial History and Culture* (Madison, WI: University of Wisconsin Press, 2003); J. Vansina, "Long-Distance Trade-Routes in Central Africa," *The Journal of African History* 3, no. 3 (1962): 375–90; Colleen E. Kriger, "Mapping the History of Cotton Textile Production in Precolonial West Africa," *African Economic History* 33 (205AD): 87–116; Miller, *Way of Death*, 62–81; Phyllis M. Martin, "Power, Cloth and Currency on the Loango Coast," *African Economic History* no. 15 (1986): 1–12; and Jan Hogendorn and Marion Johnson, *The Shell Money of the Slave Trade* (New York: Cambridge University Press, 2003).

[26] Further analysis in Chapters 3 and 7. See also Miller, *Way of Death*, 54–7; Colleen E. Kriger, *Making Money: Life, Death, and Early Modern Trade on Africa's Guinea Coast* (Athens: Ohio University Press, 2017).

[27] Vansina, *Paths in the Rainforests*, 207; Jane I. Guyer, "Wealth in People, Wealth in Things – Introduction," *The Journal of African History* 36, no. 1 (2009): 83–90; Guyer and Belinga, "Wealth in People as Wealth in Knowledge"; Miller, *Way of Death*, 43–52.

[28] John K. Thornton, *Africa and Africans in the Making of the Atlantic World, 1400-1800* (New York: Cambridge University Press, 1998), 87.

[29] Miers and Kopytoff, *Slavery in Africa*, 7.   [30] Miers and Kopytoff, *Slavery in Africa*, 9.

Wealth in people became so central to understanding West Central African societies since it was presumably the system behind the expansion of productivity and control of people. According to Joseph Miller in 1988, "Permanent, real wealth resides in dependents' abstract collective obligations to provide future material goods upon command, in respect, and in prestige."[31] Two years later, Jan Vansina argued that "wealth in goods was still converted into followers."[32] The goods, such as alcohol, gunpowder, or textiles, that rulers demanded in exchange for captives or signatures on vassalage treaties were acquired with the intention of creating a larger pool of dependents as free or enslaved subjects.[33] Historians propose that the main goal of lineage heads was to accumulate people, which explains warfare in the region but also the fact that during the Atlantic slave era male captives were sold to overseas markets while women were retained as captives locally. Anthropologist Wyatt MacGaffey argues that women were the source of wealth in people since they could expand lineages.[34]

Owning people and controlling their labor was important, which explains the broad existence of slavery as an institution in West Central Africa by the time Europeans arrived at the end of the fifteenth century. Thornton also links wealth in people with the fact that landownership did not exist. According to Thornton, "their only recourse was to purchase slaves, which as their personal property could be inherited and could generate wealth for them. They would have no trouble in obtaining land to put these slaves in agricultural production, for African law made land available to whoever would cultivate it, free or slave, as long as no previous cultivator was actively using it."[35] Yet it is important to stress that people faced restrictions as to where they might cultivate land since raids, warfare, and political instability made people vulnerable to slave raiders.[36] Also, as the sobas' complaints from earlier in this chapter

---

[31] Miller, *Way of Death*, 52.   [32] Vansina, *Paths in the Rainforests*, 251.

[33] For more on vassalage treaties and the demand for imported commodities, see Heintze, 'The Angolan Vassal Tributes,'57–78; and Carvalho, *Sobas e homens do rei*, 82–100.

[34] Wyatt MacGaffey, *Kongo Political Culture: The Conceptual Challenge of the Particular* (Bloomington, IN: Indiana University Press, 2000), 215–16.

[35] Thornton, *Africa and Africans in the Making of the Atlantic World, 1400-1800*, 87.

[36] Roquinaldo Ferreira, "Slaving and Resistance to Slaving in West Central Africa," in *The Cambridge World History of Slavery*, vol. 3 (Cambridge University Press, 2011); Mariana P. Candido, "African Freedom Suits and Portuguese Vassal Status: Legal Mechanisms for Fighting Enslavement in Benguela, Angola, 1800–1830," *Slavery & Abolition* 32, no. 3 (2011): 447–59; and Mariana P. Candido, "The Transatlantic Slave Trade and the Vulnerability of Free Blacks in Benguela, Angola, 1780-1830," in *Atlantic Biographies: Individuals and Peoples in the Atlantic World*, ed. Mark Meuwese and Jeffrey A. Fortin (Leiden: Brill, 2013), 193–210.

reveal, rulers had a clear understanding about land rights, such as the case of Caculo Cacahenda discussed before.

Wealth in people as a concept eventually became a model to explain West Central African societies, even though specialists in other regions of the African continent emphasized the existence of slavery and other forms of dependency as different categories rather than lumping them together with wealth in people.[37] Control of people was part of a system in which people were seen as property that could be bought and sold, yet those who could accumulate people could also acquire things such as alcohol, weapons, and copper manillas. A husband with several wives and children could expand cultivation and produce more food to feed more dependents. In different farming societies, seeds and later the harvested crops were individually owned.[38] As traders amassed dependents, they were socially perceived as wealthier, gained status in the community, and could aspire to political roles. Linda Heywood showed how Ovimbundu traders who profited from long-distance trade displayed their recently acquired wealth by marrying additional wives, expanding their families, acquiring cattle and slaves, and incorporating material possessions associated with Western style, such as wearing pants and shoes.[39] This process inevitably eroded old political elites and led to the rise of merchants as the new political leaders in the highlands of Benguela. Héli Chatelain, a Swiss missionary and linguist who lived in Angola from 1885 to 1889 and returned to Luanda later, stated, "In the absence of metal or paper money to represent capital, a large number of wives, of children, and hence a wide circle of blood-connection and influence, is considered the best investment and most substantial element of wealth." This influenced how later scholars understood property and wealth in West Central Africa as, solely, the accumulation of dependents.[40] Yet, if wealth was solely expressed in the accumulation of

---

[37] Paul E. Lovejoy, "Concubinage and the Status of Women Slaves in Early Colonial Northern Nigeria," *The Journal of African History* 29, no. 2 (1988): 245–66; Lovejoy, *Slow Death for Slavery*, 226–33; Mann, *Slavery and the Birth of an African City*, 200–35; James F. Searing, "Aristocrats, Slaves, and Peasants: Power and Dependency in the Wolof States, 1700-1850," *International Journal of African Historical Studies* 21, no. 3 (1988): 475–503; Megan Vaughan, *Creating the Creole Island: Slavery in Eighteenth-Century Mauritius* (Durham: Duke University Press, 2005), 150–51.

[38] For examples from other parts of the continent, see Jane Guyer, "Female Farming in Anthropology and African History," in *Gender at the Crossroads of Knowledge: Feminist Anthropology in the Postmodern Era*, ed. Micaela di Leonardo (Berkeley, CA: University of California Press, 1991), 260–62; Goheen, *Men Own the Fields, Women Own the Crops.*

[39] Linda M. Heywood, *Contested Power in Angola, 1840s to the Present* (Rochester, NY: University of Rochester Press, 2000), 16–18.

[40] Héli Chatelain, *Folk-Tales of Angola Fifty Tales, with Ki-Mbundu Text, Literal English Translation, Introduction, and Notes* (Boston, MA: The American Folklore Society by

dependents, it is difficult to understand the economic motivations of rulers to sell their most prized investment.

It is problematic to mix slavery with other forms of control of people, such as marriage, patronage, parenthood, overlordship, and so on, under the umbrella of wealth in people because not all types of relationships necessarily share the same coercion and employ violence as in slavery.[41] Wealth in people and slavery were important forms of accumulation in West Central Africa, yet they are not so different from how planters in Brazil, Cuba, or Jamaica, who also invested in enslaved people, enriched themselves. West Central Africans produced things and accumulated wealth in goods before contact with Europeans and during the centuries of the transatlantic slave trade and the Portuguese presence in the region, as evidenced by the ivory carvings and masks displayed in museums around the world.[42] Thus, wealth in people and wealth in things were not different but part of systems of accumulation that had gone through transformations for centuries, in part due to their connection to the global markets.

Changes Related to Possession and Ownership

It is only with the European liberal revolutions of the eighteenth century that the notion of land as belonging to an individual, rather than a collective possession, prevailed.[43] That is, the concept of individual property has a history. In Europe or in Africa, before the consolidation of liberalism in the nineteenth century, land was held and not owned. For England and France, it was during the eighteenth century that small landholders lost rights over communal use of land and exclusive property rights to land emerged.[44] In Portugal and Spain, it was during the nineteenth century that land was centralized on single owners and common rights disappeared. Land acquired an economic aspect related

Houghton Mifflin, 1894), 9. For more on Chatelain, see Gerald Moser, "Héli Chatelain: Pioneer of a National Language and Literature for Angola," *Research in African Languages* 14, no. 4 (1983): 516–37.

[41] Mann, *Slavery and the Birth of an African City*, 3–4; Paul E. Lovejoy, *Transformations in Slavery* (New York: Cambridge University Press, 2000), 4–22.

[42] Jane I. Guyer made this point in her 'Wealth in People and Self-Realization in Equatorial Africa', *Man* 28, no. 2 (1993), 243–65. For the goods produced in West Central Africa, see *Portugal e o mundo nos séculos XVI e XVII: Encompassing the Globe* (Lisbon: Instituto dos Museus e da Conservação, 2009), 145–60.

[43] Peter Garnsey, *Thinking about Property: From Antiquity to the Age of Revolution* (New York, Cambridge: Cambridge University Press, 2007), 182–84.

[44] E. P. Thompson, *The Making of the English Working Class* (New York: Pantheon Books, 1964), 215–23.

to production and its value as an asset, a commodity that could be rented, bequeathed, or mortgaged. Yet land also had, and has, social and political values that cannot be easily measured, and its value is associated with one's relationship with another. The economic value of land rests on individuals enjoying rights to it on the principle of occupation. We can argue that "property is theft" as defined by the nineteenth-century French philosopher Pierre-Joseph Proudhon since it assumes that not everyone enjoys the same rights.[45] But it is more than this. As defined by Sara Berry, property rights were "negotiable and contested – shaped and reshaped over time by multiple, sometimes conflicting forces."[46] In West Central Africa, as well as in Portugal and other European monarchies before the nineteenth century, property claims over land, people, and things were based and shaped by notions of kinship, community membership, and context. The difference between the public and the private were blurred, and occupation and use rights were never stable, with rulers keeping land in tenure for ancestor, and subjects securing occupation recognitions.[47]

During the process of conquest in the fifteenth and sixteenth centuries, Portuguese explorers and the monarchy employed the principle of territorial occupation and subjugation to justify claims of sovereignty, classifying some use of land as legitimate, such as cultivation or mining, while dismissing others, such as burial rights or spirit occupation, as unused land or empty territory. However, it was necessary to recognize the rights of the local population to the land and its use due to the limited power of the European invaders as well as the lack of an idea, in Europe, of individual property rights. In the context of expansion and conquest, European empires made claims over lands and their people, the concept of dominium, but did not necessarily treat land as belonging to an individual. In the case of Angola, the idea was that unlike in the Kingdom of Kongo where a monarch could clearly be identified as the

---

[45] Pierre Joseph Proudhon, *What Is Property? An Inquiry into the Principle of Right and of Government* (Princeton, MA: B. R. Tucker, 1876), Chapter 1.

[46] Berry, *Chiefs Know Their Boundaries*, xxvi.

[47] Berry, "Debating the Land"; Pierre Bourdieu and Abdelmalek Sayad, "Colonial Rule and Cultural Sabir," *Ethnography* 5, no. 4 (2004): 449–51; Saliha Belmessous, "Introduction: The Problem of Indigenous Claim Making in Colonial History," in *Native Claims: Indigenous Law against Empire, 1500-1920*, ed. Saliha Belmessous (New York: Oxford University Press, 2012), 3–18; Goheen, *Men Own the Fields, Women Own the Crops*, 108–12. For an important discussion on the changing meaning of wealth, see Stephens, "'Wealth', Poverty and the Question of Conceptual History." See also Herzog, *Frontiers of Possession*; Mariana Armond Dias Paes, "Terras em contenda: Circulação e produção de normatividades em conflitos agrários no Brasil império," *Revista da Faculdade de Direito UFMG* 74 (2019): 379–406.

legitimate occupant of the territory, in the regions north and south of the Kwanza River the land was classified unused and unoccupied. It was thus the moral duty of Europeans to conquer and colonize it, similar to the debate regarding land occupation in the colony of Brazil, where the indigenous population was also seen as incapable of making the land productive and profitable.[48]

Different conceptions of sovereignty and jurisdiction were at the center of these interactions. According to Thornton, "slaves were the only form of private, revenue-producing property recognized in African law. By contrast, in European legal systems, land was the primary form of private, revenue-producing property, and slavery was relatively minor."[49] It must be noted, however, that even in several parts of Europe, particularly in Portugal, land was held, not necessarily individually owned, before the nineteenth century – thus, European and African land regimes were closer than nineteenth- and twentieth-century jurists and colonial officers projected into the past. According to the interpretation of these jurists, private property had always existed and was a hegemonic concept in European law.[50] In contrast, land on the African continent was abundant, labor was scarce, and tenure regimes were unknown. Primary sources, however, reveal that African rulers exercised dominium over their territory, employed their power to control people, free or enslaved, in order to clear and cultivate the land, and presented indigenous claims. There is plenty of evidence that demonstrates the clashes of different conceptions of land use, access, and tenure between African rulers and

---

[48] I am very grateful to Mariana Dias Paes who helped me to make the links between land seizure in West Central Africa and Portuguese America. See Dias Paes, "Escravos e terras," 48–51. See also Anthony Pagden, "Law, Colonization, Legitimation, and the European Background," in *The Cambridge History of Law in America*, ed. Michael Grossberg et al. (Cambridge: Cambridge University Press), 1–31; and Eugénia Rodrigues, *Portugueses e africanos nos Rios de Sena. Os prazos da coroa em Moçambique nos séculos XVII e XVIII* (Lisbon: Imprensa Nacional-Casa da Moeda, 2014), 355–62 and 551–80. See also Toby Green, "Baculamento or Encomienda? Legal Pluralisms and the Contestation of Power in the Pan-Atlantic World of the Sixteen and Seventeenth Centuries," *Journal of Global Slavery* 2 (2017): 310–36.

[49] Thornton, *Africa and Africans in the Making of the Atlantic World, 1400-1800*, 74. Valentim Alexandre and Jill Dias, *O Império africano* (Lisbon: Estampa, 1998), 330–334; Lauren A Benton, *Law and Colonial Cultures Legal Regimes in World History, 1400-1900* (New York: Cambridge University Press, 2002), 50–2; and Miller, *Way of Death*, 40–54 and 115–26.

[50] António Gil, *Considerações sobre alguns pontos mais importantes da moral religiosa e sistema de jurisprudência dos pretos do continente da África Ocidental Portuguesa além do Equador* (Lisbon: Tipografia da Academia, 1854); Lopo Vaz de Sampaio e Melo, *Regime da propriedade indígena, separata da "Revista Portugueza Colonial e Marítima"* (Lisbon: Ferin Editora, 1910). For more on this, see Congost, "Property Rights and Historical Analysis."

Portuguese conquistadores, especially in the seventeenth and early eighteenth centuries when European military and demographic power was limited. In theory, however, the conquered land was under the domain of the Portuguese Crown, which claimed rights over taxation and distribution, even if it was difficult to implement it.[51]

In 1571, a Portuguese royal decree named explorer Paulo Dias de Novais as representative of the interests of the Catholic Monarchy in its attempt to expand and conquer the world. A nobleman, a *fidalgo*, he was instructed to "submit and conquer the Kingdom of Angola, [to impose] Catholic worship and celebrate the Holy Catholic Faith and enact the Holy Gospel."[52] The decree authorized Dias de Novais to conquer land along the coast and in the interior, and whatever he encountered – land, people, or mineral wealth – would be considered part of the land grants (*sesmarias*) issued by the Portuguese Crown in the form of hereditary possession. The language employed is very similar to the land grants issued to the *capitão donatários* in Brazil during the same time.[53] The land that came under the management of Paulo Dias de Novais was occupied land. Seven settled groups lived on the island of Luanda. Without their knowledge or consultation, they were assigned as the property of Paulo Dias de Novais in 1571. They did not accept these arbitrary decisions, and decades of conflict followed Novais' arrival, known in the Angolan historiography as *guerras de conquistas*. These were in fact conflicts of jurisdiction sparked by the refusal of local chiefs to recognize any Portuguese dominium rights over land and people. Luanda was not

---

[51] For more on this, see Pagden, "Law, Colonization, Legitimation, and the European Background," 1; Edmundo O'Gorman, *La invención de América*, 88; Lauren Benton, "Making Order out of Trouble: Jurisdictional Politics in the Spanish Colonial Borderlands," *Law & Social Inquiry* 26, no. 2 (2001): 373–401; Graubart, "Shifting Landscape," 65–68; Caetano Gonçalves, "O regime das terras e as reservas indígenas na colonização portuguesa," *Boletim Geral das Colônias* 2, no. 13 (1926): 26–27; Aida Freudenthal, "Benguela – da feitoria à cidade colonial," *Fontes & Estudos* 6–7 (2011): 197–229; James C. Scott, John Tehranian, and Jeremy Mathias, "The Production of Legal Identities Proper to States: The Case of the Permanent Family Surname," *Comparative Studies in Society and History* 44, no. 1 (2002): 4–44.

[52] "Carta de doação a Paulo Dias de Novais," in Alfredo de Felner, *Angola. Apontamentos sobre a colonização dos planaltos e litoral do Sul de Angola. Extraídos de documentos* (Lisboa: Agência-Geral do Ultramar, 1940), 407. See also Ilidio do Amaral, *O consulado de Paulo Dias de Novais: Angola no último quartel do século XVI e primeiro do século XVII* (Lisbon: Ministério da Ciência e da Tecnologia/ Instituto de Investigação Científica Tropical, 2000) 54–72

[53] Carmen Margarida Oliveira Alveal, "Converting Land into Property in the Portuguese Atlantic World, 16th–18th Century" (Ph.D., Johns Hopkins University, 2008); Rafael Chambouleyron, "Plantações, sesmarias e vilas. Uma reflexão sobre a ocupação da Amazônia seiscentista," *Nuevo Mundo Mundos Nuevos.*, 2006; Maria Sarita Mota, "Sesmarias e propriedade titulada da terra: o individualismo agrário na América Portuguesa," *Sæculum – Revista de História* 26, no. 1 (2012): 29–45.

empty land, and its seizure by Portugal was the product of territorial conquest and exclusion of the indigenous inhabitants.[54]

Novais distributed his land grant to fellow conquistadores, most of them noblemen, and the Society of Jesus received land grants in the form of *sesmarias* in recognition of their service and collaboration with the conquest. In the language of the time, the *sesmeiros*, the grantees, became *amos* or masters, a term used for European kings and princes but which was also used for new feudatories in the Kingdom of Angola, the imaginary space created by the Portuguese empire. Masters held control over the land and the people who occupied it, with the ability to enslave, exploit, and even sell people. Although the Crown could cancel the donation in the case of ill practice, the grantees, the *capitão donatários*, enjoyed full authority and power over the lands granted to them. These land grants also became a hereditary possession that excluded any claims that native chiefs and their subjects could have over their properties. In fact, African rulers were distributed among conquistadores and the Catholic clergy as part of the *sesmarias* and could be put to work. In many ways, this territorial occupation and political subjugation were part of the same process of establishing dominium claims at the expense of the native population.[55]

Among many obligations, African authorities had to pay taxes to the new landowners, in most cases in the form of enslaved people. In 1590, for example, the tributes that the Society of Jesuits collected from local chiefs and the population over "their" lands totaled at least 300 captives of war.[56] Portuguese conquistadores blurred the lines between land grants and rights over land occupants, claiming control over people. The *amo*, master, Garcia Mendes Castelo Branco requested from the Portuguese Crown "the soba [the ruler] Caculo Quehacango, with all his *canda* (his clan)."[57] Due to his land grants, Castelo Branco was able to

---

[54] For a different interpretation, see Catarina Madeira Santos, "Luanda: A Colonial City between Africa and the Atlantic, Seventeenth and Eighteenth Century," in *Portuguese Colonial Cities in the Early Modern World*, ed. Liam M. Brockey (New York, NY: Ashgate Publishing, 2008), 249–50.

[55] Bárbara Direito, "African Access to Land in Early Twentieth Century Portuguese Colonial Thought," in *Property Rights, Land and Territory in the European Overseas Empires*, ed. José Vicente Serrão et al. (Lisbon: CEHC-IUL, 2014), 256–63, http://hdl .handle.net/10071/2718.

[56] Heintze, *Angola nos séculos XVI e XVII*, 440.

[57] Caculo Quehacango was probably Caculo Cacahenda. See David Wheat, "Garcia Mendes Castelo Branco, Fidalgo de Angola y Mercaders de Esclavos en Veracruz y el Caribe a Principios del siglo XVII," in *Debates Históricos Contemporáneos: Africanos y Afrodescendientes en México y Centroamérica*, ed. María Elisa Velázquez (Mexico City: INAH, 2011), 90. For more on Caculo Cacahenda, see *Almanak statistico da Província d'Angola e suas dependencias para o anno de 1852* (Luanda: Imprensa do Governo, 1851),

organize at least three slave voyages between Luanda and the ports of Cartagena de Índias, Veracruz, and Jamaica between 1599 and 1618, transporting, in a single voyage in 1599, more than 500 enslaved Africans to Cartagena de Índias. Many of these enslaved people were subjects or enslaved by ruler Caculo Cacahenda, discussed earlier. By the end of the sixteenth century, land grants and the slave trade were intertwined, which favored the consolidation of the *amos* as the largest slave traders of Angola.[58]

The land concessions eventually led to disputes between the conquistadores, the Jesuits, and the administrators, who saw the rise of the *amos* as slave traders as a threat to the Crown's control over trade. Under the unification of the Iberian Crown, the system of *amos* was eliminated and the sobas were put under the direct control of the Crown.[59] In the regulation of the new governor of Angola, D. Manuel Pereira Forjaz, the King of Portugal stated on March 16, 1607, that "sobas suffered extortion and abuses, including enslavement, at the hands of the *amos*, which was against justice, law, and what was convenient to the services of God and the Portuguese Crown, which impairs the good will and the piece in the land ... sobas deserve to be treated with respect and the same liberty enjoyed by other vassals."[60] The comparison between sobas' and vassals' rights led to the creation of a new juridical space. The *sesmaria* model was abandoned, in part due to the limitation of the Portuguese Crown in establishing territorial claims beyond Luanda. Eventually, the administrative efforts focused on controlling and taxing the trade in human beings to address the demand in the Americas for coerced labor.

Dominium also represented control over any mineral resources in the territory. In 1666, after the signature of the vassal treaty between the Portuguese Crown and the ruler of Wandu, the assumption was that the soba had lost control over the copper mines in his territories, a clear indication that his legal claims over his territory's mineral resources were terminated.[61] In a similar case, the vassal treaty of 1682 forced the ruler of Kakonda to allow the settlement of Portuguese officers and the

---

95; Ana Paula Tavares and Catarina Madeira Santos, "Fontes escritas africanas para a história de Angola," in *Africae Monumenta. A apropriação da escrita pelos africanos*, vol. 1 (Lisbon: Instituto de Investigação Científica Tropical, 2002), 471–509.

[58] For more on how this system was enforced and how rulers and subjects resisted, see Beatrix Heintze, "The Angolan Vassal Tributes of the Seventeenth Century," *Revista de História Econômica e Social* 6 (1980): 62; Heintze, *Angola nos séculos XVI e XVII*, 339–40.

[59] Heintze, *Angola nos séculos XVI e XVII*, 441.

[60] Amaral, *Consulado de Paulo Dias de Novais*, 243.

[61] Heintze, *Angola nos séculos XVI e XVII*, 462.

construction of a fortress in his territory.[62] So the debate over occupation and jurisdiction could not have been initiated in the nineteenth century. In fact, when changes over property rights occurred in the nineteenth century, they happened in a context of intense disputes and negotiations going back to the sixteenth century in what constituted the colony of Angola, in West Central Africa.[63]

The lack of recognition of the African land-tenure system was a constant theme, going back to *Carta de doação* of Paulo Dias de Novais by the end of the sixteenth century. However, as Assan Saar notes, "the generalization about the absence of land ownership in Africa is risky."[64] The fact that Europeans did not recognize African claims or co-opt indigenous legal systems is the result of colonialism that naturalizes occupation and expropriation of indigenous peoples. Before the nineteenth century, African rulers and their subjects who showed loyalty and established alliances with the Portuguese conquerors were recompensed with the recognition of their territorial claims, although they were required to open their territories to traders and Catholic priests and pay tributes to the Portuguese Crown, among other obligations.[65] Yet local notions of land occupation and tenure were far from guaranteed under colonial rule. Although the colonial administration recognized sobas' territories and their control over resources, foreign settler pressure to expropriate land undermined their jurisdiction claims and allowed expropriation of land during the nineteenth century.[66]

Land was initially perceived as abundant and, after the initial land removals around Luanda and Benguela in the late sixteenth and early seventeenth centuries, the Portuguese empire focused its economic interests on the transatlantic slave trade. The removal of people from the

---

[62] Rosa Cruz e Silva, "The Saga of Kakonda and Kilengues: Relations between Benguela and Its Interior, 1791-1796," in *Enslaving Connections: Changing Cultures of Africa and Brazil during the Era of the Slavery*, ed. José C. Curto and Paul E. Lovejoy (Amherst, MA: Humanity Books, 2004), 245–59.

[63] Amaral, *Consulado de Paulo Dias de Novais*, 117 and 226; Heintze, *Angola nos séculos XVI e XVII*, 253; 7

[64] Sarr, *Islam, Power, and Dependency*, 5.

[65] For more on the disregard and adoption of indigenous legal systems, see Green, "Baculamento or Encomienda?" See also Beatrix Heintze, "Luso-African Feudalism in Angola? The Vassal Treaties of the 16th to the 18th Century," *Separata da Revista Portuguesa de História* 18 (1980): 111–31; Heintze, "Angolan Vassal Tributes"; Roquinaldo Ferreira, *Cross-Cultural Exchange in the Atlantic World: Angola and Brazil during the Era of the Slave Trade* (New York: Cambridge University Press, 2012), 52–85.

[66] Freudenthal, "Questão da terra em Angola," 22–23; Freudenthal, *Arimos e fazendas*, 140–141; David Birmingham, "The Coffee Barons of Cazengo," *The Journal of African History* 19, no. 4 (1978): 523–538; Cristina Nogueira da Silva, *Constitucionalismo e império: a cidadania no ultramar português* (Lisbon: Almedina, 2009), 305–30. Similar situations happened in the Americas; see Graubart, "Shifting Landscape," 70–73.

territory became a privileged activity, which brought about depopulation and increased the availability of land above and beyond its already perceived abundance. However, there were concerns related to learning about the territory and its people. The 1676 Regulation of the Government of Angola, for example, suggested that governors should "inquire about all land grants, who oversaw the distribution, who had the power to grant land, and who owned it."[67] The concern was to verify whether the granted lands were cultivated, not necessarily to determine the legitimate occupants or who had rights over land. In the case of disputes, whoever was able to present a title would be recognized as the landowner, a system that clearly prioritized a single form of land rights, the enclosed model in which land was owned. In the case of Ilamba and Lumbo, where the Portuguese Crown intended to establish steel production, the Royal Foundry of Nova Oeiras, this decision led to the dismissal of the local Mbundu population, who were spread across several different polities, as the legitimate occupiers and colonial occupation of the territory.[68] Land-control struggles were constant, and it was through occupation and dispossession that colonial administrative centers were created along the coast, such as Luanda and Benguela, as well as in the interior, the inland *presídios*, casting the conquered as outsiders in their own land.

In the second half of the eighteenth century, efforts were made by Portuguese officials to identify territories and their occupants, as well as the way property and land tenure operated in an attempt to increase governability.[69] In the context of the Enlightenment and territorial expansion, and the enumeration of population, maps, residential lists, African states, and their political organizations spread in the late

---

[67] AHU, Códice 544, fl. 8v. "Regimento do Governo do Reino de Angola dado em Lisboa," February 12, 1676. I am very grateful to Crislayne Alfagalli who shared her transcription of this document with me.

[68] Crislayne Alfagali, *Ferreiros e fundidores da Ilamba: uma história social da fabricação do ferro e da Real Fábrica de Nova Oeiras (Angola, segunda metade do século XVIII)* (Luanda: Fundação Agostinho Neto, 2018) is a careful detailed study of the *Fábrica de Nova Oeiras* and African knowledge over steel production. For more on expropriating knowledge, see Walter D. Mignolo, "Epistemic Disobedience, Independent Thought and Decolonial Freedom," *Theory, Culture & Society* 26, no. 7–8 (2009): 159–81.

[69] Scott, *Seeing like a State*; Sherwin K Bryant, *Rivers of Gold, Lives of Bondage: Governing through Slavery in Colonial Quito* (Chapel Hill, NC: University of North Carolina Pr, 2013). See also Catarina Madeira Santos, "Entre deux droits: Les Lumières en Angola (1750-v. 1800)," *Annales. Histoire, Sciences Sociales 60*, no. 4 (2007): 817–48; Catarina Madeira Santos, "Administrative Knowledge in a Colonial Context: Angola in the Eighteenth Century," *The British Journal for the History of Science* 43, no. 4 (2010): 539–556; and Mariana P. Candido, *Fronteras de esclavización: Esclavitud, comercio e identidad en Benguela, 1780-1850* (Mexico City: El Colegio de Mexico Press, 2011).

eighteenth century in efforts to increase colonial knowledge about the African population and how ownership rights operated. In 1750, the colonial administration organized an inventory of the local authorities of the district of Calumbo, identified as *sobas*, *quilambas*, and *quimbares*, increasing the hands each ruler had to provide as labor to the *Fábrica de Ferro de Novo Belém*, the Royal Foundry of Novo Belém, as part of their taxation. According to the list, sixty-eight rulers were able to provide from 3 to 1,000 dependents who could work for the benefit of the Portuguese Crown. In addition to labor, the rulers' taxation also included a percentage of the crops they cultivated; some also had to provide animals such as goats, chickens, or pigs. Sobas Gola Quimbi Antonio da Silva and Caciata Cacavungu, who had salt mines in their territories, were required to pay their taxes with salt.[70]

The efforts to count and control did not necessarily lead to collection of information about existing land regimes. For example, in 1772, Governor Antonio de Lencastro ordered the demarcation, description, and inventory of the property belonging to all Black and white subjects in the colony of Angola, in alphabetical order.[71] Along the coast and in the inland *presídios*, colonial officers enumerated residents, the number of inhabitants in each household, as well as the production of crops and cattle in a clear process of land enclosure under the rubric of better administration and expansion of agriculture.[72] The lists are meticulous, providing information on the location of each household, their type of construction (one or two floors, bricks, *pau a pique*, or thatched roof), and the number of free and enslaved dependents. It is unclear whether the house or the piece of land was perceived as personal property, but the fact is that some of the lists include information such as "houses that

[70] IHGB, DL81,02.19, "Inventario dos Sovas, Quilambas e Quimbares do Distrito do Calumbo que servem no serviço das Fabricas de Ferro de Novo Belém e Nova Oeiras donde se mandarão anexar todos por ordem do Ilm.o e Exm.o Snr. General, sobre os Dízimos que pagavam antes de serem isentos, e pelo que Regularão na Regulação que se fez, e o número de Filhos capazes, que cada um tem, e os que dão por Mês," 1750.
[71] BNL, Res. Cód. 8744, "Carta circular," fl. 239-239v., May 1, 1772.
[72] Among others, see IHGB, DL32,02.02, "Relação de Manuel José de Silveira Teixeira sobre os moradores da cidade de São Felipe de Benguela separados por raça, idade, emprego, título de habitação, ofícios mecânicos e quantos mestres e aprendizes existem, 1789;" IHGB, DL32,02.10, "Relação de moradores do Distrito das Vilas de Icau, Muquiama e Quilengues contendo nome, idade, estado, emprego, gados, petrechos de sua majestade, órfãos, sobas e seu território que reconhecem e tributam vassalagem, 1789;" IHGB, DL32,02.01, "Relação dos sobas potentados, souvetas seus vassalos e sobas agregados pelos nomes das suas terras, que tem na capitania de Benguela. Dividindo em sete partes e províncias para melhor conhecimento da capitania: 1º. província da cidade de Benguela; 2º. província de Quilengues; 3º. província do Presídio de Caconda; 4º. província do Ambo; 5º. província de Galangue; 6º. província de Bailundo e 7º. província do Bié," 1798.

belonged to Joaquim José de Andrade," or "owned by the tavern keeper Amaro."[73] This suggests efforts to generalize a Portuguese land tenure system built around restrictions. It privileged smallholder plots where agriculture was practiced. Decades later, many of these residents put their land plots up for sale, demonstrating that the land had been privatized and commodified.[74]

At the borderlands outside of Portuguese jurisdiction, officers listed the names and sizes of African states and made efforts to delimit territories, incorporating local notions of fluid frontiers and mobile capitals. Expressions such as "land of Galangues," "soba Canina's lands," and "territories of Ginga and Cassange" in official documents (as well as in Map I.2 in the Introduction) reveal how Portuguese officers had limited knowledge of the territory, recognized African jurisdiction over their countries, and incorporated local practices of using trees, rocks, and rivers as political limits in the colonial space.[75] It also suggests that these lands were not under colonial control but under the jurisdiction of African rulers, as their dominium, and that the administration recognized them as such.

Vague notions of lands and territories accord with how the landscape was mapped: The local power struggles between African rulers, their neighbors, and the colonial presence created an imaginary political space for Europeans. In 1798, an unidentified colonial officer produced a report about the land possession of the soba of Humbe and his disputes with his neighbors. In this rich report, there is a clear recognition of Humbe's territory and his rights over his land and people. According to the account, "previously, the sobas of Humbe, Kiluanji, Mutahucamba, Kilombo Kiacatubia, Bango A Kitamba, Bumba Danla, Gonguembo, and Mussuço Hembo were vassals of Queen Njinga, who later came under the control of the [Portuguese] Majesty. They had and have their

[73] IHGB, DL32,02.03, "Relação de José Caetano Carneiro, primeiro tenente, da metade dos moradores da parte do norte da cidade de São Felipe de Benguela, de ambos os sexos, cor, escravos sem nomes, empregos e estados. Relação de senzalas às quais pertencem," November 29, 1797, fl. 21.
[74] Arquivo Nacional de Angola (ANA), Cod. 7182, fl. 137, N. 1445, 20 March 1829; ANA, cx. 3340, Dombe Grande, doc. 53, Letter from Chefe do Dombe Grande [Francisco José Brito] and Governor of Benguela, April 20, 1865; Boletim Oficial do Governo Geral da Província de Angola (BOGGPA), n. 32, 11 August 1866, p. 315;
[75] AHU, Angola, cx. 70, doc. 5, February 24, 1785; AHU, Angola, cx. 70, doc. 43, August 7, 1785; AHU, Angola, cx. 72, doc. 14, March 26, 1787. For more about land as country, see Ana Lúcia Sá, "The Concept of 'Land' in Bioko: 'Land as Property' and 'Land as Country,'" in Doing Conceptual History in Africa, ed. Axel Fleisch and Rhiannon Stephens (New York: Berghahn, 2016), 138–61; Vincent Hiribarren, A History of Borno: Trans-Saharan African Empire to Failing Nigerian State (New York: Oxford University Press, 2017).

lands from the south to the north, crossed by the Kwanza River, until the shores of the river Lombige."[76] Ruler Mussuço began to slowly settle his people within the limits of Humbe, sending *macotas* (the heads of lineages and the ruler's advisers) to establish themselves there. They later tried to claim Humbe's territories as their own "without having rights over them." The account continues, "In the lands of the Soba Mutta Hucamba, between the rivers mentioned earlier, the intrusion of macotas from Dembo Caculo is not allowed."

In the lands of the soba Quilombo Quiacatubia, there was an alliance with smaller rulers, the *sobetas*, regarding who could settle. Afraid of what the Dembo Caculo Cacahenda intended, the soba of Humbo then "under a strange way against the laws of the [Portuguese] Majesty and the law of his state, usurped most of his lands, lands that [Humbo] owns since the establishment of his state, securing possession in time immemorial by his ancestors as the natural lords of their land. [The soba] cannot accept that the Dembo [Caculo Cacahenda], who is unable to secure access to the land through justice (or the law), unfairly removed [Humbe and his people] from the land due to the fact that [Dembo] is [militarily] stronger and more powerful." The soba requested the King of Portugal to "order the Dembo Caculo Cacahenda to stay in his lands, and to not usurp the land of others."[77] This account was probably produced by the ruler of Humbe and stresses his conception of land use rights, and his role as the legitimate occupant transmitted through his ancestors. In his own words, he was the natural lord of the communal land, with usage and tenure rights based in generations of remembered history. Yet the colonial archive does not recognize the authorship of the letter or even how colonial officers apprehended local knowledge to justify land expropriation.[78] Humbo, located south of the Kwanza River but north of Benguela and east of Benguela-Velha, was at the borderland of the Portuguese empire, a clear space in which rulers could claim dominium and negotiate them with the colonial powers and neighboring leaders who aspired to occupy the land and claim rights. As the ruler said, conflicts could arise: "If he does not secure the restitution of his land, there will be war between him and his allies and the Dembo

---

[76] IHGB, DL81,02.31, "Comunicação para o Rei de Portugal sobre a possessão das terras dos Sobas do Humbo, e as disputas com outros povos," 1798.

[77] IHGB, DL81,02.31, 1798.

[78] For similar cases, see Hanson, *Landed Obligation*, 41–53. For more on the importance of decolonizing the archive and the past, see Mignolo, "Epistemic Disobedience, Independent Thought and Decolonial Freedom."

Caculo Cacahenda, with death, violence, and cruelty, that your excellency can avoid among your vassals."[79]

Before the nineteenth-century enclosure, conflicts over land use and occupation relied on customs and practice drawn from de facto occupation, not necessarily recognized as legitimate by all the actors involved. The competition for land increased in the nineteenth century with the end of slave exports and the establishment of the plantation economy, as well as the consolidation of the idea in Europe that "property is the most absolute way of possessing things."[80] In this moment of transformation, legislation was established to guarantee de jure rights, that is, officially sanctioned. The process in which de facto rights are transformed into de jure rights was and is inherently political and privileges the claims of those in power. The debates over land use before the nineteenth century centered on the negotiations between law, colonization, and the claims for sovereignty that both Portuguese and local rulers employed.

Conclusion

Contested land regimes, natural resources, and wealth accumulation have been the norm in West Central African history. Before and even during Portuguese colonialism, rulers and commoners collected material goods and invested in items associated with expanding networks of free and enslaved dependents. Conflict over land use and occupation rights predates the nineteenth century, and different actors clashed over rights and claims. Firstcomers, latecomers, and Europeans disputed rights over land, cattle, and people due to their different and competing views regarding legitimate actors of conquest, possession, use, and control.

Ideas about accumulation, wealth, and rights underwent profound changes over three centuries. Since the early seventeenth century, local rulers and colonial officers contested and negotiated rights, jurisdiction, and control. Competing frameworks for origins, access, and occupation rights existed in the pre-nineteenth-century period. However, the consolidation of the liberal idea of individual rights over land and people in the nineteenth century privileged the notion that things and people belong to an individual rather than the possibility of shared communal use as was the case in most of the African continent. The fact that African societies did not dispose of or sell land, or that land was not commodified, does not indicate the absence of the idea of use and occupation

[79] IHGB, DL81,02.31, 1798.
[80] Congost, "Property Rights and Historical Analysis," 88; Garnsey, *Thinking about Property*, 169–73. See also Dias Paes, "Escravos e terras," 7–10.

rights. Scholars' assumption that things belong to an individual, or even to a state, reinforces the intrinsically violent aspect of asserting rights: If there is a recognized right over land or a person, it is at the expense of someone else who cannot enjoy this privilege.

One of the challenges of understanding local practices of wealth and rights is the paucity of records privileging how West Central African societies, among them the Ndombes, Kilengues, Kakonda, Bailundu, and Bienos, exercised these rights. By the time evidence about customary law was recorded in the late nineteenth and early twentieth centuries, local societies had been transformed by three hundred years of conquest and colonialism. Scholars repeated the idea that West Central Africans lacked property rights or notions of individual ownership produced by colonial bureaucrats, without questioning how this colonial knowledge was created and for what purpose. Scholars also embraced the notion, introduced by the liberal revolutions in the eighteenth century, that land can be bought and sold and treated as a commodity. Yet the evidence available in colonial archives reveals that African rulers claimed jurisdiction and occupation rights, and they exercised land tenure.

Rights over land and people, in many ways the consolidation of individual ownership over communal rights, are not a stable category but the result of an intense negotiation among social groups and between elites and the lower classes. Historicizing the notion of property is central to any understanding of knowledge production about the past. Evidence, observations, and history itself have changed over time. Assumptions that landed property is a mark of a superior system must be decentered. The risk is falling into a pattern of acclaiming the existence of ownership notions and rights before the nineteenth century as something positive, as if owning land indicates a rational economic system. Ownership of land, of people, in the end reveals that the history of accumulation corresponds with dispossession and the exacerbation of inequalities.

2   Property Rights in the Nineteenth Century

In many ways, Portuguese and West Central African land regime rights shared characteristics before the nineteenth century. Possession through land occupation and labor often intertwined and guaranteed rights to groups that could have used both strategies on the territories under dispute. Group support and neighboring recognition of employed labor and territory transformation were key in asserting possession rights for those who had been clearing and grazing land, cultivating, and burying the dead. Any consonance between West Central African rulers and the Portuguese Crown on the subject of land possessions and jurisdiction power evaporated by the mid-nineteenth century. As a replacement for the common law (*ius commune*) that had prevailed until then, codified Portuguese law invoked major changes regarding recognition of occupation and rights for first settlers, in European territories as well as their colonies. The supposedly universal code created the illusion that European jurists were entitled to modify normative order in the colonies, replacing legal arrangements that had prevailed until then with a codified set of laws established in the metropole. Territorial occupation was consolidated with this legal imposition, which established, de facto, a legislative occupation.[1]

Changes in legislation during the nineteenth century meant the rejection of the legal pluralism that had prevailed until then, including dismissing landscape transformation as a sign of rights. The use and occupation rights that West Central African employed and recognized did not require written records privileged in European codes. Through the examples available from the Angolan archives, it is possible to scrutinize the process of legal transformations experienced in West Central Africa and, to a certain extent, Portugal. Possession rights established by customs and common law slowly gave way to codified norms that

---

[1] I borrow the term *ocupação legislativa*, legislative occupation, from Cristina Nogueira da Silva. See Cristina Nogueira da Silva, *A construção jurídica dos territórios ultramarinos portugueses no século XIX. Modelos, doutrinas e leis* (Lisbon: Imprensa da Ciências Sociais, 2017), 14.

privileged legal codes and not necessarily consensus among first settlers and their neighbors. During the nineteenth century, land was commodified and privatized at the expanse of the common good. This process, however, was experimented with first in Angola and then implemented in Portugal: The history of legal changes in the colonies affected law developments in the metropole.[2] Land was used as collateral, as well as a source of income and investment. These changes happened first at colonial urban centers but eventually also spread to the areas out of colonial control, stimulating competition for land. West Central African elites redefined their claims to protect their rights, entangling different land regimes, definitions, and legal practices.

African Land Claims during the Nineteenth Century

Reading against the grain, colonial records reveal how African rulers understood their possession and land regimes. Although colonial notaries and secretaries wrote down these reports and legal opinions, the historical documents provide information on sobas' claims and allocation of land among subjects. The records reveal that West Central Africans adapted Portuguese naming practices and norms, when convenient, to translate and secure their property rights, as in a case brought to the colonial administration in Luanda in 1824. The dembo Caculo Cacahenda, also known as Sebastião Miguel Francisco Xeque after his baptism, received an official certificate recognizing his legitimacy in power and over his lands due to "the former possession from your ancestors."[3] The colonial certificate clearly recognized his jurisdiction and rights over his land and people.

A few years later, a land dispute between neighboring rulers in the interior of Luanda was settled without employing the colonial judicial structure. The result of the legal dispute was recorded in Portuguese.

---

[2] Since the publication of the influential study *Law in Colonial Africa* in 1991, several scholars have interrogated how colonized populations worked as laboratories for legal transformations in Europe. For more on this, see Kristin Mann and Richard L. Roberts, eds., *Law in Colonial Africa* (Portsmouth, NH: Heinemann, 1991); Lauren A. Benton, *Law and Colonial Cultures Legal Regimes in World History, 1400-1900* (New York: Cambridge University Press, 2002); Rachel Jean-Baptiste, *Conjugal Rights: Marriage, Sexuality, and Urban Life in Colonial Libreville, Gabon* (Athens: Ohio University Press, 2014); Saliha Belmessous, ed., *Native Claims: Indigenous Law against Empire, 1500-1920* (Oxford ; New York: Oxford University Press, 2012).

[3] Ana Paula Tavares and Catarina Madeira Santos, eds., *Africæ Monumenta: Arquivo Caculo Cacahenda* (Lisbon: Instituto de Investigação Científica Tropical, 2002), doc. 33 a "Ordem citatória passada a favor de D. Sebastiao Miguel Francisco Cheque, Dembo Caculo Cacahenda contra Dom Francisco Affonso da Silva, 15 November 1824," 99–101.

The certificate and the land title it generated provided evidence of first settlers' land claims. In 1836, the ruler Nbango Acaputu, located nearly the Ambaca fortress more than 230 kilometers inland from Luanda, presented a petition against a neighbor, Caculo Cacabasa. Nbango Acaputu accused Caculo Cacabasa of illegally exercising rights over Acaputo's land, including trying to buy it with captives and clothes and transfer its ownership to one of his nephews. Nbango Acaputu presented testimonies of neighbors who did not recognize Caculo Cacabasa as the rightful occupant of the territory.[4] This single territorial dispute lasted over nine years and required the intervention of the neighboring rulers to arbitrate the internal political dispute.

Colonial documents were presented in local courts and served as evidence of possession and land rights. Land right recognition implied control over its natural resources and labor of its inhabitants. Although the colonial documents recognized Nbango Acaputo as the legitimate land occupant, Caculo Cacabasa insisted in his claims and established an earth shrine, *dambo* in Kimbundu, in the disputed land, and made sure some of his own advisors were buried in the disputed land after their death. After nine years of ongoing disputes, the case concluded in 1847. By then, Caculo Cacabasa was deceased and his nephew, Dom Francisco António, ruled over his uncle's territory and people. In an official statement, in Portuguese, Dom Francisco António declared, "I am the nephew of the deceased [Caculo Cacabasa and] I do not want any more disorder with Nbango Acaputu because he is the owner of the land. Therefore, I write him this letter about recognizing [his rights] and transferring his land."[5] This case is rich and reveals matrilineal inheritance practices among Mbundu populations north of the Kwanza River. Clearly, Portuguese and African courts debated legitimate occupancy of territories before the introduction of the Portuguese Civil Code in mainland Portugal in 1868. West Central African rulers produced legal documents to reinforce land rights in an attempt to prove first settler claims, legitimize possession, and settle disputes, as this case indicates.

Political succession disputes indexed changing attitudes toward inheritance rights. When the soba Monpala, under the jurisdiction of Dombe Grande, died in 1858, his nephew succeeded him. The new ruler refused to allow an inventory of the deceased's property to be carried out,

---

[4] "Manuscript from Bango Acaputo, 29 March 1847," in Éve Sebestyén, "Legitimation through Landcharters in Ambundo Villages, Angola," in *Perspektiven Afrikanistischer Forschung* eds. Thomas Bearth, Wilhelm Mohlig, Beat Sottas and Edgar Suter (Cologne, Germany: Rudiger Koppe Verlag, 1994), 373.

[5] "Manuscript from Bango Acaputo, 11 July 1836," in Sebestyén, "Legitimation through Landcharters," 377–78.

threatening to relocate to distant lands with his people. While most of the elders and the ruling council recognized the legitimacy of the new ruler, the biological children of Monpala requested Portuguese support to inherit their father's property, exploiting the fact that Portuguese inheritance norms, which privileged biological male heirs, clashed with matrilineal practices, which favors male nephews from the deceased's sisters. According to the governor of Benguela, "the nephew of the deceased soba refused to allow an inventory, which is against our [colonial] law, and the children of the deceased were cheated of their property, which in our law belongs to them. The eldest son not only lost property but also the right to rule."[6] Multiple understandings of inheritance and ownership regimes coexisted, as this case indicates, and matrilineal and patrilineal inheritance practices clashed in several instances during the nineteenth century.[7] Apparently, local political elites were seizing the opportunity to alter inheritance regimes when it was convenient, embracing legal pluralism to dismiss heirs and challenge the legitimacy of competing factions.

First settlers claimed land rights based on the belief that ancestors had led them to a specific location; lineages became landholding authorities with inalienable rights. The founding of a settlement or a village, a *mbanza*, was a step toward the consolidation of political power and landholding rights.[8] Among the Mbundu north of the Kwanza River, "the landowners are the most ancient kin groups in their territories. The lunga-holding lineages, where they survive, govern the use of the land, authorizing changes in residence, selecting the sites for new villages, locating water by divining techniques based on manipulation of the physical lunga-object, as well as summoning the rains at the end of each dry season."[9] South of the Kwanza River, among several

---

[6] ANA, Cod. 471, E – 7 – 5, Registro de oficios expedidos 13 de junho de 1857 a 22 de janeiro de 1859, fl. 189, December 2, 1858, Governador de Benguela to governador geral da província. See also Martin Chanock, *Law, Custom, and Social Order: The Colonial Experience in Malawi and Zambia* (New York: Cambridge University Press, 1985), 37–38.

[7] Max Weber, *The Theory of Social and Economic Organization* (New York, NY: Oxford University Press, 1947), 346; Ifi Amadiume, *Male Daughters, Female Husbands: Gender and Sex in an African Society* (London: Zed Books, 1987), 30–35; Sandra E. Greene, "Family Concerns: Gender and Ethnicity in Pre-Colonial West Africa," *International Review of Social History* 44 (1999): 21–22; Nwando Achebe, *The Female King of Colonial Nigeria: Ahebi Ugbabe* (Bloomington: Indiana University Press, 2011), 136–38; Kathryn M. de Luna, *Collecting Food, Cultivating People: Subsistence and Society in Central Africa* (New Haven: Yale University Press, 2016), 140–46.

[8] Sebestyén, "Legitimation through Landcharters," 367.

[9] Joseph C. Miller, *Kings and Kinsmen: Early Mbundu States in Angola* (Oxford: Clarendon Press, 1976), 60. According to Miller, lunga were power regalia associated with ancestors who controlled water resources.

Umbundu-speaking groups, migration narratives dating back generations or centuries also guaranteed occupancy rights and were carefully
remembered by rulers and their custodians of history and knowledge.
While living in Bihé among the Bienos in the 1850s, the trader Ladislau
Magyar noticed that their

> customary law (*bikola*) legislated individual freedom and equality among the
> individuals. Each free adult man able to carry weapons enjoys his own
> individual possessions as well as his family members and his belongings.
> However, the head of lineages shared common interests and mutual protection,
> and the movable goods are considered individual property, and its protection, as
> well as any violation is considered a family affair. Only topics that affect all are
> legislated by the entire community.[10]

Twenty years later, the travelers Roberto Ivens and Hermegildo
Capelo collected a series of firstcomer narratives that revealed that the
Bienos were migrants from the north who settled in a fertile and generous
landscape that "provided everything."[11]

The Mbailundu narratives reveal first settler narratives dating back to
the 1700s, in which settlement led to state formation. Most of the
narratives, however, were collected in the twentieth century and refer
back to previous centuries, which generates a series of methodological
problems familiar to Africanist historians. Gladwyn Murray Childs, a
missionary from Union Theological Seminary, collected firstcomers'
accounts, outlining dynastic origins, migrations, and resettlement.
Although he recorded these accounts during the period he was in
Angola (1933–1938), they reference events that took place 200 years
before. According to the Mbailundu first settler account, Katyavala,
originally from Cipala (Quibala), migrated south to Mbonga where he
met the ruler Mbulu. There, Katyavala married Mbulu's daughter,
sealing their alliance and unifying lineages. While Mbulu was away on
a hunting trip, Katyavala occupied the village and began ruling Mbailundu
as head of a dynasty.[12] It is an account of conquest and removal from the

---

[10] László Magyar, *Reisen in Süd-Afrika in den Jahren 1849 bis 1857* (Leipzig: Lauffer &
Stolp, 1859), 277. I am thankful to Esteban Alfaros Salas who translated this passage
to me.

[11] Hermenegildo Capelo and Roberto Ivens, *De Benguela às terras de Iaca. Descrição de uma
viagem na África Central e Ocidental*, vol. 1 (Lisbon: Europa-América, 1996), 114.

[12] Gladwyn Murray Childs, *Kinship & Character of the Ovimbundu: Being a Description of the
Social Structure and Individual Development of the Ovimbundu of Angola, with Observations
Concerning the Bearing on the Enterprise of Christian Missions of Certain Phases of the Life
and Culture Described.* (London: Witwatersrand University Press, 1969), 172. For
methodological problems with reconstructing the past with limit data, see Kathryn
M. de Luna and Jeffrey B. Fleisher, *Speaking with Substance. Methods of Language and
Materials in African History* (Cham, Switzerland: Springer, 2019), 1–30; Achebe, *The*

power of competing groups. These stratagems solidified Mbailundu's rule over the territory and claims over land. Politically dramatic accounts like this also exist for nearby states. The Bihé dynastic origins, for example, date to the 1750s when an elephant hunter, the son of the soba of Humbe, fell in love with Cahanda, the beautiful daughter of the soba Bomba who occupied the lands at the left edge of the river Luando, an affluent of the Kwanza River. Once again, from this union of the Humbe with the Bomba, a new settlement originated that provided dynastic and land rights to the descendants of the ruling elite.[13]

Movements of migration, marriage with different lineages, and settlement provided the historical justification for political conquest, dynastic rule, and land rights way before the consolidation of colonial law regarding land use. They conferred on the ruler the power to grant land access to his subjects as well as to foreigners and visitors, lands that were occupied de facto. In all kinds of societies, including European ones, orally transmitted narratives have played a decisive role in legitimizing land and property regimes. Late arrivals could settle on the land, and the fact that they paid taxes and followed a series of obligations reinforced the idea that first settlers held the land and enjoyed possession rights. In many ways, communal rights over land became individual rights as some kin passed occupancy rights to their heirs, without consulting group members, as we saw in the case of Caculo Cacabasa trying to sell land that belonged to Nbango Acaputu.[14]

Female King of Colonial Nigeria, 14; Sean Hanretta, "Women, Marginality and the Zulu State: Women's Institutions and Power in the Early Nineteenth Century," *The Journal of African History* 39, no. 3 (1998): 395–413; Patricia Romero Curtin, "Laboratory for the Oral History of Slavery: The Island of Lamu on the Kenya Coast," *The American Historical Review* 88, no. 4 (1983): 858–82; Rhiannon Stephens, "'Wealth', 'Poverty' and the Question of Conceptual History in Oral Contexts: Uganda from c.1000 CE," in *Doing Conceptual History in Africa,* ed. Axel Fleisch and Rhiannon Stephens (New York, L: Berghahn, 2016), 21–48; Jan Vansina, "Memory and Oral Tradition," in *The African Past Speaks: Essays on Oral Tradition and History,* ed. Joseph Calder Miller (Folkestone, Eng: Dawson, 1980), 262–79.

[13] Alexandre Alberto da Rocha de Serpa Pinto, *Como eu atravessei a África,* vol. 1 (Lisbon: Europa-América, 1980), 142.

[14] On the importance of power and land access, see Luna, *Collecting Food, Cultivating People,* 17–20. For more on obligations between first settlers and late arrivals, see Greene, "Family Concerns," 22–23; Susan Newton-King, *Masters and Servants on the Cape Eastern Frontier, 1760-1803* (Cambridge: Cambridge University Press, 1999), 99; Assan Sarr, "Land, Power, and Dependency along the Gambia River, Late Eighteenth to Early Nineteenth Centuries," *African Studies Review* 57, no. 03 (December 2014): 111–15; Carola Lentz, *Land, Mobility, and Belonging in West Africa* (Bloomington: Indiana University Press, 2013), 101–02. For the similarity between oral claims in Portuguese empire, see Mariana Armond Dias Paes, "Terras em contenda: circulação e produção de normatividades em conflitos agrários no Brasil império," *Revista da*

Not every single firstcomer narrative casts backward to settlements in earlier centuries. Domingos Chacahanga, a former captive of the Portuguese trader António Francisco Ferreira da Silva Porto, was the first arrival in one of the newly established villages in the Benguela highlands. In the 1860s or 1870s, Chacahanga founded Caquenha, a small village within two hours' walking distance from Cuionja, next to the lands of the soba of Cabir. Chacahanga became the lord of his territory, with the power to authorize settlement and land use.[15] Old, such as Mbailundu, or new, such as Cacahanga's, narratives consolidated migrants as rulers and landholders who controlled access to the landscape, including the soil for farming and rivers and streams for fishing, and distributed plots to lineages in systems of obligation and reciprocity. Foreigners could receive access to available land but had to pay tribute to the landowners. The explorer Serpa Pinto reported that when setting up camp to spend the night in Bihé while crossing the continent, it was "necessary to notify the ruler who owns the land, sending him a small gift, which protects the visitors against eventual raids and theft. As soon as the owner of the land receives the gift, he is also responsible for the safeguarding of the caravan."[16] In the Benguela highlands, a region shaped by mobility and resettlement, as the soil became exhausted, periods of drought affected the regions, or neighbors disturbed the peace, groups searched for new available fields elsewhere. Rulers allotted plots of land when villages were founded, and the right to use it depended on its occupation and cultivation, and the ability to claim firstcomer rights.[17] Access to land was vital to a group's economic survival but was also a marker of social belonging. Lineage elders, *ngangas*, and chiefs played central roles in disputes over land access and rights.

The tomb of ancestors and religious practices associated with spirits and burial sites were crucial in the assertion of authority and power, including in the access and use of land.[18] This probably predates the nineteenth

Faculdade de Direito UFMG 74 (2019): 379–406; Boaventura de Sousa Santos, *O Direito Dos Oprimidos* (Lisbon: Almedina, 2014), 86–93.
[15] Serpa Pinto, *Como Atravessei a África*, 1, 171.
[16] Serpa Pinto, *Como Atravessei a África*, 1, 153.
[17] Wilfrid Dyson Hambly, *Ovimbundu of Angola* (Chicago: Field Museum of Natural History, 1934), 201; Miller, *Kings and Kinsmen*, 45–46; Neil Kodesh, *Beyond the Royal Gaze: Clanship and Public Healing in Buganda* (Charlottesville, VA: University of Virginia Press, 2010), 91–96; Lentz, *Land, Mobility, and Belonging in West Africa*, 122–25.
[18] For more on this, see Anne Hilton, *The Kingdom of Kongo* (Oxford; New York: Oxford University Press, 1985), 35–37; Assan Sarr, *Islam, Power, and Dependency in the Gambia River Basin: The Politics of Land Control, 1790-1940* (Rochester, NY: University of Rochester Press, 2016), 90–109; Jared Staller, *Converging on Cannibals: Terrors of Slaving in Atlantic Africa, 1509-1670* (Athens: Ohio University Press, 2019), Chapter 1.

century, but historical evidence is clear on the meaning of burial sites related to land occupation. While in Bihé in 1877, Serpa Pinto observed and described a ceremony in which ancestors and spirits continued to occupy the land and inhabitants constantly interacted with the deceased lineage members.[19] In the late 1870s, Capello and Ivens remarked on the burial places of hunters that were distinguished by the skulls of antelopes, buffalo, or hippo, which were stuck on upright poles and mixed with skulls of oxen killed in honor of the deceased.[20] The living and the dead occupied the land.

Land had a political but also a social use, and it was the control over these resources that defined hierarchy, wealth, and political legitimacy.[21] As I examine in Chapter 6, rulers and commoners challenged land rights and disputed the idea that land was necessarily communal. Spirits prevented or protected land use in other regions of the African content too. Among the Mandika in Senegambia, for example, women enjoyed ownership rights of land, particularly rice swamps.[22] In areas in West Central Africa, far from the coastal areas under Portuguese jurisdiction, the Ovambo who lived along the Kunene River had individual inheritable landownership. However, the plots were not necessarily put up for sale. Women could own their own fields separately from their husbands, and they also enjoyed ownership over the grains cultivated.[23] The trope of abundant land held in uncontested communal ownership with no existence of property right claims clashes with empirical evidence demonstrating that political elites and commoners fought for rights and competed for resources. Land was never free and plentiful in West Central Africa.

Tensions between the End of the Slave Trade and the Need to Remain a Profitable Colony

West Central Africans had clear understanding about possession, land use, and occupation rights, but the mid-nineteenth century introduced

---

[19] Serpa Pinto, *Como Atravessei a África*, 1, 124–125; see also Hambly, *Ovimbundu of Angola*, 121–22. For more on the importance of burial sites for Central African populations, see Luna, *Collecting Food, Cultivating People*, 64–65; David M. Gordon, *Invisible Agents : Spirits in a Central African History* (Athens: Ohio University Press, 2012), 26–29.

[20] Hambly, *Ovimbundu of Angola*, 121

[21] Sarr, *Islam, Power, and Dependency*, 9–16; Lentz, *Land, Mobility, and Belonging in West Africa*, 212–50; Gordon, *Invisible Agents*, 22; Luna, *Collecting Food, Cultivating People*, 139–40.

[22] Assan Sarr, "Women, Land, and Power in the Lower Gambia River Region," in Mariana Candido and Adam Jones, eds., *African Women in the Atlantic World: Property, Vulnerability and Mobility, 1680-1880* (Woodbridge: James Currey, 2019), 38–53.

[23] Emmanuel Kreike, *Re-Creating Eden: Land Use, Environment, and Society in Southern Angola and Northern Namibia* (Portsmouth, NH: Heinemann, 2004), 23.

legal changes. Legal transformation in West Central Africa was linked with pressures to end the transatlantic slave trade, which operated in Luanda and Benguela well into the 1860s, despite its ban. From the 1810s to the 1850s, colonial authorities engaged in debates about agriculture productivity, land use, and occupation within urban centers and nearby territories. The pressures to end the profitable export of enslaved West Central Africans forced colonial authorities to envision new economic uses for the colony. This was not a linear project; it was riddled with disputes and conflicting visions, and reactions and pushback from nearby sobas who had been involved in the slave trade.[24]

A series of treaties left ripple effects in the social-economic configurations that had earlier been hammered out less formally. The 1810 Anglo-Portuguese treaty limited exports of captives to Costa da Mina and the Portuguese possessions in West Central Africa and Southeast Africa. The governor of Angola, Saldanha da Gama (1807-1810), claimed that "the agricultural revolution should be prepared and conducted by the civilized proprietor, who owns lands in the hinterland."[25] Agriculture became intimately linked with colonialism and a civilizing mission; Europeans claimed to be the only civilized people to implement these ideas in the rest of the colonized world. A few years later, in 1815, a new agreement was signed that abolished the trade north of the Equator. Two years later, as part of the negotiations of the Congress of Vienna, the British Navy was granted the right to inspect Portuguese ships suspected of involvement in the illegal trade of human beings.[26] These changes

---

[24] For more on the competition and disputes during the first half of the nineteenth century, see Roquinaldo Amaral Ferreira, *Dos sertões ao Atlântico: tráfico ilegal de escravos e comércio lícito em Angola 1830-1860* (Luanda: Kilombelombe, 2012); Daniel B. Domingues da Silva, *The Atlantic Slave Trade from West Central Africa, 1780–1867* (Cambridge: Cambridge University Press, 2017); Vanessa S. Oliveira, *Slave Trade and Abolition. Gender, Commerce and Economic Transition in Luanda* (Madison: University of Wisconsin Press, 2021). For an important insight into enlightenment's ideas about civilization and progress and its effects on ordinary folks in Central Africa, food, and land access, see Luna, *Collecting Food, Cultivating People.*

[25] António de Saldanha da Gama, *Memória sobre as colónias de Portugal: situadas na costa occidental d'Africa* (Paris: Casimir, 1839), 30–32. For more on the colonial trope of Africans as lazy and undisciplined people, see Frederick Cooper, *Decolonization and African Society: The Labor Question in French and British Africa* (Cambridge: Cambridge University Press, 1996); Moore and Vaughan, *Cutting down Trees.* For more on the Portuguese civilizing process, see Maria Paula Meneses, "O 'Indígena' Africanos e o colono 'Europeu': A construção da diferença por processos legais," *E-Cadernos CES* 7 (2010), 68–93.

[26] Roquinaldo Ferreira, "A supressão do tráfico de escravos em Angola (ca. 1830-ca. 1860)," *História Unisinos* 15, no. 1 (2011): 3–13; Arlindo Manuel Caldeira, *Escravos e traficantes no império português: o comércio negreiro português no Atlântico durante os séculos XV a XIX* (Lisbon: Esfera do Livro, 2013); Daniel B. Domingues da Silva, *The Atlantic*

happened in a single decade. As a result, traders originally from Ouidah and Porto Novo, loosely labeled as Costa da Mina in Portuguese records, settled in Benguela, increasing the competition for real estate in town.[27] Besides these treaties, the Portuguese empire suffered major setbacks in the first decades of the nineteenth century. Brazil became an independent state in 1822, and a conspiracy in Benguela threatened succession from the Portuguese Empire and annexation with Brazil. Joining the empire of Brazil would allow traders in Benguela to continue trading captives. Benguela traders were jailed, those born in Brazil deported, and their property seized.[28]

In this context of external and internal challenges and imbibed in an environment of expansion of liberal ideas, such as the defense of property and rule of law, major legal and economic changes were implemented in the colony of Angola. While some merchants continued to defend and engage in trafficking human beings even after the promulgation of 1826 prohibiting the exports of captives, new European immigrants and administrators defended investment in agriculture. Nicolau Abreu Castelo Branco, the governor of Angola in 1826, encouraged the production of sugarcane to replace the export of enslaved human beings in the colonies' budget. He also recommended rewarding any trader engaged in new economic activities with an honorary induction into the Order of Christ, a highly prestigious honor in the Portuguese empire.[29] The people who would otherwise have been exported would be put to work in the newly established plantations. In addition to sugarcane, the Portuguese Crown and its representatives in Angola envisioned expanding the production of cotton and indigo, but also tapping into natural resources such as beeswax, gum copal, and orchil (a lichen used for dying) – products highly demanded in industries in Europe and North America.[30] Despite British pressure to bring the slave trade to an end and the progressive abolition of slavery in the Americas, there were

---

Slave Trade from West Central Africa, 1780–1867 (Cambridge: Cambridge University Press, 2017). a

[27] Mariana P. Candido, "Os agentes não europeus na comunidade mercantil de Benguela, c. 1760-1820," *Saeculum - Revista de História* 29 (2013): 97–123.

[28] ANA, Cod. 7183, fl. 13v. January 31, 1824. See also Roquinaldo Ferreira, "Echoes of the Atlantic: Benguela (Angola) and Brazilian Independence," in *Biography and the Black Atlantic*, ed. Lisa A. Lindsay and John Wood Sweet (Philadelphia: University of Pennsylvania Press, 2013), 224–47.

[29] AHU, Angola, Cod. 542, fl. 111v, December 30, 1826 and AHU, Cod. 452, fl. 130V, May 5, 1827. New attempts were made in the 1830s see AHU, Correspondência dos Governadores (old reference), Pasta 2, December 12, 1836 and ANA, Cod. 221, fl. 17, December 10, 1839.

[30] AHU, Angola, Cod. 452, fl. 130v, May 5, 1827; and AHU, Angola, Correspondência dos Governadores, Pasta 2, December 12, 1836.

protests that without enslavement it would be very difficult to maintain production since the local population was believed to be rebellious and colonial officers defended that the only way to obtain labor was through slavery.[31]

The Portuguese Crown was convinced that it was entitled to promote changes in agriculture in order to bring "civilization," and a new way of life to Africans, combating migration and what was perceived as a lack of an appreciation for labor or discipline. The local population was expected to act solely as cheap labor and accept the power of the Portuguese to transform their lifestyle, renouncing rights to their land, their dependents, and their goods. The strengthening of Portuguese colonialism, after losing the colony of Brazil, favored more land grabbing in West Central Africa, particularly in regions close to the coast where the Portuguese presence was stronger. This territorial colonial expansion was considered essential and inevitably led to clashes with the interests of local rulers. In the 1820s, Ndombe sobas claimed that the Portuguese had enough land and did not need to conquer more territory from their holdings, land used for grazing and cattle raising.[32] With the imposition of arbitrary and new territorial limits that ignored the social and political value of land to African actors, the process of territorial interiorization and occupation continued.[33]

The growing demand for agricultural land imposed new relationships between the colonial power and the local population. The colonial economic goal previously had been to export people, but after the end of the transatlantic slave trade, the Portuguese Crown focused on employing local labor, free or not, in agriculture production. The relationship regarding property, including land and people, as well as new economic enterprises, changed dramatically during the nineteenth century, in part due to the pressure to establish farms and produce crops in demand in the expanding industries in Europe and North America.[34] Pamphlets

---

[31] AHU, Angola, Correspondência dos Governadores, Pasta 2 C, September 30, 1839; and AHU, Angola, Correspondência dos Governadores, Pasta 18, December 15, 1852.

[32] ANA, Cod. 220, fl. 100, Setember 9, 1826, Nicolau de Abreu Castelo Branco. Senhor Alexandre José Botelho.

[33] Freudenthal, "Benguela," 208–209; for more on this, see Assan Sar, *Islam, Power, and Dependency*, 59–78 and Kristin Mann, *Slavery and the Birth of an African City: Lagos, 1760-1900* (Bloomington: Indiana University Press, 2010), 263–74.

[34] Freudenthal, *Arimos e Fazendas*; Dias, "Changing Patterns of Power in the Luanda Hinterland;" Valentim Alexandre and Jill Dias, *O Império Africano* (Lisbon: Estampa, 1998); W. G. Clarence-Smith, *Slaves, Peasants, and Capitalists in Southern Angola, 1840-1926* (Cambridge: Cambridge University Press, 1979). This situation was not exclusive to Angola. For cases in West Africa, see, among others, Robin Law, ed., *From Slave Trade to "Legitimate" Commerce: The Commercial Transition in Nineteenth-Century West*

and booklets were published to advance the idea that enslaved people should remain in West Central Africa to help consolidate Portuguese colonialism and agricultural production.[35] Lisbon-sponsored projects supported agricultural expansion, relying, ironically, on the labor of enslaved people, such as the *Projeto de Regulamento da Companhia de Agricultura e Indústria de Angola e Benguela*. This suggests a shift from slave exports to what was interpreted as a legitimate trade: the production of coffee and sugarcane, and the exploitation of natural resources within the Portuguese colonies in Africa, which generated conflict with the surrounding sobas over land rights and use. There was a rush to occupy arable land at the expense of the local population.[36] Pastoral people's grazing land was particularly targeted since the transhumant aspect of cattle raising included land that could be interpreted as vacant, albeit temporarily. Authorities in Lisbon issued ordinances to pressure colonial authorities into securing new lands in better locations, close to rivers

> where industry and commerce could prosper and produce wealth due to the fertility of the soil, and the exploitation of the copper mines located next to Quilengues, and the collection of orchil. Your Majesty recommends the government of Benguela support the legal commerce in colonial staples and the distribution of plots of lands. The best suited plots should be reserved for settlers from Azores and Madeira, who will soon arrive there.[37]

In the arbitrary rights established by conquest, plots within colonial urban limits were distributed to individuals who intended to expand agriculture, particularly freeborn Brazilians and soldiers who had served for three years in the colonial army. Collectors and subsistence populations were also targeted as uncivilized, lacking the ability to embrace farming power and privileging hunting and gathering. The colonial state

---

Africa (Cambridge: Cambridge University Press, 1995); Martin A. Klein, *Slavery and Colonial Rule in French West Africa* (New York: Cambridge University Press, 1998), 160–62; Gareth Austin, *Labour, Land, and Capital in Ghana: From Slavery to Free Labour in Asante, 1807-1956* (Rochester, NY: University of Rochester Press, 2005); Mann, *Slavery and the Birth of an African City*, 237–76.

[35] Joaquim Antonio de Carvalho e Menezes, *Memória geografica, e política das possessões portuguezas n'Affrica occidental, que diz respeito aos reinos de Angola, Benguela, e suas dependencias...* (Lisbon: Typografia Carvalhense, 1834), 27–52; Arsênio P. P. de Carpo, *Projecto de uma companhia para o melhoramento do Commércio, Agricultura e Indústria na Província de Angola* (Lisbon: Typografia da Revolução de setembro, 1848).

[36] AHU, Angola, Correspondecia dos Governadores, Pasta 2, April 8, 1836. For more on this, see Freudenthal, *Arimos e fazendas*, 298; Alexandre e Dias, *O Império africano*, 383–89; Mariana P. Candido, "Trade, Slavery and Migration in the Interior of Benguela: The Case of the Caconda, 1830-1870," in *Angola on the Move: Transport Routes, Communications, and History*, ed. Beatrix Heintze e Achim von Oppen (Frankfurt am Main: Lembeck, 2008), 63–84.

[37] ANA, Cod. 7183, fl. 76v-77, March 17, 1836.

recognized these foreign farmers' rights to land, distributing seeds and tools to help them be successful. The Lisbon government also covered transportation costs for moving their wives and families from Portugal to West Central Africa.[38] The colonial government issued rights of exploitation of sulfur mines, ignoring any claims that local rulers had over them, and advanced the enclosure of natural resources, redefining the conditions for access and control of resources.[39]

Combined economic and political pressures to transform the nature of Portuguese presence in West Central Africa created the context for new legislation to be implemented regarding land use and distribution. Although land conflicts predated the nineteenth century, it was after the ban on exports of enslaved human beings that disputes were exacerbated. The colonial government imposed a new regime of landed property in the colony of Angola, ignoring communal ownership, before a similar project was implemented in mainland Portugal. This stands in contracts to use and occupation rights that had prevailed before the initial pressures to bring slave exports to an end in the 1830s.

Codification Fever

During the nineteenth century, while West Central Africans were dealing with major economic and political rearrangements related to the expansion of plantations and exploitation of labor, European countries went through a codification fever, modifying previous understandings about law and its goals. While *ius commune* that had prevailed until the late eighteenth century was seen as the right way to settle conflicts and a law common to all subjects, the legal codes of the nineteenth century projected the idea that law was clear and objective, based on reason and rights, rather than an invented legal tradition. Profoundly influenced by the eighteenth-century liberal revolutions, civil codes were elaborated, embodying the aspirations of the bourgeoisies, such as protection of private property, and the will of people (at the exclusion of anyone not seen as a full member of the nascent European bourgeoisies, such as enslaved and freed people, non-Europeans, and women in general). Although rooted in specific contexts, European civil codes were

---

[38] AHU, SEMU, DGU, Angola, 477, 1840–1843, Registro de Correspondência Expedida, fl. 6, n. 174, October 10, 1838; n. 179, October 12, 1838; and fl. 7v, n. 194. For more on the dismissive approach to subsistence economies, see Luna, *Collecting Food, Cultivating People*, 6–9.

[39] AHU, SEMU, DGU, Angola, 477, 1840–1843, Registro de Correspondência Expedida, fl. 7v. This process is very similar to what Kristin Mann described as taking place in Lagos decades later. See Mann, *Slavery and the Birth of an African City*, 249–58.

transplanted to their colonies, claiming a universality use over peoples that, paradoxically, were ignored and dismissed as inferiors in these same codes. The promulgation of civil codes was followed by the imposition of new codifications, such as criminal, fiscal, and commercial codes, that were also transplanted to the overseas colonies. Although *ius communes* and the new legislations of the nineteenth century shared much in common, jurists advanced the ideas that they were intrinsically different, defending the notion that the nineteenth-century codes were objective and neutral. The bourgeoisie's interests shaped legal codes and the legal narratives created to defend their imposition and implementation.[40]

In West Central Africa, the process of codification led to conflicts regarding land rights and their applicability to sobas' jurisdictions. Even if the colonial control and jurisdiction were limited to the few colonial urban centers along the coast (Luanda and Benguela), and to the inland administrative centers such as Ambaca, Quilengues, and Caconda, by the early nineteenth century the Portuguese Crown claimed control over a vast territory. Even if imaginary, this control meant the imposition of its new civil code, approved in 1867 and implemented in Portugal in 1868, to all inhabitants. Yet, codification about landed property rights in the colony of Angola predated the promulgation of the 1868 Portuguese civil code that also legislated property rights, *O Direito das Coisas.* According to the *Direito das Coisas,* disputes over goods and land were presented to the magistrate, who then had to listen to the parts and arbitrate the conflict. In many ways, codification and privatization of common land were experienced first in the overseas territories. Before the 1868 civil code, a multiplicity of rights coexisted and clashed, mostly based on land use and access, which allowed aristocrats, the Monarchy, and institutions, such as the Catholic Church or military orders, to control access and charge rent, without owning the land, as a commodity, that could be sold to another owner.[41] Around Lisbon, a land market existed since the late eighteenth century where landlords leased plots to tenants in contracts signed in notaries. Many of

---

[40] For more on this, see Cristina Nogueira da Silva, *Constitucionalismo e império: cidadania no ultramar português* (Lisbon: Almedina, 2009); Tamar Herzog, *A Short History of European Law: The Last Two and a Half Millennia* (Cambridge, MA: Harvard University Press, 2018); Dias Paes, "Terras em contenda."

[41] A good overview, in English, is the Dulce Freire, ed, *An Agrarian History of Portugal, 1000-2000: Economic Development on the European Frontiers* (Leiden: Brill, 2017), as well as José Vicente Serrão, "Introduction," In *Property Rights, Land, and Territory in the European Overseas Empires,* edited by José Vicente Serrão, Bárbara Direito, Eugénia Rodrigues, and Susana Munch Miranda (Lisbon: ISCTE-IUL, 2014).

these contracts were oral agreements since "written form was not compulsory."[42]

In many ways, Portuguese aristocracy and West Central Africans shared the idea that first settlers enjoyed rights over land rather than have it as a tangible property. They also shared the recognition of the legality of oral agreements. In Portugal, institutions such as the Catholic Church relied on the principles of inalienability, curiously denied to individuals, particularly colonial subjects. The law in Portugal was therefore very flexible and recognized leasing and a variety of land use and rights (such as *enfiteuse*, foros, and sesmarias), although the attacks on common land (*baldios*) started to take place with the 1821 liberal revolution, then transformed the ideas about rule of law, property rights, and state's role. Administrators and jurists who embraced liberal ideas defended the seizure of uncultivated land and individual ownership; however, it was not until the 1926–1974 period that the Portuguese government effectively and systematically seized common land.[43]

In Angola, the Portuguese Crown claimed control and sovereignty, relying on a system of written evidence such as population counts, reports, nominal lists, and maps that could prove nominal jurisdiction. In fact, most West Central Africans lived outside of Portuguese jurisdiction, in territories controlled by sobas, somas, or dembos (as can be seen in Map I.2 in the Introduction), as West Central African rulers were recorded in colonial documents. Nonetheless, European colonial governability relied on the existence of written records such as surveys, land registrations, wills, and inventories to impose new order and make jurisdiction claims even in spaces where the Portuguese Crown had no force to impose its demands.[44] Paradoxically, this was

---

[42] José Vicente Serrão and Rui Santos, "Land Policies and Land Markets," 16.

[43] For concrete examples, see on the multiple legal arrangements that protected land access; see, for example, Francisco Nunes Franklin, *Memória para servir de índice dos foraes das terras do Reino de Portugal e seus domínios* (Lisbon: Tipografia da Academia Real das Ciências, 1825). For more on the attacks on common land as an obstacle to capitalism, farming output, and progress, see Manuel Rodrigues, *Os Baldios* (Lisboa: Caminho, 1987). For a good summary, in English, see Luis Filipe Gomes Lopes, João Manuel R. dos Santos Bento, Artur F. Arede Correia Cristovão, Fernando Oliveira Baptista, "Institutionalization of common land property in Portugal: Tragic trends between "Commons" and "Anticommons," Land Use Policy, 35 (2013), 85–94,

[44] Benton, *Law and Colonial Cultures Legal Regimes in World History, 1400-1900*, 33–59; Ann Laura Stoler, "'In Cold Blood': Hierarchies of Credibility and the Politics of Colonial Narratives," *Representations* no. 37 (1992): 153–54; Graubart, "Shifting Landscapes"; Peter Pels, "The Anthropology of Colonialism: Culture, History, and the Emergence of Western Governmentality," *Annual Review of Anthropology* 26 (1997): 170–73; Eugénia Rodrigues, *Portugueses e africanos nos Rios de Sena. Os prazos da coroa em Moçambique nos séculos XVII e XVIII* (Lisboa: Imprensa Nacional-Casa da Moeda, 2014), 675–713.

the same time when colonial subjects were using the colonial bureau-cracy to strategically survive the new legal order and claim rights dating back to the seventeenth century. The colonial administrative apparatus produced new information about the conquered land and people and ended up reorganizing and imposing rights, not necessarily recognizing the first settlers' claims. These news ways of governance introduced new ideas, crystallized others, and altered first settler/ immigrant relationships, also known as landlord/stranger, as well as gender relations and women's roles in the second half of the nineteenth century.

New forms of administration and governability during the nineteenth century transformed the relationship African societies maintained with their territories, by introducing practices seen as more suitable for the colonial project, such as abandoning the mobile capital for the territori-ally bound organization aligned with Portuguese notions of power and land control. The social use of territory that had prevailed until then had to be replaced by a utilitarian use that privileged economics over society's needs. As a result, after three centuries of contact, the imposition of new policies regulating land access and ownership rights transformed West Central African polities into bounded territorial units in which the regime of landed property prevailed, with clear limits of rights and exclusion. The colonial administration replaced modes of possession and rights regulation based on common law, which prevailed in Portugal until the introduction of the 1868 Civil Code, for one that privileged written documents and rights established in codified form. The Portuguese administration established itself as the sole and central-ized arbiter over rights and access, including over land and its distribu-tion, and dismissed other forms of norms.[45] We know that West Central African rulers also mediated disputes regarding who could enjoy land rights, and competing neighbors or lineages could contest these rights, which required negotiation and recognition. When Dembo Caculo Cacahenda requested confirmation of his land rights from the Portuguese administration in 1826, or when the captain of Dembo requested that the ruler not "settle outside of his lands," there was clearly an understanding between the colonial administration and the Dembo

---

[45] Nogueira da Silva, *Construção jurídica*, 42–47; Martin Chanock, "A Peculiar Sharpness: An Essay on Property in the History of Customary Law in Colonial Africa," *The Journal of African History* 32, no. 1 (1991): 65–88; Amrita Malhi, "Making Spaces, Making Subjects: Land, Enclosure and Islam in Colonial Malaya," *The Journal of Peasant Studies* 38, no. 4 (2011): 727–46.

regarding where he and his people should live, and that he, not his competing neighbors, enjoyed rights over the land.[46]

By the midcentury, the colonial administration had created policies to make the local rulers' control over their lands part of their subjugation to the colonial administration. According to the order from the palace of the governor in Luanda, Pedro Alexandrino da Cunha, *capitão-mores* in the interior had baptized and recognized sobas in ceremonies known as *undamento*, with all pomp and solemnity, but also emphasized the conditions under which the land was assigned, i.e., the sobas were responsible for collecting tributes, maintaining order and respect toward the Portuguese authorities, and, in the case of the sobas under Caconda jurisdiction, providing labor for the construction of the fortress of Dombe. There was also recognition of the sobas' jurisdiction to distribute land among their subjects.[47] Confronted with Portuguese legal intrusion, African subjects and local rulers maintained their understanding of land rights and possession. Attempts to regulate land tenure and land distribution brought more rulers and individuals to colonial bureaucracy during the nineteenth century in search of protection for their rights. In most cases, their interests were dismissed to the benefit of Portuguese settlers and colonial officers.

The late nineteenth-century and early twentieth-century idea that Africans were people without ownership (or property) knowledge is historically wrong. It dismisses the legitimacy and validity of West Central African notions of land use and occupation. Nineteenth-century European notions of property shaped by liberalism and codified law code naturalized property-constituting acts and dismissed West Central African's land regimes as valid. Before nineteenth-century codification,

---

[46] Tavares and Madeira Santos, *Africa Monumenta*, doc. 33 a "Ordem citatória passada a favor de D. Sebastião Miguel Francisco Cheque, Dembo Caculo Cacahenda contra Dom Francisco Afonso da Silva," November 15, 1824, 99–101; and doc. 55, "Carta do Capitão chefe do Quartel do comando dos Dembos para Caculo Cacahenda sobre recuperação das terras," January 27, 1863, p. 160.

[47] BGGOPA, 1847, n. 85, April 24, 1847. For more on the *undamento* ceremony and vassal treaties, see Mariana P. Candido, *An African Slaving Port and the Atlantic World: Benguela and Its Hinterland* (New York: Cambridge University Press, 2013), 51–53. Recognition of belonging or not to Catholicism secured rights and status. See, among others, Lucilene Reginaldo, *Os Rosários dos Angolas: Irmandades de africanos e crioulos na Bahia setecentista* (São Paulo: Alameda, 2011); Mariza de Carvalho Soares, *People of Faith: Slavery and African Catholics in Eighteenth-Century Rio de Janeiro* (Durham, NC: Duke University Press Books, 2011); Linda M Heywood, "Portuguese into African: The Eighteenth Century Central African Background to Atlantic Creole Culture," in *Central Africans and Cultural Transformations in the American Diaspora*, ed. Linda Heywood (New York: Cambridge University Press, 2002), 91–114; Linda M. Heywood and John K. Thornton, *Central Africans, Atlantic Creoles, and the Making of the Foundation of the Americas, 1585–1660* (New York,: Cambridge University Press, 2007).

European courts also recognized the de facto occupation, tilling of soil, and oral agreements as legitimate ways to exercise ownership and rights. European law purposefully ignored that fact. The consolidation of property rights during the nineteenth century created a juridical illusion that individual rights over land had always existed in Europe and needed to be codified elsewhere. But these were also new ideas in Portugal and other European countries. In many ways, the universalization of European property rights over land implied that any resources (land, water, air) could be monetized and available for a cash amount, an ideal conceived as part of the consolidation of liberal values in European law by the early nineteenth century.

The Boundaries of Dispossession

The pressure to expand the plantation economy and increase trade in natural resources accelerated competition for land. The colonial administration started issuing land titles in the 1840s recognizing individual rights over urban plots and consolidating the dispossession of individuals who could not prove occupation rights. This new policy responded to the promulgation of the October 10, 1838, Royal decree that directed colonial officers to distribute unoccupied land to anyone interested in using it for cultivation.[48] As a result, on May 30, 1843, the town council of Benguela (Câmara Municipal) claimed rights to a two-story house, a *sobrado* located in the Fortaleza Plaza, that belonged to the Brotherhood of the *Santíssimo Sacramento*. According to the document, the brotherhood was unable to maintain the house, which was in ruins, and the town council acquired the property for *um conto de réis* that entailed "ownership, rights, and property over the house."[49] Luanda and Benguela residents, including many women, began to request permission to build or run agricultural plots, known as *arimos*.[50] Residents rushed to petition

---

[48] Portaria Régia de 10 de outubro de 1838.
[49] Biblioteca Província de Benguela (BPB), "Termo de Terreno, 1843– 1833," fl. 1, May 20, 1843
[50] BPB, "Termo de Terreno, 1843-1883." In several Bantu languages kurima or kulima, means to cultivate. In Kimbundu, "agriculturar - - rima," see José Pereira do Nascimento, *Diccionario Portuguez-Kimbundu* (Huíla, Angola: Typographia da Missão, 1907), 4. For women as land owners, see Selma Pantoja, "Donas de 'arimos': um negócio feminino no abastecimento de gêneros alimentícios em Luanda (séculos XVIII e XIX)," in *Entre Áfricas e Brasis*, ed. Selma Pantoja (Brasilia: Paralelo, 2001), 35–49; Vanessa dos Santos Oliveira, "Donas, pretas livres e escravas em Luanda (Séc. XIX)," *Estudos Ibero-Americanos* 44, no. 3 (2018): 447–56; Oliveira, *Slave Trade and Abolition. Gender, Commerce and Economic Transition in Luanda*, 44–54. Aida Freudenthal, *Arimos e fazendas: A transição agrária em Angola, 1850-1880* (Luanda: Chá de Caxinde, 2005).

for land in order to assert individual property and make these claims legitimate with the colonial state, including locally born men and women such as in the case of João Teixeira, identified as a Black man.[51] Teixeira was not the only one. José Luiz da Silva Viana, Manoel Rodrigues da Silva, and João Martins de Paiva are some of the residents who requested plots of land; their background or their intents are unclear in the registers.[52]

With land use and delimitation becoming stricter in colonial centers such as Benguela, alliances with new rulers began to affect administrative attitudes about local rulers' jurisdiction of their territory. Royal instructions included orders to delimit West Central Africa rulers' terrain and conditions under which potentates could use that land.[53] By 1847 it was clear that the subjugation of new *sobas* under Portuguese control also meant the appropriation of their territory. From that moment onward, it was the Portuguese who decided whether West Central African rulers could cultivate crops or raise cattle, or even whether they could leave the land to lie fallow between agricultural cycles. The intention of the colonial state was to determine how leaders and their subjects made use of their land.

In August 1856, a new law was approved granting individuals, including foreigners, the possibility of acquiring land concessions in Angola. Thus, besides the land enclosure in the colonial center, the colonial *Junta da Fazenda*, the treasury board, began granting three-year concessions to individuals who showed interest in exploiting cultivation or salt mining. In 1856, Manoel de Azevedo Ramos received a three-year concession to explore the land and the salt mines in Catumbela, and the lands of the local ruler were classified as vacant.[54] Effectively, by the 1850s, the Portuguese Crown was legislating land occupation in its overseas colonies beyond the colonial urban centers. According to an 1857 law, all the uncultivated lands were labeled *terrenos baldios*, or vacant lands.[55] Since they were considered unoccupied, the Portuguese colonial state appropriated these lands and rented them to private individuals.

---

[51] BPB, "Termo de Terreno, 1843–1894," fl. 8v, February 4, 1846. Similar process happened elsewhere. See Malhi, "Making Spaces, Making Subjects."

[52] BPB, "Termo de Terreno, 1843–1894," fl. 1v, March 13, 1845; fl. 2, March 13, 1845; and fl. 3, March 18, 1845.

[53] BOGGPA, n. 85, April 24, 1847, p. 1.

[54] BOGGPA, n. 372, November 13, 1852, p. 4; and BOGGPA, n. 554, May 10, 1856, p. 6. For more on this, see Freudenthal, *Arimos e fazendas*.

[55] BOGGPA, n. 597, March 7, 1857, p. 1‑3. BOA, n. 598, March 14, 1857, p. 1‑4. For more on colonialism and the idea of vacant land, see Berry, "Debating the Land," 641–42. For more detail on the Portuguese division of land in other African territories, see Rodrigues, "Chiponda, 103–04.

According to this regulation, any Portuguese subject could petition and receive land. Any land bought or rented (*aforada*) had to be occupied and cultivated in a specific period determined in the contract (usually five years). Anyone who did not occupy the land they had claimed would be fined and eventually lose the right of occupation and inheritance. Lands were sold to European buyers or offered to private societies that intended to exploit them for commercial use, including the development of mineral resources. Absent from this legislation was any recognition of the rights of the local population and their access to agricultural and pastoral land for their own survival, or even their right to live on the land. In fact, the 1857 decree recognized the rights of *sesmaria* or *prazo* grantees, who had their landownership recognized at the presentation of the original land title, privileging, once again, individuals who had insertion into the colonial government and bureaucracy and could generate written titles.

Setting boundaries and establishing territorial limits reinforced enclosure projects, the rule of property, and the commodification of land. It rewarded the violence going back to the early seventeenth century that excluded Ndombe populations from the place where Benguela was founded. The territorial delimitation of Benguela in 1848 established colonial power over all the land and the environment. According to the 1848 law, the limits of Benguela, as can be seen in Plan 2.1, were

the north of the town will be from the fortress of São Felipe to the center to a straight line to the center. A straight line from the beach to the center, passing through the house of Manuel da Silva Pilartes Pena Leão at the Largo de São Felipe, will set the south limits of the town. And a line from the north to the South in front of the house of Bento Janhes Pataca, at the Quitanda street, will set the [eastern] limits of the town. The town of Benguela will be between the beach and the two lines.[56]

These demarcations reflect the daily relationships between the colonizer and the colonized in which power, legitimacy over land, and knowledge and right of occupation were defined and favored Europeans and not the ancestral settlers of the land. Officers established maps and land charts that framed the occupation of land as legitimate and restricted where Africans could live. Colonial power was at the center of the project of establishing the territorial limits of the colonial center, and local populations, including the Ndombe, who were the landlords in the seventeenth century, were no longer considered part of the landscape.[57]

---

[56] ANA, Cód. 326, fl. 57, October 10, 1848, "From Governador of Benguela [Francisco Joaquim da Costa e Silva] to general secretary."
[57] For more on this, see Ann Laura Stoler, "Colonial Archives and the Arts of Governance," *Archival Science* 2 (2002): 87–109; Clifton Crais, "Chiefs and Bureaucrats in the Making of

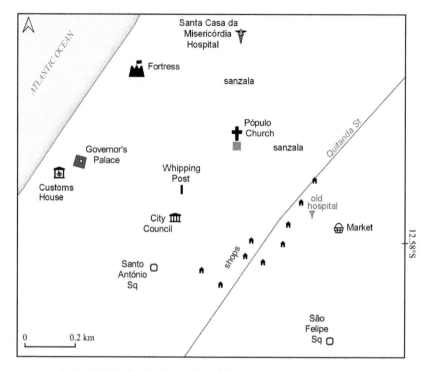

Plan 2.1 Limits of Benguela, 1848

Colonial officers aimed to define the limits of colonial towns but also of the colony, setting arbitrary limits of what was within Benguela or Mossamedes jurisdiction and what was out of colonial control.[58] In the process, colonial bureaucrats framed the people and territories as conquered and controlled. The ruler of Galanga was described as occupying "a vast territory east of the town of Benguela, six days away. His territory had abundant beeswax and copal gum."[59] The economic perspective shaped interiorization colonial policies of building more fortresses on

Empire: A Drama from the Transkei, South Africa, October 1880," *American Historical Review* 108, no. 4 (2003): 1034–56; Malhi, "Making Spaces, Making Subjects"; Luna, *Collecting Food, Cultivating People*, 222–29.

[58] AHU, SEMU, CU, Processos das Consultas, Cx. 22, doc. 754, "Informação a respeito dos limites dos governos de Benguela e Moçâmedes," L. 2, n. 100, May 12, 1855; and doc. 2, May 14, 1855; and AHU, SEMU, CU, Processo das Consultas, Cx. 5, doc. 136, 3a repartição, "Oficio do Conselho Ultramarino sobre os limites do distrito de Benguela," L. 1, N. 158, November 6, 1852.

[59] AHU, Correspondência dos Governadores, Pasta 38, December 21, 1868. "Relatório do Governo de Benguela referente a 1864-1868." For more on earlier reports, see Beatrix

the lands of conquered African rulers, or at least vassal sobas. A new fortress was built in Dombe Grande to control important trade coming from there, including wax coming from Galanga, as well as whitewash/lime and sulfur produced around Dombe Grande.[60] The territorial expansion also included buying properties. In 1857, the governor of Benguela and the treasury acquired a house and farm belonging to the widow Viana at the Egito hill, close to Egito beach. The house could be used as lodging for soldiers and colonial troops, but its surrounding farmland was not in good condition. Even so, it is but one case showing that ownership of land and houses was changing hands and had been commodified by the second half of the nineteenth century.[61]

In theory, any residents could petition land concessions to the city council or to the overseas council in Portugal. In practice, the law privileged colonial officers and residents familiar with colonial law, such as with the 1859 case of José Joaquim Geraldo do Amaral, inspector of Benguela customs. Amaral applied for land, referring to an 1838 ordinance that recommended the distribution of land plots to military personnel.[62] Amaral received 2 léguas, or 8.4 kilometers, by 1 légua of width of land declared to be empty between the River São Francisco and Luacho. With his business partner Manoel Ferreira Torres, he intended to establish cotton and sugarcane plantations. Missing is any information on the Ndombe people who inhabited this region.[63] The colonial administration granted land to Amaral as *aforamento*, that is, transferred in perpetuity through the payment of an annual tax. In 1862, when facing a series of difficulties in launching his plantation, Amaral requested dispensation from his official duties at Benguela customs to focus on his agricultural enterprise. The partnership with Ferreira Torres did not last and that failure compromised Amaral's attempts to carry out his agricultural

Heintze, *Angola nos séculos XVI e XVII. Estudo sobre fontes, métodos e história* (Luanda: Kilombelombe, 2007); Bárbara Direito, "African Access to Land in Early Twentieth Century Portuguese Colonial Thought," in *Property Rights, Land and Territory in the European Overseas Empires*, ed. José Vicente Serrão et al. (Lisbon: CEHC-IUL, 2014), 256–63, http://hdl.handle.net/10071/2718..

[60] ANA, Cod. 471, fl. 25, n. 383, August 7, 1857, "Letter from the Governador de Benguela to governador geral"

[61] ANA, Cod. 471, fl. 42v, September 15, 1857, "Letter from the Governador de Benguela to governador geral da província." For more on land tenure changes in Angola, see Aida Freudenthal, "A questão da terra em Angola. Ontem e Hoje.," *Cadernos de Estudos Sociais* 1 (2005): 15–33.

[62] AHU, SEMU, DGU, Angola, 477, 1840–1843, Registro de Correspondência Expedida, fl. 6, n. 174, October 10, 1838.

[63] Armindo Jaime Gomes, *As civilizações lacustres das margens do Kupololo* (Benguela: KAT, 2007).

plans. He lacked the necessary manpower since Torres owned most of the enslaved people who would clear the land and cultivate the soil. Amaral had twelve enslaved people, mostly women – not enough to work the vast piece of land.[64] Witnesses brought to testify stated that the land required at least 200 people to work the fields and that the few enslaved individuals Amaral owned were occupied in "cutting wood and building furniture to attend to the demands of the residents of Dombe and Cuio."[65] Two years later, the merchant dona Teresa Ferreira Torres Barruncho challenged Amaral's right to the property, arguing that he did not have the means to cultivate the land and his plots were preventing the expansion of her cotton production. Wealthy and well connected, dona Teresa Barruncho was the widow of Amaral's former business partner Manoel Ferreira Torres. She had since married the governor of Benguela, Vicente Barruncho. The overseas council intervened and ruled that Amaral could maintain property rights to the small amount of cultivated land, plus additional land four times the cultivated area. The colonial administration seized the uncultivated land and offered to dona Teresa Barruncho to expand her agricultural production.[66] Nowhere in this land dispute there is a reference to any group or individuals claiming rights to the territory before José Joaquim Geraldo do Amaral occupied it. Pushed away from the bay where Benguela was founded in the early seventeenth century, the Ndombe chiefs had moved to the arid lands in what became known as Dombe Grande and no reference to their presence, needs, or rights are discussed in the legal exchanges between authorities in Lisbon, Benguela, and Dombe Grande. Occupation was normalized, and local inhabitants became invisible in the colonial records.

African-owned land was alienated in favor of Portuguese subjects, as seen in this case, as if territories in West Central Africa were empty. In the process, land registries and demarcation favored those with Portuguese names even if they had been born on the African continent,

---

[64] AHU, SEMU, DGU, Consultas do Conselho Ultramarino, cx. 36, doc. 1651, 2 September 1862; and AHU, SEMU, DGU, Consultas do Conselho Ultramarino, cx. 39, doc 1812, "Consultando novamente sobre um Aforamento de terrenos em Benguela a Jose Joaquim Geraldo do Amaral, guarda mor da alfandega da dita cidade 1864," Doc. 5, "Auto de investigação," September 18, 1861.

[65] AHU, SEMU, DGU, Consultas do Conselho Ultramarino, cx. 39, doc. 1812, September 18, 1861. For more on this, see *Relatório dos Governadores da Provincias Ultramarinas. Relatório do Governador Geral da Provincia de Angola, 1887* (Lisbon: Imprensa Nacional, 1889), 42.

[66] AHU, SEMU, DGU, Consultas do Conselho Ultramarino, cx. 39, doc. 1812, April 19, 1864.

such as the case of Teresa Ferreira Torres Barruncho. In policies that continued to be revised years later, land demarcation involved identifying limits to occupied land. African-born women took advantage of the changes in land regimes, and those who were well positioned petitioned for land. In Serafina Barros Cunha's request, she stated her intent to build a house with a thatched roof behind José da Silva's dwelling, close to the *quitanda*, the market, as can be seen in Plan 2.1.[67] Residents also requested licenses to install tombstones in the Calundo cemetery, as was the case with Joaquim Correia da Conceição who wanted to memorialize his deceased wife, dona Florinda Perpetua da Conceição, and dona Teresa de Jesus Ferreira Torres Viana, later known as Teresa Barruncho, who requested ownership of the grave site of her former husband, José Luis da Silva Viana.[68]

By the mid-nineteenth century, the colonial state had advanced toward common land and natural resources, enclosing sulfur mines south of Benguela under the rubrics of resource management, conservation, and property rights. The colonial state sought to create a division between land that was under state management that was free from cultivation and privately owned agricultural plots in the hands of smallholders.[69] Individual ownership of land became naturalized, very different from the historical experiences of those on the ground. The colonial administration accused individuals of illegal occupation of the lands and of cutting trees without authorization, a resource considered "very important."[70] Even ownership of palm trees was contested, as shown in the notification from the secretary of the governor to the commander of Novo Presidio fortress, Francisco João da Costa Silva. According to the secretary, "the heathens planted 274 palm trees in our territory, and illegally control them." These were "state property and the heathens

---

[67] ANA, cx. 1376, November 15, 1869. For the case of Serafina Barros Cunha, see BPB, Termo de terreno, fl. 3v-4, May 7, 1845. For similar arbitrary decisions, see *Sara Berry, No Condition Is Permanent. The Social Dynamics of Agrarian Change in Sub-Saharan Africa* (Madison: University of Wisconsin Press, 1993); Lentz, *Land, Mobility, and Belonging in West Africa.*

[68] BPB, "Termo de terreno," fl. 55 and 55v, July 2, 1855. Dona Teresa is the same woman who later challenged the land concessions of José Joaquim Geraldo do Amaral in 1864. By then she had married twice, first to Manoel Ferreira Torres, who was involved in illegal slave trading, and then to Vicente Ferrer Barruncho. She had become one of the largest land and slave owners of Benguela, with properties in Dombe Grande, Luacho, and Lisbon. For more on Dona Teresa Barruncho, see Mariana P. Candido, "Women, Family, and Landed Property in Nineteenth-Century Benguela," *African Economic History* 43, no. 1 (2015): 136–61.

[69] This is not different from other processes of enclosure and state land appropriation described in Malhi, "Making Spaces, Making Subjects," 729.

[70] ANA, Cod. 166, B-14–2., fl. 132v, July 7, 1846.

could not enjoy any usufruct over them."[71] Private and Crown interests were intertwined. Francisco António Flores, a resident of Benguela, received a license to exploit sulfur and lead mines south of Benguela, with the goal of exporting these minerals. The Ndombe and subjects of Mani Capembe and Mani Mama, the lords of the lands under the rule of Dembo of Kizamba, mined sulfur there but lost their rights of access with the 1857 mining concession to Francisco António Flores.[72] The salt mines south of Benguela were also exploited as a concession to individuals, despite their location in the lands of Mani-Calunda. Lourenço Carlos Marques Batista mined them for several years. When Sousa Lara and Company Abraham Benckimol petitioned in 1886 to rent them for fifty years, the overseas council denied the request.[73]

On top of the changes associated with the end of the slave trade, the push for agricultural expansion was based on the settlement of free and poor immigrants from Azores, Brazil, and Madeira. Many arrived without tools or other resources and relied on the Portuguese government not only for access to the land but also to survive in Luanda and Benguela and the newly founded southern coastal town of Mossamedes.[74] The growing demand in Europe and North America for goods such as wax and ivory as well as tropical crops changed the colonial interests in the region. Demand for cotton, coffee, and sugar and the decline of the slavery plantation complex in the Americas favored the establishment of plantations on the African continent. Land had to be redistributed to favored European interests.[75] The Portuguese Crown's refusal to

[71] ANA, Cod. 326, fl. 70, February 10, 1849,

[72] AHU, SEMU, CU, Processos das Consultas, Cx. 40, doc. 1403, 1857, "Processo relativo a pretensão do marques de bemposta sobre a concessão da propriedade de umas minas de enxofre ao sul de Benguela," February 11 and August 31, 1857; and AHU, SEMU, CU, Processos das Consultas, Cx. 70, doc. 2460, "Pedido de Antônio Flores para licença para lavrar minas de cobre e chumbo, 1860." For more on the local rulers and their role in the mining activities, see José Joaquim Lopes de Lima, *Ensaios sobre a statistica das possessões portuguezas na África occidental e oriental; na Ásia occidental; na China e na Oceania* (Lisbon: Imprensa Nacional, 1844), 42–43.

[73] AHU, SEMU, Junta Consultiva do Ultramar, Processos de Consultas, cx. 12, doc. 509, "Arrematação de salinas de Benguela," September 24, 1886

[74] BOGGPA, n. 224, January 12, 1850. This situation was quite different from other regions of Atlantic Africa, such as Sierra Leone, where Liberated Africans provided a new labor force after 1808. For more on this, see Suzanne Schwarz, "From Company Administration to Crown Control: Experimentation and Adaptation in Sierra Leone in the Late Eighteenth and Early Nineteenth Centuries," In *Slavery, Abolition, and the Transition to Colonialism in Sierra Leone*, edited by Paul E. Lovejoy and Suzanne Schwarz (Trenton: Africa World Press, 2015), 163–88.

[75] Law, *From Slave Trade to "Legitimate" Commerce*; Martin Lynn, *Commerce and Economic Change in West Africa: The Palm Oil Trade in the Nineteenth Century* (Cambridge University Press, 2002).

recognize that land used for pasture and grazing was communal, as well as its disregard for land lying fallow, eventually led to the displacement of Africans. Over time, the lack of recognition of the ownership rights of the local population and their rulers created absurd situations in which Brazilian and Madeira settlers became landlords and the local population were strangers in their own land, labeled as squatters. Agriculture for export expanded at the expense of the local population, who were suddenly stripped of their communal land and forced to sell their labor on the newly established plantations.[76]

While in the early nineteenth century there was a recognition that sobas owned land and could impose their jurisdiction over their territories and their subjects, by the end of the century their rights had been erased. In theory, there was a distinction between land occupied by African authorities and vacant land. However, the colonial administration seized land and denied the access rights to local rulers, as seen in the case of Quipola, a ruler near Mossamedes removed from his community lands in the 1860s despite his people's long history of occupation of the territory. According to the report of the governor of Benguela, João António de Neves Ferreira,

The soba Quipola claimed that all the land his people occupied had been given to the whites. He and his people had no space to establish their *libatas* [villages] and raise their cattle. The only small piece of land available was at the *varzeas dos carpinteiros* [carpenter's cultivated plain or meadow], which was not productive. Yet he was willing to accept this land where he could establish the corrals for the cattle, but he needed the approval of the governor of Mossamedes to resettle his people there.[77]

Portuguese authorities reported the clashes and events as a matter of fact, as a legitimate legal procedure rather than an episode of dispossession. To guarantee the long-term use of the land, the *soba* of Quipola requested that the governor of Mossamedes grant him "the land title, so he and his successors and his people could occupy the land without the risk of losing it later on." However, the governor refused to grant Quipola the land title, arguing that these were "public lands," although he gave them permission to build the cattle pens on the land. In compensation, Quipola sent a cow to the governor, understanding this

---

[76] Freudenthal, *Arimos e Fazendas*, 145. BOGGPA, n. 308, August 23, 1851, p. 1–2. For similar examples in the 1860s in West Africa, see Emmanuel Kwaku Akyeampong, *Themes in West Africa's History* (Athen: Ohio University Press, 2006), 219–22.

[77] AHU, Angola, Correspondência dos Governadores, Pasta 35, doc. October 11, 1865. For more on the history of Moçâmedes in the 1840s-1860s, see W. G. Clarence-Smith, *Slaves, Peasants, and Capitalists in Southern Angola, 1840-1926* (Cambridge: Cambridge University Press, 1979), 14–23.

as a payment for the use of the land.[78] Eventually, the increased number of white settlers and their expanding farms in the *várzea do carpinteiro* forced the relocation of Quipola's subjects. By 1865, the failure of the colonial authority to protect Quipola's access to land forced the soba to relocate with his people to the interior, away from the Portuguese-occupied lands. As refugees in the land of the ruler of Capangombe, Quipola's subjects had inferior status and established relationships of dependency with the landlords of the territory. Destitute after the loss of their lands, some of the youth attacked Europeans and white traders who traveled inland. Quipola's subjects claimed that "whites always came to rob their lands."[79] Episodes of land conflict such as Quipola's case are abundant in the colonial archives, clearly indicating that West Central Africans understood their land rights and resisted Portuguese advances, mainly in unsuccessful revolts.[80]

The Portuguese monarchy issued new laws, which resulted in the land alienation of the local population. On March 28, 1877, the *Ministério dos Negócios da Marinha e Ultramar* issued a law "authorizing the government to cover any necessary expenses to transport any potential immigrants to our territorial possession in Africa, providing them with the means for the establishment of the first farm, as long as they reside in any of the African colonies for at least five years."[81] Individuals were granted land along rivers, such as the case of Joaquim Afonso Lage who received fifteen hectares on the left bank of river Nene in Huíla, and in Ambriz, Calumbo, and Mossamades, as well as the case of Aristides Urbano do Amaral, awarded 500 hectares in the Cuio to cultivate sugarcane.[82] Most of the ordinances published in the *Boletim Geral da Província de Angola*, the colonial gazette, favored men, but some women also requested land, such as the case of Rufina Rosa, a resident of Huíla, who received two hectares to expand her compound.[83] In colonial documents, emigrants are qualified as landowners and free, while the local Black population was expected to work as forced labor in this new colonial enterprise.[84]

---

[78] AHU, Angola, Correspondência dos Governadores, Pasta 23 (1), doc. October 1, 1857.
[79] AHU, Angola, Correspondência dos Governadores, Pasta 35, doc. October 11, 1865.
[80] Ver Freudenthal, *Arimos e Fazendas*, 134.
[81] BOGGPA, 1881, n. 42, October 15, 1881, p. 643.
[82] BOGGPA, 1881, n. 11, March 11, 1881, p. 145-6.
[83] BOGGPA, 1881, n. 21, May 21, 1881, p. 302.
[84] For the expansion of the forced labor regimes in Angola in the late nineteenth century, see Jeremy Ball, *Angola's Colossal Lie: Forced Labor on a Sugar Plantation, 1913-1977* (Leiden; Boston, MA: Brill, 2015), 3–4; Aharon Grassi and Jesse Salah Ovadia, "Trajectories of Large-Scale Land Acquisition Dynamics in Angola: Diversity, Histories, and Implications for the Political Economy of Development in Africa," *Land Use Policy* 67 (2017): 117.

To make sure the emigrants were successful, by the 1880s, the colonial administration distributed to each settler a firearm and its supplements; tools for agricultural work such as an axe, two hoes, and an iron shovel; and items for personal use such as pillows, a mattress, four cotton sheets, a blanket, two cotton towels, a comb, two zinc bowls, a small mirror, a brush, a shoe brush, a pan, a casserole, four plates, two bowls, two mugs, one spoon, one fork, and a knife.[85] By the end of the nineteenth century, European occupation of the territory was considered legitimate, and West Central Africans' notions of possession, ownership, and rights that had prevailed until the beginning of the 1800s were ignored. The consequence was that land was concentrated in only a few hands, and these individuals – usually of Portuguese descent – exploited African labor. West Central African rulers and their subjects became landless and forced to work in the colonial labor projects of the late nineteenth century.

Land Rights Misrepresented

West Central Africans expressed land rights in first-settler narratives. European authors (jurists, missionaries, and colonial officers), however, misrepresented these property regimes, portraying them as nonexistent. In his account of his years in Angola in the 1880s, the linguist and missionary Héli Chatelain made several observations about property. The late-nineteenth-century missionaries' and anthropologists' accounts relied on the premise that African norms, or customs, did not change over time, and that landed property had always existed in Europe, which is not true.[86] Chatelain spent most of his time north of the Kwanza River among the Mbundu and noticed that chiefs had power over subjects' personal property, indicating the existence of personal and collective rights. He also described Mbundu kinship links as well as hereditary practices. According to him, "A fatherhood is never absolutely certain, while there can be no doubt about motherhood; it is the mother, not the

---

[85] BOGGPA, 1881, n.42, 16 August 1881, p. 644–45.

[86] There is extensive scholarship on how anthropologists and missionaries created the myth of static African societies. See V. Y. Mudimbe, *The Invention of Africa. Gnosis, Philosophy, and the Order of Knowledge* (Bloomington: Indiana University Press, 1988), 12–20; Cynthia Hoehler-Fatton, *Women of Fire and Spirit. History, Faith, and Gender in Roho Religion in Western Kenya* (New York: Oxford University Press, 1996). On the rise of the landed property discourse among jurists in Europe in the nineteenth century, see Rosa Congost, "Property Rights and Historical Analysis: What Rights? What History?," *Past & Present*, no. 181 (2003): 73–106; Mariana Armond Dias Paes, "Escravos e terras entre posses e títulos: A construção social do direito de propriedade no Brasil (1835–1889)" (Ph.D., São Paulo, SP, Universidade de São Paulo, 2018).

father, that determines consanguinity or kinship, and secession or heredity. ... The uncle owns his nephews and nieces; he can sell them, and they are his heirs not only in private property, but also in chieftaincy if he be a chief."[87] Despite Chatelain's assertions that property rights were nonexistent, his account proves otherwise that Mbundu societies had a clear sense of property regimes and inheritance practices.

Besides missionary anthropologists like Héli Chatelain, jurists, such as António Gil, also made bold claims about customary law in the mid-nineteenth century. Gil, for example, categorically affirmed that West Central Africans did not recognize land rights, yet, his ethnological accounts recorded that, among all West Central African populations, regardless of their linguistic or political differences, inheritance passed through the maternal line. Gil described an odd system that supposedly did not recognize individual property but surprisingly had strict rules about its transfer.[88] Colonial administrators repeated the assertions of early missionaries, anthropologists, and jurists, perpetuating the idea of the absence of private property and forms of wealth accumulation in African societies.[89] While denying the existence of land regimes among West Central Africans, these jurists created and continued to propagate the illusion that private property had always existed in Portugal, and in European societies in general, accepting and reproducing liberal ideas that land could be commodified and expropriation since African societies did not have land regimes that recognized occupation, use, and possession.

To recognize and defend in writing that West Central Africans had land tenure regimes by the late nineteenth and early twentieth centuries would have questioned a basic tenet of imperialism and the Portuguese

[87] Héli Chatelain, *Folk-Tales of Angola: Fifty Tales, with Ki-Mbundu Text, Literal English Translation, Introduction, and Notes* (Boston, MA: The American Folklore Society by Houghton Mifflin, 1894), 8.

[88] António Gil, *Considerações sobre alguns pontos mais importantes da moral religiosa e sistema de jurisprudência dos pretos do continente da África Ocidental Portuguesa além do Equador* (Lisbon: Tipografia da Academia, 1854). For missionaries, see, for example, Hambly, *Ovimbundu of Angola*, 199–200.

[89] See, for example, Caetano Gonçalves, "O regime das terras e as reservas indígenas na colonização portuguesa," *Boletim Geral das Colónias* 2, no. 13 (1926): 26 and 42; and Gil, *Considerações sobre alguns pontos*, 11; .These ideas are also available at colonial gazettes, such as *Boletim Oficial do Governo Geral da Província de Angola*, 1857, no. 611, June 13, 1857, pp. 6–7. Also cited in João de Castro Maia Veiga de Figueiredo, "Política, escravatura e feitiçaria em Angola (séculos XVIII e XIX)" (Ph.D., Coimbra, Portugal, Universidade de Coimbra, 2015), 257–58. For an analysis of fluid movement between colonial service and higher education appointments in Portugal, see Aaron deGrassi, "Provisional Reconstructions: Geo-Histories of Infrastructure and Agrarian Configuration in Malanje, Angola" (Ph.D., Berkeley, University of California, Berkeley, 2015), 110–14.

colonization of Angola. In that sense, it is not surprising that Portuguese jurists made these claims discounting land regimes and notions of land occupation and possession. If African societies had such rights, then they had the legitimacy to challenge Portuguese land expropriation and question the entire colonial system. Colonialism was based on the expropriation of land and resources, in part because colonialists claimed that non-Europeans were incapable of apprehending and protecting the basic concept of land holding, despite extensive evidence to the contrary. Ethnographers and jurists provided the evidence for colonial claims and ideologies with their cumbersome theories, feeding colonial bureaucrats the notion of European legitimacy to occupy and colonize the world, ignoring testimonies and proofs that showed African populations did have conceptions of land rights, occupation, and use. In African Islamic societies, it was clear that notions of private property existed and thus legislation protected it, but in non-Islamic African societies, the opinion prevailed that land was communal, and no one exercised full control over it, or was able to dispose of, sell, or mortgage it.[90]

Despite the supremacy of the jurists' opinions about property and rights, colonial reports and anthropologist accounts indicate that local populations continued to defend their land rights. By the early twentieth century, anthropologists and missionaries noticed similar practices among the Nkumbi, or Humbe, on the southern border between Angola and Namibia. In a 1904 report, an unidentified colonial officer wrote,

The land belongs to those who live in it, and [even] less important advisors (*sekulos*) enjoy property rights over the land they occupy. The ruler can reappropriate occupied lands if the occupier does not have heirs at the time of his death or if he moves to another location. He can also be expelled from the community due to a troublesome character. If the landowner proves to be incompatible with the chief, he can be expelled without any indemnity. This rule is rarely employed for women.[91]

---

[90] Martin Chanock, "Paradigms, Policies and Property: A Review of the Customary Law of Land Tenure," in *Law in Colonial Africa*, ed. Kristin Mann and Richard L. Roberts (Portsmouth, NH: Heinemann, 1991), 74–75; Peter Pels, "The Anthropology of Colonialism: Culture, History, and the Emergence of Western Governmentality," *Annual Review of Anthropology* 26 (1997): 173; Anthony Pagden, "Law, Colonization, Legitimation, and the European Background," in *The Cambridge History of Law in America*, ed. Michael Grossberg et al. (Cambridge: Cambridge University Press, 2008), 22–24; José Vicente Serrão, "Property, Land and Territory in the Making of Overseas Empires," in *Property Rights, Land and Territory in the European Overseas Empires*, ed. José Vicente Serrão et al. (Lisbon: CEHC-IUL, 2014), 8–9.

[91] ANA, cx. 1338, Humbe, 1906, "Dos povos em geral," n. 35–47, pages not numbered.

Thus, quite contrary to the ideas circulating in Lisbon and Luanda, the Nkumbi had been exercising and defending their land.

A few years later, when studying the people who inhabited the district of Benguela, the auto-didactic ethnologist Augusto Bastos suggested the existence of land rights among the Kilengues, Ndombes, Bienos, and Mbailundu. Bastos stated, "the land belongs to the person who can be a chief or a subject, who built on it a *cubata* (house) or planted a tree. And with the agreement of the owner of the land, the tree fruits can be sold. Among the Ndombe, land can be rented, with the renter paying an annual tribute calculated over the harvest production."[92] As in earlier centuries, the Ndombe recognized planting trees, clearing bush, and cultivating the land as an indication of first settler rights.

Even though evidence to the contrary was all around them, colonial bureaucrats kept producing treaties and legal opinions about the absence of property rights among West Central African populations. The Portuguese jurist Lopo Vaz de Sampaio de Melo published *Política Indígena* in 1910. In this booklet, Sampaio de Melo argued there was no notion of private property in Angola and contrasted it with ahistorical European law that recognized individual rights over land. According to Sampaio de Melo, in West Central Africa, land belonged to a clan, it was inalienable and could not be sold, and chiefs distributed access among their subjects.[93] Sampaio de Melo never visited Angola or interacted with West Central African chiefs to come up with these arguments, yet he taught at the *Escola Superior Colonial,* an institution that trained colonial officers, for twenty years (1926–1946) and was instrumental in the elaboration of a colonial science to improve governability and control over colonialized populations. Sampaio de Melo oversaw preparing colonial administrators to serve overseas in matters related to jurisdiction and indigenous laws and taught courses on "Indigenous Politics," where he covered issues related to property rights in the Portuguese Empire, as well as courses on colonial ethnography and ethnology.[94] His reflections,

---

[92] Augusto Bastos, "Traços geraes sobre a ethnographia do districto de Benguella," *Boletim da Sociedade de Geografia de Lisboa* 26, no. 1 (1908): 86; Freudenthal, *Arimos e fazendas*, 89.

[93] Lopo Vaz de Sampaio e Melo, *Política indígena* (Porto: Magalhães & Moniz, 1910), 376.

[94] Besides his book, *Política Indigena*, Sampaio de Melo published articles and was the editor of the Escola Superior Colonial annual publication, *Anuário da Escola Superior Colonial,* and the founder of *Revista de Estudos Colonias.* Both operated as a colonial and imperial propaganda publications. See Lopo Vaz de Sampaio e Melo, *Regime da propriedade indigena, separata da "Revista Portugueza Colonial e Maritima"* (Lisbon: Ferin Editora, 1910) and "O problema social nas colónias e as modernas correntes da política indígena," *Boletim da Sociedade de Geografia de Lisboa,* 45 (7–8) (1927): 170–191. For more on Lopo Voz de Sampaio e Melo and his influence on colonial education, see

teaching, and publications influenced generations of colonial officers in matters related to the so-called colonial sciences, from ethnography to jurisprudence. Besides, alongside other jurists and colonial officers, Sampaio de Melo helped create and perpetuate the narrative that private property had always existed in European legal codes. Rather than historicizing landed property rights as a creation of nineteenth-century codification, colonial science jurists elaborated creative understandings of European civil codes as a direct influence of Roman Law, perpetuation of liberal economic agenda that land had always had monetary value.[95]

By the early twentieth century, the idea that African populations had no known land regimes or property rights had been consolidated in European palaces and universities. Colonial bureaucrats, missionaries, and jurists wrote extensive reports and treaties on the "backward" African land tenure regimes. A colonial science of administration justified land seizure and the European project of economic dominance. Africanists reproduced these ideas in their studies without disentangling knowledge production from ideologies that justified colonialism.[96]

Conclusion

First settlers and immigrant populations historically constructed and negotiated land rights. While the codification of civil codes in Europe created the narrative of objective and clear legislation, as well as the naturalization of privatization of land, an analysis of West Central African rulers' claims reveals a more conflictive narrative. Sobas, dembos, and manis held clear understandings of land regimes based on occupation, transformation of the landscape, and burial of ancestors. Neighboring rulers contested these rights, and disputes between rulers were constant for most of the 1800s. The novelty, by the midcentury, was the competition with Portuguese and Brazilian immigrants and the introduction of the colonial administration as an arbiter regulating land access

Carlos Manoel Pimenta Pires, "A educação dos neocolonizadores: a Escola Colonial e a investigação no ultramar no Império Português (séculos XIX e XX)" (Ph.D., Lisbon, Universidade de Lisboa. Instituto de Educação, 2016), 112–21 and 144–50.

[95] Herzog, *Short History of European Law*; Dias Paes, "Terras em contenda."

[96] For more on this, see Barbara Direito, "The land question in early twentieth-century Portuguese legal colonial thought," *Portuguese Journal of Social Science* 16, no. 2 (2017), 181–93. For scholars who helped perpetuate the colonial ideology of absence of land ownership rights, see Jack Goody, *Technology, Tradition, and the State in Africa* (London: Oxford University Press, 1971), 21–37; J. D. Fage, "Slaves and Society in Western Africa, c. 1445- c.1700," *Journal of African History* 21, no. 3 (1980): 289–310; Antony G. Hopkins, "Property Rights and Empire Building: Britain's Annexation of Lagos, 1861," *The Journal of Economic History* 40, no. 4 (1980): 777–98.

and rights. Despite more than two centuries of colonial agents recognizing West Central African rulers' sovereignty over land and jurisdiction, Portuguese missionaries and jurists were promulgating claims that Africans did not have land tenure. With that misbegotten notion, jurists guaranteed the power of colonialists.

Property rights were codified in the second half of the nineteenth century in Portugal, yet in Angola colonial judges, secretaries, and administrators registered land titles and settled land rights going back several decades. In many respects, the imposition of written titles took place earlier in the overseas colonies than in Portugal. Initially limited to the colonial towns, due to the expansion of plantation and commercial development as well as population growth, land titles eventually expanded to areas under African rulers' jurisdiction. European bureaucrats who never set foot in African territories wrote expansive treaties about African land tenure and (the absence of) property rights, which had a profound influence on later generations of colonial officers and historians. Land use and landscape transformations that had until then been accepted as proof of occupation rights were dismissed as valid forms of ownership rights.

Dispossession in West Central Africa, however, began even earlier. With the introduction of paper evidence, colonial administrators required West Central African rulers to back up immigration narratives with land titles, creating a rush for hard documentation and filling archives with rich information about local understandings of wealth, accumulation, and inequalities. Rulers and commoners registered their claims in written records, which protected their individual interests but unintentionally helped erode collective ones and legitimized Europeans as arbitrators of their rights.

3   Written Records and Gendered Strategies to Secure Property

By the mid-nineteenth century, the existence of physical paper created ownership – a "papereality," or "a world of symbols or written representations, that take precedence over the things and events represented."[1] The existence of the written register created the idea that land use and occupation could be proven, that ownership, being a farmer and a respectable colonial resident, was anchored on written evidence. In contrast to poor or enslaved urban residents, those who made use of the colonial administration had written documents recording their legal identity and inserting them as official subjects. Encoded in these documents were expressions that legitimated a narrative about the past: These were free people with Catholic names, vassals of the Portuguese Crown, and hardworking individuals who understood the importance of agriculture. Missing from these documents was any reference to skin color or a past that could jeopardize social standing or threaten someone's prestige.[2] Recording was selective, yet these documents are rich and allow historians to reconstruct the lives of West Central African men and women and their claims to property.

Written documents were more than symbolic: They were a weapon of control for colonizers and tools in the hands of the colonized, who tapped into the power of government to assert their rights. Colonial conquest

---

[1] David Dery, "'Papereality' and Learning in Bureaucratic Organizations," *Administration & Society* 29, no. 6 (1998): 678; and Bhavani Raman, *Document Raj: Writing and Scribes in Early Colonial South India* (Chicago: University of Chicago Press, 2012).

[2] Rebecca J. Scott and Michael Zeuske, "Property in Writing, Property on the Ground: Pigs, Horses, Land, and Citizenship in the Aftermath of Slavery, Cuba, 1880-1909," *Comparative Studies in Society and History* 44, no. 4 (2002): 669–99; Ann Laura Stoler, "Colonial Archives and the Arts of Governance," *Archival Science* 2 (2002): 87–109. Selective recording also took place in other locations in Atlantic Africa. See, for example, Ademide Adelusi-Adeluyi, "To Be Female & Free. Mapping Mobility & Emancipation in Lagos, Badagry & Abeokuta 1853-1865," in *African Women in the Atlantic World. Property, Vulnerability and Mobility, 1680-1880*, ed. Mariana P. Candido and Adam Jones (Woodbridge: James Currey, 2019), 131–47; Suzanne Schwarz, "Reconstructing the Life Histories of Liberated Africans: Sierra Leone in the Early Nineteenth Century," *History in Africa* 39 (2012): 175–207.

and occupation in West Central Africa were a victory of paper over memory and of writing over oral claims.[3] Written records became tools for the colonized to assert their rights and property ownership, particularly with respect to African women. Colonial records for the nineteenth century suggest that West Central African women enjoyed a series of rights and made extensive use of the colonial courts to protect their assets. In official lists of traders or owners or in traveler accounts, African women were not recognized as such, but their activities and actions determined their ability to claim rights. African women relied on the colonial bureaucracy to register their belongings, demonstrating how written records could prove ownership and conserve any disputes or negotiations behind property acquisition and transmission. The will or the land record gained new meaning, representing people, events, desires, and networks. In fact, petitions, land records, wills, and inventories reveal colonial subjects' ability to navigate the colonial legal system and pass on their possessions to relatives and friends.[4] These records legitimated women as property owners, which bolstered their status and power in the colonial urban center. Women are not invisible or hard to find in legal cases or ecclesiastical records. In fact, they are everywhere, and it is hard to write about the Angolan past without mentioning the key roles women have played, including registering claims over things, people, and land.

Colonial authorities in Angola were accustomed, by the mid-nineteenth century, to tallying people, taxing residents, and accounting for the sale, transport, and export of human beings shipped as captives. Although earlier attempts to legislate and intervene in local practices of ownership existed, during the late eighteenth and early nineteenth centuries there was a rush to survey land, people, and customs in order to facilitate colonial seizure and control. The introduction of new forms of registers, such as land registrations, indicates how notions of land use

---

[3] For more on this, see Walter Mignolo, *The Darker Side of the Renaissance: Literacy, Territoriality, and Colonization* (Ann Arbor: University of Michigan Press, 1995); Frederick Cooper and Ann Laura Stoler, eds., "Between Metrople and Clony. Rethinking a Research Agenda" (Berkeley: University of California Press, 1997), 1–56; Hawkins, *Writing and Colonialism in Northern Ghana*; Catarina Madeira Santos, "Escrever o poder. Os autos de vassalagem e a vulgarização da escrita entre as elites africanas Ndembu," *Revista de História* no. 155 (2006): 81–95; Rachel Jean-Baptiste, *Conjugal Rights: Marriage, Sexuality, and Urban Life in Colonial Libreville, Gabon* (Athens: Ohio University Press, 2014), 114–122.

[4] Dery, "'Papereality'," 682–3; Karen B. Graubart, *With Our Labor and Sweat: Indigenous Women and the Formation of Colonial Society in Peru, 1550-1700* (Stanford, CA: Stanford University Press, 2007), 80–84; Eugénia Rodrigues, "Chiponda, a Senhora que tudo pisa com os pés. Estratégias de poder das donas dos prazos do Zambeze no século XVIII," *Anais de História de Além-Mar* I (2000): 110.

and occupation had changed and become associated with written registration. Paper records were integral to the Portuguese Empire. Only when land registration and wills were recorded by the official colonial scribe and not by local Africans did the Portuguese accept the documents as authentic and legitimate.[5] Once land occupation recognition was subject to formal colonial validation and moved away from local chiefs' control, the local population was pushed to use the colonial bureaucracy to defend and acquire new rights.[6]

West Central African rulers did keep land records orally, but by the early eighteenth century, several rulers began to register their territory in written documents aware of colonial changes regarding occupation and legitimacy. Record keeping about land registration indicated that Portuguese officials felt the necessity and the authority to claim land and categorize its use. In this context, West Central African rulers struggled to establish their rights; however, some Ndembu authorities created their own state's archives, such as Caculo Cacahenda, embracing the idea that written evidence proved ownership claims.[7] In urban areas, individuals were required to identify the piece of land they intended to use, explain their plan for its use, and pay for it. Colonial bureaucrats sent agents to verify the size of the terrain and produced documents related to land possession. These pieces of paper legitimated the use of property, consolidated power over the population living in the colonial urban center, and took precedent over any other form of proving occupation.

The creation of land registries and the regulation of plots responded to changes in perceptions of governance and commodification in the nineteenth century. The local population, including West Central African

---

[5] Éve Sebestyén, "Legitimation through Landcharters in Ambundo Villages, Angola," in *Perspektiven Afrikanistischer Forschung*, eds. Thomas Bearth, Wilhelm Mohlig, Beat Sottas and Edgar Suter (Cologne, Germany: Rudiger Koppe Verlag, 1994), 368.

[6] James C. Scott, John Tehranian, and Jeremy Mathias, "The Production of Legal Identities Proper to States: The Case of the Permanent Family Surname," *Comparative Studies in Society and History* 44, no. 01 (2002): 4–44; Amrita Malhi, "Making Spaces, Making Subjects: Land, Enclosure and Islam in Colonial Malaya," *The Journal of Peasant Studies* 38, no. 4 (2011): 727–46; Bhavani Raman, "The Duplicity of Paper: Counterfeit, Discretion, and Bureaucratic Authority in Early Colonial Madras," *Comparative Studies in Society & History* 54, no. 2 (2012): 229–50; Karen B. Graubart, "Shifting Landscape. Heterogenous Conceptions of Land Use and Tenure in the Lima Valley," *Colonial Latin American Review* 26, no. 1 (2017): 62–84.

[7] For more on the Caculo Cacahenda's state archive, see Ana Paula Tavares and Catarina Madeira Santos, eds., *Africæ Monumenta: Arquivo Caculo Cacahenda* (Lisbon: Instituto de Investigação Científica Tropical, 2002). It is important to notice that documents from other West Central African state archives exist, but their access was not available to the public until very recently.

rulers, articulated their own understandings of land rights and the importance of the documents they needed to maintain their social standing. Ndembu rulers, identified as *Dembos* in Portuguese records, Ilamba lords, Kakonda sobas, and other West Central Africans, including Luso-Africans[8] and Portuguese officers, reinforced paper's power through the creation of records whose existence served as proof of ownership. Community ownership or the power of neighbors and peers to recognize occupation and use rights over land, people, and cattle was no longer enough, a clear disadvantage for those who had no access to literacy or a scriber. From the perspective of the Portuguese empire at large, there was an effort to expand knowledge about conquered people, including their jurisprudence and land regimes. Although customs, referred to as *usos e costumes*, collected in West Central Africa in the nineteenth century were not as detailed and rich as the local jurisprudence codified in Mozambique, Guiné, or Goa, they inform us about local ideas on right and wrong, what constituted crime, and local land regimes.[9] Setting down local laws in writing was part of the effort to define rights and citizenship in Portugal and its overseas empire. They defined who qualified as a Portuguese citizen in Angola, Mozambique, and Goa and indicated how the metropolitan law was applied over non-Catholic subjects.

Colonial administrators were committed to recording information that confirmed European claims, stereotypes, and political demands. As a result, there is an abundance of written documents in Portuguese about the economic, political, and social lives of the colonized. Jurists went to the colonies to collect ethnographic information in order to construct colonial knowledge. Much of the information collected was used in the

[8] For a discussion of Luso-African identity, see Mariana P. Candido, *An African Slaving Port and the Atlantic World: Benguela and Its Hinterland* (New York: Cambridge University Press, 2013), 122–39.

[9] For more on the problematic approach to *usos e costumes* in colonial jurisprudence, see Cristina Nogueira da Silva, *Constitucionalismo e Império. A cidadania no ultramar português* (Lisbon: Almedina, 2009), 212–29. There is a vast scholarship in English on the limitations and inventions associated with customary law. See, among others, Sara Berry, "Debating the Land Question in Africa," *Comparative Studies in Society and History* 44, no. 4 (2002): 638–68; Martin Chanock, *Law, Custom, and Social Order: The Colonial Experience in Malawi and Zambia* (New York: Cambridge University Press, 1985); Kristin Mann, "African and European Initiatives in the Transformation of Land Tenure in Colonial Lagos (West Africa), 1840-1920," in *Native Claims: Indigenous Law against Empire, 1500-1920*, ed. Saliha Belmessous (Oxford; New York: Oxford University Press, 2012), 223–58; Kristin Mann and Richard L. Roberts, eds., *Law in Colonial Africa* (Portsmouth, NH: Heinemann, 1991); Richard L Roberts, *Litigants and Households: African Disputes and Colonial Courts in the French Soudan, 1895-1912* (Portsmouth, NH: Heinemann, 2005).

"civilizing mission" projects.[10] Produced in a context of evolutionist theories in which African populations were portrayed as uncivilized and barbaric, *usos e costumes* still reflect local jurisprudence, although they likely remained fluid until they were crystallized in the written codes of the nineteenth century. Not surprisingly, West Central African populations apprehended the importance of the written document and began to organize their own archives to document rights and debts that could legitimize later claims.[11] Many property records are mixed in the bundled books available at the Arquivo Nacional de Angola, and in the wills, deeds, and inventories available at the Tribunal da Comarca de Benguela. In these records, Africans claimed property, which allows an understanding on the dynamics of access to resources in the colonial centers and elsewhere. Local people, including several women, made use of multiple strategies to protect their rights, calling on local norms in conjunction with the colonial system of property recognition.

These records reveal that West Central Africans acquired real estate and material goods, which allowed accumulation and consolidation of wealth. The governor of Angola in the late eighteenth century, Francisco Inocêncio de Sousa Coutinho, remarked that the Luandan elite lived luxurious lives, surrounded by "an excessive number of Black and mixed race women that follow them anywhere, dressed in expensive outfits, adorned with gold, silver, and precious stones jewelry, carried in little chairs or hammocks around town."[12] While there was a recognition that colonial elites and African subjects accumulated property in the form of enslaved people, clothes, and luxurious items, registering these items in writing and extending claims to land became a concern. Besides material items, West Central Africans claimed landed properties, as can be seen in "Termo de Terreno," available at the *Biblioteca da Província Benguela* (Library of the Benguela Province). This document lists the individuals who requested land in Benguela from 1843 to 1894 (see Table 3.5, Granted Land in Benguela). Although property records were not introduced to protect the rights of colonial subjects, many of these individuals, including a surprising number of women, were able to access the colonial bureaucracy and claim rights.[13]

[10] Maria Paula D. Meneses, "O Indígena 'africano' e o colono 'europeu': A construção da diferença por processos legais," *E-Cadernos CES*, http://hdl.handle.net/10316/36165.

[11] This is very clear in the case of the Caculo Cacahenda archives. See Tavares and Santos, *Africæ Monumenta*; Sebestyén, "Legitimation through Landcharter."

[12] Arquivo Nacional da Torre do Tombo (ANTT), Condes de Linhares, mç. 44, doc. 2 "Memórias do Reino de Angola e suas conquistas escritas por D. Francisco Inocêncio de Sousa Coutinho, governador e capitão general do Reino de Angola," 1773–1775.

[13] Rodrigues, "Chiponda," 108; Mariana P. Candido and Eugénia Rodrigues, "African Women's Access and Rights to Property in the Portuguese Empire," *African Economic History* 43, no. 1 (2015): 1–18.

Property claims in the nineteenth-century colonial records should not be taken as representative of the condition of every West Central African, but they do suggest the complexities of ownership negotiations. In addition, they reveal how, long before the Berlin Conference, European colonial violence resulted in local people losing access to land and movable property. West Central African women addressed questions of dispossession and made new appeals, employing colonial tools to advance their claims.[14]

The Population under Control: Property, Law, and Its Limits

In most places, colonizing powers sought to extend their jurisdiction over territories and populations that they knew very little about. In West Central Africa, the colonial administration erected jurisdictional boundaries that gave the illusion of clear and precise control, such as labeling West Central Africans as vassals or heathens, yet these boundaries were inherently unstable and constantly under renegotiation, as attested in several cases of local rulers who challenged the Portuguese claims.[15] While during the late nineteenth and early twentieth centuries there was a concern of European agents elsewhere in Africa to record customary laws as if they were immutable, the same cannot be said about the Portuguese colonies. Portuguese agents appropriated some elements of local jurisdiction such as the *mucano* tribunal, in the case of West Central African societies, but also sought to impose Portuguese law on its subjects.[16] A multi normative system of local and colonial laws coexisted for three centuries, which included some recognition of West Central

---

[14] Saliha Belmessous, "Introduction: The Problem of Indigenous Claim Making in Colonial History," in *Native Claims: Indigenous Law against Empire, 1500-1920*, ed. Saliha Belmessous (New York: Oxford University Press, 2012), 5–8; Scott and Zeuske, "Property in Writing," 673–74; Clifton Crais, "Custom and the Politics of Sovereignty in South Africa," *Journal of Social History* 39, no. 3 (2006): 721–40.

[15] See, for example, Beatrix Heintze, "Ngonga a Mwiza: Um sobado angolano sob domino português no século XVII," *Revista Internacional de Estudos Africanos* 8–9 (1988): 221–34; Linda M. Heywood, *Njinga of Angola: Africa's Warrior Queen* (Cambridge, MA: Harvard University Press, 2017).

[16] For the mucano tribunal, see Roquinaldo Ferreira, *Cross-Cultural Exchange in the Atlantic World: Angola and Brazil during the Era of the Slave Trade* (New York: Cambridge University Press, 2012), 88–124; Candido, *An African Slaving Port and the Atlantic World*, 215; Catarina Madeira Santos, "Esclavage africain et traite atlantique confrontés: Transactions langagières et juridiques (à propos du tribunal de mucanos dans l'Angola des XVIIe et XVIIIe siècles)," *Brésil (s). Sciences Humaines et Sociales* 1 (2012): 127–48. For the consolidation of customary law, see Chanock, *Law, Custom, and Social Order*; Mann and Roberts, eds., *Law in Colonial Africa*, 3–15.

African juridical norms. Besides the incorporation of the *mucano* tribunal, colonial agents recognized the validity of unwritten contracts, such as debt practices that allowed long-distance trade to operate for most of the transatlantic slave trade era. Nonetheless, the unwritten practices were gradually dismissed by the second half of the nineteenth century and, as a result, some ethnography collected in the early twentieth century claimed that local groups such as the Ndombe did not have "any law or law courts and when they cannot settle cases in a friendly manner, they complain to the local authority."[17]

Colonial courts were not instituted to solve disputes among colonial subjects and African rulers, yet residents requested the arbitration of colonial judicial officers. In August 1828, Dona Joana Coelho de Magalhães presented a formal complaint against the *sekulo*, an adviser of the soba of Bisova, who had failed to pay acquired debts. The judge ordered the corporal of Catumbela to settle the dispute in favor of Dona Magalhães, demonstrating that colonial law could side with African women.[18] While Dona Joana Coelho de Magalhães's background is not clear, she appears in ecclesiastical records as the godmother of several children, including Escolástica, a Black girl baptized in Benguela in 1801; Teresa, baptized in 1805 with no mention of her color or status, daughter of the enslaved woman Lourença; and Francisca, daughter of the free woman Marcela da Costa Arouco.[19] The ecclesiastical records also reveal that Magalhães married Francisco António da Luz Abreu in 1805, but they are silent on her color or "*naturalidade*," her birth place.[20] African subjects, particularly women and young people who would not be privileged in societies ruled by elders, flocked to colonial institutions to solve issues that were ignored by local rulers, elders, or African elites.

---

[17] Arquivo Nacional de Angola (ANA), cx. 3340, Dombe Grande, Maço 2 – Dombe Grande governo 1863 a 1915, "Concelho do Dombe Grande. Questionário acerca dos usos e costumes gentílicos da província de Angola," 20 March 1907, p. 15. For more on unwritten practices in the coastal West Central Africa, see Joseph C. Miller, *Way of Death: Merchant Capitalism and the Angolan Slave Trade, 1730-1830* (Madison: University of Wisconsin Press, 1988), 133–37; Lauren A. Benton, *Law and Colonial Cultures Legal Regimes in World History, 1400-1900* (New York: Cambridge University Press, 2002), 56.

[18] ANA, Cod. 7182, fl.101v, 18 August 1828 requerimento n. 1049. See Mann, "Women's Right in Law and Practice."

[19] Bispado de Luanda (BL), Benguela, Livro de Batismo, 1794-1832, fl. 147, May 8, 1801; fl. 216 v, March 27, 1805, fl. 258 v, October 17, 1808; fl. 260v, November 17, 1808; fl. 261v. November 19, 1808; fl. 280, December 18, 1809; fl. 287v, August 5, 1810; fl. 296v, February 4, 1811;

[20] BL, Benguela, Livro de Casamento, fl. 4 April 23, 1805; see also the records. She is identified as married to Francisco António Luz de Abreu in ABL, Livro de Batismo, 1794–1832, fl. 322, November 8, 1812; fl. Not numbered, May 5, 1813.

For their own protection, residents registered before traveling between the colonial centers to avoid kidnapping, seizure, and enslavement. In one case, Catarina António de Glória requested authorization to travel as a free person between Benguela and Luanda.[21] In another, Captain Raimundo had to prove that Maria, a Black woman traveling with him to Luanda, was a freed person. Like freedpeople in the Americas, these cases suggest the risks that Black individuals faced and the mechanisms they had to employ to preserve their freedom. It is not clear whether people carried written documents with them to prove status, as happened in other slave societies.[22]

By the 1820s, written documents and courts had become the method and venue for solving disputes from real estate to ownership of human beings, and several women used the colonial courts to settle conflicts over assets. Leonor da Costa Monteiro requested an audience with Captain Benites to solve issues related to the ownership of an enslaved woman.[23] In the same year, 1827, Caetano, a Black man, complained to the Benguela judge that the soldier André das Salinas (probably referring to his place of residence or birth, as das salinas means from the salt mines) had failed to deliver an enslaved woman he had inherited from a deceased relative. The judge warned Salinas he could be physically punished if he refused to deliver the captive to Caetano, her legitimate

---

[21] ANA, Cod. 7182, fl.8, August 5, 1826, requerimento n. 463. Roquinaldo Ferreira and Roberto Guedes argued that women with a masculine second name, such as Catarina António de Glória, tended to be enslaved. According to them, free women had a feminine name and a last name. The practice of adding a masculine second name to locally born women linked them to bondage. See Roquinaldo Ferreira and Roberto Guedes, "Apagando a nota que diz escrava: Efigênia da Silva, os batismos, os compadrios, os nomes, as cabeças, as crias, o tráfico, a escravidão e a liberdade (Luanda, c. 1770–c. 1811), *Almanak* 26 (2020), 30–36.

[22] ANA, Cod. 7182, fl.8, August 5, 1826, requerimento n. 466. For more on this, see Mariana P. Candido, "The Transatlantic Slave Trade and the Vulnerability of Free Blacks in Benguela, Angola, 1780–1830," in *Atlantic Biographies: Individuals and Peoples in the Atlantic World*, ed. Mark Meuwese and Jeffrey A. Fortin (Leiden: Brill, 2013), 193–210; Roquinaldo Ferreira, "Slaving and Resistance to Slaving in West Central Africa," in *The Cambridge World History of Slavery*, ed. David Eltis and Stanley L. Engerman, vol. 3 (Cambridge: Cambridge University Press, 2011), 111–31; Candido, "African Freedom Suits and Portuguese Vassal Status"; Scott, Tehranian, and Mathias, "The Production of Legal Identities Proper to States"; Rebecca J. Scott and Jean M. Hébrard, *Freedom Papers: An Atlantic Odyssey in the Age of Emancipation* (Cambridge, MA: Harvard University Press, 2012).

[23] ANA, Cod. 7182, fl.47v, April 30, 1827, requerimento n. 88. The fact that women claimed landed property in Angola is very different from other contexts in the African continent, which tended to favor men's claims. See, for example, Clifton Crais, *Poverty, War, and Violence in South Africa* (New York: Cambridge University Press, 2011), 102–3.

owner.[24] The local population understood that colonial institutions were appropriate venues for pursuing old and new claims, even when dealing with questions of ownership recognition over human beings.

In 1827, Margarida, a free Black woman, requested an audience with the judge of Benguela to settle a dispute with a ship captain.[25] Margarida had sold a female captive to the captain. Lather, the unnamed captive, while on board, claimed to be a free person. This type of dispute needed to be settled before sailing, as I had examined elsewhere, since the sale of free individuals was a topic of intense dispute and legal debate in Angola.[26] In this specific case, Margarida argued she enjoyed ownership rights over the sold captive, so any freedom claim was unjustified. A few months later in 1828, another Black woman resident of Benguela, Bando, also known as Filipa, went to the colonial judge to settle a dispute. Bando requested an audience with the magistrate to address a conflict with a Quibanda resident, António Xavier, regarding some goods he had stolen from her. The judge ordered both sides to attend a meeting to solve the feud.[27] West Central African women enjoyed a series of rights and made extensive use of the colonial courts to protect their property.

While the colonial administration was committed to protecting the interests and the property of Portuguese subjects, residents of West Central African societies appropriated the use of paper documents to gain their own advantage. The Secretaria do Estado da Marinha e Ultramar (SEMU) sent regulations to the overseas colonies ordering that in the absence of a magistrate (*juiz de paz*), the highest civil or military authority should protect the inheritance of Portuguese citizens who died without clear heirs.[28] However, the courts and the administration ended up arbitrating conflicts about rights in part because West Central Africans understood that colonial power was committed to creating

---

[24] ANA, Cod. 7182, fl.48, April 30, 1827, requerimento n. 94.
[25] ANA, Cod. 7182, Cota 23-1-40, Registro de requerimentos – Benguela, 1825 a 1829, fl.47, April 26, 1827, requerimento n. 77.
[26] For more on freedom suits in West Central Africa and for other cases, see José C. Curto, "Struggling against Enslavement: The Case of José Manuel in Benguela, 1816-1820," *Canadian Journal of African Studies* 39, no. 1 (2005): 96–122; Roquinaldo Ferreira, "Slaving and Resistance to Slaving in West Central Africa," in *The Cambridge World History of Slavery*, vol. 3 (New York: Cambridge University Press, 2011); Mariana P. Candido, "African Freedom Suits and Portuguese Vassal Status: Legal Mechanisms for Fighting Enslavement in Benguela, Angola, 1800–1830," *Slavery & Abolition* 32, no. 3 (2011): 447–59.
[27] ANA, Cod. 7182, fl.78v, 14 January 1828, requerimento n. 649.
[28] Arquivo Histórico Ultramarino (AHU), Secretária do Estado da Marinha e do Ultramar (SEMU), Direção Geral do Ultramar (DGU), Angola, 477, 1840-1843, Registro de Correspondência Expedida, fl. 8, November 28, 1838.

paper evidence.[29] Courts adjudicated payment disputes for land sale or services. This was the case with Filipa, a free Black woman who had provided domestic services to Joaquim Inácio de Couto for nine months. They had agreed on a salary of four *réis* per month, but Couto failed to pay Filipa, who requested the intervention of the judge. The judge sided with Filipa and ordered her immediate payment.[30] Colonial courts intervened to protect owners, no matter if people claimed ownership over people, service, or land. Josefa Manoel Joaquim, for example, had sold a house in Catumbela and requested that the purchaser, Ana, filed the sales letter. This case reveals that land sales were taking place by the late 1820s, suggesting that a small-scale land market existed and that these sales were recorded in sales letters.[31]

With the expansion of the colonial presence in the newly founded town of Mossamedes, due to its "good pastures and rich flora, optimal for cultivation [and] … rich in fresh water and cattle,"[32] the administration rushed to control access to the urban space. The southern settlement was central to the colonial vision of agricultural expansion, with impoverished Portuguese immigrants occupying African land at the expense of the local population. In the 1840s, there was an established market for urban houses, with the colonial administration in charge of registering property transmission and collecting taxes for the transaction.[33] Portuguese immigrants were advised that they could build houses in unoccupied lots. However, the houses where Europeans lived could not look like the houses in which the Black population resided, and immigrants from Portugal and Brazil received notifications from the colonial state that they had to refrain from buying enslaved people.[34]

---

[29] Berry, "Debating the Land Question in Africa," 638–68; Martin Chanock, "A Peculiar Sharpness: An Essay on Property in the History of Customary Law in Colonial Africa," *The Journal of African History* 32, no. 1 (1991): 65–88; Dery, "'Papereality.'" 685–87.

[30] ANA, Cod. 7182, fl.77, January 2, 1828 requerimento n. 522.

[31] ANA, Cod. 7182, fl.47v, April 30, 1827, requerimento n. 86. Unfortunately, it is not clear if these sales letter have survived and if so, where they are currently stored. For similar cases, see Mann and Roberts, *Law in Colonial Africa*, 24–26; Scott and Zeuske, "Property in Writing."

[32] Biblioteca da Sociedade de Geografia de Lisboa (BSGL), Res 1- Pasta D – 14 "Memória sobre o estado actual d'Africa Occidental seu comercio com Portugal e medidas que convinha adoptar em 1841," January 1841. For the foundation of Mossamedes, see W. G. Clarence-Smith, *Slaves, Peasants, and Capitalists in Southern Angola, 1840-1926* (New York: Cambridge University Press, 1979), 14–16.

[33] ANA, Cod. 326, fl. 17, May 19, 1847.

[34] ANA, Cod. 326, fl. 37, March 16, 1848. For more on the profile and the policies regarding the arrival of Portuguese and Brazilian immigrants in Southern Angola, see W. G. Clarence-Smith, "Capitalist Penetration among the Nyaneka of Southern Angola, 1760 to 1920s," *African Studies* 37, no. 2 (1978); Aida Freudenthal, *Arimos e fazendas: A transição agrária em Angola, 1850–1880* (Luanda: Chá de Caxinde, 2005), 177–78; Anabela Cunha, "Degredo para Angola: sentença de morte lenta," *Locus (Juiz de Fora)* 18, no. 2 (2013): 87–104.

As much as they wanted to be in charge of property registration and transmission, administrators and judges had no practical authority over territories ruled by African rulers (sobas or *dembos*). In 1848, the secretary of Angola notified the governor that it was impossible to collect the debt owned by Portuguese subjects who lived outside of Portuguese-controlled areas. José de Oliveira Rezende owed 1:600$000 to Vicente António Fatia, who had died in Benguela. In an effort to settle the inventory, Rezende had to honor his debt, yet he was "away from the conquered land." If he returned to Benguela, the governor was expected to seize his goods in order to pay off his debts.[35] As much as they wanted to project unity, coherence, structure, and intentionality, the state bureaucracy and its machinery were limited. In practice, the colonial bureaucracy, including its efforts to regulate law and legislate over property, was fragmented and disunited, in part due to the resistance of African rulers and their subjects who refused to negotiate with the intruders.

The colonial administration had a limited number of officers available to protect the property of colonial subjects and arbitrate conflicts. The 1866 population census presents a neat picture of a colonial society, with people classified into specific categories in the colonial centers such as Benguela and Catumbela (see Table 3.1). However, the officer in charge, Eduardo A. de Sá Nogueira, recognized its limitations since "no population counting can be exact due to the difficulties associated with [collecting data] in this type of work."[36]

The colonial administration lacked knowledge regarding the population that lived in the interior in territories nominally under Portuguese control. Houses were enumerated as well as the rulers who lived under Portuguese nominal control (see Table 3.2). These were divided into three categories: *dembos avassalados*, sobas independent from the *dembos avassalados*, and the sobas under the jurisdiction of vassal *dembos*, in a confusing hierarchy of subjection to colonial rule and West Central African rulers. The preoccupation with counting people, houses, and rulers was an old one and derives from concerns about collecting taxes,

---

[35] ANA, Cod. 326, fl. 60V, Ilmo. Sr. Governador de Benguela from Francisco Joaquim da Costa e Silva, secretário geral da província Benguela. November 7, 1848.

[36] AHU, SEMU, Conselho Ultramarino (CU), Estatísticas, cx. 2, 1854–1866 – Estatísticas população de Angola. For more on the weakness of the colonial state, see Ann Laura Stoler, "'In Cold Blood': Hierarchies of Credibility and the Politics of Colonial Narratives," *Representations*, no. 37 (1992): 151–89; Clifton Crais, "Chiefs and Bureaucrats in the Making of Empire: A Drama from the Transkei, South Africa, October 1880," *American Historical Review* 108, no. 4 (2003): 1034–56.

Table 3.1. *Population of Angola, 1866*

| Locations | Houses | People | | Civil Status | | | | | |
| | | Men | Women | Married | | Widow/Widower | | Single | |
				Men	Women	Men	Women	Men	Women
Benguela	4,325	7,312	8,388	316	316	33	4	6,963	8,027
Catumbela	1,484	2,470	2,850	4	3	1	0	2,485	2,847
Dombe Grande	2,200	2,917	3,883	3	3	1	0	2,913	3,879
Quilengues	6,000	10,200	22,875	0	0	0	0	11,535	16,540
Caconda	3,500	5,500	6,800	1	1	1	0	5,498	6,797
Egito	46	318	290	1	0	0	0	317	290
Total	17,555	28,717	45,086	325	323	36	4	29,711	38,380

Source: AHU, SEMU, CU, Estatísticas, cx. 2, 1854–1866, "Estatísticas população de Angola" 1866.

Table 3.2. *African Authorities and population according to religion and literacy, 1866*

Locations	Vassal dembos	Independent sobas	Sobas subordinated to dembos	Religion		Literacy
				Christians	Heathens	
Benguela	0	0	2	13,921	1,779	346
Catumbela	0	2	0	1,130	4,190	115
Dombe Grande	0	3	1	2,450	4,350	100
Quilengues	4	4	0	122	32,945	10
Caconda	0	1	0	2,400	9,900	22
Egito	0	0	0	608	0	9
Total				20,695	53,172	602

Source: AHU, SEMU, CU, Estatísticas, cx. 2, 1854–1866, "Estatísticas população de Angola" 1866.

identifying owners, and solving disputes. The numbers fed the illusion of control and of a territory under colonial rule.[37]

The population was broken down by gender, civil status, place of birth, and religious affiliation (with only two categories available: Christians, meaning Catholics, and heathens). In a moment of expansion of bureaucracy and written documents, the population counting identified few literate individuals. In 1866, only 346 individuals were able to read and write Portuguese out of Benguela's population of over 15,000. Yet this small group of literate agents created a vast number of records, including court records, in which many of the property litigations were presented. The Tribunal da Comarca de Benguela, established in the early 1850s, contains over 2,000 legal cases, most of them dealing with property litigation.[38] The court, which was initially under Luanda's colonial administration and later made autonomous alongside the Câmara Municipal, holds the records related to litigation, rights, wills, and inventories.[39] Before the creation of the Tribunal da Comarca de Benguela, property and court records were registered among the official correspondence dispersed in the codices at the Arquivo Nacional de Angola. After the establishment of an autonomous courthouse in Benguela, records were stored at the Tribunal da Comarca de Benguela.

Colonial records are filled with cases of African women – classified as white, Black, or mixed race – who asserted ownership rights in writing, showing how colonialism, writing, and power were connected. These women exerted not only control over controlled subjects but also the ability to fight against the violence of occupation and denial of colonized rights. In some instances, the records are simple summaries of cases and not the entire procedure with details that could provide more clues about the nature of these disputes. However, they reveal that West Central Africans who lived in colonial centers, including women, negotiated their

---

[37] Arjun Appadurai, "Number in the Colonial Imagination," in *Orientalism and the Postcolonial Predicament: Perspectives on South Asia*, ed. Carol A. Breckenridge and Peter van der Veer (Philadelphia: University of Pennsylvania Press, 1993), 314–40.

[38] An inventory of the 2,100 legal cases is in progress. See Mariana Candido, Mariana Dias Paes, and Juelma Mattos, "Inventário do Arquivo do Tribunal da Província de Benguela." See also "Decreto de 16 de janeiro de 1837 para a África Ocidental," 1837, First Paragraph; and "Decreto de 30 de dezembro de 1852, aprovou o regimento de administração da justiça de Angola, São Tomé e Príncipe," 1852 available at http://www .fd.unl.pt/ConteudosAreasDetalhe.asp?ID=40&Titulo=Biblioteca%20Digital&Area= BibliotecaDigital

I am thankful to Mariana Dias Paes for bringing this online collection to my attention.

[39] For the role of the Tribunal and the Camara Munipal de Bengela, see AHU, SEMU, CU, Processos das Consultas, Cx. 27, n. 911. 1 repartiçao, "Processo sobre as queixas da camara municipal de Benguela dos excessivos emolumentos e tributos que são obrigados a pagar," November 2, 1855.

rights. The effort to settle disputes over property and clarify ownership claims, though limited in scope, provided African women in Benguela and Luanda, in West Central Africa, as well as in Lagos and Abeokuta, in the British colony of the Gold Coast, and Bathurst, in Gambia spaces to assert new economic and legal rights.[40] Still, customary law recorded in the early twentieth century stated that

> Ndombe women did not enjoy any rights [to property], except to their children. She can remain living in the *cubata* (a wooden house with straw roof) that belonged to her husband after his death only if the heir authorizes [her residence]. Otherwise she returns to her family, and in the case of not having enough [resources] to maintain her children, her brothers oversee feeding them.[41]

There is a clear disconnect between the nineteenth-century evidence and the customary law recorded later.

Gendering Property

Empires did not aim to empower colonial subjects, particularly women; however, by the nineteenth century, many West Central African women, especially those in the elite, generated a new form of legal subjectivity that privileged the written document as a legitimate claim. The colonial judge was not the only possible site of justice for colonized subjects in the nineteenth century, yet African women made efforts to secure audiences with judges and court arbitration.[42] African women engaged with the

---

[40] Scholars have noticed African women's ability to use colonial courts elsewhere. See Kristin Mann, "Women's Right in Law and Practice: Marriage and Dispute Settlement in Colonial Lagos," in *African Women & the Law: Historical Perspectives*, ed. Margaret Jean Hay and Marcia Wright (Boston: Boston University Press, 1982), 151–71; Margaret Jean Hay and Marcia Wright, eds., *African Women & the Law: Historical Perspectives* (Boston: Boston University Press, 1982); Kristin Mann, *Marrying Well: Marriage, Status, and Social Change among the Educated Elite in Colonial Lagos* (New York: Cambridge University Press, 1985); Judith Byfield, "Women, Marriage, Divorce, and the Emerging Colonial State in Abeokuta (Nigeria), 1892-1904," in *"Wicked" Women and the Reconfiguration of Gender in Africa*, ed. Dorothy L. Hodgson and Sheryl A. McCurdy (Portsmouth, NH: Heinemann, 2001), 27–46; Bala Saho, *Contours of Change: Muslim Courts, Women, and Islamic Society in Colonial Bathurst, the Gambia, 1900-1965* (Lansing: Michigan State University, forthcoming).

[41] ANA, cx. 3340, Dombe Grande, Maço 2 – Dombe Grande governo 1863 a 1915, "Concelho do Dombe Grande. Questionário acerda dos usos e costumes gentílicos da província de Angola," March 20, 1907, p. 15.

[42] ANA, Cod. 7182, fl.45, 4 de abril 1827, requerimento n. 45. Vanessa Oliveira has examined this from Luanda. See her Vanessa S. Oliveira, "Spouses and Commercial Partners: Immigrant Men and Locally Born Women in Luanda (1831-1859)," in *African Women in the Atlantic World. Property, Vulnerability and Mobility, 1680-1880*, ed. Mariana P. Candido and Adam Jones (Woodbridge: James Currey, 2019), 217–32; Oliveira, *Slave Trade and Abolition*. There is a rich scholarship on Africans and the courts in Latin America. See, for example, Cristina Nogueira da Silva and Keila Grinberg, "Soil

colonial judicial system to establish claims and protect their property, including against their husbands. The petitions, appeals, and lawsuits disclose the methods and arguments African men and woman employed. Although their motivations are not clear, women looked for spaces to settle disputes, including the Portuguese imperial legal system, ironically consolidating the notion of rights as formal and written practices and solidifying colonial control. The writing culture, or the practice of registering property in writing, affected sovereignty, legitimacy, and identity, and transformed law and oral record keeping.[43]

Despite the historical evidence, the discussion of property rights in the Angolan historiography has not addressed gender, without any clear analysis of how men's and women's rights were similar or different, or how these rights changed over time.[44] The customary law recorded in the twentieth century shows that local rulers tried to prevent women from claiming land rights, despite clear indications that West Central African women had ownership rights recognized before the Berlin Conference and asserted them under different contexts. In West Central Africa, as elsewhere, possession or occupancy was at the origin of property in the

---

Free from Slaves: Slave Law in Late Eighteenth- and Early Nineteenth-Century Portugal," *Slavery & Abolition* 32, no. 3 (2011): 431–446; Karen B. Graubart, "The Limits of Gender Domination. Women, the Law, and Political Crisis in Quito, 1765–1830," *Colonial Latin American Review* 24, no. 1 (2015): 114–16; Herman L. Bennett, *Africans In Colonial Mexico: Absolutism, Christianity, and Afro-Creole Consciousness, 1570-1640* (Bloomington: Indiana University Press, 2005); Bianca Premo, "Before the Law: Women's Petitions in the Eighteenth-Century Spanish Empire," *Comparative Studies in Society and History* 53, no. 2 (2011): 261–89; Joseli Maria Nunes Mendonça, *Entre a mão e os anéis: A lei dos sexagenários e os caminhos da abolição no Brasil* (Campinas, SP: Editora da Unicamp/ CECULT/ FAPESP, 1999); Gabriela dos Reis Sampaio, Lisa Earl Castillo, and Wlamyra Ribeiro de Albuquerque, *Barganhas e querelas da escravidão: tráfico, alforria e liberdade (séculos XVIII e XIX)* (Salvador: Edufba, Editora da Universidade Federqal da Bahia, 2014).

43 Martin Chanock, "Paradigms, Policies and Property: A Review of the Customary Law of Land Tenure," in *Law in Colonial Africa*, ed. Kristin Mann and Richard L. Roberts (Portsmouth, NH: Heinemann, 1991), 61–84; Hawkins, *Writing and Colonialism in Northern Ghana*, 32–35.

44 Caetano Gonçalves, "O regime das terras e as reservas indígenas na colonização portuguesa," *Boletim Geral das Colônias* 2, no. 13 (1926): 26–45; Valentim Alexandre and Jill Dias, *O Império africano* (Lisbon: Estampa, 1998), 438–57; Olympia Perry Vidal Pereira Bastos, "A colonização portuguesa no planalto de Benguela" (Tese apresentada ao concurso de admissão, Lisbon, Escola Normal Superior, 1920); Elisete Marques da Silva, *Impactos da ocupação colonial nas sociedades rurais do sul de Angola* (Lisbon: Centro de Estudos Africanos ISCTE, 2003); Francisco Liberal Fernandes, "O direito de propriedade em Angola: aspectos gerais da lei de terras," *Boletim de Ciências Econômicas* 57, no. 2 (2014): 1463–78; Aurora da Fonseca Ferreira, "Ocupação de terras: problemas de ontem e hoje," *Cadernos de Estudos Sociais* 1 (2005): 35–99; Aharon Grassi and Jesse Salah Ovadia, "Trajectories of Large-Scale Land Acquisition Dynamics in Angola: Diversity, Histories, and Implications for the Political Economy of Development in Africa," *Land Use Policy* 67 (2017): 115–25.

sense that whoever claimed rights got to enjoy ownership. This privileged the act of possession, those who made claims, and the system that recognized notions of private property, such as the colonial court. Inevitably the interests of those who did not care or who did not have the resources to make the original claim of occupancy suffered, as well as those without access to literacy in Portuguese.[45]

Colonial governance encountered various inheritance practices in West Central Africa. Several groups along the coast and in the interior of Benguela followed matrilineal inheritance practices, in which nephews, the children of sisters, were the natural heirs. This custom regulated transmission and political rights in the case of ruling lineages, although, as seen in Chapter 2, some groups challenged the system if and when patrilineal inheritance was more convenient.[46] However, the existence of matrilineal inheritance did not guarantee women access to land or cattle. Among the Ndombe, for example, cattle accumulation indicated wealth by the late eighteenth century. Like other pastoral societies, the Ndombe did not consume the meat but used the hides for bags and the horns to make pipes, manufactured cheese and yogurt with the milk, and used the manure to enrich the soil. Cattle were a measure of wealth for pastoralists and farmers, who used it to pay taxes and settle debts, but also as part of marriage arrangements and offerings to the spirits and to honor the dead.[47] However, it is not clear whether men and women had different access to cows, pigs, and sheep. Despite the lack of information on gender accumulation, cattle had an economic value and could be disposed of, sold, or held as collateral, although few families owned large herds. As a result, by the

[45] Carol M. Rose, *Property and Persuasion: Essays on the History, Theory, and Rhetoric of Ownership* (Boulder, CO: Westview Press, 1994), 17–19; Rosa Congost, "Property Rights and Historical Analysis: What Rights? What History?," *Past & Present*, no. 181 (2003): 73–106; Mariana Armond Dias Paes, "Escravos e terras entre posses e títulos: A construção social do direito de propriedade no Brasil (1835-1889)" (Ph.D., São Paulo, SP, Universidade de São Paulo, 2018).

[46] António Gil, *Considerações sobre alguns pontos mais importantes da moral religiosa e sistema de jurisprudência dos pretos do continente da África Ocidental Portuguesa além do Equador* (Lisbon: Tipografia da Academia, 1854), 41; Augusto Bastos, "Traços geraes sobre a ethnographia do districto de Benguella," *Boletim da Sociedade de Geografia de Lisboa* 26, no. 1 (1908): 51; Wilfrid Dyson Hambly, *Ovimbundu of Angola* (Chicago: Field Museum of Natural History, 1934), 199–201. For the case of heirs challenging the matrilineal system in Portuguese courts, see AHA, Cod. 471, E – 7 – 5, Registro de ofícios expedidos 13 de junho de 1857 a 22 de janeiro de 1859, fl. 189, December 2, 1858, Governador de Benguela to governador geral da província, and the cases discussed in Chapter 2. For the problematic of matrilineal systems, see Wyatt MacGaffey, "Crossing the River. Myth and Movement in Central Africa," in *Angola on the Move. Transport Routes, Communications and History*, ed. Beatrix Heintze and Achim von Oppen (Frankfurt am Main: Verlag Otto Lembeck, 2008), 228–32.

[47] Paulo Martins Pinheiro de Lacerda, *Annaes Maritimos e Coloniaes*, Quinta Série, (1845), 486–87. For other cattle societies, see Hambly, *Ovimbundu of Angola*, 153.

late eighteenth century, herders in Kilengues hid the number of cattle they owned when investigated by colonial officers to avoid taxation.[48] In terms of land access, Ndombe women secured land rights after marriage, and these could be forfeited in the case of divorce.[49] The situation was different in the twentieth century, as anthropologists noticed.[50]

To control and manage such flux of inheritance practices, colonial administrators imposed written records, such as wills and registers, to provide a record of ownership. There are very few wills dating to the eighteenth century, but most of those are for Portuguese men who died while in Luanda or Benguela, and all of them refer to personal property including clothes and luxury items such as silverware, tobacco cases, objects made of turtle shell, and enslaved people.[51] Some of them refer to real estates, such as the case of the postmortem will of the Portuguese trader Aurélio Veríssimo da Silva. In 1805, da Silva declared that he owned a tile-roofed house on the beach of Benguela that had previously belonged to the priest Francisco de Santa Anna Barros, revealing commercialization of real estate in the colonial urban center.[52] I have not been able to locate eighteenth-century wills or postmortem inventories of locally born people, including *filhos da terra*, the locally born whites who enjoyed much of the privilege and status of Portuguese-born individuals. However, burial records reveal the existence of wills. Tomé Rodrigues, for example, started writing a will while sick but died in 1792 before he could finish it.[53] Most of the wills and property transfer contracts available are

---

[48] Biblioteca Nacional do Rio de Janeiro (BNRJ), doc. I-28, 28, 29, "Notícias de São Filipe de Benguela e costumes dos gentios habitantes naquele sertão," 10 November 1797. For more on cattle raising, see Childs, *Kinship & Character of the Ovimbundu*, 109.

[49] Bastos, "Traços Geraes," 86. For similar practices in other places, see Chanock, "Paradigms, Policies and Property: A Review of the Customary Law of Land Tenure," 73.

[50] Hambly, *Ovimbundu of Angola*, 119; Luisa Mastrobueno, "Ovimbundu Women and Coercive Labour Systems, 1850–1940: From Still Life to Moving Picture" (M.A., Toronto, University of Toronto, 1992), 17, 25–26.

[51] See the inventories available at ANTT, Feitos Fintos, Justificações Ultramarinas, África, mç 2, doc. 3 B, "Autos de habilitação de Ana Isabel e outros para a herança de José de Sousa falecido em Benguela," 1791; and mç 2, doc. 3A, "Autos de Habilitação e Justificação de D. Ana Maria Batista, viúva para a levar a levar a herança dele de seu filho o sargento mor António José de Barros, falecido em Cabo Negro," 1800; mç 9, doc. 12, "Autos de habilitação de D. Francisca Xavier da Cunha, viúva, e seus filhos para a herança do marido e pai José António Ferreira, falecido em Benguela." 1802; mç 12, doc. 4, "Autos de habilitação de Gastão José da Camara Coutinho e mais herdeiros do Exmo. José Gonçalo da Camara, governador que foi de Angola, onde faleceu," 1784.

[52] ANTT, Feitos Findos, Justificações ultramarinas. Africa, mç. 14, doc., 1, fls. 8 a 14v, September 2, 1805.

[53] BL, Livro de óbito, Benguela 1770-1796, fl. 175v-176, July 6, 1792. For more on the *filhos da terra*, see Beatrix Heintze, "A Lusofonia no interior da África Central na era pré-colonial. Um contributo para a sua história e compreensão na actualidade," *Cadernos de Estudos Africanos* 6/7 (2005): 179–207; Jacopo Corrado, "The Fall of a Creole Elite?

for the post-1850 period, although fragmentary evidence suggests how West Central African men and women accumulated wealth.

Women also registered property in writing, although few recorded land ownership in the early nineteenth century. Most focused on protecting their interests as slave owners, preventing the escape or seizure of human property, in systems of ownership very similar to slavery in the Americas or in other colonial centers along the African coast. In 1814, Catarina da Costa appealed to the governor of Benguela that Manoel Candido de Melo had illegally taken one of her enslaved boys (*moleque*), Justino, to a ship bound for Luanda and requested the restitution of her human property. With the collaboration of the governor of Angola, the young Justino was located and sent back to serve in da Costa's house.[54] Catarina da Costa was from Bailundu in the central highlands and outside of colonial control, yet she was fully integrated into colonial society and used the colonial system to win small victories such as recuperating Justino. As this case indicates, written documents became a physical manifestation of elite women and men's subjectivity as legal agents and colonial subjects. Yet these documents silence the experience of those who were considered property, the enslaved men and women, such as Justino, who constituted an important portion of the West Central African population for most of the nineteenth century.

The colonial administration did not aspire to empower colonial subjects, yet many colonized women privileged the written document. However, access to colonial bureaucracy had limits. It was predominantly an urban phenomenon for women and men culturally exposed to the Portuguese world even if they were locally born. For example, the Benguela-born Catarina Rosa, married to the soldier Manoel de Souza, demanded that her husband return her clothes since she did not intend to cohabit with him anymore due to the "bad life she had while in his company."[55] It is important to stress she did not seek alimony, indicating she was able to support herself. One did not have to be an elite woman to

Angola at the Turn of the Twentieth Century: The Decline of the Euro-African Urban Community," *Luso-Brazilian Review* 47, no. 2 (2010): 100–19; C. Pacheco, *Arsénio Pompílio Pompeu de Carpo: Uma vida de luta contra as prepotências do poder colonial em Angola*, 1992; Carlos Pacheco, *José da Silva Ferreira: O homem e a sua época* (Luanda: União dos escritores angolanos, 1990); Carlos Pacheco, "Leituras e bibliotecas em Angola na primeira metade do século XIX," *Locus (Juiz de Fora)* 6, no. 2 (2000): 21–41.

[54] She was probably the same Catarina da Costa who married Alexandre José de Melo from Bihé in 1819. BL, Livro de Casamento, Benguela, fl. 17v, 3 February 1819. For details on the legal dispute, see ANA, Cod. 323, fl. 104v, Gov de Angola, José de Oliveira Barbosa to Governador de Benguela, Senhor de Alvelos Leiria, April 13, 1814; and fl. 108v, Gov de Angola, José de Oliveira Barbosa, to Governador de Benguela, Senhor de Alvelos Leiria. July 13, 1814.

[55] ANA, Cod. 7182, fl.20v, 28 de setembro 1826, requerimento n. 608.

present a demand to the colonial judge. In 1826, Caraxima, identified as a Black woman, requested actions against Gira, Humba, Chacabara, and Dumba, all Black men, who had seized three children of João, one of her dependents. In this case, a woman with a clear Umbundu name presented her case to the judge in Benguela after the colonial authority in Dombe Grande failed to address her concerns.[56]

Africans successfully used colonial authority and institutions for their own ends, ensuring their economic well-being and gaining access to social and legal identities. They also sought to protect their economic interests, as in the case of Andreza Leal do Sacramento, who presented a petition against Joaquim Inácio da Costa for failing to deliver an enslaved woman,[57] or Francisca Xavier Ramos, who demanded Dionisio Barbosa de Melo provide a proof of sale for the peanut barrel he sold on her behalf to the priest Tomás.[58] The records do not mention the color or place of origin of Andreza or Francisca, but in the population census of 1826 only two white women are listed as residing in Benguela. The white classification referred to those born in Portugal or locally born descendants of Portuguese individuals. In 1833, the number of women classified as white had dropped to one.[59] The small number of white women recorded as residing in Benguela and the considerable number of legal cases presented by West Central African women suggest that color classification did not prevent legal actions in the colonial courts.

In 1827, Dona Lucrécia Ferres Lobato demanded a payment of 651,828 *réis* from José Apolinário. To support her claim, she presented eight different sale bills and promissory notes, indicating that she had advanced enslaved people to Apolinário, who had failed to pay their value. "Facing these legal documents," the governor issued that "Apolinário had 24 hours to honor his payment and present a receipt

[56] ANA, Cod. 7182, fl.27v, 27 de outubro 1826, requerimento n. 691.
[57] ANA, Cod. 7182, fl.29, 22 de novembro 1826, requerimento n. 706.
[58] ANA, Cod. 7182, fl.27v, 22 de novembro 1826, requerimento n. 694.
[59] AHU, Angola, 1 seccao, cx 156. Doc. 16, June 20, 1827 (old reference); and AHU, Angola, cx. 176, doc .17, "Mapa dos habitantes da Paróquia de São Felipe de Benguela" 1833 (old reference). For more on the demography of Benguela, see Mariana P. Candido, *Fronteras de esclavización: Esclavitud, comercio e identidad en Benguela, 1780-1850* (Mexico City: El Colegio de Mexico Press, 2011). For more on color hierarchies and classifications in the Portuguese empire, see Eduardo França Paiva, *Dar nome ao novo: Uma história lexical da Ibero-América entre os séculos XVI e XVIII (as dinâmicas de mestiçagens e o mundo do trabalho)* (Belo Horizonte: Autêntica, 2017); Hebe Mattos, "'Black Troops' and Hierarchies of Color in the Portuguese Atlantic World: The Case of Henrique Dias and His Black Regiment," *Luso-Brazilian Review* 45, no. 1 (2008): 6–29; Hebe Maria Mattos, *Das cores do silêncio: Os significados da liberdade no sudeste escravista: Brasil Século XIX* (Rio de Janeiro: Arquivo Nacional, 1995). Also see the special number of *Estudos Ibero-Americanos* 44, no. 3 (2018) organized by Eugénia Rodrigues and Mariana P. Candido.

for it."[60] Bills, notes, and formal processes against debtors became physical artifacts as the papers assumed the role of evidence that could be used later.

The colonial courts also became spaces to solve domestic disputes since Portuguese law favored the interests of heirs, recognizing wives' rights to half of the couple's property.[61] In 1827, Dona Antónia Rodrigues de Abreu submitted a divorce petition to the judge of Benguela, in order to end her marriage to Manuel Barbosa Coutinho. The divorce petition included an alimony request. Dona Antónia Rodrigues de Abreu had moved into the house of a poor relative who offered a roof, yet she "was living in misery." Abreu also claimed that her husband had expelled her from their house to host his lover, Ana de Sousa. The judge replied that he could not arbitrate on ecclesiastical matters such as divorce, but "knowing the priest, I am convinced he will favor justice and not allow such scandalous behavior to take place."[62] The judge stated that since the couple were legally married, husband and wife shared all the assets. In the case of divorce, it was necessary to identify all the goods and property acquired since their union, pay any eventual debts, and the remaining assets had to be divided between husband and wife. Until the division of property was settled, the judge ordered Barbosa Coutinho to provide Abreu 300 *réis* daily to cover her meals and needs. The end of this case is unknown, but a few months later Abreu passed away at the local hospital. According to the burial record, she was identified as coming from Luanda and married to Manuel Barbosa Coutinho. The divorce was apparently not settled before her death. However, her husband continued to cohabit with Dona Ana de Sousa in the following years, burying a child, Isabel, the newly couple

---

[60] ANA, Cod. 7182, fl. 46, April 9, 1827, requerimento n. 67.
[61] For the Portuguese Law and wives inheritance rights, see *Código Philippino, our Ordenações e Leis do Reino de Portugal*, Livro 1, 88 (Lisbon: Fundação Calouste Gulbenkian, 1985), 206–15. See also Eugénia Rodrigues, *Portugueses e africanos nos Rios de Sena. Os prazos da coroa em Moçambique nos séculos XVII e XVIII* (Lisboa: Imprensa Nacional-Casa da Moeda, 2014), 599–612; Alida C. Metcalf, "Women and Means: Women and Family Property in Colonial Brazil," *Journal of Social History* 24, no. 2 (1990): 277–98; Mariana L. R. Dantas, "Succession of Property, Sales of Meação , and the Economic Empowerment of Widows of African Descent in Colonial Minas Gerais, Brazil," *Journal of Family History* 39, no. 3 (2014): 222–38; Mariana L. R. Dantas, "Miners, Farmers, and Market People: Women of African Descent and the Colonial Economy in Minas Gerais," *African Economic History* 43 (2015): 82–108; Candido and Rodrigues, "African Women's Access and Rights to Property in the Portuguese Empire."
[62] ANA, Cod. 7182, fl. 50, May 21, 1827, requerimento n. 128. Unlike other European systems, Portuguese laws protected the interest of wives and daughters. Jutta Sperling, "Women's Property Rights in Portugal under Dom João I (1385-1433): A Comparison with Renaissance Italy," *Portuguese Studies Review* 13, no. 1–2 (2005): 27–59.

had together, in 1831.[63] Despite the protection offered by Portuguese laws regarding property rights, African wives had to overcome extra hurdles and were denied a series of rights to which they were entitled, such as property or alimony, as this case suggests.

In these records, we see the variety of assets West Central African women accumulated and their ability to make sure their ownership was recognized in the colonial law, in a clear indication that any discussion about property in Angola needs to place women at the center of the debate. In 1828, Josefa de Carvalho, a free Black resident in Benguela, complained to the colonial authorities that one of her captives, Maria, had fled from her *arimo* (agricultural plot) in Catumbela.[64] In a single document, Josefa de Carvalho claimed ownership over a plot of land and a person. In the same year, another woman identified as Black, Laureana António, reported that one of the *sekulos* (advisers) of the ruler of Dombe Grande, named Candele, had seized one of her cows and beaten Teresa, one of her slaves.[65] Others complained about men who had seized their belongings, such as the case of the Black woman Filipa, also known as Bando, examined earlier.[66] Historical records reveal that several colonial residents employed Umbundu and Portuguese names.

A vast number of records list African women as owners, but colonial lists project the notion that property was a male domain. Colonial agents did not recognize women as legitimate owners or able to manage their property. In 1822, the bishop of Angola reported that "the widespread practice of concubinage led to the extreme weakness of black women, some who were enslaved Christians who belong to their own partners, others who were heathen vassals of the neighboring sobas. The Caconda priest informed me that one of his parishioners, a white man, had already baptized 75 of his own children."[67] The Portuguese traveler António Francisco Ferreira da Silva Porto saw concubinage as an expansion of slavery since men "paid" for their wives and put them to work to increase their wealth, with the ability to reject and sell them. For him, as for many other European agents, concubinage, female enslavement, and prostitution were intertwined and synonyms, confusing bridewealth and dowry

---

[63] For Dona Antónia Rodrigues de Abreu burrial record, see BL, Benguela, Livro de Óbitos, 1797-1831, fl. 195, December 5, 1827. For Manuel Barbosa Coutinho's daughter record, see BL, Benguela, Livro de Óbitos, 1797–1831, fl. 231v-232, May 24, 1831.

[64] ANA, Cod. 7182, fl. 78, 14 de janeiro 1828, requerimento n. 648.

[65] ANA, Cod. 7182, fl. 78v, 14 de janeiro 1828, requerimento n 651.

[66] ANA, Cod. 7182, fl. 78v, 14 de janeiro 1828, requerimento n 649.

[67] ANTT, Ministério do reino, mç 499, cx 622, Correspondência recebida de Índia, Moçambique, Angola, Guiné, "Memoria do Bispo de Angola enviada a Rainha sobre o estado da Igreja e pede a sua demissão," fl. 2v, Vicente de Prazeres Costa, Cacheu, 1822.

practices with bondage.[68] In the process, women's strategies to navigate and occupy spaces in colonial societies were dismissed as sex work, and the emotional ties and collective economic effort behind their actions were denied or seen as a moral transgression. Fundamentally, West Central African women were not seen as legitimate owners, property holders, or contributors to the colonial economy, despite clear indications of their roles.

Throughout the nineteenth century, the colonial administration collected lists of traders who lived in Benguela. Inevitably, these lists (Tables 3.3 and 3.4) identified male, white traders, neglecting the role of the local population in commerce.

In the list of larger traders and owners who lived in Benguela in 1869, fourteen names were identified, as can be seen in Table 3.4. Some of these clearly represented companies such as Conchoix & Freres, which probably referred to a corporation headed by Eugenio Caicoix, a French entrepreneur.[69] Only one was a woman – Dona Teresa Barruncho, the leading exporter of cotton in Benguela in the 1860s. Despite her importance, she was represented by a man, José Gonçalves da Silva Soares, as was necessary in the Portuguese Empire.[70]

Similar to the West Central African rulers who embraced written culture to assert their rights during the eighteenth and nineteenth

---

[68] BSGL, Res – 2-C-7 – Silva Porto, "Notas para retocar a minha obra logo que as circunstancias permitam," 1866, fl. 59-62, "Mancebia entre os quimbundos." There is an important scholarship on women's sexuality and colonialism in Africa, challenging the use of prostitution to dismiss African women economic and social initiatives. See Jean-Baptiste, *Conjugal Rights*, 145–48; Benedict B. B. Naanen, "'Itinerant Gold Mines': Prostitution in the Cross River Basin of Nigeria, 1930-1950," *African Studies Review* 34, no. 2 (1991): 57–79; Nwando Achebe, *The Female King of Colonial Nigeria: Ahebi Ugbabe* (Bloomington: Indiana University Press, 2011), 77–84; Hilary Jones, "Women, Family and Daily Life in Senegal's Nineteenth-Century Atlantic Towns," in *African Women in Atlantic Coast Societies, 1680-1880*, ed. Mariana P. Candido and Adam Jones, p. 233–47 (James Currey, 2019).

[69] For more on the Coichoix & Frères society, see TCB, "Traslado d'uns autos cíveis de execução: Banco de Portugal; Espólio de Eugenio Coichoix" 1879; "Traslado de uns autos cíveis de execução: Agente do banco Nacional Ultramarino e Casal do súbdito francês Eugenio Caichoix," 1879; and "Traslado de parte das peças constantes do processado na execução," 1882.

[70] Boletim Oficial do Governo Geral da Província de Angola (BOGGPA), 1869, n. 31, July 31, 1869, p. 362. For the importance of male representatives, see Eugénia Rodrigues, "As donas de prazos do Zambeze. Políticas imperiais e estratégias locais," in *VI Jornadas Setecentistas: Conferências e comunicações*, ed. Magnus Pereira and Nadalin (Curitiba: Aos Quatro Ventos, 2006), 15–34; Rodrigues, *Portugueses e Africanos*, 771–80; Philip J. Havik, "Gender, Land, and Trade: Women's Agency and Colonial Change in Portuguese Guinea (West Africa)," *African Economic History* 43, no. 1 (2016): 162–95. For more on Dona Teresa Barruncho, see Mariana P. Candido, "African Businesswomen in the Age of Second Slavery in Angola," *The Atlantic and Africa: The Second Slavery and Beyond*, edited by Paul E. Lovejoy and Dale W. Tomich, p. 179–201 (Albany, NY: SUNY Binghamton Press, 2021)

Table 3.3. *Benguela traders, 1821*

José Nicolau Ferreira
Alexandre José da Silva
José Joaquim Teixeira
João Pedro de Andrade
Diniz Vieira de Lima
Joaquim Lopes dos Santos
José Apolinário Alvares
Manoel Pires Chaves
João Batista Benites
José Rodrigues de Magalhães
Francisco Ferreira Gomes

Source: Arquivo Histórico Militar (AHM),
2-2-1-36, "Requerimento dos Negociantes
da Praça de Benguela."

Table 3.4. *List of Benguela traders and owners, 1869*

António Coimbra
Caetano Alberto de Sousa
Custódio José de Sousa Veloso
Conchoix & Frères
Domingos Joaquim Pereira
Ferreira & Costa
Francisco José de Freitas
Francisco César da Horta
João Ferreira Gonçalves, representing Joaquim Lopes de Castro's business
Joaquim Gonçalves de Azevedo Castro and João Maria Carreira, representing Manoel
    António Teixeira Barbosa's business
José Gonçalves da Silva Soares, representing D. Teresa Barruncho's business
José Joaquim Teixeira, representing Joaquim Pereira Galino's business
José Joaquim Vieira da Silva
Manuel António dos Santos Reis

Source: BOGGPA, 1869, n. 31, July 31, 1869, p. 362

centuries, women resident in Luanda and Benguela also seized the
opportunity. Colonial administrators produced lists of merchants (see
Tables 3.3 and 3.4) that privileged recognition of men as merchants and
property owners, but even so African women had a central role in
exerting property rights in the first half of the nineteenth century.

African Women, Property Claims, and Written Documents

Colonial laws and courts were employed when there were disputes over property, in the form of resources such as land or, in the case of free and enslaved dependents, labor. The existence of multiple legal spheres affected colonial subjects who could employ different judicial spaces when it suited them, such as in marriage, divorce, or ownership rights. Although the introduction of colonial adjudication over local disputes, which replaced the role of elders and sobas, may have made it more difficult for West Central African men and women to access the court, elite women took advantage of the new urban legal system to insert themselves into the colonial space and claim rights, as in other African contexts.[71]

Although the Portuguese legal code theoretically guaranteed women's right to property as wives and daughters, that is, in relationship to men, the colonial administration did not necessarily view African women as capable and trustworthy in managing inheritances. Colonial officer Elias Alexandre da Silva Correa expressed doubt that women could exercise any control over their human property: "If the slaves do not agree with her choice of a husband they run away, afraid of possibly experiencing severe treatment from a new owner."[72] Colonial observers condemned the behavior of powerful women and portrayed them as simultaneously standing up to male power, unable to manage their properties, and under the influence of their male dependents. These attitudes were not exclusive to West Central Africa, as similar public discredit of women as landholders was widespread in Mozambique from the eighteenth to nineteenth centuries.[73]

West Central African women invested in urban real estate, enslaved people, luxury goods, and animals, combining different strategies to accumulate property, including controlling dependents who cultivated their land. This was the case with Joana Martinho Lopes, who died in Benguela in 1864. Although Martinho Lopes's will has not been located, the inventory of her properties at the time of her death is available. Lopes's

---

[71] Kristin Mann and Richard Roberts, "Law in Colonial Africa," in *Law in Colonial Africa*, ed. Kristin Mann and Richard L. Roberts (Portsmouth, NH: Heinemann, 1991), 3–58; Daisy Hilse Dwyer, "Outside the Courts: Extra-Legal Strategies for the Subordination of Women," in *African Women & the Law: Historical Perspectives*, ed. Margaret Jean Hay and Marcia Wright (Boston: Boston University Press, 1982), 90–109; Kristin Mann, "Women, Landed Property, and the Accumulation of Wealth in Early Colonial Lagos," *Signs* 16, no. 4 (1991): 682–706; Byfield, "Women, Marriage, Divorce."

[72] Elias Alexandre da Silva Corrêa, *História de Angola* (Lisbon: Ática, 1937), 1, 113–4. See also Oliveira, *Slave Trade and Abolition. Gender, Commerce and Economic Transition in Luanda*, 61–79 and 90–101.

[73] Rodrigues, "Chiponda," 110–11.

inventory was considered "small" and consisted of a plot along the Cavaco River in Benguela, an *arimo* with ten *cubatas* in Dombe Grande, gold, an old trunk, a piece of golden lace, six pieces of textile, and an old blanket.[74] Most of her wealth was invested in controlling labor, or wealth in people, a system based on the rights over someone's labor and reproduction. Her assets included a small boy, five older women, two women, two girls, a man who worked as a mason who was freed in the terms of her will, a fisherman, two men without skills, and a woman with her baby.[75] Men and elders may have had control over women's labor, but cases such as this demonstrate certain women had rights to someone else's labor, accumulating free and unfree dependents.[76] If the control of women's labor was central to different systems of stratification, the ability of women to control labor favored their economic expansion. Their wealth allowed them to accumulate dependents from communities of impoverished people in troubled circumstances. Personal wealth, social prestige, and security relied on being able to control labor through ties of marriage, patron–client links, and allegiance.[77] Hence, women achieved economic independence as landowners and labor recruiters, using the labor of their children and dependents to secure prestige and safety. Married or widowed, women retained control over the products of their and their dependents' labor. They were able to invest in trade opportunities, pay land taxes, and purchase household items for themselves and their businesses.[78] Yet Portuguese men, such as Bishop Vicente Prazeres da Costa and Silva Porto, both mentioned earlier, portrayed African women as lazy, irresponsible, or exclusively sexual beings.[79]

In archival records, West Central African women appear as social actors who participated in the economic and social life of their communities. However, colonial officers viewed the enrichment of Africans,

---

[74] TCB, "Inventário de Joana Martinho Lopes," 1864, fl. 4–6.

[75] TCB, "Inventário de Joana Martinho Lopes," 1864, fl. 2–6.

[76] For more on wealth in people, see Joseph C. Miller, *Way of Death: Merchant Capitalism and the Angolan Slave Trade, 1730-1830* (Madison: University of Wisconsin Press, 1988), 61–63. For the idea that men were the only accumulators of wealth in people, see Caroline H. Bledsoe, *Women and Marriage in Kpelle Society* (Palo Alto: Stanford University Press, 1980), 46–9.

[77] Bledsoe, *Women and Marriage*, 48; Bourdieu, *Pascalian Meditations*, 193–8; Bourdieu and Wacquant, *An Invitation to Reflexive Sociology*, 118–9.

[78] Schmidt, *Peasants, Traders, and Wives*, 15; Hodgson and McCurdy, "'Wicked' Women," 2–5; Bledsoe, *Women and Marriage*, 3–4.

[79] António Francisco Ferreira da Silva Porto wrote lengthy statements about Black women's inferiority as well as their resistance to pain. See BSGL, Res 2-C 6, "Silva Porto, apontamentos de um portuense em África. Vol 2. Bié 25 de outubro de 1860 a 1 de julho de 1861," fl. 129, May 27, 1861; and fl. 261, April 5, 1862. Jennifer Morgan has written on these problematic and conflicting visions of Black women in European imaginary. See Jennifer L. Morgan, *Laboring Women: Reproduction and Gender in New World Slavery* (Philadelphia: University of Pennsylvania Press, 2011).

particularly women, with ambivalence. The colonial administration approved the growing production of cotton or sugarcane and portrayed it as in harmony with civilizing goals, yet at the same time African involvement competed with the enterprises of European farmers.[80] In 1877, António Ignácio Ruas requested a renewal of his two-year license for his position as administrator of the post office of Luanda. His license allowed him to work on the farm of his daughter, Ambrozina Ismánia Ruas, in the Golungo Alto.[81] Even on the eve of the Berlin Conference, when the destinies of Africans changed dramatically, women in West Central Africa were managing farms and gaining wealth through their labor. By the second half of the nineteenth century, access to property was gendered. Its access defined social status and economic power. Land ownership also structured relationships within and outside of households. More importantly, examples indicate that some West Central African women played an important role in claiming property and increased their social prestige and wealth in the process at the expense of legitimate trade.

One of the ironies of the colonial obsession with writing down property records is that it provided space for West Central African women to claim rights. Unlike in other contexts in which women's presence in court records seems to be limited to women who were property belonging to male actors, in the Portuguese colonial records African women are everywhere, including as property owners.[82] Free Black women owned houses, plots of land, and small businesses such as taverns and shops and conducted business in the streets of colonial towns selling prepared food, fruits, fish, and water, a pattern that was replicated elsewhere in Atlantic ports.[83]

---

[80] These ambivalent colonial policies were not exclusive to Angola. See the case of the British in Kenya and the Gold Coast. Sara Berry, "Hegemony on a Shoestring: Indirect Rule and Access to Agricultural Land," *Africa: Journal of the International African Institute* 62, no. 3 (1992): 327–55.

[81] AHU, Angola, Pasta 47, doc 146, March 22, 1877.

[82] Hawkins, *Writing and Colonialism in Northern Ghana*, 290–91. For the prevalence of women in Portuguese colonial records, see Mariana P. Candido, "Engendering West Central African History: The Role of Urban Women in Benguela in the Nineteenth Century," *History in Africa* 42 (2015): 7–36.

[83] Selma Pantoja, "Quintandas e quitandeiras: história e deslocamento na nova lógica do espaço em Luanda," in *África e a Instalação do Sistema Colonial (c. 1885-c. 1935): Actas da III Reunião Internacional de História de África*, ed. Maria Emília Madeira Santos (Lisbon: Centro de Estudos de História e Cartografia Antiga, 2000), 175–86; Vanessa S. Oliveira, "Trabalho escravo e ocupações urbanas em Luanda na segunda metade do século XIX," in *Em torno de Angola. Narrativas, identidades e conexões atlânticas* (São Paulo: Intermeios, 2014), 265–67; Jane Landers, "Founding Mothers: Female Rebels in Colonial New Granada and Spanish Florida," *Journal of African American History* 98, no. 1 (2013): 7–23; David Wheat, *Atlantic Africa and the Spanish Caribbean, 1570-1640* (Chapel Hill: University of North Carolina Press, 2016), 142–80; Ty M. Reese, "Wives, Brokers, and Laborers: Women at Cape Coast, 1750-1807," in *Women in Port: Gendering*

After acquiring a debt with Dona Joana Rodrigues Magalhães and having difficulty honoring it, the Black woman Dionísia requested that an agent in Quilengues send her a young girl (a *moleca*) to liquidate Dionísia's debt to Magalhães.[84] African women with Portuguese names had many economic roles. In the 1820s, at the height of Atlantic commerce, Francisca Lopes Pereira owned the house in which she cohabited with José Pólilo. After their relationship ended, she demanded that Pólilo vacate the house and pay for the services that the young enslaved boy and girl, who belonged to her, had provided. In colonial documents, Pereira claimed her role as the owner of a house and of enslaved children who served her and her guests, including her domestic partner. As in other relationships in the Atlantic African ports, a wealthy woman could host visitors by offering companionship, lodging, and a variety of services, such as translation, access to her networks, and even the use of her own enslaved personnel. Compensation and the return of her property were thus a legitimate claim. The primary sources that register Francisca Lopes Pereira's rightful existence in colonial society are silent about her skin color and place of origin, thus allowing her a chance to enjoy the rights from which Black people and their descendants were usually excluded in an empire preoccupied with blood purity, status, and origin.[85]

Free Black women controlled a substantial portion of the economic resources in Benguela. For example, Josefa Manoel Joaquim owned and sold houses.[86] Dona Mariana António de Carvalho, from Galangues and married to Lieutenant Colonel José Justiniano dos Reis, had canoes that sailed between Benguela and Lobito. She also exploited limestone in Lobito, an important resource for the construction of brick houses, overseeing its commercialization in Benguela and Catumbela.[87] Other residents invested in fishing and transporting goods, such as the case of

---

Communities, Economies, and Social Networks in Atlantic Port Cities, 1500-1800, ed. Douglas Catterall and Jody Campbell (Leiden: Brill, 2012), 291–314.

[84] ANA, Cod. 7182, fl. 50v, May 21, 1827, requerimento n. 132. For Francisco Lopes Pereira's burial record, see BL, Benguela, Livro de Óbitos, 1797-1831, fl. 221-221v, 27 February 1830. For more on silences regarding color and origin, see Elizabeth Anne Kuznesof, "Ethnic and Gender Influences on 'Spanish' Creole Society in Colonial Spanish America," *Colonial Latin American Review* 4, no. 1 (1995): 153–76; Candido, "Engendering West Central African History," 22–26.

[85] ANA, Cod. 7182, fl. 55, June 7, 1827, requerimento n. 192. For more on restrictions associated with skin color, see João Figueiroa-Rêgo and Fernanda Olival, "'Cor da pele, distinções e cargos: Portugal e espaços atlânticos portugueses (séculos XVI a XVIII),'" *Tempo* 16, no. 30 (2011): 115–45; Ronald Raminelli, "Impedimentos da cor: Mulatos no Brasil e em Portugal c. 1640-1750," *Varia História* 28, no. 48 (2012): 699–723.

[86] ANA, Cod. 7182, fl. 137, 20 de marco 1829, requerimento n. 1445.

[87] ANA, Cx. 151, Secretaria Geral do Governo de Benguela, fl. 178v, 23 September 1845, n. 620; and ANA, Cx. 151, Secretaria Geral do Governo de Benguela, fl. 185, October 15, 1845, n. 674; fl. 194v, n. 749, April 17, 1845. For her marriage record, see BL, Benguela, Livro de Casamento, 1806-1853, fl. 46, May 31, 1838.

Dona Ana Martins de Santa Ana who owned at least two boats that sailed to Quicombo, Cuio, Lobito, and Rio Tapado.[88]

Women could also access property through inheritance. Probate documents available at the Tribunal da Comarca de Benguela show that some women inherited land, enslaved people, and goods from their relatives. This was the case with Matilde, a three-year-old girl who inherited property from her father, the Guimarães (Portugal) born trader João Batista da Silva. Her mother, Joana Luiz Borges César, acted as administrator of the probate estate since Matilde was a minor. Batista da Silva left his daughter a *cubata* divided into three rooms, with four doors and four windows. Young Matilde also inherited five enslaved individuals, furniture, a variety of textiles, and beads.[89] Due to the young age of the heir, her mother continued to live in the *cubata* and administered the inheritance on behalf of her daughter.

Probate estates also reveal that women transmitted property, including land, to nonrelatives. Dona Joana Rodrigues da Costa was the widow of Lieutenant Colonel Domingos Pereira Diniz. Her children had already died by the time she made her will, which led her to bequeath her property to Dona Florinda José do Cadaval, her "spiritual sister," although the nature of this bond is not clear in the document.[90] Besides her house within the fortress of Caconda, Dona Joana Rodrigues da Costa owned cotton and linen textiles, a single soup bowl, three teacups, a teapot, a silver candleholder, and a set of silver cutlery for six people. Among her human property were two women skilled in leatherwork.[91] Her belongings were not luxurious, but by donating them to another woman she allowed a fellow merchant woman, Florencia José do Cadaval, to accumulate material goods and increase her wealth. This gendered strategy protected the interests of female friends and associates.

Through their wills, women such as Dona Joana Rodrigues da Costa guaranteed the distribution of goods and transmission of property. Women who wrote down their wishes and identified their property displayed a great deal of control over their lives. They were skilled enough to learn how to navigate within the colonial system and protect their relatives by preventing male family members or sobas from seizing their belongings. However, not every woman who lived in the colonial centers had the opportunity to leave a will. Josefa Soares, a single thirty-

[88] ANA, Cx. 151, Secretaria Geral do Governo de Benguela, fl. 188v, October 28 1845; fl. 189, n. 703, October 28, 1845; fl. 192, n. 729, October 28, 1845; fl. 192, n. 729, October 18, 1845; and fl. 193v, n. 740, November 13, 1845; fl. 198, n. 776, November 24, 1845; fl. 198, n. 778, November 24, 1845; and fl. 199v, n. 778, November 24, 1845.
[89] TCB, Inventários, "Inventário de João Batista da Silva," 1863, fls. 1–14.
[90] TCB, Inventários, "Inventário de Joana Rodrigues da Costa," May 13, 1850, fl. 6v.
[91] TCB, Inventários, "Inventário de Joana Rodrigues da Costa," May 13, 1850, fl. 14–16v.

Table 3.5. *Granted land in Benguela, 1845–1894*

Years	Men	Women	Total
1845–54	75	13	88
1855–64	14	13	27
1865–74[94]	17	11	28
1886–94	10	3	13
Total	116	40	**156**

Source: Biblioteca Província de Benguela, Termo de Terrenos 1845–1894

year-old woman from Libolo, died in 1864 while in Benguela.[92] Colonial authorities noticed that although she did not have a will, she had assets and seized them. It is not clear what happened to her estate.

Land registration documents also reveal the efforts of African men and women to record ownership and petition for property within the limits of the colonial bureaucracy. Even though the demarcation of land predated the nineteenth century, it was only then that the colonial government assumed the responsibility of controlling and registering it. One of Cazengo's planters, for example, reported buying a farm from a free Black woman.[93] By 1845 men and women in Benguela were requesting permission from the colonial government to build or manage plots of land. Of the 156 land plots granted, women petitioned and registered forty of them, as can be seen in Table 3.5.

Among them was Dona Florinda Josefa Gaspar, the daughter of Joanes José Gaspar who had served as the soba in Catumbela and corporal in Dombe Grande in the early nineteenth century. Dona Gaspar married the Brazilian *degredado* Francisco Ferreira Gomes and established a large transcontinental family with him.[95] Women who were well positioned

---

[92] BOGGPA, 1869, n. 13, 27 March 1869, p. 198. For a different opinion that emphasizes the victimization of women, see Cutrufelli, *Women of Africa*, 61–64.

[93] David Birmingham, "The Coffee Barons of Cazengo," *Journal of African History* 19, no. 4 (1978): 526.

[94] No records are available from 1874 to 1886.

[95] Biblioteca da Província de Benguela (BPB), Termos de Terrenos, 1843–1894, fl. 61–2, "Alvará de terreno concedido a Florinda Joanes Gaspar," November 20, 1861. For more on Dona Florinda Gaspar and her family, see Mariana P. Candido, "Women, Family, and Landed Property in Nineteenth-Century Benguela," *African Economic History* 43, no. 1 (2015): 136–61; Roquinaldo Ferreira, "Biografia como história social: O clã Ferreira Gomes e os mundos da escravização no Atlântico Sul," *Varia Historia* 29, no. 51 (2013): 679–719; Roquinaldo Amaral Ferreira, "Atlantic Microhistories: Mobility, Personal Ties, and Slaving in the Black Atlantic World (Angola and Brazil)," in *Cultures of the Lusophone Black Atlantic*, ed. Nancy Prisci Naro, Ro Sansi-Roca, and D. Treece (New York: Palgrave Macmillan, 2007), 99–127. Mariana P. Candido and Monica Lima, "Florinda Josefa Gaspar," *Oxford Research Encyclopedia of African History*, forthcoming.

were able to guarantee access through inheritance but also through colonial venues, such as petitioning for access to land and paying for it. In 1861, Dona Gaspar requested and received a land plot of twenty fathoms, i.e., 36.5 m^2, along the Cavaco River. Her intentions were to build a house and a garden. Dona Joaquina Martins Ramos Abreu also secured a land plot in the Cavaco neighborhood, with 45.7 m facing the west, bordering the backyard of Clementina Rodrigues da Costa's and Dona Júlia Miguel Pereira's houses. The back of the plot measured 78.6 m and shared a border with Dona Isabel da Luz Abreu's house. Dona Joaquina Martins Ramos Abreu paid 1$538 reis fortes to the Benguela city hall.[96] Not far from them, Felipa Martins de Castro also acquired a plot of 36.5 m facing north and 67 facing south, where Dona Rodrigues da Costa had built her house.[97]

Several women were richer and in better economic and social positions than their spouses, and their real estate and slave holdings offered them a series of advantages as lenders and credit holders.[98] In 1805, for example, the Portuguese trader Aurelio Veríssimo Vieira died after having contracted debts with a series of consolidated merchants. In his will, he declared, "I have a series of credit letters with Dona Joana Gomes Moutinho related to several slaves I shipped to Rio de Janeiro and my executor will pay her."[99] By the early nineteenth century, Dona Moutinho was one of the most successful merchants in Benguela. She was the daughter of Dona Francisca Gomes Moutinho, another African woman who played the role of cultural broker and intermediary between Europeans and African rulers. In the late eighteenth century, Dona Joana Gomes Moutinho married the captain of the Benguela colonial army, José Ferreira da Silva, who also operated as a private trader. This relationship was apparently brief, as by 1798 she was already a widow.[100]

---

[96] BPB, termo de Terreno, fl. 67v, December 5, 1864.

[97] BPB, termo de Terreno, fl. 69v, December 27, 1865.

[98] Vanessa de Oliveira, "Spouses and Commercial Partners: Immigrant Men and Locally Born Women in Luanda (1831-1859), in *African Women in Atlantic Coast Societies, 1680-1880*, ed. Mariana P. Candido and Adam Jones (James Currey, 2019g), 217-32. For the importance of credit in the West Central African economy, see Miller, *Way of Death*, 95–98; Mariana Candido, "Merchants and the Business of the Slave Trade at Benguela, 1750-1850," *African Economic History* 35 (2007): 1–30; Filipa Ribeiro da Silva, "Private Business in the Angolan Trade, 1590s-1780s," ed. David Richardson and Filipa Ribeiro da Silva (Leiden: Brill, 2015), 71–101; Daniel B. Domingues da Silva, *The Atlantic Slave Trade from West Central Africa, 1780–1867* (Cambridge: Cambridge University Press, 2017), 52–55.

[99] ANTT, Feitos Findos, Justificações Ultramarinas, África, Maço 14, doc. 1, f. 10, September 2, 1805.

[100] For her mother's information, see BL, Benguela, Livro de Óbito, fl.222v-223, March 31, 1788. For reference to her marriage to Jose Ferreira da Silva, see BL, Benguela, Livro de Batismo, 1794-1806, fl. 44, April 17, 1796; and AHU, Angola, cx. 76, doc. 45,

Due to her family and marital connections, she established herself as a powerful merchant and resident of the colonial center. She owned a two-story house surrounded by farmland and a residential compound where fifty slaves lived. Among her dependents was her nephew, Caetano de Carvalho Velho, who ran the town's butcher shop. Between 1795 and 1801, she was named the godmother of at least seventeen children baptized in the local Catholic Church, *Nossa Senhora do Populo*.[101] She also helped to reproduce values associated with colonialism, such as Catholicism, and guaranteed her economic position and social status through her interaction with colonial agents, foreign traders, and poor residents. Dona Moutinho economic status translated into social capital, reinforced by her liaisons with foreign men.

Wealth and social prestige offered Dona Moutinho the chance to be seen not only as a wealthy merchant woman but also as a lender and business partner.[102] Entrepreneur, slave owner, and landlord, Dona Moutinho was part of the local merchant community that maintained links with the interior (in her case, the region of Kilengues); she could easily accommodate recently arrived traders with the infrastructure she had in place. Despite her wealth, the fact that she was a woman forced her to use attorneys or proxies to represent her in official matters. Her power was also expressed in her choice of proxy (*procurador*) who managed her businesses on her behalf. In 1799 João Mendes de Oliveira, a priest from the island of Príncipe, and in 1806 Nazario Marques da Silva, an important Benguela-based trader, represented her in church matters.[103]

Credit was central to economic transactions on the African coast, and foreigners and locals were active participants in advancing merchandise

---

June 22, 1791. For the reference to her as a widow, see AAL, Benguela, Livro de Obitos, April 11, 1798.

[101] For references to her property, see IHGB, DL, 32, 02.02 (1797), fl. 13-13v. For her godchildren, see BL, Benguela, Livro de Batismo, 1794-1806, fl. 25 v, July 29, 1795; fl. 39, November 19,1795; fl. 44v, May 2, 1796; fl. 68v, July 4, 1797; fl. 69v-70, July 3,1797; fl. 71v, August 25,1797; fl. 73v-74, October 31, 1797; fl. 77, November, 27, 1797; fl. 94, August 31, 1798; fl. 95v, September 10, 1798; fl. 102, November 26, 1798; fl. 108, May 4, 1799; and fl. 110, June 3, 1799.

[102] For more on Dona Joana, see Mariana P. Candido, "Las donas y la trata de esclavos," *Mujeres Africanas y Afrodescendientes em el Mundo Atlántico, siglos XVII al XIX*, Maria Elisa Velázquez and Carolina González (México City: DEAS-INAH, 2016), 243–278. For other cases in Angola, see Júlio de Castro Lopo, "Uma Rica Dona de Luanda," *Portucale* 3 (1948): 129–138; Selma Pantoja, "Gênero e Comércio: As Traficantes de Escravos na Região de Angola," *Travessias* 4/5 (2004): 79–97; Pantoja, "Donas de 'Arimos'"; Candido, "Marchande de Benguela."

[103] ABL, Benguela, Batismo, fl. 110, June 3, 1799; and fl. 227, April 26, 1806. In 1805, the Portuguese merchant Aurélio Veríssimo Viana acknowledged his debts with her in his will. Years before Dona Joana had advanced him slaves to be sold in Rio de Janeiro Arquivo Nacional da Torre do Tombo (ANTT), Feitos Findos, Justificações Ultramarinas, África, Maço 14, doc. 1, fl. 10.

and acquiring debts. African women appear in colonial records as loaners. In the 1820s, Rosa Chamires sued Caetano de Morais, a resident of Catumbela who owed her 12$800 *réis*.[104] She expected the colonial authorities to help her in recuperating the loan she had provided months before. Similarly, Rita Jorge lent 7$200 *réis* to the soldier Pedro António. António managed to pay part of his debt, 6$300 *réis*, before he deserted the army and ran away. Unable to collect the remaining 900 *réis*, Rita Jorge filed a complaint with the colonial judge requesting that Cecilia, who cohabited with António, honor his debt. The Benguela judge sided with Jorge and demanded the payment, making Cecilia responsible for her partner's debts.[105]

The absence of local banks propelled trustworthy people with enough cash to the position of moneylenders for residents who did not have access to the credit provided by transatlantic slave traders. The credit arrangements were informal and probably unwritten and are accessible to historians only when creditors failed to recuperate their money and requested the intervention of colonial authorities or in inventories that regularly included lists of money out at interest and debt owing. For example, Maria Braxel, a Black woman, advanced 2$400 *réis* to the sailor Luis, and Andreza Leal do Sancramento lent 10$450 reis to José, a Black resident of Dombe Grande.[106] The motivation or goals are not stated, but it is fair to assume these men had limited access to other creditors, and both women had cash and connections. Dona Joana Francisca de Sousa acted as a guarantor and assumed the risk for her son, Manoel de Sousa Marques, who failed to pay 84$000.[107] African women's roles as moneylenders and creditors indicate that they had control over their earnings from surplus production, petty trade, and services they provided. As a result, they had cash to lend and the autonomy to sue debtors or customers who refused to pay for their services. Ana Freire Joaquim, a Black woman who worked for Pedro António, demanded their agreed-upon payment of 32$000 *réis*.[108] It is not clear what type of service she performed, yet, she could sue Pedro Joaquim. In a similar case, Josefa solicited the help of the administrator of Catumbela to recover the amount of 12$000 *réis* for services she had provided to Juliana Gonçalves de Siqueira.[109]

---

[104] ANA, Cod. 7182, fl. 114v, October 22, 1828, requerimento n. 1221.
[105] ANA, Cod. 7182, fl.54, June 6, 1827, requerimento n. 178.
[106] ANA, Cod. 7182, fl. 137, March 20, 1829, requerimento n. 1447; and ANA, Cod. 7182, fl. 82v, February 13, 1828, requerimento n. 734.
[107] ANA, Cod. 7182, fl.11v, August 5, 1826, requerimento n. 498.
[108] ANA, Cod. 7182, fl. 9, August 5, 1826, requerimento n. 474.
[109] ANA, Cod. 7182, fl. 9v, August 5, 1826, requerimento n. 479.

With the monetization of the economy and the expansion of the paper register, both men and women lent and collected money. It is not clear how these practices differed from those prior to the nineteenth century. In 1846, Mariana Antónia de Carvalho made a formal request to Eleutério Treisse to pay the remaining value of a house in Mossamedes, indicating not only that she was a homeowner but also that she had sold it on credit.[110] Lenders accepted enslaved people as pawns for those who needed credit. In 1849, the Luanda-based Dona Maria dos Reis Dionísia offered three female slaves as collateral to Dona Ana Joaquina dos Santos e Silva, the largest slave trader in Luanda by the mid-nineteenth century. Failing to return the advance, Dona Maria dos Reis Dionísia lost her slaves to a more-powerful resident who increased her wealth by accumulating the dependents and debts of others.[111]

Women not necessarily registered loans and credit arrangements in notaries with promissory notes. Yet some did, such as the case of Joana Rodrigues da Costa, who died in 1850. Among her belongings were listed four credit bills for merchandise she had advanced to inland traders and two bills related to loans acquired with Manuel de Barros Cunha.[112] Women employed the courts to collect debts but not necessarily registered loans on the town's notaries. Men, however, tended to register formal loans in notaries, with debtors and creditors presenting written documents and recognizing the importance of paper evidence. In his 1862 will, Agostinho António Ramos, a resident of Cuio, declared he owed 40$000 réis to Dona Teresa Ferreira Torres Barruncho and the same amount to Joaquim Ferreira, a resident of Novo Redondo, and both "had documents." He also noted, "If any document shows up with debts from Bento Joanes Papata, they should not be considered since he owns me nothing."[113] Tomé Ribeiro Antunes initiated a legal action to collect a debt from João Henriques Teixeira's estate. Ribeiro Antunes had lent the Teixeira couple 206$936 *réis* to help them settle and start a farm in Luaxi/Luacho, close to Dombe Grande. He presented seven written documents registered in notaries detailing the expenses and items

---

[110] ANA, Cod. 455, "Correspondência Expedida do Governo," fl. 191, June 15, 1846.
[111] BGGOPA, n. 179, March 3, 1849, p. 4, "Edital, March 1, 1849. For more on Dona Ana Joaquina, see Carlos Alberto Lopes Cardoso, "Ana Joaquina dos Santos Silva, industrial angolana da segunda metade do Século XIX," *Boletim Cultural da Câmara Municipal de Luanda* 3 (1972): 5–14; Júlio de Castro Lopo, "Uma rica dona de Luanda," *Portucale* 3 (1948): 129–138; Douglas Wheeler, "Angolan Woman of Means: D. Ana Joaquina dos Santos e Silva, Mid-Nineteenth Century Luso-African Merchant-Capitalist of Luanda," *Santa Barbara Portuguese Studies Review* 3 (1996): 284–97.
[112] TJB, Inventários, "Inventário de Joana Rodrigues da Costa," May 13, 1850, fl. 16v.
[113] ANA, cx. 5251, Dombe Grande, "Junta da Fazenda Pública de Benguela [Luis Teodoro França] to Chefe do concelho do Dombe Grande], July 1, 1862.

lent between June 1863 and July 1866, which included over 1,101 *cazongueis* of manioc flour (15,414 kilos), six cows, and fish to feed his people, as well as a variety of textiles, three *pipas* of firewater, and enslaved adults and twelve children. In March 1867, the court recognized the debt due to "proof presented in several documents" and awarded Ribeiro Antunes the right to receive repayment.[114]

Despite these cases, European traders did not necessarily have the financial upper hand and relied on local traders with more cash to borrow money. The Portuguese trader Inácio Teixeira Xavier accumulated debts with several Benguela residents, many of them born locally. One was Rufina Angélica do Céu (105$415), who had married at least twice before 1850 and owned several enslaved men and women. Céu was able to sign her own name, which was uncommon among women in West Central Africa.[115]

Since the colonial bureaucracy did not necessarily resolve all credit-related disputes, some individuals became frustrated and seized goods in retaliation for the lack of repayment, a practice that resembled the kidnapping of free people along the African coast to settle debt payments. In 1860, Isabel Soares da Silva, a Black woman, and José Gonçalves de Almeida, whose skin color was not identified in the documents, trespassed on the *arimo*, the garden of Domingos Marcelino Galvão, and removed some planted manioc. Galvão initiated a legal proceeding against the two, but it soon emerged that the couple was unhappy with Galvão's failure to repay a debt and the slow process of the colonial bureaucracy in helping them regain their money. Silva had provided Galvão six and a half bottles of *aguardente* (firewater), and the Benguela judge estimated its value at 1$950. The manioc they seized and the damage to the soil and garden were evaluated at 12$000. As a result, the judge ordered the couple to pay the difference or face jail time.[116] The stories held in colonial records shed some light on the mechanisms that local men and women employed to collect loans.

[114] TCB, "Ação comercial Autor Tomé Ribeiro Antunes Réu Casal de João Rodrigues Teixeira" December 1867.

[115] Teixeira Xavier's other creditors included José Balahala (77$015), José Manuel Ribeiro (1:020$525), José Manuel Ribeiro (110$485), and José Marques Pereira da Silva (1:620 $066). See BGGOPA, 1869, n. 4, 23 January, p. 39–40. For more on Dona Rufina Angélica do Céu's marriages to João Batista Correa Peixoto and Manoel Maria Conceição da Silva, both from Luanda, see BL, Benguela, Livro de Casamento, fl. 55 v, April 20, 1850. For Rufina Angélica do Céu's slaves, see BL, Benguela, Livro de Batismo 1846–1849, fl. 45v, February 22, 1847; Benguela, Livro de Batismo 1849-1850, fl. 111v, October 27, 1850 and Benguela, Livro de Batismo, 1851-1853, fl. 7v, October 12, 1851.

[116] ANA, cx. 1373, Dombe Grande, doc. 3 – "Processo referido de Autos civis, Juizo ordinario provisório Autos de Exame e vistoria a requerimento do Domingos Marcelino Galvão. Reus José Gonçalves de Almeida e preta Isabel Soares da Silva," July 9, 1860.

Similar to the *signares* or *nharas* in Senegal and Guinea, West Central African women achieved the position of intermediaries and became important business owners during the era of the transatlantic slave trade.[117] Very few European women ever settled in Benguela, and the colonial administrators did not prevent the rise of West Central African women entrepreneurs. The collaboration favored both sides. On the one hand, local women provided foreign traders access to commercial networks, acting as traders and translators, and mediating the contact between slave traders based on the coast and internal commercial elites. On the other hand, foreign traders facilitated African women's access to imported goods, which they would then market at a profit.[118] More interesting is the fact that the available colonial documents reveal that a number of these African women were single and did not necessarily rely on the capital of powerful men to establish themselves as business owners. Many had agents in the internal markets, such as Maria António da Silva

---

For cases when goods and people were seized as a result of criminal solutions, see Ferreira, "Slaving and Resistance to Slaving in West Central Africa," 111–130.

[117] George E. Brooks, "A Nhara of Guine-Bissau Region: Mãe Aurélia Correia," in *Women and Slavery in Africa*, ed. Claire C Robertson and Martin A Klein (Madison: University of Wisconsin Press, 1983), 295–317; George E Brooks, "The Signares of Saint-Louis and Gorée: Women Entrepreneur in Eighteenth Century Senegal," in *Women in Africa. Studies in Social and Economic Change*, ed. Nancy Hafkin and Edna Bay (Stanford, CA: Stanford University Press, 1976), 19–44; Philip J. Havik, *Silences and Soundbites: The Gendered Dynamics of Trade and Brokerage in the Pre-Colonial Guinea Bissau Region* (Munster: LIT Verlag Münster, 2004); Pernille Ipsen, *Daughters of the Trade: Atlantic Slavers and Interracial Marriage on the Gold Coast* (Philadelphia: University of Pennsylvania Press, 2015); Reese, "Wives, Brokers, and Laborers: Women at Cape Coast, 1750-1807"; Natalie Everts, "A Motley Company: Differing Identities among Euro-Africans in Eighteenth-Century Elmina," in *Brokers of Change: Atlantic Commerce and Cultures in Precolonial Western Africa*, ed. Toby Green (Oxford: The British Academy/ Oxford Universty Press, 2012), 53–69. For the scholarship on merchant women in West Central Africa, see Selma Pantoja, "Gênero e comércio: as traficantes de escravos na Região de Angola," *Travessias* 4/5 (2004): 79–97; Cesaltina Abreu, "'Xé, minina, não fala política!', cidadania no feminino: sine die?," in *Angola e as angolanas. Memória, sociedade e cultura*, ed. Selma Pantoja, Edvaldo Bergamo, and Ana Claudia da Silva (São Paulo: Intermeios, 2016), 167–86; Mariana P. Candido, "Aguida Gonçalves da Silva, une dona à Benguela à la fin du XVIIIe siècle," *Brésil(s). Sciences Humaines et Sociales* 1 (2012): 33–54; Candido, "Merchants and Business."

[118] There is an important scholarship on the partnerships between African women and Atlantic traders. See Pamela Scully, "Malintzin, Pocahontas, and Krotoa: Indigenous Women and Myth Models of the Atlantic World," *Journal of Colonialism and Colonial History* 6, no. 3 (2005); Adam Jones, "Female Slave-Owners on the Gold Coast. Just a Matter of Money?," in *Slave Cultures and the Cultures of Slavery*, ed. Step Palmié (Knoxville: University of Tennessee Press, 1995), 100–111; Hilary Jones, *The Métis of Senegal: Urban Life and Politics in French West Africa* (Bloomington: Indiana University Press, 2013); Jean-Baptiste, *Conjugal Rights*; Carina E. Ray, *Crossing the Color Line: Race, Sex, and the Contested Politics of Colonialism in Ghana* (Athens: Ohio University Press, 2015); Lorelle Semley, *To Be Free and French: Citizenship in France's Atlantic Empire* (Cambridge: Cambridge University Press, 2017), 24–56.

who employed trade agents in Quilengues, and Isabel Francisca Antónia Viera who had representatives in Caconda.[119] Andreza Leal do Sacramento experienced a series of problems with José Gongo, a Black man who acted as her commercial agent in Dombe Grande.[120]

Women also acted as itinerant traders, acquiring goods and people in the interior on behalf of coastal traders. This was the case with Dona Ana Teixeira de Sousa, a resident of Benguela who received goods on behalf of Manuel Ribeiro Alves to acquire enslaved people in Caconda in 1856, despite the official ban on slave exports from Portuguese territories in West Central Africa. Alves presented three witnesses, all male traders living in Benguela, who testified in favor of Alves. Dona Ana Teixeira de Sousa was ordered to pay the 1:038$150 réis she had received from Alves.[121] She had at least two enslaved young people working for her, Antonio from Bihé and Francisco from Hanha, a region near the fortress of Caconda.[122]

Colonial records are not necessarily clear on the economic activities of local women but do provide some clues. In the 1840s, for example, Dona Ana Martins de Santa requested a series of licenses to send boats and as many as thirty-four enslaved individuals with fishing nets to Lobito. The judge in Benguela recommended that the regent of the fortress of Catumbela allow them to cross his jurisdiction without any problems.[123] The number of people and boats involved suggests she operated a fishing business, although the official documents never disclosed her economic activities. Many of the lists of taxpayers from the 1860s and 1870s reveal that women operated agricultural businesses in Benguela, Dombe Grande, and Egito, as can be seen in Tables 3.6 through 3.8. A list of taxpayers indicates the importance of slave and land holdings in Dombe Grande from 1857 to 1860, though the size of the landed property or the number of enslaved people owned is not known. In those three towns, forty-two people were identified as having paid or owing taxes to the Crown, including eleven women.[124]

---

[119] ANA, Cod. 7182, fl. 89, May 16, 1828, n. 873; and ANA, Cod. 7182, fl. 99v, August 4, 1828, n. 994.

[120] ANA, Cod. 7182, Cota 23-1-40, Registro de requerimentos – Benguela, 1825 a 1829, fl. 150v, June 19, 1829, requerimento n. 1660.

[121] TCB, "Ação commercial Autor Manuel Ribeiro Alves Réu Ana Teixeira de Sousa, 1856," fl. 17–19v, February 15, 1856.

[122] ABL, Benguela Batismo 1846-1849, fl. 3v–4, August 1, 1846 and June 13, 1847.

[123] ANA, cx. 151, fl. 6v, June 9, 1842; ANA, cx. 151, fl. 8V, June 19, 1843, n. 133; ANA, cx. 151, fl. 164V, August 11, 1845, n. 133.

[124] ANA, cx. 5251, doc. 126 "Relação dos indivíduos coletados neste concelho para pagarem dízimos e impostos de escravos, os quais indivíduos se acham residindo em Benguela, e que nunca tratam de satisfazer suas importâncias," Dombe Grande Aprill 23, 1863.

Table 3.6. *Top ten Benguela taxpayers, 1857–1860*

	Total tax paid
Manuel da Costa Souza	54,830
Luiz Teodoro da Silva	37,950
D. Teresa Ferreira Barruncho	36,700
Mariana Antonio Carvalho	30,800
Domingos Rodrigues Viana	29,940
Paulo Fernandes da Silva	23,190
D. Dionísia Josefa Fernandes	22,500
Maria Barboza	17,300
D. Isabel António da Luz e Abreu	15,250
Francisco António da Glória Júnior	13,950

Source: ANA, cx. 5251, doc. 126

Table 3.7. *Cotton plantations in Egito County, District of Benguela, January 1862–May 1864*

Growers	Plantation	Location	# cotton plants	# enslaved people
António Pereira Barbosa	Sta. Maria	Quilundo	4,000	15
Bastos	Caôllo	Caôllo	3,000	45
	S. Joaquim	Gando	10,000	40
António Joana	St. Justa	Quilundo	60,000	30
	St. António	Quinpunga	3,000	10
Carolina Joana da Silva	Cauhita	Cauhita	3,000	10
	Quinpunga	Quinpunga	5,000	15
José Fernandes do Porto	Quicanjo	Quicanjo	2,000	8
	Quinpunga	Quinpunga	6,000	8
D. Elena Ferreira de Carvalho	S. Germano	Quilundo	50,000	50
António Joaquim Teixeira de Carvalho	S. João	Camballa	50,000	50
Domingos Ribeiro Alves	S. Domingos	Mottetto	200,000	80
Cipriano Manuel Sardinha	Gando	Gando	3,000	12
Roque Maria da Silva	Cauhita	Cauhita	5,000	9
José Cristovão Bastos	Mogollo	Mogollo	3,000	9
António Ribeiro da Silva Guimarães	Caôllo	Caôllo	40,000	39

Source: Aida Freudenthal, *Arimos e Fazendas*, 377

After the 1850s, cotton plantations expanded along the West Central African coast in response to growing demand in Europe and North America for cheap raw materials. The outbreak of the US Civil War in 1861 affected the availability of cotton for European industry and drove

Table 3.8. *Cotton plantations in Dombe Grande, 1864*

Growers	Location	Year established	Number of cotton plants	Number of enslaved people
Tomé Ribeiro Antunes	Mama	1863	41,000	120
Francisco Marcelino Galvão	Tumbo	1864	1,000	40
João Esteves de Araújo	Luaxe	1862	40,000	100
Manuel da Costa Souza	Luaxe	1862	20,000	60
José Joaquim Geraldo do Amaral	Luaxe	1862	20,000	48
D. Teresa Ferreira Torres Barruncho	Luaxe	1862	NA	439
D. Isabel António da Luz Abreu	Dombe	1863	NA	74
João Henriques Teixeira	Mama	1863	12,000	48
D. Maria Dias de Jesus	Dombe	1862	20,000	46
Custódio José de Sousa Veloso	Dombe	1863	16,600	62
José Manuel Ribeiro	Dombe	1863	1,356	50
Francisco Pacheco de Sousa e Silva	Dombe	1864	3,000	30
Casal de Inácio Teixeira Xavier	Equimina	1863	4,000	200

Source: Aida Freudenthal, *Arimos e Fazendas*, 379

cotton prices up. The growing textile industries in Europe searched for new sources of cotton, and Angola was one of the options.[125] Local residents set up plantations relying on enslaved labor diverted into the new legitimate business, as can be seen in Tables 3.7 and 3.8. The expansion of agriculture and the plantation economy transformed the landscape, with environmental changes not yet examined. According to the Governor of Benguela report, in 1868, "The great plains that used to be covered by dense woods and served as refuge for wild animals are now clear of trees, and almost all of the land along the coast is now plantations of cotton and sugarcane."[126]

As can be seen in Table 3.7, among the eleven owners of cotton plantations in Egito were two women, Carolina Joana da Silva and Dona Elena Ferreira de Carvalho, and Table 3.8 shows that in Dombe Grande there were three women-controlled plantations: Dona Teresa Ferreira Torres Barruncho, Isabel António de Luz Abreu, and Dona Maria Dias de Jesus, who also appear in ecclesiastical and judicial records.

[125] For more on cotton production in Angola, see W. O. Henderson, *The Lancashire Cotton Famine 1861-1865* (Manchester: Manchester University Press, 1934), 48–9; Clarence-Smith, *The Third Portuguese Empire, 1825-1975*; Anne Pitcher, "Sowing the Seeds of Failure: Early Portuguese Cotton Cultivation in Angola and Mozambique, 1820–1926," *Journal of Southern African Studies* 17, no. 1 (1991): 43–70.
[126] AHU, Correspondência dos Governadores, Pasta 38, "Relatório do Governo de Benguela referente a 1864-1868," December 21, 1868. (old numeration)

The prospects of economic gain were so attractive that important business owners, such as the versatile Ana Joaquina dos Santos Silva, also invested in plantations in Mossamedes and Novo Redondo, acquiring boats and enslaved individuals to help expand her business.[127]

Conclusion

In 1878, the captain of Dombe Grande warned the governor of Benguela that the rush to register land in people's names would lead to conflict. The captain stated that Floriano José Mendes da Conceição was "bragging that he is connected to the Mendes Machado family from Ambaca, and that he knows the laws, which will favor him to continue stealing as he has been doing for a long time. ... Floriano claims to have documents, but these are simple pieces of paper with shallow requests making vague use of the articles from the penal code." The captain continued that while serving in the administration Floriano took advantage of his position to acquire a plot of land for his daughter Florinda, who was a minor. Floriano argued that wasteland surrounded the plot, which allowed him to occupy a larger territory than that originally assigned to his daughter. The captain of Dombe Grande concluded, "I am convinced that this will never be solved [and will affect] the peaceful interaction with the people who inhabit this region."[128] This case makes it clear that the first settlers were disregarded as legitimate occupiers by the simple presence of a piece of paper and the statement that their lands were wastelands. Indeed, as Conceição stated, those who knew the laws and had social connections took advantage of the system at the expense of the local inhabitants, who experienced dispossession and exclusion.

Colonial courts emerged as an alternative for West Central African subjects who failed to achieve their goals in local courts controlled by African rulers. As a result, the colonial court became a site of conflict over rights and jurisdiction between Portuguese and soba authorities. The colonial court also became the space to settle civil cases related to credit and debt that went beyond the jurisdiction of the Portuguese colonial state. Colonial subjects went to court to verify their legitimacy as property holders. While in some instances African rulers lost their land when it was labeled as unproductive or unoccupied, in other cases

<hr/>

[127] ANA, Cod. 326, fl. 63, November 19, 1848; and ANA, Cod. 326, fl. 82v, July 9, 1849. For more on Dona Ana Joaquina dos Santos Silva, see Oliveira, *Slave Trade and Abolition.*, 61–74 and 90–101.

[128] ANA, cx. 3340, Dombe Grande, maço 3, Concelho do Dombe Grande, Correspondência Expedida, January 1, 1878–October 1, 1878, Letter Exchange between Manoel Jose da Silva, captain of Dombe Grande and Secretario do governo de Benguela, February 12, 1878.

colonizers and colonized fought over the best solution for implementing the colonial civilizing views.

The rush to create paper trails to legitimize ownership led to the expansion of the colonial archives, containing wills, postmortem inventories, land registers, deeds, tax collections, and legal disputes. These historical documents operated as ownership evidence and reveal the changes associated with governance and property claims during the nineteenth century. Local rulers and residents embraced written evidence to protect their interests, which resulted in the creation of new traditions and the consolidation of written evidence as the only valid and legitimate way to prove property rights. West Central Africans made use of multiple strategies to protect and pursue their rights, involving customary rights and the use of colonial law and a system of property recognition. The establishment of written records and venues for petition, such as courts, allowed colonial subjects to make use of colonial apparatus to strategically survive the new legal order and claim their rights.

The colonial archives also reveal that property claims were a gendered process, and men and women employed different strategies to protect their rights. The written documents and courts allowed African women to bypass the authority of male elders or local rulers and settle disputes in a space that would favor them. The recognition of women's right to property and inheritance in the Portuguese legal code created the space for African women to make ownership claims and accumulate assets. West Central African women were owners of human beings, goods, and real estate, but they also operated as moneylenders, debt collectors, and business owners. They were more than business partners to husbands, partners, or fathers; they administered businesses, managed farms and shops, and had active economic roles.

As a technique, writing created new spaces of power and new ways to insert colonized people into history. The resourcefulness of different individuals in adapting to the writing culture and turning it to their own ends makes the persistent commodification of West Central Africans, which will be examined in Chapters 4 and 5, more distressing. It is important to realize that not every West Central African had the opportunity to use the colonial bureaucracy and make petitions, yet the historical evidence available discloses how some contested and negotiated ownership rights. The documents show how colonial violence and dispossession operated and how certain groups of people were favored. West Central Africans, both rulers and commoners, addressed questions of dispossession and new claims, in many ways employing colonial tools to advance their claims and establish new rights. Those expelled from their lands remain silent in documentation, reinforcing their dispossession from history as well as from their land.

4   Commodification of Human Beings

By the early nineteenth century, control over people's labor was well established in West Central Africa and linked to land access and rights. Societies in the region included highly centralized and hierarchical societies, such as the states of Kongo, Matamba, and Bihé; pastoralist groups, such as the Ndombe and Kilengues; and collectors (gathering-hunting groups), such as the !Khu and Kwadi, characterized by smaller population and transhumance. The range of political and economic organizations challenge any simplistic generalization yet reveal the complexities of this region and its populations. Several of these groups clashed over resources and territories and incorporated defeated individuals and refugees fleeing war and famine into their societies into servile status. Such newcomers were excluded from a variety of rights, including access to land.

For impoverished men, women, and children who lived in that region, the nineteenth century was not a time of freedom and expansion of rights, but quite the opposite. Slavery remained a legal institution in Portuguese overseas territories until 1878, with enslaved people performing most of the productive tasks in urban towns and new plantations installed along the coast. Free people bought and sold individuals who were responsible for a variety of tasks in urban and rural spaces, in areas controlled by local sobas or by the Portuguese colonial administration. Captive labor generated profit and social prestige, enriching others through dispossession and exploitation.

Many enslaved people legally contested their bondage, using colonial courts to seek and sometimes secure their freedom. Gender mattered in slavery and in achieving freedom. Similar to slave societies in the Americas, manumission and freedom contracts were negotiated, always privileging the interests and profits of owners. Men and women employed different strategies and had different outcomes. Mostly, formerly enslaved people financially compensated their former captors, perpetuating inequality, and dispossession. The paths to freedom were never easy, genderless, and trouble free. Alongside the expansion of slavery during the nineteenth century, other mechanisms of exercising control over financial transactions and labor expanded, such as pawnship and *panyarring* or seizing people when debts were not repaid. Both mechanisms protected the interests and investment of owners at the expense of poor people in search of security and access to resources. Free dependents, in most cases destitute people, were held as collateral, or pawns, for goods or services. Women and girls faced a higher threat to their status as pawns, and the inability of their relatives and hosts to repay debts resulted in their enslavement. As will be examined later, pawnship was linked to the control of trade and markets and the need to generate labor, including farming output. The abolition of slavery facilitated the spread of pawnship as a form of mobilizing unfree labor, with young women and junior members of society absorbed into creditors' households. In West Central African and colonial courts, debts were serious business, intimately related to the protection of property. If courts failed to address debt payments, money lenders or traders resorted to panyarring. The labor of enslaved individuals, as well as those in liminal situations, such as pawns, allowed the free population, elite members or not, to enjoy relative comfort and leisure, and to maintain social hierarchies that privileged control over labor and the commodification of people, land, and goods. The debates about property and commodification of land during the nineteenth century examined in the earlier chapters also expanded to the arbitration of individuals treated as property.

There is an ongoing debate among scholars about the nature of slavery in African societies. While some argue that slavery within Africa was milder and less violent than in the Americas because it often held the possibility of upward social mobility, recent scholarship has emphasized the role of violence, exclusion, and their lasting legacies, stressing how enslaved individuals and their descendants continued to be alienated from political and social rights.[1] By the nineteenth century, slavery in

---

[1] Martin A. Klein, "Studying the History of Those Who Would Rather Forget: Oral History and the Experience of Slavery," *History in Africa* 16 (1989): 209–17; Elisabeth McMahon, *Slavery and Emancipation in Islamic East Africa: From Honor to Respectability* (New York: Cambridge University Press, 2013); Alice Bellagamba, Sandra E. Greene, and Martin A. Klein, eds., *African Voices on Slavery and the Slave Trade* (New York: Cambridge University Press, 2013); George Michael La Rue, "Zeinab from Darfur: An Enslaved Woman and Her Self-Presentation in Egypt and the Sudan," in *African Voices of Slavery and the Slave Trade*, ed. Alice Bellagamba, Martin A. Klein, and Sandra E. Greene (New York: Cambridge University Press, 2013); Martin A. Klein, "African Traditions of Servitude and the Evolution of African Society," *Ab Imperio* 2014, no. 2 (2014): 27–45; Sandra E. Greene, *Slave Owners of West Africa: Decision Making in the Age of Abolition* (Bloomington: Indiana University Press, 2017) and Marie Rodet, "Escaping Slavery and Building Diasporic Communities in French Soudan and Senegal, ca 1880–1940," *The International Journal of African Historical Studies* 48, 2 (2015), 363–386.

West Central Africa, both within the colonial centers and the *sobados*, had been profoundly transformed by three centuries of interaction with the Atlantic World. The institution of slavery along the coast and in the interior went through changes and adaptation in part because of local contexts, but also due to the pressure and nature of the Atlantic market. Sobas and their subjects did not hold to a static precolonial form of slavery, profoundly different from the capitalistic and racialized American version. Capture, debt bondage, and pawnship had changed and expanded in response to the growing demand for enslaved human beings, particularly in the region that exported the largest number of enslaved Africans to the Atlantic World.[2]

This chapter examines the commodification of people in West Central Africa and the expansion of ownership over human beings during the nineteenth century. The records available in the colonial archive expose the extent of people's commodification during the nineteenth century. The brutality of property claims over human beings is unambiguous in inventories, registers, bills of sale, and waybills, paper documents created to deny humanity and protect the interest of owners. These documents continue to reproduce the violence and legal and extra-legal exclusion that enslaved individuals experienced in the past by limiting their historical existence to records that categorized them solely as commodities. The records were created to facilitate control of property, and their survival discloses the commitment to register people's exclusion and dispossession. One example is the case of Engrácia, a nine-year-old enslaved girl, who was included in a travel registry when she was taken on a small two-masted boat (*sumaca*) from Luanda to Benguela in the company of her owner, Romana Antónia Zurarte. Zurarte was a Black woman and slave owner, who enjoyed the freedom to travel between two colonial ports and therefore could compel Engrácia to accompany her, an act that reinforced her proprietorship and rights.[3] The existence of the travel registry suggests that free and enslaved people needed colonial authorization to move between colonial centers. It also alludes to the

---

[2] For the debate over the nature of slavery in Angola, see Isabel de Castro Henriques, *Percursos da Modernidade em Angola: dinâmicas comerciais e transformações sociais no século XIX* (Lisbon: Instituto de Investigação Científica Tropical, 1997); W. G. Clarence-Smith, "Slavery in Coastal Southern Angola, 1875-1913," *Journal of Southern African Studies* 2, no. 2 (1976): 214–23; Joseph C. Miller, "The Paradoxes of Impoverishment in the Atlantic Zone," in *History of Central Africa*, ed. David Birmingham and Phyllis Martin, vols. 1, 2. (London: Longman, 1983), 118–59; John Thornton, "The Slave Trade in Eighteenth Century Angola: Effects of Demographic Structure," *Canadian Journal of African Studies* 14, no. 3 (1980): 417–27.

[3] Arquivo Nacional de Angola (hereinafter ANA), Codice (Cod.) 277, C-16-1, fl. 116v, March 19, 1814.

fact that colonial subjects carried papers stating their legal status, in case they needed to prove their freedom or that they had authorization to travel.

While Portuguese colonial forces moved freely, West Central Africans, enslaved or free, had to request authorization to travel on their own (occupied) land. The colonial state was invested in controlling movements and generating documents to assist control over colonized people. In the case of enslaved people, paper documents proved ownership and dependency. For example, in the mid-1810s, two women arrived in Benguela to work in the local hospital. They had been convicted of crimes in Luanda, and they were sentenced to forced labor at Benguela's hospital. Both traveled with permits (*guias*), which authorized their movement and recognized their legal status. Joaquina Fernandes was identified as a free woman while Silvana was an enslaved woman. Although both faced control over their travel, Silvana's documents stressed her bondage and the fact that she belonged to somebody else.[4] These practices of movement control continued well into the twentieth century in Southern Africa, with perhaps the South Africa Pass Law the most known case, although labor mobility was carefully controlled in other colonial spaces.[5]

Owning People, Accumulating Wealth

Ownership over human beings was common and widespread in West Central Africa since early contacts with Europeans, revealing that wealth in things, such as land, and wealth in people were connected and part of the same system that valued social and economic stratification. When the Portuguese arrived in the Kingdom of Kongo in the fifteenth century, they encountered captives of war. Upon contact with the Ndongo and Matamba, Portuguese sources also indicated the presence of enslaved people, mainly war captives, foreigners, and outlaws.[6] Political and

---

[4] ANA, Cod. 323, D – N- 6, fl. 121v, "From Governor of Angola, José de Oliveira Barbosa, to Governador de Benguela, Senhor de Alvelos Leiria," February 18, 1815. For more on the registers and the commodification of Black bodies, see Johnson, "Markup Bodies"; Morgan, "Archives and Histories of Racial Capitalism."

[5] Clifton Crais, *Poverty, War, and Violence in South Africa* (New York: Cambridge University Press, 2011), 141–47; Zachary Kagan Guthrie, *Labor, Mobility, and Colonial Rule in Central Mozambique, 1940-1965* (Charlottesville: University of Virginia Press, 2018); Zachary Kagan Guthrie, "Introduction: Histories of Mobility, Histories of Labor, Histories of Africa," *African Economic History* 44, no. 1 (2016): 1–17.

[6] Linda M. Heywood, "Slavery and Its Transformation in the Kingdom of Kongo: 1491–1800," *The Journal of African History* 50, no. 1 (2009): 1–22; John K. Thornton, *A Cultural History of the Atlantic World, 1250-1820* (New York: Cambridge University

territorial disputes between West Central African rulers often led to war and resulted in the enslavement of free people. Enslavement and slavery were legal in the Portuguese empire dating back to the Papal Bull *Dum Diversas* (1452), which sanctioned attacks led by the Catholic Portuguese kingdom against heathens, Saracens, and enemies of Christ. *Dum Diversas* and later *Romanus Pontifex* (1455) recognized the right of the Portuguese Crown and its agents to enslave its enemies, seize their possessions, and occupy their lands. Thus, conquest and slavery acted hand in hand.[7] Upon arriving in West Central Africa, Portuguese agents acquired slave individuals from Kongo merchants and nobles. They also had an active role in kidnapping and enslaving free people.[8] While some enslaved individuals were exported into the transatlantic slave trade, others remained in captivity in Luanda, Benguela, the inland colonial centers, and African states. Colonial officers, traders, local elites, and others with the ability to acquire an enslaved person did so, investing in acquiring captives and putting them to work in private or public spaces, exploiting their labor while advancing their own social standing. Despite the nineteenth-century expansion of abolitionist movements that brought increasing pressure to end the slave trade, slavery expanded in West Central Africa. It was a time when slavery intensified across the African continent, in part due to the expansion of commercial agriculture after the 1830s.[9]

Press, 2012), 183–85 and 209–10; Linda M. Heywood, *Njinga of Angola: Africa's Warrior Queen* (Cambridge, MA: Harvard University Press, 2017), 11–13.

[7] A. J. R. Russell-Wood, "Iberian Expansion and the Issue of Black Slavery: Changing Portuguese Attitudes, 1440-1770," *The American Historical Review* 83, no. 1 (1978): 16–42; Mariana P. Candido, "O limite tênue entre a liberdade e escravidão em Benguela durante a era do comércio transatlântico," *Afro-Ásia* 47 (2013): 251; Bárbara Direito, "African Access to Land in Early Twentieth Century Portuguese Colonial Thought," in *Property Rights, Land and Territory in the European Overseas Empires*, ed. José Vicente Serrão et al. (Lisbon: CEHC-IUL, 2014), 256–63.

[8] Roquinaldo Ferreira, "Slaving and Resistance to Slaving in West Central Africa," in *The Cambridge World History of Slavery*, ed. David Eltis and Stanley L. Engerman, vol. 3 (Cambridge: Cambridge University Press, 2011), 111–31; Mariana P. Candido, *An African Slaving Port and the Atlantic World: Benguela and Its Hinterland* (New York: Cambridge University Press, 2013), 191–227.

[9] Paul E. Lovejoy, *Transformations in Slavery* (New York: Cambridge University Press, 2000); Paul E. Lovejoy, *Jihād in West Africa during the Age of Revolutions* (Athens, OH: Ohio University Press, 2016); Gareth Austin, *Labour, Land, and Capital in Ghana: From Slavery to Free Labour in Asante, 1807-1956* (Rochester, NY: University of Rochester Press, 2005); Robin Law, ed., *From Slave Trade to "Legitimate" Commerce: The Commercial Transition in Nineteenth-Century West Africa* (Cambridge: Cambridge University Press, 1995); Robin Law, Suzanne Schwarz, and Silke Strickrodt, "Introduction," in *Commercial Agriculture, the Slave Trade and Slavery in Atlantic Africa*, ed. Robin Law, Suzanne Schwarz, and Silke Strickrodt (Woodbridge: James Currey,

Slavery became central for the organization and functioning of local economies, and enslaved men and women performed most of the productive tasks, from cultivating, preparing, and selling food to offering services in the colonial towns, such as shoemakers, washers, and sailors, as well as domestic tasks associated with housekeeping and tending children. Bondage was also widespread within local states, with elite and nonelite members securing unfree dependents to increase production and prestige.[10] In the process, captives became commodified; they were treated as property who belonged to someone and they could be sold and bought. While the primary sources do not privilege the perspective of the enslaved individuals, this chapter tries to overcome the limitations of the historical evidence and attempts to avoid replicating the commodification of people. In many ways, enslaved individuals tend to be erased from West Central African histories, as if captivity and bondage only happened in the Americas. Thus, focusing on people considered as property in West Central Africa is an effort to overcome archival numbness and mischaracterizations that deny the role and violence of slavery within African societies. Writing about the commodification of men,

2013), 1–27; Roquinaldo Amaral Ferreira, "Agricultural Enterprise and Unfree Labour in Nineteenth Century Angola," in *Commercial Agriculture, the Slave Trade and Slavery in Atlantic Africa*, ed. Robin Law, Suzanne Schwarz, and Silke Strickrodt (Woodbridge: James Currey, 2013), 225–42; Samuël Coghe, "The Problem of Freedom in a Mid Nineteenth-Century Atlantic Slave Society: The Liberated Africans of the Anglo-Portuguese Mixed Commission in Luanda (1844–1870)," *Slavery & Abolition* 33, no. 3 (2012): 479–500. For scholars who emphasize the nineteenth century as an age of freedom, see Janet L. Polasky, *Revolutions without Borders: The Call to Liberty in the Atlantic World* (New Haven: Yale University Press, 2015).

[10] Joseph C. Miller, "Imbangala Lineage Slavery," in *Slavery in Africa: Historical and Anthropological Perspectives*, ed. Suzann Miers and Igor Kopytoff (Madison: University of Wisconsin Press, 1977), 205–33; Linda M Heywood, "Slavery and Forced Labor in the Changing Political Economy of Central Angola, 1850-1949," in *The End of Slavery in Africa*, ed. Suzanne Miers and Richard Roberts (Madison: University of Wisconsin Press, 1988), 415–35; Joseph C. Miller, "Women as Slaves and Owners of Slaves. Experiences from Africa, the Indian Ocean World, and the Early Atlantic," in *Women and Slavery.*, ed. Gwyn Campbell, Suzanne Miers, and Joseph C. Miller, vol. 1, 2 vols. (Athens, OH: Ohio University Press, 2007), 1–40; Roquinaldo Ferreira, "Escravidão e revoltas de escravos em Angola (1830-1860)," *Afro-Ásia* 21–22 (1998): 9–44; Beatrix Heintze, *Angola nos séculos XVI e XVII. Estudo sobre fontes, métodos e história* (Luanda: Kilombelombe, 2007); Vanessa S. Oliveira, "Trabalho escravo e ocupações urbanas em Luanda na segunda metade do século XIX," in *Em torno de Angola. Narrativas, identidades e conexões atlânticas* (São Paulo: Intermeios, 2014), 265–67; Vanessa S. Oliveira, "Notas preliminares sobre punição de escravos em Luanda (século XIX)," in *O colonialismo português - novos rumos da historiografia dos PALOP*, ed. Ana Cristina Roque and Maria Manuel Torrão (Porto: Húmuss, 2013), 155–76; Mariana P. Candido, "Concubinage and Slavery in Benguela, c. 1750-1850," in *Slavery in Africa and the Caribbean: A History of Enslavement and Identity Since the Eighteenth Century*, ed. Olatunji Ojo and Nadine Hunt (London: I.B.Tauris, 2012), 65–84.

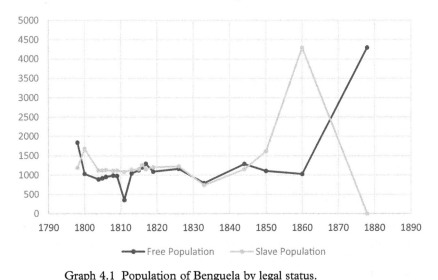

Graph 4.1 Population of Benguela by legal status.
Source: AHU, Angola, 1 sec., cx. 88, d. 46; ANA, Cod. 442, fl 161v-162; AHU, Angola, 1 sec., cx. 113, d. 6; AHU, Angola, 1 sec., cx. 116, d. 87; AHU, Angola, 1 sec., cx. 118, d. 21; AHU, Angola, 1 sec., cx. 120 d. 21; AHU, Angola, 1 sec., cx. 121, d. 32; AHU, Angola, 1 sec, cx, 124, d. 8; AHU, Angola, 1 sec., cx. 127, d. 59; AHU, Angola, 1 sec., cx. 131 d. 45; AHU, Angola, 1 sec, cx 133, d. 32; AHU, Angola, 1 sec., cx. 136, d. 19; AHU, Angola, 1 sec., cx. 138, d. 1; AHU, Angola, 1 sec., cx 156 d. 16; AHU, Angola, 1 sec., cx, 176, d. 17; Lopes de Lima, p. 4-A; *Almanak estatístico da província de Angola*, p. 9; ANA, cx 5568; AHU, Pasta 48.

women, and children in West Central Africa is an opportunity to address exclusion, silences, and the gendered nature of narratives about the past and reflect on its reverberations into our present.[11]

For most of the nineteenth century, enslaved people represented half or more of Benguela's population. The number totaled around 1,118 enslaved individuals in 1804 and reached its height in 1860 when around 4,300 people were in captivity, after the official ban of slave exports and the closure of the Brazilian market (see Graph 4.1).

[11] Marisa J. Fuentes, *Dispossessed Lives: Enslaved Women, Violence, and the Archive* (Philadelphia, PA: University of Pennsylvania Press, 2016); Jennifer L. Morgan, "Archives and Histories of Racial Capitalism. An Afterword," *Social Text* 33, no. 4 (2015): 153–61; Jessica Marie Johnson, "Markup Bodies: Black [Life] Studies and Slavery [Death] Studies at the Digital Crossroads," *Social Text* 36, no. 4 (2018): 57–79; Lorelle Semley, "Writing the History of the Trans-African Woman in the Revolutionary French Atlantic," in *African Women in the Atlantic World. Property, Vulnerability and Mobility, 1680-1880*, ed. Mariana P. Candido and Adam Jones (Woodbridge: James Currey, 2019), 191–215.

The expansion of written culture in the nineteenth century led to the registration of people's residency, skills, and movements. These records facilitated control of human property and replicated the vocabulary used by slave owners to patrol and surveil their possessions. Enslaved people were carefully observed and identified by gender, skills, and bodily features that could facilitate their recognition or economic value. These documents indicate that women, men, and children were commercialized in markets, public auctions, taverns, and along the docks, despite the lack of a centralized system of human property registrations. The presence of enslaved women, men, and children was listed in population enumerations, slave registers, official correspondence, and travel accounts. In all these documents, their oppression and legal status were reinforced even in the case of those, such as Francisco, who had an important skill. Francisco was a skilled blacksmith who provided a key service to the colonial state. Yet, his existence in Benguela in 1811 is associated with the fact that he belonged to Dona Maria Domingos de Barros and did not enjoy freedom.[12]

In 1837, in a case that emphasizes a woman's skills and her physical shape, the thin Black woman Dorotéa disappeared from Benguela. Her owner, José Rodrigues Guimarães, a lieutenant in the Benguela army, suspected Dorotéa had fled toward Novo Redondo, which may indicate she was originally from there. Dorotéa was one of several captives of his and had valuable medical skills, having tended one of Guimarães's wounds after an accident. After nine years of trying to locate her without any luck, Guimarães decided to report her disappearance. In fact, a few days after the announcement, Guimarães heard that Dorotéa had settled in Novo Redondo, north of Benguela, where she had been living as a merchant who traveled to inland markets.[13] It was through the public announcement of Dorotéa's flight, along with the collaboration of other slave owners, that her former owner was able to identify her.

Colonial efforts to control human property continued in the second half of the nineteenth century. In the 1850s, the *Registro de Escravos* (Slave Register) was compiled to gather information on the slave population, and the data found there provides clues on the accumulation of human property. According to a decree of December 14,1854, slave

---

[12] ANA, Cod. 445, fl. 123v, February 1, 1812.

[13] ANA, Cod. 166, B-14-2., fl. 133v, "From Governor of Angola Secretary to Governor of Benguela, João de Roboredo," April 22, 1846, and July 17, 1846; and AHA, Cod. 326, "From Commander of Quicembo to Governor of Benguela, João de Roboredo," fl. 16, April 21, 1847. See also José C. Curto, "Resistência à escravidão na África: O caso dos escravos fugitivos recapturados em Angola, 1846-1876, " *Afro-Ásia*, no. 33 (2005): 67–86; Ferreira, "Slave Flights."

owners had to register their slaves within thirty days. Those who failed had to free their captives, revealing how compliance with registration recognized ownership rights. One of the surviving slave registers lists 2,588 individuals in bondage living in Benguela in 1859 (Table 4.2).[14] Slave owners brought 1,382 enslaved women and 1,199 enslaved men to be registered, providing much information about their age, occupation, and place of origin. The register shows the heterogeneity of the Benguela enslaved population, with people coming from the coastal region, nearby places, and *sobados* in the highlands.[15] The register also exposes the activities enslaved women and men performed in Benguela. Out of the fifty people listed as farmers in the slave register, forty-two were women. The remaining eight were men from regions other than Benguela. Among the individuals registered, there were sailors, shoemakers, cooks, carpenters, stonemasons, and seamstresses, such as Rufina, Damásia, Lusia, Leonor, Delfina, and Feliciana, who were listed as under sixteen years old and belonging to a single owner, Dona Isabel Rodrigues da Costa.

Outside Benguela, in inland *presídios* such as Caconda, the enslaved population was also enumerated and identified (see Table 4.3). In 1854, colonial officers carefully recorded the presence of 568 enslaved people and identified seventy-one slave owners. Most of the slave owners (fifty-four people) owned fewer than ten captives, while fifteen of Caconda's slave owners had more than ten enslaved people, as can be seen in Table 4.3. One of these slave-owning Caconda residents was Tomé Ribeiro de Antunes. In the 1860s, Antunes advanced goods and captives to recent Portuguese arrivals in West Central Africa, with business and commercial partners in Luanda, Dombe Grande, Benguela, Catumbela, and Mossamedes.[16]

Slave registries had the goal of identifying and locating enslaved women, men, and children in a unique and definite way in order to protect the interests of owners as well as to enhance colonial governability. The process of aggregating data coincided with the expansion of colonial control, which reinforced the commodification of people and celebrated control and ownership. However, in some instances, careful identification failed, suggesting the inability of the colonial state to

[14] ANA, Cod. 3160, "Registro de Escravos (Benguela), 1859. For the regulation, see ANA, Cod. 444, fl. 185v-186, April 5, 1849; and *A Abolição da Escravatura*, 35–36. For an analysis of the Luanda's slave register, see Coghe, "Problem of Freedom"; Oliveira, "Notas preliminares."

[15] This document has been analyzed in detail in Candido, *Fronteras de Esclavización*, 206–22.

[16] ANA, Cod. 3159, and TCB, "Ação comercial Tomé Ribeiro Antunes vs João Rodrigues Teixeira," January 9, 1867.

Table 4.2. *Benguela slave ownership, 1859*

Slave owners	Total
Bento Pacheco dos Santos	122
Joaquim Luis Bastos	84
D. Ana Muniz de Santana	78
Dionísia Josefa Fernandes	74
Joaquim Correa da Conceição	55
José Vieira da Silva	52
D. Isabel Rodrigues da Costa	40
António Gomes Vidal César	35
Jácomo Vitor	32
Félix José Ferreira Campos	31
Feliciana Meneses de Santana	31
José António Campina	30
António da Costa Covelo	30
D. Ana Moniz de Santana	29
João Mateus da Costa	29
Vitória de Moura Soares	27
Rosa Francisca Joanes	27
José Joaquim da Silva	25
Maria Marcelina Fernandes	23
Bernardo Ferreira Pinheiro	23
Florinda Rodrigues da Costa	22
Francisco Geraldo Ferreira de Sousa Guimarães	22
Gertudes Maria da Conceição	21
D. Maria de Jesus do Nascimento Amado	21
Manoel José Rebelo de Matos	20
Luis António de Sousa Monteiro	20
José Dias da Silva	20

Source: ANA, Cod. 3160 "Registro de Escravos, Benguela," 1859

manage vast territories. In the Caconda slave register, for example, only one enslaved person was listed with a skill. Francisca was a seamstress. Although the remaining 567 enslaved people did not have skills recorded, they probably worked in the gardens and houses, performing a variety of tasks from cleaning, pounding grain, tending animals, and taking care of children to manufacturing baskets, clothes, or leather products, which clearly required specialization. The presence of specific skills is seen in the case of two enslaved women, Hucamba and Engrácia, who belonged to Joana Rodrigues da Costa, a Caconda resident who manufactured leather goods such as saddles.[17] It is likely that her slaves

---

[17] TCB, "Autos cíveis do inventario de Joana Rodrigues da Costa," April 12, 1850, fl. 15v. For more on colonialism, paper records, and property control, see Bhavani Raman,

Table 4.3. *Slave owners in Caconda, 1854*

Slave owners	Total
Estevão Fernandes da Silva	79
Aurélio José Antonio	68
Maria Ferreira da Silva	61
José Lopes Chaves	36
Luis Batista Fonseca	32
Martinho José Lopes Cordeiro	17
Rita da Conceição	17
Luis Gonzaga Cordeiro	17
Rita Ferreira Torres	16
Félix Pinto da Silveira	14
Antonio Gomes Pereira	14
Severino Coelho Santiago	14
João Pinto	13
Tomé Ribeiro de Antunes	10
Antónia José Coelho de Sousa	10

Source: ANA, Cod. 3159 "Registro de Escravos, Caconda," 1854

were performing the actual leather-working. Knowledge and skills increased the economic and social value of enslaved people, benefiting people who controlled their labor and bodies. It is puzzling that notaries and owners left off valuable information from the registries.

Slavery remained alive in the 1860s and 1870s when it was being abolished elsewhere in the Atlantic World, with Cuba and Brazil as the last bastions of slavery in the Americas well into the 1880s. In Luanda and Benguela, ownership of human beings expanded in the second half of the nineteenth century, with residents placing announcements in the *Boletim Oficial do Governo Geral de Angola,* the official gazette, offering or requesting the services of enslaved people. For example, in 1864, Eugénio Felipe Tomas Massi was interested in hiring a "young black woman with good appearance, able to wash clothes."[18] Queirós

"The Duplicity of Paper: Counterfeit, Discretion, and Bureaucratic Authority in Early Colonial Madras," *Comparative Studies in Society & History* 54, no. 2 (2012): 229–50; James C. Scott, John Tehranian, and Jeremy Mathias, "The Production of Legal Identities Proper to States: The Case of the Permanent Family Surname," *Comparative Studies in Society and History* 44, no. 1 (2002): 4–44; Crais, *Poverty, War, and Violence in South Africa*, 133–35.

[18] Boletim Oficial do Governo Geral da Província de Angola (hereinafter, BOGGPA), 1864, n. 39, September 14, 1864, p. 342.

announced the sale of two registered slaves, a bad stonemason, and a barber/bleeder who specialized in treating ulcers.[19] Some enslaved people were also advertised by their language skills, such as a registered enslaved cook, around eighteen to twenty years old, who spoke Portuguese well.[20] These announcements stress good behavior and the ability to wash, sew, and iron without any regard for captives' humanity.[21] Rather than a system that recognized personhood and offered social and economic mobility to former captives, slavery in West Central Africa was based on fear and violence. Along the coast and inland, predatory commercial exchanges resulted in commodification of human beings, who could be acquired for a relatively small amount of money. Yet traders complained about the increased value of enslaved individuals. According to the trader António Ferreira da Silva Porto, an *upica*, a slave in Umbundu, was exchanged for a cow or sixty pieces of mixed textiles in 1860. He claimed that earlier in the nineteenth century, captives had lower value, since an entire family could be acquired with this same quantity and quality of goods.[22]

Aligned with the expansion of paper culture, the colonial state instituted the keeping of records to monitor the movement of colonial subjects and, in the process, facilitated policing enslaved people in and around the colonial territories. Free West Central Africans relied on the colonial state to prove and assert ownership of others. They also relied on the colonial state to patrol and protect their property and interests. In 1826, for example, Manuel de Barros e Cunha, requested the help of the Quilengues administrators in capturing nine of his captives.[23] His slaves had fled, and Barros da Cunha was unable to retrieve them; thus, he requested colonial support. In fact, the colonial archives

[19] BOGGPA, 1864, n. 39, September 14, 1864, p. 343.
[20] BOGGPA, 1866, n. 17, April 28, 1866, p. 115.
[21] BOGGPA, 1866, n. 3, January 20, 1866, p. 16; 1866, n. 43; October 27, 1866, p. 345; 1870, n. 19' May 7, 1870, p. 307.
[22] Biblioteca da Sociedade de Geografia de Luanda (hereinafter, BSGL), Res – 2-C-7 – Silva Porto, "Notas para retocar a minha obra logo que as circunstâncias permitam," April 1, 1866, fl. 64–69, "Escravidão." For studies that underestimate the violence and overestimate social integration of slavery in African societies, see Suzanne Miers and Igor Kopytoff, eds., "African Slavery as an Institution of Marginality" (Madison: University of Wisconsin Press, 1977), 1–78; Basil Davidson, "Slaves or Captives? Some Notes on Fantasy and Fact," in *Slavery and Muslim Society in Africa: The Institution in Saharan and Sudanic Africa, and the Trans-Saharan Trade*, ed. Allan George Barnard Fisher (C. Hurst, 1970), 54–73; Jan Vansina, *Paths in the Rainforests: Toward a History of Political Tradition in Equatorial Africa* (Madison: University of Wisconsin Press, 1990).
[23] ANA, Cod. 7182, fl. 5, July 29, 1826, n. 444. For the debate on the duties and responsibilities of colonial officers, see Carlos Couto, *Os capitães-mores em Angola no século XVIII* (Luanda: Instituto de Investigação Científica de Angola, 1972), 323–28. For efforts of movement and sovereignty control in other African contexts, see Clifton

are filled with petitions of West Central African men and women, who owned people, and requested colonial support to locate and recapture their human property.

One year after Barros da Cunha's petition, the Benguela resident Marcela Joaquina requested help in locating Fita, one of the enslaved women in her house. Fita had fled in 1827 and had been seen living in Dombe Grande, not far from Benguela, under the protection of soba António Muene Canha. Unable to challenge Muene Canha's power, Marcela Joaquina appealed to the colonial state for help in recuperating Fita.[24] The petitions do not provide information on how and when these captives were acquired or even their place of destiny, which was probably unknown. Petitions expose that free West Central Africans, wealthy or not, accumulated slaves and profit from their labor in a variety of economic activities. These owners also expected the colonial state to patrol the movement of their property and acted as a private security, protecting individual ownership.[25]

This control, however, had to be carefully exercised in order to avoid the mistaken apprehension of property, which could hurt the interests of slave owners. To navigate the thin line between control and recognition of ownership rights, colonial subjects filled out notifications to protect their property. Afraid that colonial authorities would seize her captives while in transit, Dona Ana Martins de Santana requested authorization to send twenty-five of her enslaved fishermen to Lobito in the 1840s. The colonial authority issued a one-month travel pass that allowed the twenty-five captives to travel between Benguela and Lobito to carry out "business," a vague term that could mean many things, yet in this context might apply exclusively to the business of working for their slavers. The authorization stressed that the movement of these twenty-five enslaved men should not be confused with any practice of illegal slave trading, since they would work solely for Dona Ana Martins de Santana's fishing business, emphasizing once more, Santana's control over their labor, movements, and bodies.[26] A few years later, in 1848, Carolina, a free Black woman, stated her plans to travel from Quicembo, near old

Crais, "Custom and the Politics of Sovereignty in South Africa," *Journal of Social History* 39, no. 3 (2006): 721–40.

[24] ANA, Cod. 7182, fl. 41v, March 13, 1827, n. 869.

[25] For similar cases in West Central Africa, see Oliveira, "Trabalho escravo"; Vanessa S. Oliveira, *Slave Trade and Abolition. Gender, Commerce and Economic Transition in Luanda* (Madison: University of Wisconsin Press, 2021); Ferreira, "Slavery and the Social and Cultural Landscape of Luanda."

[26] ANA, cx. 151, "Secretaria Geral do Governo de Benguela. Fragmento de códices, correspondência de 1843 a 1846," fl. 8V, June 19, 1842, n. 133.

Benguela, to Luanda with her female slave, Joaquina. Carolina's concern was to protect her free status while maintaining Joaquina in captivity. As in other slave societies, free people of color worked hard to differentiate themselves from enslaved people and exercised their privileges as free people.[27] In the process, they exerted ownership over others and perpetuated inequalities. Their status as free people relied on their ability to exploit the labor of other individuals who were commodified.

Written documents reveal the processes of commodification, where women and men were considered someone else's property, who could be legally acquired, exploited, or exchanged. In West Central Africa, slaves were property whose worth was measured in age, skill, and gender and whose economic value was openly discussed. In 1827, Diogo Vieira de Lima requested a written document to attest that a young girl, Teodora, belonged to him. Teodora was the daughter of a freed Black woman, Maria Luz; however, Vieira de Lima claimed ownership over Teodora since she was born while her mother belonged to him, before she was able to buy her own freedom.[28] With a legal document that recognized his rights as a slave owner, Vieira de Lima could sell Teodora, disregarding the opinion and wishes of Teodora's mother. Family separation was a theme that dominated the accounts of British abolitionists, yet slave owners in Angola do not seem to have shared the same concerns. As this case indicates, written records protected property owners and their assertion of ownership at the expense of family bonds. Written documents, such as Vieira de Lima's statement, solidified people's legal status and established ownership.

As property, enslaved people could be transferred from one owner to another. In 1825, Manuel João Matias requested the prompt delivery of the three male captives he had inherited.[29] Unable to solve this

---

[27] ANA, Cod. 326, fl. 42, "From regent of Quicembo, Francisco Joaquim da Costa e Silva, to Government of Angola secretary, João de Roboredo," May 25, 1848. For more on Quicembo, its market, and its importance as an illegal slave embarkation site, see "Minister of Marine to the Duke of Loulé," Lisbon, January 30, 1865, *Correspondence with the British Commissioners at Sierra Leone, Havava, the Cape of Good Hopes, Loanda, and New York Relates with the Slave Trade*, vol. 75 (London: Harrison and Sons, 1865), 59–60. For more on legal status and social hierarchies, see Gabriela dos Reis Sampaio, Lisa Earl Castillo, and Wlamyra Ribeiro de Albuquerque, *Barganhas e querelas da escravidão: Tráfico, alforria e liberdade (séculos XVIII e XIX)* (Salvador: Edufba, Editora da Universidade Federal da Bahia, 2014); Hebe Maria Mattos, *Das cores do silêncio: Os significados da liberdade no sudeste escravista: Brasil Século XIX* (Rio de Janeiro: Arquivo Nacional, 1995); Juliana Barreto Farias, "'Diz a preta mina…': cores e categorias sociais nos processos de divórcio abertos por africanas ocidentais, Rio de Janeiro, século XIX," *Estudos Ibero-Americanos* 44, no. 3 (2018): 470–83.

[28] ANA, Cod. 7182, fl. 44v, April 3, 1827, n. 38. For more on the commodification of individuals and slavery in Africa, see Lovejoy, *Transformations in Slavery*, 1–11.

[29] ANA, Cod. 7182, fl. 1, July 19, 1825, n. 429.

inheritance within his family, he relied on the colonial administration to protect his interests as a slave owner. Several other cases from the 1820s reveal that enslaved individuals were treated as commodities, without any reference to their identity or personal experiences. João Batista Benites claimed he had rights over one of the female slaves of the trader Florinda Francisca. Francisca had died before settling debts with Benites; thus, he demanded financial compensation and the delivery of one of Francisca's captives.[30] Also, in the 1820s, Mariana Pilarte Silva requested the delivery of some captives she had inherited from her deceased mother. According to Pilate Silva's account, two of her commercial agents at Dombe Grande, António and Hamba Mocoacha, had seized the captives and refused to honor her mother's wishes.[31] Public announcements of inherited slaves ensured that slave ownership was public knowledge, protected by social convention.

As in the case of land examined earlier, these cases expose the establishment of the colonial administration as arbiter over property conflicts. Colonial agents ensured that slave owners were satisfied, strengthening terror and fear among enslaved individuals. Dona Inês Xavier de Almeida denounced her husband for selling one of her slaves who helped her in domestic activities, while another woman, Rosa Xavier, claimed that one of her neighbors, a Black man named Vitano, had seized one of her slaves, thus damaging production in one of her gardens in Catumbela.[32] In a similar situation, Catarina Simoa Gonçalves required help to recuperate Susana, her property who had been kidnapped by her neighbor, Rosa.[33] The situation was not different in the second half of the nineteenth century. In 1865, two individuals owned by Dona Maria Joaquina da Cunha, a resident of Luanda, were placed under the care of the judge of Angola until an inventory was carried out and the inheritance was clarified.[34] Thus, these cases indicate that women and men were treated as property in West Central Africa, commodified in a sense that they could be inherited, used as debt payments, and bought and

---

[30] ANA, Cod. 7182, fl.12, August 5, 1826, n. 502.
[31] ANA, Cod. 7182, fl. 110, October 4, 1828, n. S/N.
[32] ANA, Cod. 7182, fl.11, August 5, 1826, n. 495; and AHA, Cod. 7182, fl. 19v, 23 September 1826, n. 598.
[33] ANA, Cod. 7182, fl. 37, February 1, 1827, n. 811.
[34] ANA, cx. 3340, Dombe Grande, doc. 168, fl. 64, "Letter from Chefe do Dombe Grande [Francisco José de Brito]," October 16, 1865. For more on the role of the colonial administration in protecting the interests of slave owners, see Freudenthal, "Quilombos de Angola," 120; João de Castro Maia Veiga de Figueiredo, "Política, escravatura e feitiçaria em Angola (séculos XVIII e XIX)" (Ph.D., Coimbra, Portugal, Universidade de Coimbra, 2015), 189–91 and 283–88.

sold. Many of these cases are about women owning other women, which exposes the gendered nature of slave accumulation and appropriation of labor.

Although, in the 1860s, colonial laws were moving toward the "slow death for slavery" and making the ownership of human beings illegal, slave owners did not feel any constraint to stop trading in human beings or even enslaving people. In fact, the governor of Angola, Menezes, stated that "slavery has been abolished, and probably it will not be revived; however, the law allows the condition of freed status."[35] In 1873, for example, Bento Augusto Ribeiro Lopes seized two free women and enslaved them, arguing that they were Black and *gentias* (heathens), as if these two conditions allowed them to be enslaved. When the news reached the governor of Benguela, he stated that "all black people are free, unless a written document proves otherwise."[36] Violence and commodification were daily threats for impoverished women and men in West Central Africa, who could not rely on community or family for protection against enslavement and sale.

Slavery did not end peacefully. Captors resisted abolition, as will be examined in Chapter 5. The promulgation of a series of decrees, including the 1869 decree that officially abolished slavery, created new registries and requirements. The 1869 decree, for example, required newly freed slaves to continue working for their former slavers for another nine years, as freed people, or *libertos*. In 1875, the *liberto* legal status was extinguished, but those who were freed were channeled to a new type of forced labor, the *contrato*.[37] Yet settlers and residents of the colonial centers continued to kidnap free West Central Africans. In 1875, for example, Joaquim António Bravo requested authorization to enslave people and transport them to his farms in São Tomé.[38] This practice goes back to the earlier centuries when

---

[35] Menezes, *Relatório do Governo*, 82. For the idea of a slow death for slavery, see Paul E. Lovejoy and Jan S. Hogendorn, *Slow Death for Slavery: The Course of Abolition in Northern Nigeria, 1897-1936* (Cambridge: Cambridge University Press, 1993).

[36] ANA, Cx. 1322, Catumbela, "Administração do Concelho, 1853–1935, Correspondência Recebida," "From governor of Benguela to chefe do concelho da Catumbela [José de Abreu Silvana]," February 17, 1873; and ANA, Cx. 1322, doc. 63, "From Governor de Benguela to chefe do concelho da Catumbela", 15 February 1873.

[37] AHU, DGU, 1112, "Extinção da condição de servil e regulamento do trabalho nas colonias (1875-1877)" and AHU, pasta 48 (648) N. 241, April 29, 1875. See also J. M. da Silva Cunha, *O trabalho indígena: Estudo de direito colonial* (Lisbon: Agência Geral das Colónias, 1956), 146–48.

[38] AHU, pasta 48 (648) N. 241, February 10, 1875, "Requerimentos em que Joaquim António Bravo, proprietário agrícola em São Tomé, pede lhe seja permitido o resgate da escravidão no interior da província."

colonial agents and traders enslaved free people, and it continued to occur despite the abolition of slavery.[39]

Even into the 1920s, evidence of slavery in Angola continued to appear. Under pressure from the *Comission de la Esclavage* of the Society of Nations, the colonial administration carried out an investigation regarding the continuation of slavery practices in its colonies. According to the report, slavery had been terminated in most of Angola due to the "colonizing power's eradication of warfare, capture, and the intertribal conflicts." The report continues, "Slavery continues to exist among certain tribes in cases of unpaid debts or as punishment for very severe crimes."[40] Similar to the narratives that justified the slave trade 300 years earlier, disciplining and patrolling Black bodies was the justification of territorial occupation, conquest, and slavery. According to the report, slavery was an "African" institution, dissociated from colonialism and the Portuguese presence. Colonial officers used these cases to denounce the "primitivism" and backwardness of West Central Africans, erasing the European role in the expansion and transformation of slavery within Africa. In 1921, four enslaved women were "considered as cattle" and listed among the property in the inventory of a deceased man.[41]

---

[39] Among the legal cases at the Tribunal da Comarca de Benguela, there are several cases of enslavement of free people. See TCB, "Processo crime por se escravizar homens livres, Ministério Público, vs. Francisco Luciano dos Santos Moura," 1855; "Processo crime tentativa de escravização de pessoas livres, Ministério Público vs Miguel Gonçalves da Cruz, 1857. See as well, José C. Curto, "Experiences of Enslavement in West Central Africa," *Histoire Sociale/Social History* 41, no. 82 (2008): 381–415; Mariana P. Candido, "African Freedom Suits and Portuguese Vassal Status: Legal Mechanisms for Fighting Enslavement in Benguela, Angola, 1800–1830, " *Slavery & Abolition* 32, no. 3 (2011): 447–59; Ferreira, "Slaving and Resistance to Slaving in West Central Africa."

[40] Arquivo Histórico Diplomático (hereinafter AHD), Ministério das Colónias – Gabinete do Ministério, May 18, 1936, C. P. Garcia, "Conforme sugeri a V Excia em parecer do conselho do Império de que fui relatos." p. 5.

[41] AHD, Serviço da República. Repartição dos Negócios políticos e de administração civil. Entrada n. 22, Antônio Lopes Mateus, "Informações prestadas pelas colónias sobre usos e costumes que podem ser interpretados como sobrevivência da escravatura, nos termos do artigo 7 da convenção de 1926," February 13, 1936, n. 12. For the idea of slavery as an African institution, see BSGL, Res-2-C-7, fl. 65. For more on the moral justifications for slavery, colonialism, and conquest, see Sylvia Tamale, "Researching and Theorising Sexualities in Africa," in *African Sexualities: A Reader*, ed. Sylvia Tamale (Cape Town: Pambazuka Press, 2011), 11–35; Clifton Crais and Pamela Scully, *Sara Baartman and the Hottentot Venus: A Ghost Story and a Biography* (Princeton, NJ: Princeton University Press, 2010); Carol E. Henderson, "AKA: Sarah Baartman, The Hottentot Venus, and Black Women's Identity," *Women's Studies* 43, no. 7 (2014): 946–59; Jennifer L. Morgan, *Laboring Women: Reproduction and Gender in New World Slavery* (Philadelphia: University of Pennsylvania Press, 2011); Rachel Jean-Baptiste, *Conjugal Rights: Marriage, Sexuality, and Urban Life in Colonial Libreville, Gabon* (Athens: Ohio University Press, 2014); Mariana P. Candido, "Conquest, Occupation, Colonialism and

In episodes that resemble the slave narratives of the eighteenth and nineteenth centuries, children were kidnapped and enslaved during the first three decades of the twentieth century. For example, while returning from a trip to Ganguelas in 1931, Tito Augusto de Carvalho seized children and offered them to Chiquito, Cangamba, and Cueriengue in exchange for cattle and pigs.[42] Slavery survived in West Central Africa because it was profitable, generated wealth, and imposed a race-based social and economic hierarchy. It was a form of property recognized by West Central Africans living in the interior and along the coast, despite the official condemnation of the practice.

Resistance to Commodification

The colonial administration policed closely the movement of subjects, particularly enslaved ones. Paper culture and identity were important tools to exercise control and police movements. Enslaved people broke from such restrictions. In many ways, individuals who were labeled as property resisted their commodification. To challenge the rights of others who exercise control over their bodies and labor, enslaved people engaged in a variety of resistant acts. Despite resorting to escape since the seventeenth century, by the mid-nineteenth century the issue of fugitives from slavery received more attention from the colonial administration, which was concerned about protecting slave owners' property.[43]

Exclusion: Land Disputes in Angola," in *Property Rights, Land and Territory in the European Overseas Empires*, ed. José Vicente Serrão et al. (Lisbon: CEHC-IUL, 2014), 223–33, http://hdl.handle.net/10071/2718.

[42] AHD, Serviço da República. Repartição dos Negócios políticos e de administração civil. Entrada n. 22, Mateus, "Informações prestadas pelas colônias," February 13, 1936, n. 11. For slave narratives describing the capture of children, the most famous case is Olaudah Equiano, *The Interesting Narrative of the life of Olaudah Equiano, or Gustavo Vassa, the African* (London, 1789), and see Paul E. Lovejoy, "'Freedom Narratives' of Transatlantic Slavery," *Slavery & Abolition* 32, no. 1 (2011): 91–107. For more on kidnaping and enslavement of children, see Diptee, *From Africa to Jamaica*; Benjamin Nicholas Lawrance, *Amistad's Orphans: An Atlantic Story of Children, Slavery, and Smuggling* (New Haven, CT: Yale University Press, 2015); W. G. Clarence-Smith, "The Redemption of Child Slaves by Christian Missionaries in Central Africa, 1878-1914, " in *Child Slaves in the Modern World*, ed. Gwyn Campbell, Suzanne Miers, and Joseph C. Miller (Athens: Ohio University Press, 2011), 173–90, and other articles in these collections.

[43] There is an increasing scholarship on fugitives from slavery in various geographical contexts, yet few studies have examined this type of resistance in Angola. See Freudenthal, "Quilombos de Angola"; Heintze, *Angola nos séculos XVI e XVII*, 507–38; Ferreira, "Slave Flights"; Aurora da Fonseca Ferreira, *A Kisama em Angola do século XVI ao início do século XX. Autonimia, ocupação e resistência*, 2 vols. (Luanda: Kilombelombe, 2012). Mariana Candido and Vanessa Oliveira, "Slavery in Luanda and Benguela," *Oxford Research Encyclopedia in African History* (2022), accessed April 24, 2022.

In the 1820s, Diogo Vieira de Lima, a resident of Quilengues, reported that one of his male slaves had run away. From the document available, it is not clear if the enslaved man was identified by his name or if any physical description was provided to the colonial authorities.[44] Decades later, in the 1840s, after years of failing to recuperate her property on her own, Maria de Menezes Benites requested the intervention of the captain of Caconda to recover a slave woman and her four daughters.[45] Claiming that their property interests had been hurt, individuals requested the support of the colonial state to retrieve their captives.

As in other slave societies, enslaved individuals were under constant surveillance and control and were subject to physical and psychological violence, which is extremely difficult to measure based on evidence in the available documents. In 1846, Manuel Ferreira Torres beat to death one of his female slaves who worked at his plantation in Equimina, nearby Dombe Grande. It is not clear what precipitated such a violent act. The victim remains nameless in the historical record, suggesting that this was a regular occurrence that did not deserve much attention from colonial officers. The legal case was recorded not because of the murder but due to the reaction of other enslaved individuals. The beating and murder galvanized three captives who had witnessed the episode into fleeing, afraid that their slaver's wife, Dona Teresa de Jesus Ferreira Torres Viana, would blame them for any responsibility in the event. The reaction of the three women suggests that threats and violence were daily practices at Torres's farm. The public punishment that resulted in death had terrorized the three enslaved women, which undercut any effort to minimize violence among those who remained in captivity in Africa. Rather than looking for the three witnesses who could potentially solve the case and bring justice to the deceased woman, the colonial state mobilized a military force to locate and apprehend the three runaways. After their arrest, the three unnamed women were placed under the care, or lack of care, of the *Curador dos Escravos e Libertos*, an institution that protected the interests of slave owners and had already become infamous by the 1850s for the appalling treatment of enslaved and freed people. The three enslaved women probably endured more fear and punishment for their actions that threatened to expose the daily violence and extra-judicial killings that took place within domestic spaces.[46] Slavers often

---

[44] ANA, Cod. 7182, fl. 1, July 19, 1825, n. 428.
[45] ANA, cx. 151, fl. 165, August 11, 1845, n. 495.
[46] ANA, Cod. 469, fl. 39, May 24, 1846. For more on physical punishment on enslaved people, see Ferreira, "Slave Flights," 71; Aida Freudenthal, "Os quilombos de Angola no século XIX: a recusa da escravidão," *Estudos Afro-Asiáticos* 32 (1997): 114–15; Oliveira, "Notas preliminares." For the prevalence of violence in slave societies, see

called on colonial authorities for assistance in managing slaves; as this last case indicates, even the institutions whose mission was to protect those in vulnerable positions failed to do so, as they sided with the owners' class in cases of conflict. The colonial archives contain numerous accounts of unnamed enslaved women and men beaten, whipped, and murdered.

While in some cases captors welcomed the intervention of colonial forces, in other instances the assertion of state power over privately owned bodies was received with suspicion and discomfort. In the 1860s, the Portuguese trader António Francisco Ferreira da Silva Porto complained that two of his female slaves had been baptized in Benguela without his authorization or knowledge and he was unaware of their Catholic names. These women may be Maria and Joaquina, two enslaved women baptized in Benguela in 1852, identified as property of António da Silva Porto.[47] Unfortunately none of the historical documents registered their Umbundu names. Silva Porto's complaint was not based on his concern for the spiritual well-being of his captives but on the fact that his rights as slave owner were not required before their baptism. By challenging the authority of the priest to baptize enslaved people without the express consent of their owner, Silva Porto insisted that the colonial state and the Catholic Church needed to publicly recognize his control and ownership over human beings.

These episodes of violence and struggle challenge any efforts to minimize slavery in West Central Africa as a milder or less-violent institution than that established in the Americas. Slavery was based on displacement, violence, and political and social exclusion.[48] The presence of enslaved people in West Central Africa states, urban centers, and colonial towns becomes visible in the historical record through the experience of bodily violence. Colonial agents and travelers related violent episodes, yet these accounts failed to identify the names or the fate of the victims. They also tended to erase any agency of enslaved people and to reinforce

---

Ana Lucia Araujo, "Black Purgatory: Enslaved Women's Resistance in Nineteenth-Century Rio Grande do Sul, Brazil," *Slavery & Abolition* 36, no. 4 (2015): 568–85; Fuentes, *Dispossessed Lives*; Trevor G. Burnard, *Mastery, Tyranny, and Desire Thomas Thistlewood and His Slaves in the Anglo-Jamaican World* (Chapel Hill: University of North Carolina Press, 2004); Audra Diptee, *From Africa to Jamaica: The Making of an Atlantic Slave Society, 1775-1807* (Gainesville: University Press of Florida, 2012).

[47] BSGL, Res 2-C 6, "Silva Porto, apontamentos de um portuense em África. Vol 2," fl. 40, January 29, 1861. For the baptism records, see Bispado de Luanda (hereinafter BL) Batismo Benguela 1851-1853, fl. 56v, March 1, 1852; and 77v May 30, 1852.

[48] Martin A. Klein, *Slavery and Colonial Rule in French West Africa* (New York: Cambridge University Press, 1998); Lovejoy, *Transformations in Slavery*; Klein, Bellagamba, and Greene, *Bitter Legacy*; Greene, *Slave Owners of West Africa*; Jennifer Lofkrantz, "Idealism and Pragmatism: The Related Muslim West African Discourses on Identity, Captivity and Ransoming," *African Economic History* 42, no. 1 (2015): 87–107.

their subjugation by emphasizing their position as property. For example, Joachim John Monteiro noticed that enslaved women collected the ore in the copper mines located six miles inland from Benguela and transported it to the port, yet he does not report the conditions of their labor.[49] László Magyar reported that enslaved women cooked and cleaned in the households of Benguela, acted as nurses, and met the sexual demands of their slavers.[50] According to Magyar, "the families [in Benguela] are complemented by Black slave women who are kept in harems, without any access to education and perform domestic tasks."[51] Despite these references, these enslaved women are nameless in both accounts, and their historical existence is only recorded in relationship to an owner. Their roles as daughters, siblings, mothers, and aunts disappear from the historical record, further stressing the kinless characteristic of slavery as an institution.[52]

In the 1840s, Pedro Alexandrino da Cunha, the governor of Angola, implied that slave flights were motivated by gender anxieties regarding forced labor. According to him, men "did not accept agricultural labor, which they see as demeaning and female work."[53] Whether motivated by gender or not, colonial records indicate that enslaved women left for the same reasons as their male counterparts: to protect their lives and loved ones, challenging perceptions that slave flights were mainly a male phenomenon.[54] In fact, available documents show that women and girls escaped from their owners, who reported their flight to the colonial authorities. A young woman, probably a teenager, belonging to Andreza Leal do Sacramento, fled to Catumbela, where her father hid and protected her. The family reunion was disrupted by an unnamed witness who denounced them to the authorities. João and his daughter were arrested in 1835 and probably separated once again.[55] The colonial administration made extensive use of violence and terror to prevent recurrent flights; however, enslaved people resisted any way possible,

---

[49] For more on this report, see Joachim John Monteiro, *Angola and the River Congo* (New York: Macmillan, 1876), 191–92.

[50] Magyar, *Reisen in Sud-Afrika*, chapter 1, "Estadia em Benguela," p. 10. I am very grateful to Maria da Conceição Neto, who shared her Portuguese translation of the original.

[51] Magyar, *Reisen in Sud-Afrika*, chapter 1, "Estadia em Benguela," p. 2.

[52] Fuentes, *Dispossessed Lives*, 124–29; Mariana P. Candido, "Engendering West Central African History: The Role of Urban Women in Benguela in the Nineteenth Century," *History in Africa* 42 (2015): 7–36; Klein, "African Traditions of Servitude and the Evolution of African Society"; Benedetta Rossi, "Slavery and Migration: Social and Physical Mobility in Ader (Niger)," in *Reconfiguring Slavery: West African Trajectories*, ed. Benedetta Rossi (Liverpool: Liverpool University Press, 2009), 182–206.

[53] Cited in Ferreira, "Slave Flights," 72.

[54] For the idea that men fled more than women, see Freudenthal, "Quilombos de Angola," 115.

[55] ANA, Cod. 509, fl. 110, August 2, 1835.

risking their lives in search of freedom. If located, these self-emancipated individuals paid a high price. Upon the death of Felizarda de Nazaré, three of her enslaved women went to Catumbela, where they managed to live for four years before the colonial army located, seized, and sold them in the Benguela public market.[56]

An unnamed enslaved woman who belonged to Dona Margarida fled in 1847 to Dombe Grande, where she was caught with a man named Zambo. The couple was accused of being romantically involved and perhaps the unnamed woman had attempted to form her own family in freedom.[57] The legal case does not provide any information about what happened to Zambo and his partner after she was arrested and returned to her slaver. In the 1850s, Naquibuacura, a captive woman, took some goods from the tavern where she worked and left.[58] Flights continued to take place after the end of slave exports in a clear indication that no one waited for abolition to end their life in captivity. Enslaved men and women resisted their capture and bondage daily, in episodes that colonial officers and traders described as "laziness" or "backwardness." It is much easier to locate episodes of flight and revolt in official documents than smaller daily resistance actions that were not necessarily registered. The fact that colonial authorities complained about the stubbornness, filth, and lazy behavior of enslaved individuals reveals how women and men in bondage resisted in nonviolent ways, challenging any colonial imposition of new morals and civilization practices.[59]

Pawnship and *Panyarring*

In the mid-nineteenth century, changes associated with the expanding bureaucracy made conflicts over human property in West Central Africa – nothing new in themselves – more visible in the colonial records. In many instances, the debate over property rights was related to the practice of pawnship, *penhor* in Portuguese, when free dependents were held as collateral for goods advanced to traders who traveled to inland

---

[56] ANA, Cod. 455, fl. 230 v, October 14, 1846, "To Governor of the Province, Pedro Alexandrino da Cunha, from Joaquim Luis Bastos, Captain and Interim Governor."

[57] ANA, Cod. 463, fl. 27, November 27, 1847.

[58] TCB, "Translado de uns autos crimes João da Silva Pereira vs Canique, Quiopa, Quipanga, and Naquibuacura," 1859. This case is also in Ferreira, "Slave Flights," 69.

[59] For more on this aspect of resistance, see *Almanak statistico da Provincia d'Angola e suas dependencias para o anno de 1852.* (Luanda: Imprensa do Governo, 1851), 22; Carlos José Caldeira, *Apontamentos d'uma viagem de Lisboa a China e da China a Lisboa* (Lisbon: G.M. Martins, 1852), 200; José Joaquim Lopes de Lima, *Ensaios sobre a statistica das possessões portuguezas na África occidental e oriental; na Ásia occidental; na China, e na Oceania* (Lisbon: Imprensa Nacional, 1844), XXXVIII..

markets to acquire captives. Failure to honor the terms of the loan, which usually meant delivering captives in exchange for the advanced credit, could lead to enslavement and sale of the pawns. Although it was not recognized as legal under colonial law, this system operated and could result in the enslavement of free people placed as pawns. Pawnship was common as a mechanism of trade protection among African traders, and several colonial officers embraced its use.[60] The fact that pawnship conflicts were registered in colonial documents reveals the coexistence of multiple norms and legal understandings in the same geographical space.

Colonial records show parents and relatives using children and women in general as collateral for credit and debt recovery during the eighteenth and nineteenth centuries. This was the case with Andre Gaspar's child, placed as collateral for a debt Gaspar acquired with a Luanda trader.[61] In local courts, debts were taken very seriously and were intimately related to the protection of property. Writing in the early twentieth century, Augusto Bastos argued that among the Ndombe, Mbailundu, Nganguela, and Kilengues, and other groups of people living in the province of Benguela, "debt is sacred, and no one can escape paying it. When a person has a debt, commercial or private, there are always witnesses who can testify, if necessary, in case the debtor refused to honor his or her obligations. As soon as a debt is proved, the debtor must pay it and the creditor can even dispose of his or her freedom, enslaving the debtors."[62]

---

[60] For more on pawnship as intrinsically linked to the operation of the slave trade, see Joseph C. Miller, *Way of Death: Merchant Capitalism and the Angolan Slave Trade, 1730-1830* (Madison: University of Wisconsin Press, 1988), 179–80; Jan Vansina, "Ambaca Society and the Slave Trade c. 1760-1845, " *Journal of African History* 46, no. 1 (2005): 6–7; Roquinaldo Ferreira, *Cross-Cultural Exchange in the Atlantic World: Angola and Brazil during the Era of the Slave Trade* (New York: Cambridge University Press, 2012), 78–79. For the enslavement of pawns and the legal debate around it, see Paul E. Lovejoy and Toyin Falola, eds., *Pawnship, Slavery, and Colonialism in Africa* (Trenton, NJ: Africa World Press, 2003); Randy J Sparks, *The Two Princes of Calabar: An Eighteenth-Century Atlantic Odyssey* (Cambridge, MA: Harvard University Press, 2004); Paul E. Lovejoy, "Pawnship, Debts, and 'Freedom' in Atlantic Africa during the Era of the Slave Trade: A Reassessment" 55, no. 1 (2014): 55–78; Olatunji Ojo, "'Èmú' (Àmúyá): The Yoruba Institution of Panyarring or Seizure for Debt," *African Economic History* no. 35 (2007): 31–58; Olatunji Ojo, "The Atlantic Slave Trade and Local Ethics of Slavery in Yorubaland," *African Economic History* 41 (2013): 73–100.

[61] Ferreira, "Slaving and Resistance to Slaving in West Central Africa," 123; Judith Spicksley, "Contested Enslavement: The Portuguese in Angola and the Problem of Debt, c. 1600–1800, " *Itinerario* 39, no. 2 (2015): 262–63.

[62] Augusto Bastos, "Traços geraes sobre a ethnographia do districto de Benguella," *Boletim da Sociedade de Geografia de Lisboa* 26, no. 1 (1908): 87. For more on the importance of debt and punishment in local legal systems, see António Gil, *Considerações sobre alguns pontos mais importantes da moral religiosa e sistema de jurisprudência dos pretos do continente da África Ocidental Portuguesa além do Equador* (Lisbon: Tipografia da Academia, 1854), 18–20; Figueiredo, "Política, escravatura e feitiçaria," 242–50.

Along with slavery, pawnship expanded in West Central Africa in the nineteenth century. The historical documents tend to include cases in which the pawnship arrangements had been violated, rather than the cases that were settled. Settled disputes never reached the colonial court for arbitration. The risk is that the documents available overrepresented conflicts. Portuguese colonial law recognized the use of human beings as a legitimate form of payment for outstanding debts.[63] In 1827, Guiomar Pacheco de Almeida placed an enslaved pawn with Cosme Lopes Pereira, a trader who had advanced her a loan. A few months later when she went to pay her loan and retrieve her captive, she found he was gone, creating a legal debate over Lopes Pereira's right to sell de Almeida's property.[64] In 1828, Isabel, a Black woman living in Dombe Grande, placed one of her slaves, Teresa, in the hands of Catumba until she secured the goods to repay a debt her uncle owed Catumba. After her uncle's death, Isabel felt responsible for honoring his debt, even if the only way to do it was placing Teresa in Catumba's household. Teresa was already enslaved, and it is not clear if she ever returned to Isabel's control. Although Isabel honored this debt, she refused to recognize the claims of Domingas, another woman who accused Isabel's uncle of failing to pay his debts before his death.[65] This episode clearly indicates that pawns could be enslaved and sold into different markets, and captives used as pawns could be placed under another person's control to settle debts. When debts were not repaid, dependents could be seized and enslaved.

There was a clear connection between pawnship and access to imported goods that were considered valuable. Pawnship was linked to participation and control of trade and markets, and the ability to generate labor. In the 1860s, a ruler in the lands of the Anduro offered two women as pawns to António da Silva Porto in exchange for textiles, gunpowder, and alcohol. Unable or unwilling to offer the goods, the Portuguese merchant returned the two pawns and interrupted the trust operation. Silva Porto claimed to be more interested in securing payment than entering pawnship conflicts, although one year earlier he had provided

---

[63] Vansina, "Ambaca"; Ferreira, "Slaving and Resistance to Slaving in West Central Africa"; Spicksley, "Contested Enslavement"; Figueiredo, "Política, escravatura e feitiçaria," 141–68.
[64] ANA, Cod. 7182, fl. 56, June 16, 1827, requerimento n. 209.
[65] ANA, Cod. 7182, fl. 85, March 14, 1828, requerimento n. 788.

the soba of Ganguela with textiles, beads, and gunpowder in exchange for pawns.[66] In extreme cases in which an individual could not provide a pawn to secure a loan, individuals were forced to work, mixing pawnship, debt enslavement, and self-enslavement.[67]

The abolition of slavery in 1869 did not result in the end of bondage and human trafficking; in fact, pawnship seems to have become more important as a tool for labor exploitation of young women or junior members of society, who ended up absorbed in the creditor's household as a wife or nondependent. In 1926, a report indicated that *penhor* was "a contract between families involving minor women. The young women could be placed under the care of a family, and she worked in the household until the loan and the interest were paid. After the payment of the terms of contract, she had to be returned to her family. If the debt was not paid, she remained in the creditor's household until she became aware of her [subordinated] condition. She could buy her own freedom or seek the intervention of an administrative authority."[68] Pawns were not considered property, and anyone held in pawnship had to be treated well; otherwise, the terms of the contract could be broken. It is important to stress that in West Central Africa women were placed as pawns, unlike the cases in the Bight of Biafra and Gold Coast where male pawns were more popular in the nineteenth century.[69] Yet, like other parts of the African continent, pawnship remained alive well into the twentieth century, despite the growing pressure from the League of Nations to eliminate any form of forced labor or situations that could easily lead to enslavement, such as the cases of debts.[70]

[66] BSGL, Res 2-C 6, "Silva Porto, apontamentos" fl. 232, January 30, 1862; and fl. 49, February 13, 1861. For similar practice elsewhere, see Lovejoy, "Pawnship, Debts, and 'Freedom,'" 61–62.

[67] José C. Curto, "Struggling against Enslavement: The Case of José Manuel in Benguela, 1816-20, " *Canadian Journal of African Studies* 39, no. 1 (2005): 96–122.

[68] AHD, Repartição dos Negócios políticos e de administração civil, Antônio Lopes Mateus, "Informações prestadas," February 13, 1936, n. 13.

[69] Paul E. Lovejoy and David Richardson, "Trust, Pawnship, and Atlantic History: The Institutional Foundations of the Old Calabar Slave Trade," *American Historical Review* 104, no. 2 (1999): 333–55; Austin, *Labour, Land, and Capital in Ghana*, 177–79; Lovejoy, "Pawnship, Debts, and 'Freedom,'" 62. For the link between women's vulnerability and pawnship, see Claire C. Roberston, "We Must Overcome: Genealogy and Evolution of Female Slavery in West Africa," *Journal of West African History* 1, no. 1 (2015): 70–71; Ugo Nwokeji, *The Slave Trade and Culture in the Bight of Biafra: An African Society in the Atlantic World* (New York: Cambridge University Press, 2010), 225–36.

[70] AHD, Ministério dos Negócios Estrangeiros, Ministério do Ultramar, Arquivo Histórico Ultramarino, U. I. 14446, AHD/3/MU-GM/GNP-RNP/S167/UI014446, processo 26/3. "Inquérito sobre a existência da escravatura nas colônias," Luanda, December 20, 1940.

Traders and free residents disputed the rights of enslaved people in the case of unpaid debts, a practice known as *panyarring*, or seizure for debt. *Panyarring* was the capture of a person, free or enslaved, to recover assets. By the early nineteenth century, this practice was widespread in West Central Africa, with *sobas*, local traders, and colonial agents resorting to it in cases where the failure to collect debts led to extrajudicial solutions. Free people could also be seized and enslaved after trials carried out in the local African courts, known generically in this region by the nineteenth century as *mucano*. Social violations such as adultery, theft, or sorcery were brought to court as cases of property transgression and settled with heavy fines or enslavement. Free people could provide free or enslaved dependents as their replacement, which could ultimately result in a life in bondage.[71] The trader Silva Porto reported cases of people enslaved through debts in courts in Bihé, such as the 1852 case of eight free young women seized as replacements to settle the debts of their powerful owner, a Bihé trader.[72] As a result, local courts often promulgated decisions that enslaved free people for crimes others had committed, feeding Atlantic and local demands for enslaved labor.[73]

In cases of individuals who acquired debts, their property, including human beings, was listed as collateral, and colonial courts were involved in resolving related disputes. Despite legislation that prevented colonial officers from enslaving anyone due to debts and the imposition of harsh penalties on anyone caught breaking the law, debt enslavement was common in the Portuguese colonial centers. Colonial authorities arbitrated in favor of creditors, allowing colonial subjects to seize free people in debts. One example is the case of the trader Marcos Vaz da Conceição who requested authorization to seize Temaqueve, an enslaved man who belonged to Eugénia Manuel Gomes. Gomes owed the trader Vaz da

---

[71] Several cases of seizure for debt are described in Curto, "Experiences of Enslavement in West Central Africa"; Ferreira, *Cross-Cultural Exchange*, 66–77; Vansina, "Ambaca"; Mariana P. Candido, "The Transatlantic Slave Trade and the Vulnerability of Free Blacks in Benguela, Angola, 1780-1830," in *Atlantic Biographies: Individuals and Peoples in the Atlantic World*, ed. Mark Meuwese and Jeffrey A. Fortin (Leiden: Brill, 2013), 193–210; Candido, "Limite tênue."

[72] BSGL, Res 1, pasta E, 2, António da Silva Porto, "Memorial de Mucanos, 1841-1885," p. 16, November 22, 1852. For more on panyarring as retributive justice, see Lawrance, *Amistad's Orphans*, 104; Lovejoy, "Pawnship, Debts, and 'Freedom,'" 58–59.

[73] This also happened elsewhere in the continent. See Nwokeji, *Slave Trade in the Bight of Biafra*; Heywood, "Slavery and Its Transformations"; Lovejoy, *Transformations in Slavery*, 4, and 81–85; Ojo, "'Èmú' (Àmúyá)"; Randy J. Sparks, *Where the Negroes Are Masters : An African Port in the Era of the Slave Trade* (Cumberland, RI: Harvard University Press, 2014), 138; Colleen E. Kriger, *Making Money: Life, Death, and Early Modern Trade on Africa's Guinea Coast* (Athens: Ohio University Press, 2017), 106–08.

Conceição 573$870, or 573 thousand and 870 *réis*. This amount would be the equivalent of £2,651 in 1828, quite an impressive amount. The colonial judge not only authorized the seizure but also demanded that Temaqueve be brought in front of the judge.[74] A few months later, Luis, a Black man, reported that Sanzala, a Black woman who lived in Dombe Grande, had seized one of his brothers due to the fact he had failed to repay twelve thousand réis she had lent him, the equivalent of £55.44 in 1820.[75]

In cases brought to the colonial courts in the second half of the nineteenth century, enslaved people continued to be used as collateral, and the inability of free people to pay debts resulted in pawning their dependents, many of them already enslaved. The merchant Manoel Ribeiro Alves presented a commercial suit in 1856 against Dona Ana Teixeira de Sousa for the recovery of 1,038$160, advanced as loans between 1847 and 1851. This corresponds to £4,671.72 in 1850 and Sousa was unable to repay her debts, which resulted in a legal case presented at the Tribunal da Comarca de Benguela. According to the three male witnesses, Bento Pacheco dos Santos, Bernardo Ferreira Pinheiro, and João Correia Evangelista, Sousa was involved in long-distance trade and had requested Ribeiro Alves provide imported goods (*fazendas*) as well as goods manufactured around Caconda as a form of cash advancement. The judge sided with the creditor and ordered Sousa to hand over seven slaves from her household. Each slave was presented and appraised by the court. Luiz, a boy, was appraised as 60$000, or £270 in the 1850s and £15,506.21 in 2017; Quiomba and her baby were valued at 60$000; Luiza, a young girl, was priced at 40$000; Catraio, a boy, was appraised at 40$000; and Herma, a woman, was valued at 60$000. While being transported from Dombe Grande to Benguela, all of them, except Herma, fled. Unable to pay her debts, Sousa decided to pawn more people to recover cash. She pawned her human property, including Florencia with her son, and two women, Quilombo and Merino, but their value was not enough to cover her debt. Sousa had to borrow cash to repay Ribeiro Alves. He accepted the cash, but let the judge know he preferred to receive enslaved people than cash, indicating

---

[74] ANA, Cod. 7182, fl. 68, October 10, 1827, n. 458. For more on the colonial prohibition regarding panyarring and its failure, see the cases presented in Curto, "Struggling against Enslavement"; Candido, *An African Slaving Port*, 224; Ferreira, *Cross-Cultural Exchange*, 79–80. For the conversion rate of reis to pound sterling, see W. G. Clarence-Smith, *The Third Portuguese Empire, 1825–1975: A Study in Economic Imperialism* (Manchester: Manchester University Press, 1985), 227.

[75] ANA, Cod. 7182, fl. 86, March 28, 1828, n. 805.

that human property was a form of currency.[76] This case reveals how *panyarring* and pawnship operated closely, and vulnerable dependents, particularly those who were enslaved, could be used not only as collateral but also as debt payment.

A few years later, another trader relied on the colonial courts to recuperate his property. In 1867, Tomé Ribeiro Antunes sued the estate of João Henrique Teixeira and his wife regarding an unpaid debt going back to 1862. Afraid, after the passing of Teixeira, that he would not recover the credit he had advanced, Antunes requested that the Benguela judge order the Teixeira's property to be seized, including their enslaved individuals. In the couple's inventory, treasury officers identified a quantity of hoes, textiles, caskets of palm oil, and jewelry and assessed their value. They also valued movable goods including animals and human beings, who were listed side by side, once again emphasizing the commodification of people and the denial of humanity to anyone enslaved. In the inventory, an unnamed old woman is listed as worth 40$000 réis; a young boy, a *moleque*, is 35$000; and an adult woman with her baby was estimated at 38$000.[77] Even a freedman, a *liberto*, was evaluated in the inventory (35$000), suggesting he could also be sold, regardless of his legal status, to pay the Teixeira's debt.[78] The judge ordered the public sale of all property to settle the debt. These cases show that the colonial court also embraced the seizure of human beings as a legitimate way of settling debts, implementing *panyarring* as a legal strategy to recover assets.

Sorcery or accusations of sorcery also resulted in court cases where the accused could face ordeals to prove their innocence. If found guilty, the accused or their dependents could be transferred and enslaved, creating disputes regarding ownership of people.[79] In 1866, the judge of Benguela brought to trial a case of three women who changed owners, even though they were freed. After a long case in which Luisa Cordeiro Bimbi was accused of enslaving Bibiana, Catumbo, and Teresa Caleço, it became

---

[76] TCB, "Autos cíveis de libelo Manoel Ribeiro Alves vs Ana Teixeira de Sousa" February 21, 1856; and "Autos cíveis de execução Joaquim Luis Bastos vs D. Ana Teixeira de Sousa," March 8, 1856. For enslaved individuals as currency, see Green, *A Fistful of Shells*, 281–86.

[77] TCB, "Ação Comercial Tomé Ribeiro Nunes vs Casal João Henrique Teixeira," 1867, fl. 16.

[78] TCB, "Ação Comercial Tomé Ribeiro Nunes vs Casal João Henrique Teixeira," 1867, fl. 19. For more on panyarring, enslavement of free people, and schemes to exploit labor, see Ojo, "'Èmú' (Àmúyá)"; Lawrance, *Amistad's Orphans*, 103–4; Enrique Martino, "Panya: Economies of Deception and the Discontinuities of Indentured Labour Recruitment and the Slave Trade, Nigeria and Fernando Pó, 1890s–1940s, " *African Economic History* 44, no. 1 (2016): 91–129.

[79] For several cases of sorcery and enslavement, see Ferreira, *Cross-Cultural Exchange*, 71–77.

clear that the case involved *panyarring* and a sorcery accusation. Their previous owner, Joaquim Quinpunduca, had killed his partner Manbella, and shortly after, his dependents were hit by a smallpox epidemic that led to several deaths. Joaquim was convinced that the two events were related, and the only way to get rid of the smallpox was to pay for Mandela's murder. He approached a healer, Luisa Bimbi, and offered her four cows and three captives to remove the sorcery from his household. Luisa accepted the payment and provided the service.[80] In the colonial court, however, the transfer of the three women's ownership led to an investigation. "In Ambundu ... any theft was a heinous crime, second only to witchcraft, and only payable by the transfer of people."[81] The purpose of the legal case was not to challenge the legitimacy of offering human beings to relieve a malady or sorcery, but to determine whether it was legitimate to transfer people who were considered free.

The widespread use of pawnship and *panyarring* reveals the extreme value that local and colonial courts placed on protecting property. The colonial court clashed with local understandings of ownership and transfer of dependents, particularly after the 1830s when the Portuguese monarchy was under pressure to disassociate itself from the slave trade and slave labor. Yet, historical documents attest to the conflation of pawnship and *panyarring* mechanisms among West Central African inhabitants, including among colonial subjects. Colonial documents show the brutal realities of property disputes, indicating that acquisition of individuals was a mechanism of wealth accumulation.

Conclusion

The expansion of bureaucracy during the nineteenth century has left us with abundant information in the historical record about disputes over human property and slave status. By that time, impoverished women, men, and children had been commodified in colonial towns as well as in African states. Individuals were bought and sold, and bequeathed and inherited, revealing the incessant disregard for people's humanity and rights. Rather than a mild form of captivity, slavery in West Central Africa was cruel, alienating, and violent. Enslaved people were forcibly transported, removed from their communities, exposed to physical and mental threats, and had limited chances of social and economic mobility. Despite the violence and dispossession, evidence from the colonial

---

[80] TCB, "Autos de deposito de duas libertas a requerimento do curador dos escravos e libertos," July 24, 1866.
[81] Vansina, "Ambaca," 13.

archives demonstrates that enslaved men and women resisted their enslavement and constantly ran away. Flight was not gendered, and enslaved women chose self-emancipation for the same reasons that their male counterparts did: to protect their lives and loved ones. The legal cases available challenge any effort to underestimate the violent nature of slavery in West Central Africa, particularly in the colonial centers of Luanda and Benguela. Slavery in that region was not a mild or less-violent institution than in the Americas. As slavery elsewhere, it was based on displacement, subjugation, brutality, and political and social exclusion that lasted well into the twentieth century.

The recognition of ownership rights over women, men, and children in West Central Africa was consolidated in the nineteenth century. The control and ownership over enslaved bodies allowed free West Central Africans to enjoy comfortable lives, leisure time, and other advantages. Slavery as an institution also maintained social hierarchies that privileged the interests of those who owned people over those who did not. In sum, people-as-property was recognized by local courts and the colonial state as legitimate. Wealth in people coexisted with other property regimes. Ownership over people was not an alternate form of property in the absence of other forms of individual property rights. Enslavement and slavery were central to the operation of local economies and the project of Portuguese territorial expansion and colonial claims. Land dispossession cannot be fully understood without considering the roles of slavery, family separations, and population removal. Accumulation of dependents, slavery, was possible because individuals were stripped of their rights and their lands. In the process, they became vulnerable to enslavement and their labor was expropriated. Ending ownership rights resulted in litigious conflicts between slavers and their human property. When the colonial state tried to end slavery, it created a new legal category, *libertos*, which represented uninterrupted work for former captors without financial compensation. The creation of the category of *liberto*, or freed person, was a maneuver to allow the ongoing exploitation of people's labor, which will be analyzed further in the next chapter.

5   Branded in Freedom
The Persistent Commodification of People

As long as European powers were imposing their written property laws on West Central Africa, and as long as people could be used as economic pawns, freedom was an ambiguous status. While legal recognition of property rights over land and goods expanded in the nineteenth century, the morality regarding ownership of human beings was challenged in courts, parliaments, and newspapers for centuries.[1] Accumulation of free and enslaved bodies, known as wealth in people, has been a fundamental framework for understanding West Central African societies' perceptions about wealth and accumulation. But ownership rights over people were contested in Angola. Coerced, unfree labor persisted, even as Portugal introduced gradual means to emancipate slaves in its possessions. Any efforts to regulate and end ownership rights over individuals had a public and a private sphere of debates, where slavers resisted the end of commodification while enslaved individuals rejected amelioration and gradual abolition projects.[2] Even freed people struggled to maintain their autonomy and avoid commodification.

In Angola, changes regarding human property started to take place during the mid-nineteenth century due to international pressure, but also due to the actions of enslaved individuals. In most instances, the interests

---

[1] For more on the long struggle for freedom in the Atlantic world, see José Lingna Nafafé, *Lourenço da Silva Mendonça and the Black Atlantic Abolitionist Movement in the Seventeenth Century* (Cambridge: Cambridge University Press, 2022); Roquinaldo Ferreira, *The Price of Emancipation: Central Africa in the Age of Global Abolition (c. 1820-1870)* (Princeton, NJ: Princeton University Press, forthcoming); Pamela Scully and Diana Paton, eds., "Introduction: Gender and Slave Emancipation in Comparative Perspective," in *Gender and Slave Emancipation in the Atlantic World* (Durham: Duke University Press, 2005), 1–33.

[2] Influential studies on the limitations of freedom are Thomas C. Holt, *The Problem of Freedom: Race, Labor, and Politics in Jamaica and Britain, 1832-1938* (Baltimore, MD: Johns Hopkins University Pres, 1992); Frederick Cooper, Thomas C Holt, and Rebecca J Scott, eds., *Beyond Slavery: Explorations of Race, Labor, and Citizenship in Postemancipation Societies* (Chapel Hill: University of North Carolina Press, 2000).

of slave owners prevailed, and legal changes were followed by many years of servitude in transitional status. On July 24, 1856, King Dom Pedro of Portugal declared that from that date onward the children of enslaved women in Portuguese colonies were automatically free in what is known as *"lei do ventre livre."* However, the next paragraph of the law stated that "the children of enslaved women freed according to the previous decree must serve their former owners until they complete 20 years-old."[3] The free-womb law also stated that *libertos* had to continue serving their former masters in exchange for a small financial compensation.[4] The political and economic elites in Portugal and Angola debated the social and economic costs of freeing children of enslaved mothers, looking for ways to prolong their servitude. Minister Marquis Sá da Bandeira signed an ordinance on November 6, 1857, in which he recognized the international pressure to end slavery and emphasized the decline of the number of enslaved individuals in Angola. Sá da Bandeira stressed the importance of recognizing "the ownership rights of the legitimate slave masters" and the need to financially compensate them in the case of losing their property. A new decree on February 25, 1869, freed all slaves, who were then subjected to a period of apprenticeship. The argument behind these laws was that a gradual emancipation was safer and less disruptive to the economy. Freedom became a moving target: whenever the deadline got closer, authorities found ways to extend the duration of the apprenticeship programs, never clarifying the types of training that freed people received. For most of the nineteenth century, Portuguese jurists defended the prolongation of freed status for former

---

[3] BGGOPA, 1866, n. 4, January 27, 1866, p. 17. *A Abolição do tráfico e da escravatura em Angola (documentos)* (Luanda: Ministério da Cultura, 1997), 41. For more on the Portuguese legislation and its meanings to be people in their colonies, see Miguel Bandeira Jerónimo, *Livros brancos, almas negras. A "missão civilizadora" do colonialismo português, c. 1870-1930* (Lisbon: Imprensa de Ciências Sociais, 2010); Miguel Bandeira Jerónimo, "The 'Civilising Guild': Race and Labor in the Third Portuguese Empire, c. 1870-1930," in *Racism and Ethnic Relations in the Portuguese-Speaking World*, ed. Francisco Bethencourt and Adrian Pearce (Oxford: Oxford University Press, 2012), 173–99; Roquinaldo Ferreira, "Abolicionismo versus colonialismo: Rupturas e continuidades em Angola (século XIX)," in *África. Brasileiros e Portugueses, séculos XVI-XIX*, ed. Roberto Guedes (Rio de Janeiro: Mauad, 2013), 95–112. Similar legislation transitions took place in the Americas. See, among others, Rebecca J. Scott, *Slave Emancipation in Cuba the Transition to Free Labor, 1860-1899* (Pittsburgh: University of Pittsburgh Press, 2000); Beatriz G. Mamigonian, "In the Name of Freedom: Slave Trade Abolition, the Law and the Brazilian Branch of the African Emigration Scheme (Brazil–British West Indies, 1830s–1850s)," *Slavery & Abolition* 30, no. 1 (2009): 41–66; Mariana Armond Dias Paes, *Escravidão e direito. O estatuto jurídico dos escravos no Brasil oitocentista (1860-1888)* (São Paulo: Alameda, 2019).

[4] BOGGPA, 1858, n° 653, April 3, 1858, p. 1; and *A abolição do tráfico e da escravatura em Angola*, 7.

slaves, known as *libertos*, and condoned the use of their forced labor to build infrastructure and economic enterprises in the overseas colonies.[5]

During the 1850s and 1860s, authorities in Lisbon debated how to end slavery with minimal impact on the colonial economy and empire treasury. The legal debate was always accompanied by discussion on how much the state would have to spend in financial compensation to slave masters and how "philanthropic campaigns" were necessary to prepare the enslaved population for a life in freedom. However, there was no discussion about financially compensating former slaves or providing resources and education that would empower people to become financially independent. Freedom did not mean inclusion. Despite this series of legal changes, *libertos* continued to be treated as slaves, bequeathed, and sold as property. Forced labor was portrayed as a civilizing agent, similar to what happened in other parts of Africa and the Americas.[6]

Primary sources that include postmortem wills, court cases, slave registers, and parish records help reconstruct the contested nature of ownership rights over people and control over their labor and bodies. The apprenticeship regimes associated with the transition from slavery evolved into the *contrato*, a forced-labor policy used as a tool of labor mobilization and taxation in twentieth-century Portuguese colonial rule in Africa.[7] Regardless of how they were released, freed people were also

[5] Marquês de Sá da Bandeira, *A emancipação dos libertos. Carta dirigida ao excelentíssimo senhor Joaquim Guedes de Carvalho Menezes, presidente da relação de Loanda* (Lisbon: Imprensa Nacional, 1874), 6–8; José de Almada, *Apontamentos históricos sobre a escravatura e o trabalho indígena nas colónias portuguesas* (Lisboa: Imprensa Nacional, 1932), 15–18; Cristina Nogueira da Silva, *Constitucionalismo e império: a cidadania no ultramar português* (Lisbon: Almedina, 2009), 351–53; Margarida Seixas, "Escravos e libertos no Boletim Oficial de Angola (1845-1875)," *E-Revista de Estudos Interculturais do CEI* 3 (2015). These debates happened elsewhere as well, see, for example, the several contributions in the volume Richard Anderson and Henry Lovejoy, eds, *Liberated Africans and the Abolition of the Slave Trade, 1807-1896* (Melton: Boydell & Brewer, 2020), in particular, Suzanne Schwarz, "The Impact of Liberated African 'Disposal' Policies in Early Nineteenth Century Sierra Leone," 45–65.

[6] AHU, DGU, 1112, *Extinção da condição de servil e regulamento do trabalho nas colonias (1875-1877)*, April 29, 1875; and BGGOPA, 1866, n. 4, January 27, 1866, p. 17. The Portuguese empire was not an outlier and the similar process took place in other European slaving powers. The database, "Legacies of British Slave-ownership," examines the profits generated in the British West Indies. The 1833 Slave Emancipation Act awarded £20 million to slave owners but nothing for the enslaved. See https://www.ucl.ac.uk/lbs/. I am grateful for Suzanne Schwarz's comments about this project. For an important analysis on the unfinished struggle for financial compensation and reparations in the Atlantic world, see Ana Lucia Araujo, *Reparations for Slavery and the Slave Trade. A Transnational and Comparative History* (New York: Bloomsbury, 2017).

[7] James Duffy, *A Question of Slavery* (Cambridge, MA: Harvard University Press, 1967); Gerald J. Bender, *Angola Under the Portuguese: The Myth and the Reality* (London: Heinemann, 1978); Linda M. Heywood, "Slavery and Forced Labor in the Changing

excluded from institutions. According to the brotherhood *Nossa Senhora do Sacramento* at the parish of *Nossa Senhora do Pópulo*, freed people could not become members and the church bell could only sound to announce the death of one of the brotherhood members. Both clauses were considered "paltry and not very Christian."[8] This chapter explores the experiences of *libertos* in a context of change related to property recognition and rights along with freed people's access to property in the second half of the nineteenth century. Although semantics suggest otherwise, there was very little distinction between the experiences of enslaved or freed people in Angola.

An Ambivalent Legal Status

For over three centuries, Europeans and Africans had been debating the legal status of Africans, particularly from a theological point of view. Since the early sixteenth century, ecclesiastical personnel questioned the legal and moral arguments regarding enslaving Africans and owning people as property who could be bought and sold.[9] By the early seventeenth century, African *sobados* and the Portuguese colonial administration viewed slavery as a legal institution with clear definitions of who could or could not be enslaved, although some individuals challenged its legality.[10] Local rulers and Portuguese agents targeted political enemies and those with different religious beliefs, the so-called heathens (*gentios* in Portuguese sources). Transgressors and criminals, including political

Political Economy of Central Angola, 1850-1949," in *The End of Slavery in Africa*, ed. Suzanne Miers and Richard Roberts (Madison: University of Wisconsin Press, 1988), 415–35; and Frank Luce, "Armed Struggles, the ILO and the Labor Institute: Suppressing Forced Labor in Angola," in Joel Quirk, ed., *Slavery, Migration and Contemporary Bondage in Africa* (Trenton, NJ: Africa World Press, 2013), 65–93.

[8] AHU, SEMU, CU, Processos das Consultas, Cx. 31, n. 1071, repartição, "Processo acerca da aprovação do compromisso da irmandade do Santíssimo Sacramento da freguesia de Nossa Senhoro do Pópulo, 1856. L. 2, n. 450, April 22, 1856.

[9] A. J. R. Russell-Wood, "Iberian Expansion and the Issue of Black Slavery: Changing Portuguese Attitudes, 1440-1770," *The American Historical Review* 83, no. 1 (1978): 16–42; Boubacar Barry, *Senegambia and the Atlantic Slave Trade* (New York: Cambridge University Press, 1998), 27–49; António Manuel Hespanha and Catarina Madeira Santos, "Os poderes num Império Oceânico," in *História de Portugal, O Antigo Regime*, ed. António Manuel Hespanha, vol. 4 (Lisbon: Estampa, 1997); António Manuel Hespanha, "Luís de Molina e a escravização dos negros," *Análise Social* 35, no. 157 (2001): 937–60; Toby Green, *The Rise of the Trans-Atlantic Slave Trade in Western Africa, 1300-1589* (New York, NY: Cambridge University Press, 2012), 177–296; Linda M. Heywood and John K. Thornton, *Central Africans, Atlantic Creoles, and the Making of the Foundation of the Americas, 1585-1660* (New York: Cambridge University Press, 2007), 70–72.

[10] See, for example, Nafafé, *Lourenço da Silva Mendonça and the Black Atlantic Abolitionist Movement*

172   Branded in Freedom: The Persistent Commodification of People

dissidents, were also at risk of being enslaved. In the early nineteenth century, the expansion of ideas related to civility and the "Civilizing Mission" also influenced who could or could not be protected from forced labor. Some West Central Africans, such as those who served as *empacaceiros* (soldiers), were considered free people and protected by the colonial state, in part because their labor as professional soldiers benefited Portuguese interests.[11] In addition to the *empacaceiros*, other subjects enjoyed some level of protection against enslavement, although free Black people remained vulnerable.[12]

Portuguese legislation contemplated manumission and the freed legal status in the *Ordenações Filipinas*, the legal code implemented in the Portuguese Empire from the early seventeenth century. Following the political changes associated with the establishment of the constitutional monarchy, legislation was altered including the creation of codes of law that affected populations in overseas colonies. However, these nineteenth-century constitutional changes struggled to address rights and protections for the enslaved and freed populations that inhabited its colonies, although abolitionist pressure resulted in changes regarding

---

[11] Initially the term *empacaceiro* was used by those who hunt mpakasa, or buffalo, in Kimbundu. Eventually, the term designated anyone skilled in arrow hunting and later African soldiers who also employed muskets and shotguns, or *guerra preta*, Black troops. See Arquivo Nacional de Angola (ANA), Cod. 455, E-4-3, fl. 70 v, "Letter to the Governor of Angola Lourenço Germando Bosolo from colonel Juan Casemiro Pereira de Vasconcelos." For more on the *empacaceiros*, see Ana Paula Tavares and Catarina Madeira Santos, eds., *Africæ Monumenta: Arquivo Caculo Cacahenda* (Lisbon: Instituto de Investigação Científica Tropical, 2002), 400–01. For the civilizing mission in the Portuguese Empire, see Maria Paula G. Meneses, "O 'indígena' africano e o colono 'europeu': a construção da diferença por processos legais," *e-cadernos ces*, no. 7 (2010), http://eces.revues.org/403; Nogueira da Silva, *Constitucionalismo e império*, 284–304; Jerónimo, "The 'Civilising Guild': Race and Labor in the Third Portuguese Empire, c. 1870-1930"; Jerónimo, *Livros Brancos, Almas Negras*; Samuël Coghe, "Reordering Colonial Society: Model Villages and Social Planning in Rural Angola, 1920–45," *Journal of Contemporary History* 52, no. 1 (2017): 16–44.

[12] For more on this topic, see Mariana P. Candido, "African Freedom Suits and Portuguese Vassal Status: Legal Mechanisms for Fighting Enslavement in Benguela, Angola, 1800–1830," *Slavery & Abolition* 32, no. 3 (2011): 447–59; José C. Curto, "Struggling against Enslavement: The Case of José Manuel in Benguela, 1816-1820," *Canadian Journal of African Studies* 39, no. 1 (2005): 96–122; Roquinaldo Ferreira, *Cross-Cultural Exchange in the Atlantic World: Angola and Brazil during the Era of the Slave Trade* (New York: Cambridge University Press, 2012), 52–87; Mariana P. Candido, "O limite tênue entre a liberdade e escravidão em Benguela durante a era do comércio transatlântico," *Afro-Ásia* 47 (2013): 239–68; Crislayne Alfagali, *Ferreiros e fundidores da Ilamba : uma história social da fabricação do ferro e da Real Fábrica de Nova Oeiras (Angola, segunda metade do século XVIII)* (Luanda: Fundação Agostinho Neto, 2018).

the *liberto* condition.[13] The problem was that the legal term *libertos* included people in different life circumstances, such as those freed by the Mixed Commissions, people freed at the baptismal font, those who were manumitted for services or in wills, and those who bought their freedom.

The 1836 ban on slave exports led to a concentration of enslaved people who could not be sent to the Americas. In 1844, under British influence, a *Tribunal de Presas* (Prize Court) was established with the goal of apprehending ships suspected to be involved in transporting enslaved Africans. If illegal embarkation occurred, the court investigated and declared all onboard to be freed. These actions resulted in the emancipation of up to 3,000 captives from barracoons and slave ships in Angola. Despite their new status as freed people, all these individuals received an official "T" iron brand on their upper arms, indicating they were under the care of the Prize Court.[14] In many ways, the branding "T" on freed individuals operated as written evidence of their new status as *libertos*, once again, showing that the writing culture was essential to exercised rights over property, land or people, including over those who no longer belonged to individuals but to colonial states or societies in charge of facilitating their transition into freedom.

---

[13] For the limitations of the abolitionism movement in Portugal, see Cristina Nogueira da Silva and Keila Grinberg, "Soil Free from Slaves: Slave Law in Late Eighteenth- and Early Nineteenth-Century Portugal," *Slavery & Abolition* 32, no. 3 (2011): 431–46; Arlindo M. Caldeira, *Escravos em Portugal. Das origens ao século XIX* (Lisbon: A Esfera dos Livros, 2017). For the long history of slavery and presence of free Africans in Portugal, see A. C. de C. M Saunders, *A Social History of Black Slaves and Freedmen in Portugal, 1441-1555* (Cambridge: Cambridge University Press, 1982); António de Almeida Mendes, "Africaines esclaves au Portugal: dynamiques d'exclusion, d'intégration et d'assimilation à l'époque moderne (XVe-XVe siècles)," *Renaissance and Reformation* 31, no. 2 (2008): 45–65; Didier Lahon, *O negro no coração do império: uma memória a resgatar: séculos XV-XIX* (Lisboa: Ministério da Educação, 1999); Lucilene Reginaldo, "'África em Portugal': devoções, irmandades e escravidão no Reino de Portugal, século XVIII," *História (São Paulo)* 28, no. 1 (2009): 289–319. For a detailed study on the constitutional changes in Portugal and its empire in the nineteenth century, see Nogueira da Silva, *Constitucionalismo e império*.

[14] *Índice do Boletim Oficial da Província de Angola comprehendendo os anos que decorrem desde 13 de setembro de 1845, em que foi publicado o N. 1 até 1862 inclusive* (Luanda: Imprensa do Governo, 1864), 264. See also Samuël Coghe, "The Problem of Freedom in a Mid-Nineteenth-Century Atlantic Slave Society: The Liberated Africans of the Anglo-Portuguese Mixed Commission in Luanda (1844–1870)," *Slavery & Abolition* 33, no. 3 (2012): 480; Nogueira da Silva, *Constitucionalismo e império*, 335–37. For different strategies of identifying liberated Africans, see Helen MacQuarrie and Andrew Pearson, "Prize Possessions: Transported Material Culture of the Post-Abolition Enslaved – New Evidence from St Helena," *Slavery & Abolition* 37, no. 1 (2016): 45–72; as well as several case studies examined in Richard Anderson and Henry B. Lovejoy, eds., *Liberated Africans and the Abolition of the Slave Trade, 1807-1896* (Melton: Boydell & Brewer, 2020).

In 1847, the Mixed Commission patrols seized the slave ship *Flor do Campos*, its crew and cargo, which included thirty-three captives identified as originating from the interior of Benguela. The general secretary of the Province of Angola, João de Roboredo, declared the captives freed, *libertos*, and assigned them to Luanda's residents, who employed them under the auspices of the *Junta Protetora de Libertos*. After some *libertos* fled, Governor Cunha decided to cancel their redistribution among Luanda residents and sent them instead to the island of São Tomé. This decision was motivated by the insecurity that Prize Court *libertos* faced. Cunha argued that some of the thirty-three liberated individuals had put their "freed" status at risk by

escaping to the bushes looking for their homelands in the interior of Benguela, where all of them had come from. Many were enslaved while running away. In order to prevent their kidnapping, and their subsequent re-enslavement, as this had already happened to many others, I ordered all to be sent to São Tomé, where they will be useful.[15]

Thus, these thirty-three individuals, who had already suffered the trauma of captivity, enslavement, and an interrupted slave voyage, had to face a new challenge: resettling in São Tomé, a place unknown to them, where their labor would enrich São Tomé planters.

The authorities who were supposedly in charge of freeing people from the slave trade were now also responsible for the practice of exporting West Central Africans. Cases like this demonstrate that the *liberto* status did not mean the end of forced migration for West Central Africans. In fact, they continued to be treated as commodities who could be forcibly transported and put to work in the expanding cocoa farms in São Tomé.[16] The Luanda public cemetery register reveals the burial of over

---

[15] Arquivo Histórico Ultramarino (AHU), Angola, Correspondência dos Governadores, 2a Seção, Pasta 12, doc. February 13, 1847. Liberated Africans fled upon arrival in Freetown as well. See Schwarz, "The Impact off Liberated African "disposal" Policies," 48.

[16] There is a vast scholarship on the importance of *liberto* labor in São Tomé. See, among others, Augusto Nascimento and Alfredo Gomes Dias, "A Importação de libertos em São Tomé no Terceiro Quartel de Oitocentos," *Revista de História Económica e Social* 25 (1989): 1–70; Catherine Higgs, *Chocolate Islands. Cocoa, Slavery, and Colonial Africa* (Athens: Ohio University Press, 2012); Alexander Keese, "Forced Labour in the 'Gorgulho Years': Understanding Reform and Repression in Rural São Tomé e Príncipe, 1945–1953," *Itinerario* 38, no. 1 (2014): 103–24; Gerhard Seibert, "Sugar, Cocoa, and Oil. Economic Success and Failure in São Tomé and Príncipe from the Sixteenth to the Twenty-First Centuries," in *African Islands: Leading Edges of Empire and Globalization*, ed. Toyin Falola, R. Joseph Parrott, and Danielle Porter Sanchez (Rochester, NY: University of Rochester Press, 2019), 68–95; Augusto Nascimento, "As fronteiras da nação e das raças em São Tomé e Príncipe: São-tomenses, Europeus e Angolas nos primeiros decênios de Novecentos," *Varia História* 29, no. 51 (2013):

Illustration 5.1 A portrait of a slave in the Portuguese settlement of
Benguela, 1813
(*Source*: National Maritime Museum, Greenwich, Michael Graham-Stewart
Slavery Collection)

100 liberated Africans between July 13, 1844, and January 1, 1845. In
several cases, a single entry registers the burial of three to six bodies
identified only by their sex and the branded letters on their bodies.
Though freed, their names, places of origin, and life experiences were
not recorded, and their existence in the colonial archive is restricted to
their enumeration, a short identification as female or male, and a description of the hot iron mark that had burned their skin. The written record
reinforced people's commodification and disposability, stressing how the
colonial state and residents had naturalized violence, as can be seen in
Illustration 5.1. Most of the deceased individuals had been seized by the

721–43; Mariana P. Candido, "Des passeports pour la liberté? Conceptions raciales et
déplacements de populations vers São Tomé (XIXe siècle)," in *Libres aprés les abolitions?
Statuts et identités aux Amériques et en Afrique* (Paris: Khartala, 2018), 71–92.

Anglo-Portuguese Mixed Commisson patrols, but some were also people who had been declared free locally.[17] The law was ambiguous in the case of people who secured their manumission, or who were declared *libertos* after captivity in the colonial centers. The colonial administration allowed the establishment of an in-between status, similar to the condition of freed people elsewhere in the Atlantic world. Every freed individual was under the tutelage of the *Junta Protetora dos Escravos e Libertos* and was forced to serve the colonial state for at least seven years. In some instances, the Junta could suspend the policy, such as the case of *libertos* who graduated from the Universidade de Coimbra or any institution of higher education (university and polytechnic colleges), as well as those who joined the clergy, served in the army and navy, or were members of the Royal Academy of Science. Those who taught at primary or secondary schools became agents of commercial houses or major traders (*comerciantes de grosso trato*), or who acquired any territorial property were also released from forced labor. In the colony of Angola, liberated Africans were bought and put to work for an excessive number of hours to expand the infrastructure and make urban improvements. They were also subjected to physical punishment.[18] Attaining the status of liberated did not mean they gained rights or protection against former slave owners or the violence of the colonial state.

The promulgation of the 1854 decree made mandatory the registration of property on human beings. Owners who failed to identify and register their slaves risked losing their property to the newly inaugurated *Junta Protetora dos Escravos e Libertos*. However, the Junta did not protect the rights of unregistered slaves but simply guaranteed a change of status to liberated Africans, which included continuing service for the state or private individuals. It also created the paternalistic figure of the *Curador*

[17] AHU, Angola, Correspondência dos Governadores, Pasta A and C (old numeration), 1845, "Livro de escritura dos libertos, Cemitério Público," January 1, 1845. For more on violence, the problem of people's disposability, and the historical narrative, see Jessica Marie Johnson, "Markup Bodies: Black [Life] Studies and Slavery [Death] Studies at the Digital Crossroads," *Social Text* 36, no. 4 (2018): 57–79; Marisa J. Fuentes, *Dispossessed Lives: Enslaved Women, Violence, and the Archive* (Philadelphia: University of Pennsylvania Press, 2016).

[18] ANA, Cod. 455, fl. 78, April 28, 1845. "Tutela dos libertos," *Boletim do Conselho Ultramarino*, vol. II (Lisbon: Imprensa Nacional, 1869), p. 488–89. See also Coghe, "Problem of Freedom," 479–80. For the challenges Black people faced to have access to higher education in Portugal, see Lucilene Reginaldo, "André do Couto Goudinho: Homem preto, formado em Coimbra, missionário no Congo em fins do século XVIII," *Revista História* 173 (2015): 141–74; Lucilene Reginaldo, "'Não tem informação': mulatos, pardos e pretos na Universidade de Coimbra (1700-1771)," *Estudos Ibero-Americanos* 44, no. 3 (2018).

dos escravos pobres e libertos, the attorney for slaves, the poor, and freed people, a problematic position that implied the legal subordination of these people.[19] The apprenticeship period for former slaves was portrayed as a transitory stage and favored the interests of owners since freed people continued to perform the same tasks as before. The colonial state sided with former owners and their request that the state mitigate the loss of their property, justifying the practice by stating that formerly enslaved people needed to learn how to live as free people and free laborers. Administrators mixed Civilizing Mission goals of self-discipline and developing a work ethic with moral ideas of Western superiority, associating African labor with slavery and backward attitudes.[20] The expansion of the paper culture also pushed for registering the enslaved population and the imposition of taxes on slave property.[21]

Irregularities occurred, suggesting the connivance of colonial authorities and slave owners, such as the case of Mariana, who lived in bondage despite having been freed upon baptism. In 1854, Mariana's godfather, António Pereira Barbosa Bastos, litigated her freedom, arguing that her former slave master, Miguel Gonçalves da Cruz, had financially profited from her manumission yet continued to keep Mariana in bondage. In the litigation process, Bastos presented copies of Mariana's baptism and slave registrations, once again showing the importance of written evidence to prove freedom and discredit property claims. Mariana's baptism had taken place in Bastos's house, located in the region known as Egito's beach north of Benguela, famous as a place where illegal slave

---

[19] ANA, Cod. 444, fl. 185v-186, April 5, 1849; *Indice do Boletim Oficial da Província de Angola*, 105 and 110; *A abolição da Escravatura*, 35–36. For more on this, see Aida Freudenthal, "Os quilombos de Angola no século XIX: A recusa da escravidão," *Estudos Afro-Asiáticos* 32 (1997): 113.

[20] For more on the conflict between supporting slavery and the civilizing mission, and the apprenticeship solution, see Sá da Bandeira, *A emancipação dos libertos*, 6–7; Kevin Grant, *A Civilised Savagery: Britain and the New Slaveries in Africa, 1884–1926* (Routledge, NY: Chapman & Hall, 2005); Suzanne Schwarz, "'A Just and Hounorable Commerce.' Abolitionist Experimentation in Sierra Leone in the Late Eighteenth and Early Nineteenth Centuries," *African Economic History* 45, no. 1 (2017): 1–45; Jerónimo, *Livros Brancos, Almas Negras*. The apprenticeship regime implemented in Angola was similar to the British, French, and Portuguese schemes imposed in the Caribbean and in Brazil. See Beatriz Gallotti Mamigonian, "O Estado Nacional e a instabilidade da propriedade escrava: A lei de 1831 e a matrícula dos escravos de 1872," *Almanack* no. 2 (2011); Beatriz G. Mamigonian, "In the Name of Freedom: Slave Trade Abolition, the Law and the Brazilian Branch of the African Emigration Scheme (Brazil–British West Indies, 1830s–1850s)," *Slavery & Abolition* 30, no. 1 (2009): 41–66; Stanley Engerman, "Comparative Approaches to the Ending of Slavery," *Slavery & Abolition* 21, no. 2 (2000): 281–300.

[21] ANA, Cod. 3160, "Registro de Escravos (Benguela), 1859. For more on the punishment, see *Indice do Boletim Oficial da Província de Angola*, 110. For this debate, see Ferreira, "Abolicionismo versus Colonialismo.

exports occurred.[22] The baptism was conducted in front of a group of witnesses, including the priest, Manoel Monteiro de Moraes; the captain of the artillery of Luanda, Joaquim Militão de Gusmão; and Mariana's godparents. Mariana, baptized as an adult woman, was identified as a heathen (*gentia*) and, under the gaze of her godparents António Pereira Barbosa Bastos and Violante Joaquina, was declared a free person.[23]

Yet the following year Miguel de Gonçalves da Cruz listed Mariana as one of his properties in the slave register.[24] According to the copy of the slave register dated November 5, 1855, Mariana came from Benguela-Velha (nowadays Porto Amboim). She was eighteen years old, of average height, with a "J" branded on both sides of her back. No explanation is available about the meaning of the Js or even on how Mariana got them. Her official economic activity was washing and ironing, and she offered her skills in the streets of Benguela and Egipto. Bastos's argument was that Cruz had deceived the state by listing Mariana as his property since she was already a free person. He claimed that Cruz was trying to take advantage of the government's financial compensation for slave owners by increasing the amount of his property, and in doing so put Mariana's freedom at risk. It is not clear how this case ended, but it reveals captors' resistance to recognizing and executing the status of freed or liberated Africans, and their interest in maximizing their property claims and profits. Freedom was often followed by arbitrary decisions to keep former slaves in bondage under the disguise of acquiring skills or learning how to live as free people. In Angola, formerly enslaved people, like Mariana, received no financial compensation for their labor. One of the paths to freedom was the use of colonial courts; the support of free people was important in processes very similar to those in Brazil, as well as later in French and British colonies on the African continent.[25] The imposition

---

[22] TCB, "Processo crime tentativa de escravizar pessoas livres, Ministério Público vs Miguel Gonçalves da Cruz, 1857." For more on Egito beach and the illegal slave trade, see AHU, Angola, Pasta 29, September 6, 1861; and Valentim Alexandre and Jill Dias, *O Império Africano* (Lisbon: Estampa, 1998), 384.

[23] Her baptism was on April 16, 1854. See TCB, Crime "Escravizar pessoas livres, Ministério Publico vs Miguel Gonçalves da Cruz, 1857," fl. 5, November 13, 1856.

[24] TCB, "Escravizar pessoas livres, Ministério Público vs Miguel Gonçalves da Cruz, 1857, fl. 6-6v. More references are available at AHU, Angola, Pasta 35, "Nota do número de libertos," December 31, 1864.

[25] Coghe, "Problem of Freedom," 484. For slaves using colonial courts in Brazil, see Keila Grinberg, *Liberata : A Lei da Ambigüidade : As Ações de Liberdade da corte de apelação do Rio de Janeiro no século XIX* (Rio de Janeiro: Relume Dumará, 1994); Chalhoub, *A força da escravidão*. For studies that stress the use of colonial courts in Africa, see Kristin Mann and Richard Roberts, "Law in Colonial Africa," in *Law in Colonial Africa*, eds. Kristin Mann and Richard Roberts (Portsmouth, NH: Heinemann, 1991); Richard L. Roberts, *Litigants and Households: African Disputes and Colonial Courts in the French*

of liberal values, such as individual property rights, however, actually increased precarity for the enslaved and freed West Central Africans.

Apprenticeship and Lingering Slaving Practices

Given the status of *liberto* and its link with so-called apprenticeship programs, former slaves saw very little difference from the institution of slavery. A series of undermining practices continued to exist even when a person was legally free. Slavers may have received financial compensation for the manumission, but many were unwilling to set their human property free. Slaveholders such as Dona Josefa Manoel Pereira da Silva resisted freeing their property, even though the 1854 decree made cases of freedom litigation mandatory. Many other cases of enslaved individuals in Angola and elsewhere in the continent stress the level of vulnerability and uncertain status that poor dependents and refugees faced in times of turmoil. Many of them were women, considered valuable workers and pawns in local disputes between political elites and merchants.[26]

In 1850, the governor of Angola sent eight freedwomen, who are not identified by their names or places of origin, to the newly established town of Mossamedes, nowadays Namibe, with the goal of putting them to work in agriculture or "wherever the governor felt their labor was needed."[27] A few months later, another group of twenty unnamed *libertos* arrived in Mossamedes to supply much of the needed labor in the newly established plantations. After the death of their former owner, José Guilherme Pereira Barbosa, twenty slaves were put under the care of the colonial state. After they were freed, all of them were moved from

Soudan, 1895-1912 (Portsmouth, NH: Heinemann, 2005); Richard Roberts, "The End of Slavery, Colonial Courts, and Social Conflict in Gumbu, 1908-1911," *Canadian Journal of African Studies* 34, no. 3 (2000): 684–713; Scully, *Liberating the Family?*; Paul E. Lovejoy, "Concubinage and the Status of Women Slaves in Early Colonial Northern Nigeria," *The Journal of African History* 29, no. 2 (1988): 245–266.

[26] For more on the importance of women's work, see Curtis Keim, "Women and Slavery among the Mangbetu C. 1800-1910," in *Women and Slavery in Africa*, ed. Claire C Robertson and Martin A Klein (Madison: University of Wisconsin Press, 1983), 144–59; Marcia Wright, "Women in Peril: A Commentary on the Life Stories of Captives in Nineteenth Century East-Central Africa," *African Social Research* 20 (1975): 800–19; Susan Herlin Broadhead, "Slave Wives, Free Sisters: Bakongo Women and Slavery C. 1700-1850," in *Women and Slavery in Africa*, ed. Claire C. Robertson and Martin A. Klein (Madison: University of Wisconsin Press, 1983); Candido, "Concubinage and Slavery in Benguela, C. 1750-1850."

[27] ANA, Cod. 326, fl. 119v, March 13, 1850. For an important study on the colonial legal apparatus in Angola see Mariana Dias Paes, "Shared Atlantic legal culture: The case of a freedom suit in Benguela," *Atlantic Studies* 17, 3 (2020): 419-440.

Cazengo to Mossamedes and continued to perform the same labor they did as enslaved people: weeding, pruning, planting, and later harvesting. The thirteen men and seven women were identified by their age, sex, place of origin, and physical marks. Miguel Gico from Cazengo was the oldest at thirty-nine years old. Nine-year-old Facesta Quilossobo from Mbailundu was the youngest. Eleven of them had the iron mark "T" of the Prize Court (*Tribunal das Presas* in Portuguese) on their bodies, a visual mark that their bodies could still be subject to physical abuse even when legally freed.[28] Perhaps their experience in the coffee plantations in Cazengo north of N'dalatando made them attractive laborers for the Mossamedes plantations that required labor, preferably enslaved labor. Five out of the thirteen men were under fifteen years old. While colonial administrators put anyone to work, West Central Africans perceived cultivation as a task for women and children.[29]

The apprenticeship system in Angola had a nominal vocational training aspect. The *Curador dos escravos pobres and libertos* oversaw the training that liberated Africans received and wrote quarterly reports. These reports reveal the failures of the program, with *libertos* working on farms and cleaning houses, exactly the same activities they performed before attaining liberated status. Despite its limitations and failures, or precisely because of them, between 1854 and 1863 more than 30,000 people were freed in the Portuguese territories in West Central Africa.[30] Among them was Júlia, a Black woman who sought help from the *Curador dos escravos pobres e libertos* to restore her freedom.[31] According to Article 6 of the 1854 decree, "every slave resident in Portuguese territory has the right to claim his or her natural freedom, as long as they are able to financially compensate their slave master for his or her service."[32] As in other slave societies, enslaved people actively looked for support and ways to pay for manumission. On October 4, 1860, Júlia

---

[28] ANA, Cod. 326, fl. 130 v, June 5, 1850. For more on the Cazengo coffee plantations, see David Birmingham, "The Coffee Barons of Cazengo," *Journal of African History* 19, no. 4 (1978): 523–38; David Birmingham, "A Question of Coffee: Black Enterprise in Angola," *Canadian Journal of African Studies* 16, no. 2 (1982): 343–46.

[29] For more on this topic, see Roquinaldo A. Ferreira, "Agricultural Enterprise and Unfree Labour in Nineteenth Century Angola," in *Commercial Agriculture, the Slave Trade and Slavery in Atlantic Africa*, ed. Robin Law, Suzanne Schwarz, and Silke Strickrodt (Woodbridge: James Currey, 2013), 238.

[30] Roquinaldo Ferreira, "Escravidão e revoltas de escravos em Angola (1830-1860)," *Afro-Ásia* 21–22 (1998): 20.

[31] For more on the *junta protetora dos escravos e libertos*, see AHU, Angola, Livro 661, fl. 6v, October 31, 1857. See also Jerónimo, *Livros brancos, almas negras*; Jerónimo, "The 'Civilising Guild'," 173–99.

[32] "Decreto de 11 de dezembro de 1854, ordenando o registro de escravos e libertos," Menezes, *Relatório do Governador Geral*, 424–25. For other cases of enslaved people

claimed her freedom. Dona Josefa Manoel Pereira da Silva refused to accept Julia's request to set a price on her manumission and failed to present herself or her representative to the court. Witnesses supported Júlia's request, including the local priest. Four days later, Dona Josefa Manoel Pereira da Silva attended the hearing and requested 120$000 *réis* for Júlia's freedom, or £540 pounds sterling, a very high amount equal to about £31,929.77 today. Júlia agreed to pay half of it, 60$000 *réis*, for her freedom, which resulted in the intervention of the attorney Van Dunen. An independent appraiser set 80$000 *réis* as the appropriate price for Julia's freedom (£360 in 1860, corresponding to £21,286.51 in 2017). It is not clear how Júlia collected this amount of money, but in twenty-four hours she brought the 80$000 *réis* to Van Dunen and was declared a free woman. Thirteen days after initiating the process, Júlia received her manumission letter.[33] It was a struggle for enslaved individuals to ensure that the *Junta Protetora* heard their cases and intervened in their favor.

Even attaining freed status, however, did not mean full control of one's own mobility. In 1858, the freedwoman Felicia Cesária requested protection against the efforts of a former owner to take her back to Luanda against her will. According to her account, the Catela family owned her for many years, and she worked in the family's home in Luanda. The family faced economic difficulties and put Felícia Cesária up for sale. One man, Tomás António Tarracão, showed interest and offered 160 $000 *réis* to buy Felicia Cesária but failed to deliver the amount (roughly £ 720 in 1856 or £ 42,573 in 2017). A Benguela lieutenant, Francisco Martins de Merenda, paid 170$000 réis (£ 765 pounds in 1860 or £ 45,233 in 2017) for her and took her to his house in Benguela. Tarracão tried to make an unsuccessful second offer. Facing resistance from Lieutenant Merenda, now Felícia Cesária's legal owner, Tarracão paid for her freedom. Now a freedwoman, Felicia refused to go to Luanda with Tarracão. She asked the *Curador* to allow her to remain under Lieutenant Merenda's care, arguing she was treated well and

---

using the Portuguese courts to challenge slavery, see Chalhoub, *A força da escravidão*; Grinberg, "Slavery, Manumission and the Law in Nineteenth-Century Brazil"; Cristina Nogueira da Silva and Keila Grinberg, "Soil Free from Slaves: Slave Law in Late Eighteenth- and Early Nineteenth-Century Portugal," *Slavery & Abolition* 32, no. 3 (2011): 431–446.

[33] TCB, "Autos cíveis de reinvindicação da liberdade da preta Julia, escrava de Josefa Manoel Pereira da Silva, October 4, 1860." The attorney, Guilherme Van Dunen, was also one of the largest slave owners of Benguela. See Delgado, *A Famosa e Histórica Benguela*, 173. Slave holders resisted emancipation in different contexts, and Angola is not an exception. For an excellent comparison between emancipation debates and policies in the Atlantic world, and one which includes and privileges the South Atlantic, see Araujo, *Reparations for Slavery and the Slave Trade*, 45–82.

enjoyed freedom at his house. The attorney stated he had seen Felicia carried in *maxilas* (palanquins) and wearing nice dresses and shoes. According to him, this demonstrated that it was false to declare that Merenda treated her as a slave.[34] One of the tasks of the *Curador dos escravos pobres e libertos* was to ensure that freed individuals were not exploited. However, his argument that access to Western wardrobes was evidence of good care erases the terror and violence that Felicia Cesária certainly experienced while in captivity.

The expressed wishes of a freedwoman were not respected, and the governor of Angola ordered Felícia Cesária to return to Luanda on board the ship *Esperança* (hope in Portuguese), an ironic name for a ship that would transport a freedwoman to captivity. On September 1858, Felicia Cesária boarded *Esperança* in her journey to Luanda to serve the man who had freed her. The *Curador* stated there was not much he could do since Tomás António Tarracão had powerful influence and access to colonial authorities. Upon arriving in Luanda, the freedwoman Felicia Cesária was delivered to the house of Tarracão against her wishes.[35] It is not clear why Cesária resisted going to Tarracão's house. Perhaps she feared violence, or she may have established a network of friends and people who supported her in Lieutenant Merenda's house. Felicia Cesária disappears from the colonial records after her arrival in Luanda; one wonders if she was ever able to exercise her freedom. Her case reveals once again the vulnerability of freed people and the incertitude they faced, but also the expectations regarding paid manumission. Tarracão presumed Felícia Cesária would be grateful and become his dependent, living under his supervision and in his household. Rather than an act of generosity, the expectation was an attitude of indebtedness, and when Felícia Cesária refused, he employed unwritten social rules, mobilized his contacts, and exercised his power.[36] The tragic irony is that although these were freed people, colonial administrators saw little difference between an enslaved individual and a *liberto*. On the subject of *libertos* in Angola, the traveler Joachim John Monteiro remarked,

---

[34] ANA, Cod. 471, E – 7 – 5, Registro de oficios expedidos 13 junho de 1857 a 22 janeiro de 1859, fl. 121, April 17, 1858, Governador de Benguela to governador geral da província; fl. 130v-131, June 7, 1858; fl. 133, June 7, 1858.
[35] ANA, 471, fl. 150v, July 31, 1858; and fl. 163v, September 5, 1858.
[36] For more on this topic, see Nogueira da Silva, *Constitucionalismo e império*, 352–53; Yacine Daddi Addoun, "'So That God Frees the Former Masters from Hell Fire:' Salvation through Manumission in Ottoman Algeria," in *Crossing Memories. Slavery and African Diaspora*, ed. Ana Lucia Araujo, Mariana P. Candido, and Paul E. Lovejoy (Trenton, NJ: Africa World Press, 2011), 237–59.

Owners were obliged to supply them with proper food, clothing, and medicine, and were not allowed to punish them; while they, on their part, were required to work for seven years as compensation to their owners, at the expiration of which time they were to be free. This has been allowed to remain virtually a dead letter, the slaves never having had the law explained to them, and the authorities not troubling themselves to enforce their liberation at the end of the seven years.[37]

In Felícia Cesária's case, sexuality and the possibility of sexual abuse might have played an important role, despite the documents' silence. The December 10, 1836, law that abolished the slave trade and the 1850s decrees that freed children of enslavement in the colony of Angola could be circumvented through a loophole that allowed Portuguese subjects to relocate to other Portuguese territories and bring up to ten *libertos* with them to facilitate agricultural expansion. In 1853, a resident of Benguela, João Maria de Sousa e Almeida, moved to the São Tomé archipelago, bringing 100 of his slaves.[38] He was not alone. During the sixteen months between February 1861 and August 1862, thirty-seven ships left the port of Luanda for São Tomé with West Central Africans of different statuses – slaves, freed, and free. Among them, there were 25 freedwomen, 124 freedmen, and 47 freed people whose gender was not identified.[39]

Colonial bureaucracy's push to enumerate and quantify colonized populations generated immense data on how Black bodies were treated, or rather mistreated, commodified, and abused. All freed people forcibly transported to São Tomé were baptized and branded on the right arm, similar to enslaved Africans being transported to the Americas. The volume of documents suggests the terror, the violence, and the commodification of freed people, who did not control their movement or their labor. Sir George Jackson, the British Commissioner in Luanda to the Foreign Office, stated that a freed person "has no voice in the matter."[40] Most freed individuals traveled with someone, sometimes a female companion. On other occasions, the annotation in the observation section could include information such as "belongs to Joaquim Gomes Vasco, who travels to São Tomé," as in the case of Pedro, listed as a freedman on board the ship *Estafânia*, clearly still in

---

[37] Joachim John Monteiro, *Angola and the River Congo* (New York: Macmillan, 1876), 40–41. There are remarkable similarities with the British apprenticeship model imposed on the British West Indies. For more on this, see Holt, *The Problem of Freedom*.

[38] Nascimento e Dias, "Importação de Libertos em São Tomé," 51.

[39] AHU, Angola, Miscelânea, Maço 771, "Escravos, Libertos e Livres. Angola e São Tomé."

[40] Carreira, *The People of the Cape Verde Islands*, p. 106–07; Duffy, *A Question of Slavery*, 14; Marques, *Os Sons do silêncio*, 308–11.

bondage.[41] This case challenges the written data and the enumeration efforts that perpetuated people's commodification and erases the violent nature of slavery and the apprenticeship regimes. Tallies and the data available in the colonial archives embrace the liberal logic that work, including forced labor, provides dignity. However, the records fail to recognize the humanity and the experiences of freed Africans, demonstrating "the promiscuous use of the term *livre* [and] *libertos*," making it difficult to distinguish the limits of each of these legal statuses.[42] Twenty-six of the people did not have their status identified in their passports. Six of them were young people between the ages of ten and sixteen years old. These individuals were treated as property.

The movement of former slaves and others continued, with colonial authorities in Benguela issuing passports to Portuguese merchants to relocate and transport supposedly freed people. One such case was Nabungo, a freedwoman who traveled with António Rodrigues Neves Júnior, as his "dependent," an ambiguous term that nonetheless indicated Nabungo's subordination to Neves Júnior. Other freed people were on the same ship, the *Paquete do Sul*, and their fate after arriving in São Tomé is not known.[43] In 1864, the governor of São Tomé, Estanislau de Almeida, remarked on the large number of people transported there, "Everybody knows that in 1861 and 1862 many black individuals of both sexes came from Angola as free people. But it is also common knowledge that these people were sold to the main slave owners of this island [of São Tomé] as soon as they landed here."[44] The colonial state and former slave owners did not treat freedmen and freedwomen as free people, and they continued to be considered valuable property. Legal loopholes and the connivance of colonial administrators kept slavery alive well into the twentieth century, regardless of its legal abolition in 1875. These freed individuals also faced a series of limitations regarding access to land and tools, which denied them a series of property rights white settlers enjoyed in São Tomé.[45]

---

[41] It is not clear if this D. Estefânia ship is the same D. Estefânia ship that belonged to the Companhia União Mercantil, subsidized by the Portuguese Crown, and responsible for communication between Western Africa and Portugal. See Alexandre and Dias, *O Império Africano*, 280. See also AHU, Angola, Miscelânia, Maço 771, "Escravos, Libertos e Livres. Angola e São Tomé," ship Estefânia, July 2, 1861.

[42] Duffy, *A Question of Slavery*, 11. See also Johnson, "Markup Bodies"; Saidiya Hartman, "Venus in Two Acts," *Small Axe* 12, no. 2 (2008): 1–14.

[43] ANA, cx. 1338, Passaportes exteriores, Luanda, August 13, 1862.

[44] Nascimento and Dias, "A Importação de libertos em São Tomé no Terceiro Quartel de Oitocentos," 56.

[45] For more on this, see Gerhard Seibert, "Colonialismo em São Tomé e Príncipe: hierarquização, classificação e segregação da vida social," *Anuário Antropológico* 2 (2015): 99–120.

While colonial authorities were discussing the nature and duration of *liberto* status, the requests of Portuguese settlers provide some information about how freedmen and freedwomen were in fact perceived. On February 20, 1875, Joaquim António Bravo, a farmer in São Tomé, requested authorization to "ransom the largest number of Black people needed to be sent to farms in São Tomé."[46] The term used by Bravo, *resgate*, is the same word employed by fifteenth- and sixteenth-century Portuguese agents who kidnapped and seized free people on the Atlantic coast of Africa. The secretary of the *Negócios da Marinha e do Ultramar* denied the request, stating that slave trading was illegal and that "heathens" who lived under slavery had to remain in Angola where they would, eventually, be civilized. However, the request exposes how planters in São Tomé viewed the employment of West Central Africans as overt slave trade. A few years later, in 1878, when the status of *liberto* had officially been abolished, 251 "ransomed settlers" signed contracts to work on farms and in homes and were shipped to São Tomé on board the steamship *China*. These individuals had been seized (*resgatado* in Portuguese) in Libolo, Novo Redondo, including Quissango, a fifteen-year-old young man, and Quilembo, a fifteen-year-old woman, the youngest people on board *China*. They were traveling with forty-four men and thirty-four women kidnapped in Novo Redondo and labeled as ransomed settlers, as if their actions were voluntary. The oldest person in the group from Novo Redondo was Vungi, a twenty-six-year-old man.[47] Under the same program, sixty-one women and ninety-three men seized in Libolo, as well as twelve men and seven women recruited in Cambambe, were sent to São Tomé. All were identified as free, single, and not baptized. On some lists, freed people were listed as belonging to a planter in São Tomé, such as the case of Muhongo, a Quisanga man who belonged to Dona Isabel de Brito Giblet.[48] One wonders if any of them understood the terms of the contract, and if they ever made it back to Angola.

As these cases from official record indicate, the 1875 law did not end servitude. In fact, it explicitly stated that freed people were obliged to offer their services for hire, preferably to former slavers. The gradual, and messy, process of establishing individual property rights encouraged de

---

[46] AHU, Pasta 45, n. 36, "Requerimento de Joaquim António Bravo, proprietário e agricultor em São Tomé," February 20, 1875.
[47] AHU, Pasta 48 (648), doc. 241, "Mapas dos colonos livres resgatados no sertão de Novo Redondo," October 19, 1878.
[48] AHU, Pasta 48 (648), doc. 241, "Mapa dos colonos livres resgatos em Libolo," October 11, 1878, See also "Mapas dos colonos livres resgatados no sertão de Novo Redondo," and "Mapa dos colonos livres resgatos em Cambambe," October 11, 1878.

facto slavery, perhaps even more surreptitious forms than before. The removal of people from their places of origin was societally destabilizing and contributed to commodification but also to notions of empty and available lands. Slavery, commodification, and displacement were intimately connected and vital to colonialism's ability to survive and generate profits. The colonial state changed the discourse regarding owning human beings to fit an international order that defended free markets yet continued to exploit African labor. Freed labor represented the continuous subjugation of Africans in the name of civilization and entrepreneurship.[49]

The Failure of Freedom

The series of 1854–1875 decrees that attempted to bring the institution of slavery to an end failed miserably, first because freed people continued to work in conditions akin to slavery, and, second, despite the change in their legal status, freed individuals de facto belonged to other people and did not enjoy autonomy and freedom. The expansion of coffee, sugar, and cotton plantations along the Bengo River, in the Cazengo Region, around Dombe Grande, and Mossamedes and their constant need for cheap and dispensable labor perpetuated many of the practices of ownership of human beings into the twentieth century. As with the freed people sent from Luanda and Benguela to São Tomé in the 1850s to 1870s, the freedmen and freedwomen south of the Kwanza River had very few opportunities to improve their condition. In 1851, Dona Vicarta Aires Gomes presented a petition to the secretary of Mossamedes to remove one of the freedwomen living in her house, Ana, from the apprenticeship program. Aires Gomes showed interest in educating Ana so she could provide more than manual labor.[50] The historical record is not clear about what Ana, or any other freed people, desired. The colonial archives that reinforce subjugation and disposability also offer some glimpses of the experiences and skills of individuals who were commodified. Even in situations where former masters requested better training for freed people, it is not clear how successful they were. By the second half of the nineteenth century, most freedmen and freedwomen continued to experience the coercion, violence, and control over their

---

[49] Nogueira da Silva, *Constitucionalismo e império*, 370–80; Frederick Cooper and Ann Laura Stoler, eds., "Between Metrople and Colony. Rethinking a Research Agenda," in *Tensions of Empire. Colonial Cultures in a Bourgeois World* (Berkeley: University of California Press, 1997), 2–5.

[50] ANA, Cod. 326, fl. 186, September 8, 1851. For more on lay people's understanding of law and justice see Dias Paes, "Shared Atlantic Legal Culture."

bodies that had marked West Central Africa since the early sixteenth century.

Colonial records show that freed people frequently fled, suggesting their refusal to accept the working conditions or continued attachment to old masters. In 1863, a group of ten freed individuals and three enslaved men fled from the plantations on which they had been working in Mossamedes. The group of freedom seekers moved to Catumbela, although the documents do not comment on their reasons for choosing that destination, located more than 400 kilometers away.[51] The following year another group of six freed people and some enslaved individuals escaped from their fishing work, taking a boat belonging to José Maria de Novais.[52] Desertions were a threat to the prosperity of plantations and the colony itself. The regent of Catumbela requested help, in 1869, from the surrounding *sobas* in locating an ox and a runaway freedman, Pedro, both belonging to the administration. The colonial forces were unable to locate Pedro and, as in many cases, relied on the local population to track down and seize fugitive individuals. This situation is like that of earlier centuries when *sobas* were prevented from offering asylum to any refugees who fled into their territories.[53]

The boundaries between free and slave statuses were blurred in nineteenth-century Angola. Despite changes in legislation that limited slavery, advertisements in the colonial gazette continued to announce the sale and acquisition of freed individuals as if they were property. In 1869, for example, Francisco Cardoso da Costa advertised for a freedwoman of good appearance who could wash and iron clothes to work outside of Luanda.[54] Free people felt no need to disguise their intentions in these advertisements, publicly displaying their disdain for the legislation.

Disputes over property expose the vulnerability and lack of options that freed people faced in the second half of the nineteenth century, in

[51] ANA, Cx. 1322, Catumbela, Administração do Concelho, 1853–1935, Correspondência Recebida, doc. 129, "From governor de Benguela to chefe do concelho da Catumbela [Augusto Ernesto da Silva Francisco]," May 7, 1863.
[52] ANA, cx. 3340, Dombe Grande, doc. 48, fl. 17v, "Letter from alferes and chefe de Dombe Grande, Emigídio Martins da Conceição," March 4, 1864.
[53] ANA, Cx. 1322, Catumbela, doc. 48, "From governor de Benguela to chefe do concelho da Catumbela [Antonio José da Silva], June 7, 1869. For more on the flight and how it was seen as a public threat, see Alberto da Costa Abreu e Costa, *Carta dirigidao ao Illmo Exmo Sr. João de Andrade Corvo sobre a questão do trabalho em África Ocidental* (Lisboa: Typographia Universal, 1875), 8–9; Aida Freudenthal, *Arimos e fazendas: a transição agrária em Angola, 1850-1880* (Luanda: Chá de Caxinde, 2005), 133–37 and 356–58.
[54] BOGGPA, 1869, n. 39, September 25, 1869, p. 467. For more on announcements, see José C. Curto, "Resistência à escravidão na África: o caso dos escravos fugitivos recapturados em Angola, 1846-1876," *Afro-Ásia*, no. 33 (2005): 67–86; Seixas, "Escravos e libertos no Boletim Oficial de Angola (1845-1875)."

ways very reminiscent of how land disputes were handled in the colonial courts. In the 1860s, due to his inability to pay a debt to António Teixeira de Melo Madureira, the *Ministério Público* (colonial prosecutor) seized the property of José Pinto da Silva Rocha, including four women who lived in his compound. However, the four women had been freed. Constância de Jesus, a Black woman, brought the case to court not to challenge the seizure of freed people but to claim that they were her property that the colonial state had illegally seized. José Pinto da Silva Rocha was her domestic partner, but although they cohabited, she claimed that the four freedwomen belonged to her, not to her partner. To prove her ownership, Jesus produced the slave register of December 14, 1854, in which two of the four women, seven-year-old Guebe and seventeen-year-old Suinge, were listed as belonging to her. Jesus had acquired the third woman, Lupeça, in a public auction in Benguela. Constância's daughter, already deceased, had been the original owner of the fourth freedwoman, Isabel. As her daughter's heir, Constância de Jesus enjoyed rights over Isabel as well. Jesus argued that she and Rocha were not married, and thus her property could not be seized to pay his personal debt. Jesus was a washer and unable to read the documents or sign her name, yet she challenged the actions of the colonial state and its agents.[55] She showed familiarity with Portuguese law that recognized women's rights to property. Although it would be tempting to stress the agency of a Black woman, a washer, a colonized subject, Constância's ability to claim property only underscores the fact that freed people remained under bondage.

Guebe, Suingue, Lupeça, and Isabel were not the only freedwomen sold and disputed after 1858. Probate records attest to the sale of freed people. Upon the death of her slaver in 1870, Guilhermina was listed as part of the estate of João, a Black carpenter resident in Benguela. Guilhermina was a freedwoman, appraised at 6$000 réis, or 6,000 réis (£27 pounds sterling in the 1870s). The inventory does not reveal her age or place of origin, nor does it describe her abilities or the period she

---

[55] TCB, "Auto cível de embargo de quatro libertas. Ministério Público vs, Constância de Jesus," January 12, 1866. For more on legislation protecting women's ability to inherit property in the Portuguese empire, see Jutta Sperling, "Women's Property Rights in Portugal under Dom João I (1385-1433): A Comparison with Renaissance Italy," *Portuguese Studies Review* 13, no. 1–2 (2005): 27–59; Mariana L. R. Dantas, "Succession of Property, Sales of Meação, and the Economic Empowerment of Widows of African Descent in Colonial Minas Gerais, Brazil," *Journal of Family History* 39, no. 3 (2014): 222–38; Vanessa S. Oliveira, "Spouses and Commercial Partners: Immigrant Men and Locally Born Women in Luanda (1831-1859)," in *African Women in the Atlantic World. Property, Vulnerability and Mobility, 1680-1880*, ed. Mariana P. Candido and Adam Jones (Woodbridge: James Currey, 2019), 217–32.

served João. It is not clear if she was his apprentice. At a public auction on February 27, 1871, Guilhermina, a freedwoman, was sold to Maria Caetana de Sousa Lopes. Sousa Lopes paid 6,000 réis, plus 4,000 related to the expenses for Guilhermina's meals and lodging for the year between João's death and the auction.[56] By the 1870s, a freewoman such as Guilhermina could be bought for 10$000 in Benguela, or £45.

In 1870, two residents of Catumbela disputed ownership over Vitorino, a Black man. João da Silva Souza claimed Vitorino belonged to his wife, and that Vitorino had fled a few days before. Bento Augusto Ribeiro Lopes argued he had bought Vitorino but was unable to produce any written evidence. Silva Souza brought the chief of Catumbela a copy of the 1855 slave register in which Vitorino was identified as a slave, and later *liberto*, who had to serve his unnamed wife until 1878. Realizing he would lose the dispute, Ribeiro Lopes decided to free Vitorino. The Benguela judge intervened and declared that Ribeiro Lopes could not manumit Vitorino since he was already a freedman; thus, only the person who held him in apprenticeship, Silva Souza, had the power to alleviate any obligations between Vitorino and his master. In the judge's ruling, the 1855 register served as proof of property and sealed Vitorino's destiny. Vitorino was declared under the legal tutelage of João da Silva and returned to his household as a human property. Although freed, Vitorino's fate was not in his hands and he missed his chance to gain freedom.[57]

Alongside legal cases, ecclesiastical and other records reveal the presence of freed people and their limited autonomy in Angola. Baptism records of Dombe Grande provide some clues about the freed population there, where several sugar and cotton plantations relied on freed labor. They cover a short period of time, November 15, 1874, to January 29, 1875, yet combined with qualitative data, the ecclesiastical records suggest the limitations of enslaved people to acquire freedom. Out of the 226 people baptized in Dombe Grande during this period, 184 of them were identified as freed people (Table 5.1). The names of the former owners are listed in this baptism book, suggesting the limits of freed-women's and freedmen's liberty. Most freed labor was controlled by a small number of residents. Manuel de Paula Barbosa and Dona Teresa Jesus Ferreira Torres Barruncho owned vast amounts of land and

[56] TCB, "Autos Cíveis de Inventário de João Preto Carpinteiro," February 27, 1871.
[57] ANA, Cx. 1322, Catumbela, Administração do Concelho, 1853–1935, Correspondência Recebida, doc. 148, "Letter from the regente of Catumbela [Jose da Silva Souza] to governor de Benguela [Antonio Silva Carvalho]," October 28, 1870.

Table 5.1. *Freed individuals in Dombe Grande baptism records, 1874-1875*

Former owners	Freed people
Manuel de Paula Barbosa	56
D. Teresa Jesus Ferreira Torres Barruncho	44
Martinho Lopes Cordeiro	9
Farm Santa Teresa	9
Luis Bernardo Tavano	8
D. Isabel António da Luz Abreu	5
2 Residents	3
8 Residents	2
30 Residents	1
Total	**184**

Source: BL, Dombe Grande, Livro de Batismo 1874–1875

controlled freed people's labor. Other powerful residents, such as Martinho Lopes Cordeiro, Luis Bernardo Tavano, and Dona Isabel António da Luz Abreu registered between five and nine freed people. Thirty residents each brought a single *liberto* to be baptized between November 1874 and January 1875.

Freed people moved between the houses and farms of Portuguese settlers and African subjects as loans, pawns, and favors. In some instances, the refusal to return *libertos* on time or as requested led to court challenges that reveal the arbitrary nature and lack of individual liberty that these individuals faced. This was the case with Ignácio, who was initially under the tutelage of Benguela resident Catarina Barros Araújo, then served in the house of João António Pilarte da Silva, and was then transferred to Luis Augusto de Brito's house in Catumbela in the 1870s.[58] Their constant displacement, their forced baptism, and their identification without a surname suggest their vulnerability and commodification, even if legally they were no longer in bondage. West Central Africans lived under instability. While the expansion of legal documents projected colonial clarity and control fixity, it is clear West Central Africans lived in ambiguity, which furthered the degradation of their societies. Destabilization and dismissal of earlier forms of property regimes favored dispossession.

[58] TCB, "Autos cíveis de ação ordinária de libelo. Catarina Barros de Araújo vs Luis Augusto de Brito," November 5, 1872. For lawyers reinforcing people's commodification see Dias Paes, "Shared Atlantic Legal Culture."

Freed People and Their Quest for Property

Holding individual property protected West Central Africans against enslavement and life in bondage. It offered individuals the possibility to cash in their belongings to secure freedom. Asserting freedom depended on individuals' ability to hold property. Portuguese law legislated freed people's access to property. According to the law, when a freed individual died *ab intestatio*, without a will or natural heirs, the former slaver could inherit his or her property, suggesting there was no legal constraint in acquiring assets.[59] The 1820s juridical debates in Portugal regarding freed individuals had to straddle the liberal ideas of freedom and the colonial spaces where unfree status was a fact. The legislation did not prevent freed people from acquiring property, yet the juridical debate in Portugal during the 1820s and 1830s prevented freedmen born in African colonies from exercising political rights. Freedmen born in Portugal who had acquired a skill and property could vote and be elected. After emancipation, freed individuals were caught between Portuguese settlers and the colonial state, and the indigenous population. The legal changes did not alter the liminal status of freed individuals, who continued to be viewed as savage, backward, and uncivilized, and as a result, were denied their rights and lost ownership of their land, similar to the cases of *libertos* in São Tomé.[60]

When manumitting slaves in wills, some owners offered them some property and capital, recognizing the difficulties freed people would encounter when trying to survive and thrive in a slave society. In 1858, Manuel Vida César freed Rita, one of his slaves, in his will and gave her 30$000 *réis*, equivalent to £135 pounds sterling. He also stated that Rita had a slave girl under her care, the young Mariana, given to Rita four months before his death.[61] In most cases, however, former slaves were freed without compensation or transmission of goods. In 1852, Manuel Oliveira Brandão freed a stonemason, João Barbosa, and José Augusto de Meireles freed twenty-four-year-old Joaquinia in their wills without any stipulation of cash or goods.[62] Sometimes enslavers quantified that the compensation was freedom, such as in the case of Joana, a thirty-year-old woman from the interior of Benguela who was freed in

[59] Manuel Borges Carneiro, *Direito civil de Portugal*, vol. 1 (Lisbon: Impressão Régia, 1826), 99–100.
[60] Seibert, "Colonialismo em São Tomé e Príncipe"; Nogueira da Silva, *Constitucionalismo e império*, 352–57. See also Lowe, *The Intimacies of Four Continents*, 63–65.
[61] TCB, "Autos cíveis do inventário de Manuel Vida César" 1858, fl. 2v.
[62] TCB, Fragmento de códice, "Registro de uma carta de liberdade passada a favor de João Barbosa, pedreiro," fl. 54, June 30, 1852.

1853.[63] Marcolina and her daughter, Leonor, were freed in 1866 and compensated with *plena liberdade*, "full freedom."[64] Freedom letters would not exist absent the concern of enslavers and formerly enslaved individuals with proving status and securing protection against re-enslavement, although libertos could be forced to continue serving former owners until their deaths before they could enjoy their freedom. Such was the case with Elena from Bihé; she received her freedom letter in 1866, but it stated she was required to continue serving her enslaver until his death.[65]

In other instances, enslavers made sure the people held in bondage remained on the land on which they lived and worked, even after manu-mission, opening the possibilities of continuous exploitation. In the 1860s, Agostinho António Ramos, a resident of Cuio, listed six enslaved individuals in his will – Maria, António, José, Ginge, Miguelina, and Margarida. He instructed that Miguelina and Margarida would be freed upon his death, and each woman would receive one plot of land (*arimo*) on which she would live. Each newly freedwoman was also given owner-ship over Ramos's slaves, with Miguelina receiving Maria and António, while Margarida was declared the new owner of José and Ginge. It is difficult to imagine this interaction between the recently freed and their new property. Ramos also gave people to two other captives he freed: Catumbo received the adult woman Catarina, while Camia received two boys, Joaquim and Cabito, and two adult women, Rita and Munano.[66] Once freed, former slaves became enslavers and increased their economic

---

[63] TCB, Fragmento de códice, "Registro de uma carta de liberdade passada a favor da preta Joana," Pages not numbered, August 8, 1853.

[64] TCB, Fragmento de códice, "Registro de uma carta de liberdade passada a preta Marcolina e sua filha Leonor," fl 169v, January 7, 1866.

[65] TCB, Fragmento de códice, "Registro de uma carta de liberdade passada a preta Elena por apelido Bissassa," fl. 171v, June 7, 1866. This practice was quite common in other slave societies, particularly in former Iberian colonies. See, for exemple, Mônica Maria da Pádua Souto da Cunha, Marcus Joaquim Carvalho, and Mateus Samico Simon, "Liberdade partida em 1/4: alforria e pecúlio em Pernambuco sob a Lei do ventre-livre," *Documentação e Memória/ TJPE* 2, no. 4 (2011): 11–28; Gabriela dos Reis Sampaio, Lisa Earl Castillo, and Wlamyra Ribeiro de Albuquerque, *Barganhas e querelas da escravidão: tráfico, alforria e liberdade (séculos XVIII e XIX)* (Salvador: Edufba, Editora da Universidade Federal da Bahia, 2014); Kimberly S. Hanger, "Landlords, Shopkeepers, Farmers, and Slave-Owners: Free Black Female Property-Holders in Colonial New Orleans," in *Beyond Bondage: Free Women of Color in the Americas* (Urbana, IL: University of Illinois Press, 2004), 219–36; Mary Caroline Craavens, "Manumission and the Life Cycle of a Contained Population: The VOC Lodge Slaves at the Cape of Good Hope, 1680-1730," in *Paths to Freedom: Manumission in the Atlantic World*, ed. Rosemary Brana-Shute and Randy J. Sparks (Columbia: University of South Carolina Press, 2009), 99–119.

[66] ANA, cx. 5251, Dombe Grande, "Letter from Junta da Fazenda Pública de Benguela [Luis Teodoro França] to Regent of Dombe Grande," July 1, 1862.

and social standing. In fact, the *Junta Protetora dos Escravos e Libertos* oversaw the protection of the estate and the collection and administration of inheritances that were left to enslaved and freed people. Legislation, including the 1853 ordinance *Regulamento sobre libertos*, stated that freed people were entitled to have assets. However, freedmen in the overseas colonies who owned property could not vote, ensuring that freed people were excluded from political rights. In practice, freed people continued to be marked by the stigma of slavery and were not considered full citizens.[67]

In the eyes of the law, for most of the nineteenth century, freed people enjoyed rights, although freedmen who owned property were not politically enfranchised. If freed individuals committed crimes, they faced trial and constraints just as a free individual would.[68] Thus, it is not surprising that freed people, particularly freedmen, could have access to land if they demonstrated that they had embraced the "Civilizing Mission" principles of cultivation, and also had access to transportation and commercialization in the colonial centers. However, this was constantly challenged based on the notion that freed people were legally considered to be minors who were under the tutelage of the colonial state.

Although free people did not face any legal constraints to acquiring assets in Angola, I was able to locate a single case among the more than 2,000 legal cases available at the Tribunal da Comarca de Benguela of a freed person presenting documents to qualify for an inheritance. Josefina Rodrigues presented her case in the court of Benguela in 1867. The notary described Josefina Rodrigues as a freedwoman who had belonged to the deceased merchant Joaquim António Rodrigues. At the time of her hearing, Josefina was a farmer and lived off her own work. Her case was an effort to claim the inheritance of her son Domingos, who had once also belonged to Joaquim António Rodrigues. In other parts of the litigation, Josefina was identified as free, single, and adult.[69] During the proceedings, it became clear that she had cohabited with Joaquim until his death in 1861. Although the record is silent, it is unlikely that this was a consensual union. The relationship was characterized by slavery dynamics of asymmetrical power: Josefina's status as an enslaved woman prevented her from resisting sexual advances from her former owner. Joaquim and Josefina had a son, Domingos, who died in 1862 when he

---

[67] Nogueira da Silva, *Constitucionalismo e império*, 355–62.

[68] *Boletim do Conselho Ultramarino. Legislação Novíssima, vol. II* (Lisbon: Imprensa Nacional, 1869), p. 676–81.

[69] TCB, "Autos cíveis de habilitação pelo casal de Joaquim António Rodrigues. Habilitante a preta Josefina Rodrigues" fl 3, November 15, 1867; and fl. 4, October 18, 1866.

was three years old. Josefina presented a series of documents to support her claim, including Joaquim's will and Domingos' baptism and burial records, indicating that she was aware of colonial law and inheritance rights and embraced the power of paper culture. In Joaquim's will, he acknowledged his paternity of Domingos and freed Josefina. He also gave Josefina a plot of land in Dombe Grande. The documents are not clear whether this was where she continued to farm and live. In addition to the written documents, Josefina brought three witnesses, all locally born men, who confirmed she was a freedwoman and had lived many years with the deceased Joaquim António Rodrigues with whom she had a son. All three men stated that Josefina could manage her property and was financially independent. In January 1869, almost fifteen months after the process was initiated, the judge recognized Josefina's right to Joaquim's estate.

Other freed people may have presented similar cases and been successful in inheriting land.[70] Freed individuals may have resorted to other strategies to secure access to real estate, such as relocating away from colonial centers to more remote areas where they could negotiate land access with local rulers, avoiding confrontation with Portuguese settlers and colonial officers. Relocation also permitted physical and social distance from places associated with their servitude and lower social status. Not all free people had the same opportunities to relocate away from the coast. While freed individuals, originally from locations in the interior, could try to settle in regions where they were familiar with language and culture, liberated Africans, those released by the Mixed Commission smuggled on slave ships, did not necessarily enjoy the same degree of knowledge to relocate. Liberated Africans were not necessarily familiar with the landscape, political organization, or even local languages, such as Umbundu or Kimbundu. Another challenge for historians is finding

---

[70] For more on African women's access to colonial courts, see Kristin Mann, "Women's Right in Law and Practice: Marriage and Dispute Settlement in Colonial Lagos," in *African Women & the Law: Historical Perspectives*, ed. Margaret Jean Hay and Marcia Wright (Boston, MA: Boston University Press, 1982), 151–71; Kristin Mann, "Women, Landed Property, and the Accumulation of Wealth in Early Colonial Lagos," *Signs* 16, no. 4 (1991): 682–706; Elke Stockreiter, *Islamic Law, Gender, and Social Change in Post-Abolition Zanzibar* (New York: Cambridge University Press, 2015), 64–68 and 110–13; Elisabeth McMahon, *Slavery and Emancipation in Islamic East Africa: From Honor to Respectability* (New York: Cambridge University Press, 2013), 70–71. For the violent nature of the relationships between slave master and enslaved women, see Megan Vaughan, *Creating the Creole Island: Slavery in Eighteenth-Century Mauritius* (Durham: Duke University Press, 2005), 171; Pamela Scully, "Rape, Race, and Colonial Culture: The Sexual Politics of Identity in the Nineteenth-Century Cape Colony, South Africa," *The American Historical Review* 100, no. 2 (1995): 335–59; Fuentes, *Dispossessed Lives*, 83–86.

evidence since relocations are not captured in the colonial records, which tend to overrepresent conflicts over property around Luanda, Benguela, and other settlements with a long history of Portuguese colonial presence.

Freed individuals also found new opportunities for earning a living; Josefina, for one, lived off her own crops. Others restructured their economic life as artisans and craftsmen or were incorporated into farms as wageworkers, although their labor and economic dependency resembled the apprenticeship regime in many ways.[71] As a result of this economic dependency, freed individuals who owned property were viewed with suspicion, as if they were unable to save money to acquire goods. In 1874, two freed people, Januário and Emilia, traveled from Benguela to Catumbela carrying several items with them. A debate arose on whether the goods belonged to them or to Dona Rita, who had control over them. The regent of Catumbela questioned their ability to own these goods, although they were not particularly rare or valuable. The items included a revolver and ammunition, three empty bottles, a water jug, metal earrings and brooch, a metal crucifix, a sewing kit in a little box, gunpowder, a mug, three tea and soup spoons, a coat, a bundle of textiles, a short spear (*zagaia*), and a small glass container of ointment.[72] Despite the law that allowed freedmen and freedwomen to own property, their assets were questioned as legitimate.

In 1875, the *liberto* status and slavery were abolished in Angola, yet the number of people who remained enslaved continued to be around 20 percent of the Angolan population. Enslavers had to register freed individuals as *serviçais*, a new term that did not bring major changes in labor relationships. *Serviçais* received a wage and continued to work in farming, porterage, and public works, regulated by the new 1899 ordinance that regulated labor. The 1899 ordinance was followed by the colonial forced-labor system that lasted until 1961.[73] Labor and legal rights precarities tracked with the undermining of any communal notion

---

[71] Freudenthal, *Arimos e fazendas*, 248–62; W. G. Clarence-Smith, *Slaves, Peasants, and Capitalists in Southern Angola, 1840-1926* (New York: Cambridge University Press, 1979), 58–66; Jelmer Vos, "Work in Times of Slavery, Colonialism, and Civil War: Labor Relations in Angola from 1800 to 2000," *History in Africa* 41, no. 1 (2014): 374–79; Maria da Conceição Neto, "De escravos a serviçais, de serviçais a contratados: omissões, percepções e equívocos na história do trabalho africano na Angola colonial," *Cadernos de Estudos Africanos*, no. 33 (2017): 107–29.

[72] ANA, Cx. 1322, "Correspondência Recebida," doc. 61, "Letter from widow Dona Rita to governor de Benguela [Antônio Martins da Rosa]," March 26, 1874.

[73] *Collecção de legislação relativa as colonias portuguezas em Africa* (Lisbon: Companhia Nacional Editora, 1899), 248; Vos, "Work in Times of Slavery, Colonialism, and Civil War," 379; Jeremy Ball, *Angola's Colossal Lie: Forced Labor on a Sugar Plantation, 1913-1977* (Leiden; Boston, MA: Brill, 2015), 30–32; Neto, "De escravos a serviçais," 113.

of property. The assertion of individualized rights, however, did not represent recognition of the humanity of West Central Africans, particularly those who had been enslaved or were descendants of people held in bondage. Destabilization of old forms of ownership and wealth favored population displacement and dispossession.

Conclusion

New laws in the nineteenth century enforced emancipation, but freed people continued to face legal challenges when attempting to exercise their freedom. While slavery as an institution expanded, courts and other legal venues were established to question property rights over human beings. Slavery was considered immoral, forced labor, but on the other hand was viewed as a necessity to maintain economic prosperity. The legal category of *libertos* included liberated Africans freed by the Mixed Commission in charge of patrolling and prosecuting cases of illegal slave embarkation, as well as the formerly enslaved individuals who had been manumitted. Enslaved people acquired freedom through a variety of ways, including manumission for services in wills or at the baptismal font, as well as people who paid for their freedom. In many ways, the freed status reproduced the conditions of bondage and perpetuated dependency links. Despite their nominal freedom, freed individuals continued to be treated as property even though they were able to acquire goods, land, and even enslaved people.

Legal changes also brought protective institutions that reproduced social hierarchies and paternalistic and patriarchal expectations that placed freed people, particularly freedwomen, as dependent on the colonial state. Judges were put in place to emphasize the legal subordination of freed people and push freed individuals into arbitrary training and apprenticeship programs that maintained their dependency on former slave owners. The colonial archives are filled with documents that register irregularities, suggesting the connivance of colonial authorities and enslavers. It became clear that in spite of a humanitarian rhetoric, the colonial state protected the interests of former owners and responded to their requests to cope with losing their property. Formerly enslaved people or liberated Africans were portrayed as helpless and needing to learn how to live as free people, who required a new work ethic and self-discipline.

Civilizing Mission goals of self-discipline and a work ethic thrived in the decisions regarding the rights and duties of freed people. The official argument in Lisbon and Luanda, aligned with the abolitionist attitudes elsewhere, was that a gradual emancipation was safer and less radical and did not risk economic instability.[74] For the *libertos*, full emancipation was a moving target: whenever a chance of freedom got closer, authorities found ways to extend the duration of the apprenticeship programs, never clarifying the types of training that freed people received. There was never any discussion on how to financially compensate formerly enslaved people for their work, or how to provide resources and education to eradicate dependency. Even after the abolition of the status of *libertos* in 1878, freed people continued to be treated as slaves, bequeathed and sold as property, and excluded from religious organizations such as Catholic brotherhoods, demonstrating the lack of political will to profoundly transform the society and eradicate slavery and the freed status that designated someone as a former slave. The case studies explored in this chapter indicate that freed people's wishes were constantly ignored, and they continued to be vulnerable people who were treated as property.

With all the contested ideas about ownership of people and practices of freedom, debates about property rights in Angola were not limited to land ownership or access to material goods. Notions of wealth in people, in many ways, run parallel to claims over land. We have seen that West Central African–born individuals, and foreigners, made extensive claims over people. The same Civilizing Mission goals of productive, work ethics and maximizing of labor that affected access to individual freedom examined in this chapter affected land claims and rights. The defense of private interests over collective one, from humans to land, collided with the interests and understanding of coastal rulers and political elites, the focus of the next chapter. Clashes over rights and property claims facilitated land dispossession and expansion of inequalities.

---

[74] See, for example, Seymour Drescher, *Abolition: A History of Slavery and Antislavery* (New York: Cambridge University Press, 2009); Philip Misevich and Kristin Mann, eds., *The Rise and Demise of Slavery and the Slave Trade in the Atlantic World* (Rochester, NY: University of Rochester Press, 2016).

6 The Erasure of Communal Rights

For most West Central African rulers, land was central to subsistence agriculture, meeting their population needs as well as guaranteeing access to future generations.[1] Land was not for individual profit. During the nineteenth century, however, in the wake of liberal reforms in Europe, land became commodified, as something that could be bought and sold by individuals who did not use it or occupied it. Land acquired monetary value, a major departure from land regimes that recognized possession based on occupation and use rights. In a way, possession went through a process of transformation that privileged written evidence and created the notion of private property. *Sobas*, the local rulers who had signed vassalage treaties in the seventeenth and eighteenth centuries, granted rights of access to their subjects as well as to foreigners, such as European settlers. *Sobas* did not necessarily sell their lands. By the mid-nineteenth century, colonial administrators and foreign settlers, however, treated those temporary loans as personal property and local occupants became undesirable. The 300 years of Portuguese contact with West Central Africa and the spread of vassalage treaties that displaced rulers who resisted colonial advances led to the placement of *sobas* who did not necessarily have the support of or legitimacy with their subjects. As a result, when changes related to land use and rights were introduced in the mid-nineteenth century, some of the coastal rulers had already been incorporated into the colonial world for generations and were unable to resist land appropriation. While farming communities could easily prove the use and occupation of soil, herders and transhumant populations had their rights challenged. As we will see in this chapter, elite women adopted and adapted to these changing legal

---

[1] Tuca Manuel, *Terra, a tradição e o poder. Contribuição ao estudo etno-histórico da Ganda* (Benguela: KAT – Aguedense, 2005); Kathryn M. de Luna, *Collecting Food, Cultivating People: Subsistence and Society in Central Africa* (New Haven, CT: Yale University Press, 2016).

regimes, making claims over land, buying real estate, and transmitting it to loved ones after their deaths.

Land rights were transformed during the nineteenth century. While some individuals profited, most of the population was displaced and came to be viewed as strangers in their own territories. This chapter ties the consolidation of land ownership in the hands of colonial settlers, foreign merchants and immigrants, and a few wealthy West Central Africa to the processes of dispossession and impoverishment that perpetuated the commodification of people, if sometimes in new guises, as discussed in Chapter 5. It stresses privatization of land in individual hands, at the expense of rulers and their subjects, who saw their rights denied or seen as illegitimate. Land dispossession created groups of landless populations, forced to relocate to sustain their families and communities.

Many African groups had strict land regimes and made extensive land transactions before the 1900s, but not much attention has been paid to land tenure in Angola.[2] Early twentieth-century jurist treatises had a profound impact on the scholarship about wealth accumulation and private property in Africa, and in Angola in particular.[3] Yet no reflection was made on the role of early twentieth-century colonial jurists' writings on the formulations of land ownership and celebration of private property as a cornerstone of European legal codes, or even on the debate about legal knowledge construction and consolidation and the use of law to solidify and perpetuate colonialism, including land alienation. Throughout this chapter, empirical evidence reveals the back-and-forth between law as written and law as a contested space, where different actors employed different arguments to protect their interests. Their

---

[2] Carola Lentz, *Land, Mobility, and Belonging in West Africa* (Bloomington: Indiana University Press, 2013); Assan Sarr, *Islam, Power, and Dependency in the Gambia River Basin: The Politics of Land Control, 1790-1940* (Rochester, NY: University of Rochester Press, 2016). For a detailed study on land grabbing in twentieth-century Angola, see Aaron deGrassi, "Provisional Reconstructions: Geo-Histories of Infrastructure and Agrarian Configuration in Malanje, Angola" (Ph.D., Berkeley, CA: University of California, 2015).

[3] See, for example, Jack Goody, *Technology, Tradition, and the State in Africa* (London: Oxford University Press, 1971), 12–13, 24–25, and 29–30; Miriam Goheen, *Men Own the Fields, Women Own the Crops: Gender and Power in the Cameroon Grassfields* (Madison, WI: University of Wisconsin Press, 1996), 110, 112, and 114. For West Central Africa in particular, see Jan Vansina, *Paths in the Rainforests: Toward a History of Political Tradition in Equatorial Africa* (Madison, WI: University of Wisconsin Press, 1990), 251; John K. Thornton, *Africa and Africans in the Making of the Atlantic World, 1400-1800* (New York, NY: Cambridge University Press, 1998), 87, 89, 95, and 105; Joseph C. Miller, *Way of Death: Merchant Capitalism and the Angolan Slave Trade, 1730-1830* (Madison: University of Wisconsin Press, 1988), 43–45 and 52; Wyatt MacGaffey, *Kongo Political Culture: The Conceptual Challenge of the Particular* (Bloomington: Indiana University Press, 2000), 215–16.

disputes reveal the tension that existed in West Central Africa regarding local rulers' interpretation of their land rights, the colonial imposition of property rights that privilege writing and land titles, and the emergence of individuals interested in accumulation of land as a private asset.

We know from Chapter 2 how changes in the legislation affected West Central African rulers' land rights; in this chapter, the attention is on the individuals, particularly West Central African women, who claimed, bought, and transferred land. The actions of West Central African individuals and colonial settlers encroached on the territories of local rulers. Crucial to justifying dispossession was the creation and consolidation of stereotypes that had profound effects on twentieth-century colonial rule, such as the notion that land was untamed and underexploited, and that Africans, particularly men, were lazy, backward, and lacked the knowledge and motivation to make land productive and engage in the cash economy.[4] Looking at how individuals seized land, it becomes clear that some land policies, such as classifying collective lands as vacant or unproductive, were implemented first in overseas colonies than in mainland Portugal. By the mid-nineteenth century, the colonial state in Angola started seizing lands classified as vacant or unproductive and leasing them to individuals who showed interest in promoting agriculture. Seizure was an important step in the process of land alienation and codifying land rights, leading to the imposition of new forms of land regimes by the mid-nineteenth century and new ways to prove and exercise those legal rights after the 1860s.

Land as Individual Property

Since their arrival on the coast of West Central Africa, the Portuguese officials engaged in disputes with local rulers regarding land use and rights. Land occupation and expropriation were central to the process of subjugating the local population and to incorporating an overseas territory into the Portuguese Empire. However, it was only after the 1830s that the Portuguese Crown actively legislated land regulation, including land tenure, in West Central Africa. Before the mid-nineteenth

---

[4] Bárbara Direito, "African Access to Land in Early Twentieth Century Portuguese Colonial Thought," in *Property Rights, Land and Territory in the European Overseas Empires*, ed. José Vicente Serrão et al. (Lisbon: CEHC-IUL, 2014), 259; Henrietta L. Moore and Megan Vaughan, *Cutting down Trees: Gender, Nutrition, and Agricultural Change in the Northern Province of Zambia, 1890-1990* (Portmouth, NH: Heinemann, 1994), 112–15; Suzanne Schwarz, "'A Just and Honourable Commerce.' Abolitionist Experimentation in Sierra Leone in the Late Eighteenth and Early Nineteenth Centuries," *African Economic History* 45, no. 1 (2017): 23.

century, the exports of enslaved individuals, not land exploitation, were the focus of the colonial policy.[5] As liberal ideas took hold in Portugal, mainly for the benefit of the elite and the protection of individual rights over collective ones, one result was rapid land enclosure and the dismissal of communal land rights. The *Revolução Liberal* in 1820 resulted in changes in Portugal as well as in its empire. Unoccupied land became a threat to the realization of liberalist doctrine and the ideals of individualism. By the late nineteenth century, Domingos Vandelli, a Paduan naturalist, claimed that Portuguese low farming productivity was related to the inexistence of a competitive land market. According to him, collective land prevented higher productivity. Alongside other Enlightened thinkers, Vandelli favored that land that was not cultivated be declared vacant. The state could seize any land labeled as unproductive, denying communal rights and transferring "vacant lands" to a "new" owner. These changes began taking place in Portugal with the implementation of laws regulating the use of communal lands in 1804 and 1815, yet it was in the African colonies that land seizure took place first.[6] There were efforts to seize land in West Central Africa before the 1830s, but the economic profits associated with the transatlantic slave trade as well as the successful resistance of African rulers and populations prevented colonial land takeovers beyond a few colonial centers in the interior such as Ambaca, Cambambe, Massangano, Caconda, and Quilengues. Changes related to conceptions of land occupation, possessions, and rights after the Liberal Revolution transformed the way the Portuguese political and commercial elite imagined its African colonies and the economic possibilities that could bring more revenue and prestige and prolong the Portuguese domain.[7] It was in this context that orders arrived in Luanda and Benguela regarding land seizure and commodification.

In 1825, the newly installed president of the chamber of Benguela received instructions to distribute land to individuals willing to promote

---

[5] Amaral, *O consulado de Paulo Dias de Novais;* Heintze, *Angola nos séculos XVI e XVII,* 243–71; and Rodrigues, *Portugueses e africanos,* 554.

[6] Manuel Rodrigues, *Os Baldios* (Lisboa: Caminho, 1987), 38–39; Marcia Maria M. Motta, "Das discussões sobre posse e propriedade da terra na história moderna: velha e novas ilações," in *O direito às avessas: por uma história social da propriedade,* ed. Marcia Maria M. Motta and María Verónica Secreto (Niterói, RJ: EDUFF, 2011), 21–24; Marcia Maria M. Motta, *Direito à terra no Brasil. A gestação de um conflito, 1795-1824* (São Paulo, SP: Alameda, 2009), 47.

[7] Valentim Alexandre, "O liberalismo português e as colónias de África (1820-39)," *Análise Social* 16, no. 61–62 (1980): 319–40; Aida Freudenthal, *Arimos e fazendas: a transição agrária em Angola, 1850-1880* (Luanda: Chá de Caxinde, 2005), 137–38; Cristina Nogueira da Silva, *Constitucionalismo e império: A cidadania no ultramar português* (Lisbon: Almedina, 2009), 311.

cultivation, privileging Portuguese outlaws (*degredados*). It is not clear whether African-born individuals could receive land plots.[8] These plots were distributed in *sesmaria* regimes, similar to what had happened in Brazil and other Portuguese colonies.[9] In the case of West Central Africa, the *sesmaria* regime goes back to the seventeenth-century instructions Paulo Dias de Novaes received, when sent to conquer and occupy land. The 1820s instructions required land cultivation in crops perceived as relevant to the colonial administration, such as sugarcane or coffee, at the expense of crops in demand locally, such as sorghum, millet, or manioc. In the following debate, the colonial administration started seizing land of religious orders, and small farmers were unable to pay back their taxes or debts. The administration bestowed these lands on individuals in a system of *aforamento*, in which tenants enjoyed the use of and harvest from the land against the payment of rent.[10] The policy favored distributing land to officers serving in the colonial army; they could request up to three years away from their military service in order to invest their time in making their new land productive. The colonial administration provided seeds and the farming tools necessary and continued to pay their salaries in addition to financing the travel and resettlement of their family members. The policy was very like those available to Portuguese subjects living in Brazil.[11]

Following the announcement, residents in Luanda and Benguela, including some elite African women, received plots of land.[12] One of the women was Joaquina Martins de Ramos e Abreu, who was authorized to build a house on Cavaco street near the house of Bento Pereira

---

[8] ANA, Cod. 7183, "Registro de correspondência recebida 1798–1851," fl. 74v-75, May 22, 1825.

[9] For more information on the sesmarias, see Carmen Margarida Oliveira Alveal, "Senhores de pequenos mundos: disputas por terras e os limites do poder local na América portuguesa," *Saeculum – Revista de História* 26 (2012): 63–77; Virgínia Rau and José Manuel Garcia, *Sesmarias medievais portuguesas* (Lisboa: Editorial Presença, 1982); Maria Sarita Mota, "Sesmarias e propriedade titulada da terra: o individualismo agrário na América Portuguesa," *Sæculum – Revista de História* 26, no. 1 (2012): 29–45; Rafael Chambouleyron, "Plantações, sesmarias e vilas. Uma reflexão sobre a ocupação da Amazônia seiscentista," *Nuevo Mundo Mundos Nuevos* (2006).

[10] Freudenthal, *Arimos e fazendas*, 138–39.

[11] AHU, Secretária do Estado do Ministério do Ultramara (SEMU), Direção Geral do Ultramar (DGU), Angola, 477, 1840–1843, Registro de Correspondência Expedida, fl. 6 – 7v, 3 November 1838. See also Eduardo dos Santos, *Regime de terras no ex-Ultramar Português: Evolução da política legislativa até 1945* (Lisbon: Universidade Técnica de Lisboa/ Centro de Estudos Africanos, 2004), 31.

[12] AHU, SEMU, DGU, Angola, 477, 1840-1843, Registro de Correspondência Expedida, fl. 23v, November 28, 1840; and AHU, SEMU, DGU, Angola, 477, fl. Not numbered, n. 634ª March 29, 1842.

Trindade. She had one year to build a fence to mark her plot.[13] Nearby
the Barros street, Vitória do Nascimento acquired a license to build a
house. The boundaries are difficult to recreate, but it stood in front of the
house of Manuel de Barros Cunha's orphan daughter, and the houses of
Joana Mendes were at the back. To the west were an empty plot and the
house of Gregório Soares de Barros. These broad delimitations suggest
that land occupation and use were contingent on negotiation and
social agreement.

The land records reveal that colonial authorities knew the inhabitants
and their places of residence.[14] The concessions allowed people to build
houses, create gardens, or simply enclose land and transformed it into
private property. In several instances, these newly awarded concessions
had been considered vacant land, a loaded and problematic term that
imagined colonial territories as empty spaces waiting for the arrival of
Europeans to fulfill their destiny of becoming a cultivated plot. Pastoral
groups used the land for grazing, or people believed that the lands
were occupied by spirits and were thus inaccessible. However, colonial
officers ignored all the reasons for land appearing to be empty and expropriated them to the benefit of the colonial state and colonial settlers.[15] Lands
considered vacant could be occupied by any one colonial subject with the
resources to cultivate or negotiate rights with the colonial government.

Even though occupying and marking boundaries of urban land predates
the nineteenth century, it was only then that the colonial government
assumed the responsibility of controlling and registering the *arimos*. In
the nineteenth century, the term *arimo* continued to be employed to
designate a plot of land where crops such as sorghum, manioc, beans,
maize, and other crops were cultivated and animals were raised with the
same meaning, including in non-Kimbundu regions such as Benguela. In
the urban *arimos*, the producers and their families consumed part of the
harvest, and the surplus was sold in the urban and internal markets and
used to supply ships and populations in transit (See Illustration 6.1).[16]

[13] BPB, Termo de Terreno, 1843–1894, fl. 12v, August 28, 1849. In Luanda, women also
started investing in real estate after the end of slave exports. See Vanessa S. Oliveira,
Slave Trade and Abolition. Gender, Commerce and Economic Transition in Luanda
(Madison: University of Wisconsin Press, 2021).
[14] BPB, Termo de Terreno, fl. 17v, December 20, 1849. For the population of Benguela,
see *Almanak statistico da Provincia d'Angola e suas dependencias para o anno de 1852.*
(Luanda: Imprensa do Governo, 1851), 9.
[15] For more on this, see Assan Sarr, "Land, Power, and Dependency along the Gambia
River, Late Eighteenth to Early Nineteenth Centuries," *African Studies Review* 57, no. 3
(2014): 101–21; Lentz, *Land, Mobility, and Belonging in West Africa*.
[16] *Quarenta e cinco dias em Angola: apontamentos de viagem* (Porto, 1862), 102; and Silva
Corrêa, *História de Angola*, 1, 113–14.

In the colonial urban center, African men and women began requesting the colonial government's permission to build on or cultivate plots of land in 1843.[17] A single land register book is available for Benguela during the nineteenth century, *Termos de Terrenos*, although more may exist for other regions and time periods. Vanessa Oliveira has identified land transactions in Luanda, including sales and mortgage records.[18] The Benguela register demonstrates the colonial effort to regulate land, but also individuals' interest in securing access. As can be seen in Table 3.5, 156 individuals requested land access between 1845 and 1894. Not a single ruler, a *soba*, was recorded as claiming land or having their territories recognized.

The colonial state registered all approved requests in this single book, which raises the question of whether other applicants had their cases rejected, and if so on what grounds. No records were written down for the 1875–85 period. The numbers are also very small compared to the traveler and contemporary accounts that describe Benguela with 500 to 605 houses in the mid-nineteenth century.[20] The register reveals that land had become commodified and had a monetary value associated with it, and its ownership had become associated with written registration. As seen earlier, written records were integral to the Portuguese Empire and its governance of overseas colonies. Colonial authorities in Angola had been counting people since the late eighteenth century, but taxation and accounting for the sale, transport, and export of enslaved Africans had been going on for over three centuries. Not all transactions were written down, but many were. By the mid-nineteenth century, record keeping regarding land registration proved that Portuguese officials embraced and implemented policies of privatizing land and categorizing its use.[21]

The creation of land registries and the regulation of landed property were responses to changes in perceptions of governance, as the colonial state encroached on local land rights. The 1857 law on vacant lands

[17] BPB, Termo de Terreno, 1843–1894.
[18] Oliveira, *Slave Trade and Abolition. Gender, Commerce and Economic Transition in Luanda.*, Chapter 4.
[20] *O Panorama. Jornal Literario e Instructivo*, vol. 16 (1858), p. 323, and José Maria de Souza Monteiro, *Os Portuguezes em Africa, Asia, America, e Oceania: Obra classica* (Lisbon: Typ. de Borges, 1850), 148.
[21] For more on land rights in other empires, see Lauren Benton, "Making Order out of Trouble: Jurisdictional Politics in the Spanish Colonial Borderlands," *Law & Social Inquiry* 26, no. 2 (2001): 373–401; Anthony Pagden, "Law, Colonization, Legitimation, and the European Background," in *The Cambridge History of Law in America*, ed. Michael Grossberg et al. (Cambridge: Cambridge University Press, 2011), 1–31; Kristin Mann, "Women, Landed Property, and the Accumulation of Wealth in Early Colonial Lagos," *Signs* 16, no. 4 (1991): 682–706; Saliha Belmessous, ed., *Native Claims : Indigenous Law against Empire, 1500-1920* (New York: Oxford University Press, 2012).

exacerbated this policy and transformed notions of land use and access. Viewing it as abandoned, the Portuguese colonial state felt entitled to claim uncultivated land and rent or sell it to private individuals. The exceptions were the lands located close to the sea and navigable rivers, within the limits of a town or inland fortresses, forests with valuable wood, territories with minerals, and any piece of land the Portuguese Crown viewed as vital to public interest. According to this regulation, any Portuguese subject could acquire land with the purpose of cultivating it within five years. Working the land operated as a mechanism to link land occupation to forms of labor considered legitimated and productive, such as farming. Cattle herding or gathering and hunting, on the other hand, were not considered a legitimate form of labor for land use and occupation rights, in a process very similar to what was happening to justify the dispossession of indigenous populations in Brazil.[22] The transfer and adaptation of legal categories and policies regarding land use and rights between Angola, Brazil, and Portuguese jurists suggest that institutional and intellectual links continue despite the political separation of Brazil from the Portuguese empire.

In Angola, European buyers and private societies acquired land with the intent to exploit it for commercial use, including the development of mineral resources. In the process, land rights of the local population were denied and their access to agricultural and pastoral land for their own survival was limited and not recognized. Even the simple right to live on the land had to be justified as productive, as defined by the colonial state. The plural legal system that had previously existed regarding possession and occupation rights gave way to the imposition of Portuguese legislation. Community use or the power of neighbors and peers to recognize occupation rights was no longer enough from a legal standpoint. Some rulers made use of the colonial bureaucracy to solidify their land claims, indicating changes in rights to the land and community interests. In 1857, for example, the *soba* Agostinho a Ndala Quitamba from Ambaca, a Portuguese fortress in the interior of Angola, sold the *arimo*

---

[22] *Boletim Oficial Geral do Governo da Província de Angola* (BOGGPA), n. 597, March 7, 1857, p. 1–3. BOGGPA, n. 598, March 14, 1857, p. 1–4. This law enacted changes approved in the Lisbon in 1856. See Santos, *Regime de terras no ex-Ultramar Português*, 23 and 57–59. For more on colonialism and the idea of vacant land, see Berry, "Debating the Land," 641–42. For more details on the Portuguese division of land in Africa, see Rodrigues, "Chiponda, 103–04. For similarities with land legislation in Brazil, see Soraia Sales Dornelles, "A questão indígena e o Império: Índios, terras, trabalho e violência na província paulista, 1845-1891," (Ph.D., Unicamp, Caminas, 2017) e Mariana Armond Dias Paes, "Escravos e terras entre posses e títulos: A construção social do direito de propriedade no Brasil (1835-1889)" (Ph.D., São Paulo, SP, Universidade de São Paulo, 2018).

called Tutu to Christovão Antunes de Souza, suggesting the land had acquired a monetary value and that individuals could buy it, even when land belonged to a community, not to a ruler.[23]

Going back to the *Termos de Terreno*, land was commodified and distributed to foreigners in exchange for cash. African women presented many of these requests for land, such as Dona Clementina Eugénia Rodrigues da Costa who in 1859 requested a license to build a house for her grandchildren at the Nossa Senhora do Pópulo Square, bordering Maria Inocência Barbosa Coutinho's garden and the property of Tomé Rodrigues Viana. It is not clear whether Viana's property was a house, a garden, or a shop.[24] The license records indicate that residents quickly claimed urban land in Benguela. It does not appear that women faced major constraints, although they had to compete with male residents and local rulers for access and rights. The arrival of white immigrants in the 1840s also exacerbated competition and new economic alliances. Demand for cotton, coffee, and sugar and the decline of the slavery plantation complex in the Americas favored the establishment of plantations on the African continent with land redistributed to European immigrants. Many of those new arrivals, however, were impoverished, and they lacked tools and resources and relied on the Portuguese government not only for access to land but also to enable their survival in their new location. The administration support included a subsidy of $300 réis daily for the first six months, around £40 pounds sterling per month in 1850, a substantial state sponsorship of private enterprises.[25]

Settlers initially set up plantations to harvest orchil (*urzela*, in Portuguese), a lichen important in the dyeing industry due to its purple-blue dye.[26] In the 1840s and 1860s, orchil exports were one of the driving forces of the Angolan economy. Realizing the economic opportunity available with the expansion of agriculture, individuals started petitioning for larger plots outside of Benguela, to take advantage of a series of colonial incentives. This goal was the case with Guilherme Haworth and Eduardo Ferreira Pinto Bastos, who submitted a request to the Secretaria de Estado dos Negócios da Marinha do Ultramar (SEMU)

---

[23] BOGGPA,n. 599, March 21, 1857, p. 10 For more on Ambaca, see Jan Vansina, "Ambaca Society and the Slave Trade C. 1760-1845," *Journal of African History* 46, no. 1 (2005): 1–27.

[24] BPB, Termo de Terreno, fl. 61v, June 1, 1859.

[25] BOGGPA, n. 224, January 12, 1850. For similar practices elsewhere, see Law, *From Slave Trade to "Legitimate" Commerce*; Martin Lynn, *Commerce and Economic Change in West Africa: The Palm Oil Trade in the Nineteenth Century* (Cambridge University Press, 2002).

[26] Maria Cristina Cortez Wissenbach, "As feitorias de urzela e o tráfico de escravos: Georg Tams, José Ribeiro dos Santos e os negócios da África Centro-Ocidental na década de 1840," *Afro-Ásia*, no. 43 (2011): 43–90.

for 100 square miles of land to cultivate cotton in Mossamedes, south of Benguela. They requested land close to the port to decrease transportation costs, a twenty-year tribute break, and another eighty miles of land if they managed to establish a productive plantation within four years. Haworth and Bastos also requested that all tariffs be waived on the machinery they imported and that the colonial state would provide armed forces to protect the settlers and their properties. The SEMU agreed to provide the land without charging payment for one or more plots in perpetuity. The land would have coastal access limited to ten miles. A contract was to be signed after the responsible parties informed the government of the name and nature of the company or society. However, taxes had to be paid annually, and eighty miles could be rewarded as a bonus even if only half of the terrain was cultivated. All imported goods were subject to tariff except the machinery. Foreigners could be employed only with the approval of the government.[27]

The requests were not only to cultivate land but also to exploit natural resources, with total disregard of the local population that inhabited the territories. In 1861, Francisco António Flores and Manuel Peres Lezano applied for authorization to exploit copper at Cuio near Dombe Grande. Their request was approved and limited to nine *léguas* (23.4 miles), even though Flores, a Luanda resident, was Brazilian and a foreign national at that time. The traveler Joachim Monteiro visited copper deposits at Cuio from 1861 to 1863 and noticed that the Ndombes brought their cattle there for grazing. The land in question was not empty, but Flores and Lezano intended to exploit its resources to the detriment of the local pastoral groups that used the lagoons and wetlands for their animals, looking for relief from the drylands and desert-like conditions a few miles inland.[28]

Women in many African societies, particularly single women, were excluded from land and cattle ownership, but the situation was different in West Central Africa.[29] In fact, in West Central Africa, women's access

---

[27] AHU, SEMU, CU, Processos das Consultas, Cx 67, doc. 2336, 1861, "Processo acerca do pedido de Guilherme Howorth e Eduardo Ferreira Pinto Bastos sobre a concessão de 100 milhas quadradas de terreno no distrito de Benguela para a cultura do algodão," February 15, 1861.

[28] AHU, SEMU, CU, Processos das Consultas, Cx. 69, doc. 2402, "Processo acerca do pedido de Francisco Antonio Flores para sque se lhe pemita lvrar minas de cobre no Cuio," August 30, 1861 and Joachim John Monteiro, *Angola and the River Congo* (New York: Macmillan and Co., 1876), 76, 197–200. For the role of Cuio as a port for shipping copper and natural resources from Dombe Grande, see *O Panorama* vol. 16 (1858), p. 325.

[29] Claire C. Robertson and Iris Berger, *Women and Class in Africa* (New York: Africana, 1986), 10; Ester Boserup, *Woman's Role in Economic Development* (London: Allen & Unwin, 1970).

to land and its inhabitants solidified women's power and prestige. Women were not necessarily marginalized, particularly elite members who could take advantage of a colonial legal code that recognized women's right to own, inherit, and transmit property. Colonialism did not protect African women's interests, especially since most women who lived in Benguela or Luanda by the mid-nineteenth century were not even considered free. However, their access to land clearly varied, based on local experiences and individual abilities, particularly for elite women with Portuguese names who lived in the colonial centers, where they could take advantage of a legal system that allowed them to enjoy property rights.[30]

Dona Teresa de Jesus Ferreira Torres Barruncho, who had already established herself as an important trader in Benguela, expanded her business toward Luacho in the Dombe Grande district (see Map 6.1). Located in a valley marked by rivers and sources of water that favored the spread of mosquito-borne disease, the area was constantly threatened by flooding. However, the abundance of water made it an ideal location to produce sugarcane and cotton, crops known for requiring unusually high quantities of water. Barruncho's initial request was delayed because she had not specified the amount of land she required nor if she intended to buy or lease it. She explained that she needed 9,259 hectares, i.e., 24.1 square miles, and she had 300 enslaved individuals employed on her farm to clear the land for cultivation and harvest the orchil. In her request, Barruncho emphasized the importance of cultivation and agricultural exports for the Angolan economy. Her husband, Vicente Ferrer, sent a letter supporting her request, suggesting that the administration had created some obstacles for her in obtaining the land.[31] Eventually, Dona Teresa Barruncho's farm, Santa Teresa, became one of the most

---

[30] Selma Pantoja, "Donas de 'arimos': Um negócio feminino no abastecimento de gêneros alimentícios em Luanda (séculos XVIII e XIX)," in *Entre Áfricas e Brasis*, ed. Selma Pantoja (Brasilia: Paralelo, 2001), 35–49; Vanessa S. Oliveira, "Slavery and the Forgotten Women Slave Owners of Luanda (1846-1876)," in *Slavery, Memory and Citizenship*, ed. Paul E. Lovejoy and Vanessa S. Oliveira (Trenton, NJ: Africa World Press, 2016), 129–47; Vanessa S. Oliveira, "The Donas of Luanda, c. 1770-1867: From Atlantic Slave Trading to 'Legitimate' Commerce" (Ph.D., Toronto, York University, 2016); Vanessa S. Oliveira, "Gender, Foodstuff Production and Trade in Late-Eighteenth Century Luanda," *African Economic History* 43, no. 1 (2015): 57–81; Mariana P. Candido, "Aguida Gonçalves da Silva, une dona à Benguela à fin du XVIIIe siècle," *Brésil(s). Sciences Humaines et Sociales* 1 (2012): 33–54; Mariana P. Candido and Eugénia Rodrigues, "African Women's Access and Rights to Property in the Portuguese Empire," *African Economic History* 43, no. 1 (2015): 1–18.

[31] AHU, SEMU, CU, Processos das Consultas, Cx. 34, Doc. 1581; October 21, 1861. See also *Índice Alfabéticos do Boletim oficial da Província de Angola* (Luanda: Imprensa do Governo, 1864,) p. 32.

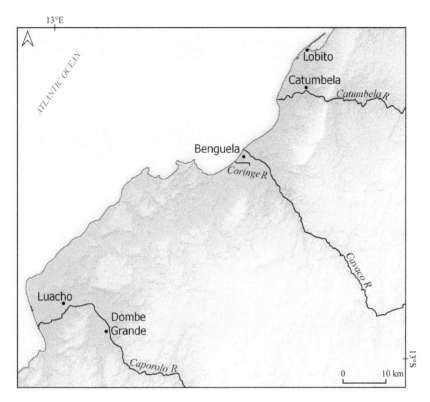

Map 6.1 Benguela, Catumbela, Dombe Grande

profitable plantations at Luacho.[32] Based on her wealth and her marriage
to the governor, she likely commanded a great deal of social and economic influence among the Benguela merchant and political elite.

Other merchant women such as Dona Ana Joaquina and Ana
Francisca, residents of Luanda, had plantations along the Bengo River
as well as in Mossamedes, where they had companies that managed their
properties; their workers, many of them enslaved; and their trade with
inland markets and the Atlantic world. Ana Joaquina dos Santos Silva,
for example, had properties in Luanda, Golungo Alto, and Guifandongo,
and more than 1,400 enslaved individuals.[33] These were all African-born
women who made extensive use of the bureaucracy to claim property and
inheritances, confer power on attorneys, and collect debts.

---

[32] *O Panorama*, vol. 16 (1858), 324–25. For Luanda traders, see Wissenbach, "As feitorias
de urzela e o tráfico de escravos," 69.
[33] Oliveira, *Slave Trade and Abolition*, 71–80.

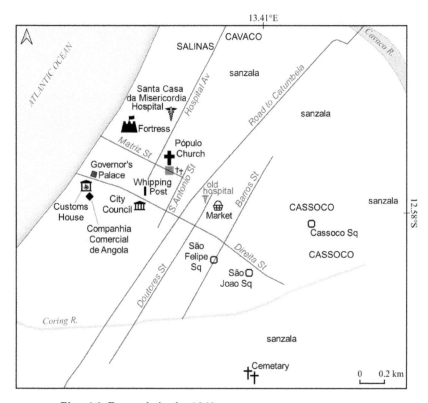

Plan 6.2 Benguela in the 1860s

Land close to the rivers was in high demand due to its potential agricultural use. In Benguela, for example, Amália Rodrigues occupied a 60.5 square-meter plot, neighboring the house of the free Black man Gabriel along the Cavaco River (see Plan 6.2).[34] Nearby in the Cassoco neighborhood, Manoel Ribeiro Alves and Florência Manoel each received a plot where Luis Teodoro de França and Dona Isabel Rodrigues da Costa had houses.[35] In the Bicocolar neighborhood, Maria Antonia Gomes Pereira's plot measured thirty-three meters in the front and eighty-three in the back and bordered the property of João Maria Carreira and the old, abandoned house of the Portuguese traveler António Francisco Ferreira da Silva Porto. Her goal was to build a mud brick house.[36]

[34] BPB, Termo de Terreno, fl. 66, August 6, 1861.
[35] BPB, Termo de Terreno, fl. 63v-64, May 11, 1861.
[36] BPB, Termo de Terreno, fl. 64v, September 6, 1861.

Illustration 6.1 An 1855 view of Morena Beach shore, with the Custom House at the center. The Custom House building still stands in Benguela and houses the National Museum of Arqueologia (*Source:* "Custom House," House of Commons Parliamentary Papers HMS Linnett, 1855)

The Benguela land register records only small plots, but the colonial gazette reveals that individuals also acquired larger plots in and around Benguela. Custódio José de Sousa Velloso received an area measuring five by two kilometers on the right shore of the Cavaco River near Benguela. Dona Eugénia Ferreira da Silva Menezes was granted six kilometers of land along the route connecting Benguela and Catumbela. Dona Antónia da Luz e Abreu was recognized as the owner of plots in Dombe Grande that she had acquired from Mariano Augusto César de Farias and his wife. Martinho Lopes Cordeiro was entitled to vacant land (*terrenos baldios*) between the Quindongo hill and the Caporolo River that included two cashew trees (*cajueiros*) in the Dombe Grande district. Manuel António dos Santos received land south of the beach, described as close to where the old fortress once stood, and thus showing the presence of an earlier military construction south of Morena beach. Manuel de Paula Barbosa could occupy as much as ten kilometers around the region Innamagando south of Benguela. Manuel Ferreira Torres, the son of Dona Teresa Barruncho (discussed earlier), also received land around Vichore in Dombe Grande.[37] António Martins Castro obtained five kilometers close to the salt mines along the Catumbela River.[38] Francisco Marques Esteves wanted land around Cuio.[39]

Absent from these official documents and requests is any discussion about the indigenous occupants of the land. Although in earlier centuries the Portuguese forces had encountered strong resistance from the Ndombe and other groups that occupied the region, by the nineteenth century these groups were absent from the colonial documents and the Ndombe were portrayed as living outside of the colonial area of influence. The colonial state claimed they maintained "good and peaceful relationships with the indigenous people,"[40] but it is difficult to imagine that these populations were removed from their land without resistance.

Those who did not obtain colonial land grants could buy land in the market. Anyone able and willing to pay could become the owner of farms of deceased owners. However, it is not clear how these earlier occupants ever secured property rights. In 1864, for example, the Santa Teresa farm, including the enslaved individuals who worked there, went up for sale after Inácio Teixeira Xavier died, and a contentious dispute emerged

---

[37] BOGGPA, 1864, n. 36-3-9, p. 305–06, p. 312. For other cases that slaves, besides real estate, were auctioned see ANA, Cx. 1322, Catumbela, Administração do Concelho, 1853–1935, Correspondência Recebida, doc. 267, "From governor de Benguela to chefe do concelho da Catumbela [Augusto Ernesto da Silva Francisco], November 5, 1863.
[38] BOGGPA 1864, n. 40-1–10, p. 345.
[39] BOGGPA 1868, n. 13, March 28, 1868, p. 15.
[40] BOGGPA 1866, n. 2, January 13, 1866, p. 9

between his creditors in Benguela and his family in Portugal. The recommendation was to liquidate his assets, a strategy that tended to hurt heirs and dissipate fortunes. There was some difficulty in selling his assets, probably because local merchants and investors waited to see if the prices would decrease and generate more gains. In such unsettled situations, people in bondage were placed under the care of the colonial state or individuals, which generated more exploitation and abuse. In the end, Teresa Barruncho bought the Teixeira Xavier's farm, expanding her land and holdings of human beings since 363 enslaved people were also acquired.[41]

The introduction and expansion of cash crop production resulted in land alienation in the name of economic progress. The shortage of available land around the colonial centers encouraged the movement of foreign settlers into southern zones, resulting in a new landscape for the articulation of land alienation, rights, and ownership claims. Portuguese settlers protested when faced with delays in obtaining land. According to them, the land was "their right."[42] The coastal territories around Cuio and Mossamedes as well as in the interior were appropriated. José Gomes, for example, received three square kilometers in Mosange around Quilengues, while Miguel Luis Duarte do Amaral and Dona Mariana Rosa do Carmo Amaral obtained four square kilometers in Kikuco, also in Quilengues.[43]

These changes occurred in the context of the transformation of land use and occupation, and the growing importance of urban space in Benguela, similar to what happened later in Lagos, Accra, Cacheu, and Freetown.[44] People fought over land, as seen in the case of a Luanda resident João Mateus, a farmer, who claimed that since 1851 he had a *musseque/museke* or country house and had been cultivating a plot of land,

---

[41] BOGGPA 1864, n. 36, September 3, 1864. AHU, SEMU, DGU, Consultas do Conselho Ultramarino, Cx. 46, doc. 2159 "Requerimento de Barbara Adelaide de Almeida Teixeira relativos à arrematação da fazenda denominada Santa Teresa de Equimina, situada no distrito de Benguela,", 13 March 1866.

[42] BOGGPA 1869, n. 12, March 20, 1869, p. 153.

[43] BGGPOA 1870, n. 2, January 8, 1870 p. 15.

[44] Gareth Austin, *Labour, Land, and Capital in Ghana: From Slavery to Free Labour in Asante, 1807-1956* (Rochester, NY: University of Rochester Press, 2005); John Parker, *Making the Town: Ga State and Society in Early Colonial Accra* (Portsmouth, NH: Heinemann, 2000); Kristin Mann, "African and European Initiatives in the Transformation of Land Tenure in Colonial Lagos (West Africa), 1840-1920," in *Native Claims: Indigenous Law against Empire, 1500-1920*, ed. Saliha Belmessous (Oxford; New York: Oxford University Press, 2012), 223–58; Naaborko Sackeyfio-Lenoch, *The Politics of Chieftaincy. Authority and Property in Colonial Ghana, 1920-1950* (Rochester, NY: University of Rochester Press, 2014); Philip J. Havik, "Gender, Land, and Trade: Women's Agency and Colonial Change in Portuguese Guinea (West Africa)," *African Economic History* 43, no. 1 (2016): 162–95; Sarr, "Land, Power, and Dependency."

Illustration 6.2 A view of Benguela's main square
(*Source*: "Vista Parcial da Cidade," Arquivo Nacional de Angola, Cartografia
e Postais, P-1-71)

in Camixe, located on the road to Mutolo. *Musseque* was used as a term
to designate a rural property; in twenty-first-century Angola, it became
synonymous with shantytowns. Mateus explained that the *musseque* was
initially vacant land, and he requested that his ownership right be recognized. He noted that his neighbors, such as Domingos Fançony, already
had land titles for their *musseques*.[45] In Benguela, the occupation of urban
land continued in the 1860s and 1870s, with authorities praising themselves for establishing large plots that could accommodate houses and
vegetable gardens, and discussing strategies to maximize house proximity
and street alignment to improve urban life.[46]

[45] BGGPOA, 1869, n. 35, August 28, 1869, p. 415. For more on *musseques*, see Luciano
Cordeiro, "1593-1631 – terras e minas africanas," in *Viagens, explorações e conquistas dos
portuguezes. Coleção de documentos* (Lisbon: Imprensa Nacional, 1881), 11. For more on
Domingos Fançony, see Oliveira, *Slave Trade and Abolition*, 26; and Carlos Pacheco, "A
origem napolitana de algumas famílias angolanas." *Anais da Universidade de Évora*, no. 5
(1995), 181–201.
[46] ANA, Cx 1376, doc. November 15, 1869 and BOGGPA 1870, n. 37, September 10,
1870, p. 529.

Land Market

Historians interested in land tenure in Africa have argued that land was abundant, failing to examine how, in specific places and times, there was competition for land and how, in different contexts, African women were able to mobilize multiple legal systems for their own interests.[47] Land was individualized and held, accumulating in fewer hands in different regions of the continent, at the expense of the local rulers and their subjects, increasing the concentration of wealth and inequalities.[48] In the Portuguese colonies, another dimension for competition was the presence of African women who claimed property rights and embraced the commodification of urban land. Portuguese inheritance law protected the rights of heirs, including wives and daughters, which allowed women access to property. Principles of joint ownership and equal inheritance allowed wives and widows to become owners and managers of their husbands' estates in their absence, although there are examples of women who had their rights denied and challenged in court.[49] While the law protected autonomy vis-à-vis their male relatives, in practice women, particularly women of color, did not necessarily enjoy the same legal protection. In theory, however, unlike other European legal systems, wives received half of the couple's estate after the husband's death, and all children, regardless of gender and legitimacy, inherited a similar share of the inheritance, which resulted in the division of family estates.[50]

---

[47] Jack Goody, *Death, Property and the Ancestors* (Stanford, CA: Stanford University Press, 1962); Thornton, *Africa and Africans in the Making of the Atlantic World, 1400-1800*; A. G. Hopkins, *An Economic History of West Africa* (New York, NY: Columbia University Press, 1973); Austin, *Labour, Land, and Capital in Ghana*; Susan M. Martin, *Palm Oil and Protest: An Economic History of the Ngwa Region, South-Eastern Nigeria, 1800-1980* (New York: Cambridge University Press, 2006).

[48] For studies that emphasize land privatization, see Kristin Mann, *Slavery and the Birth of an African City: Lagos, 1760-1900* (Bloomington: Indiana University Press, 2010); Kristin Mann, "Women, Landed Property, and the Accumulation of Wealth in Early Colonial Lagos," *Signs* 16, no. 4 (1991): 682–706; Mann, "African and European Initiatives"; Marie-Hélène Knight, "Gorée au XVIIIe siècle du sol," *Revue française d'histoire d'outre-mer* 64, no. 234 (1977): 33–54; Eugénia Rodrigues, "As donas de prazos do Zambeze. Políticas imperiais e estratégias locais," in *VI Jornadas Setecentistas: conferências e comunicações*, ed. Magnus Pereira and Nadalin (Curitiba: Aos Quatro Ventos, 2006), 15–34; Eugénia Rodrigues, *Portugueses e africanos nos Rios de Sena. Os prazos da coroa em Moçambique nos séculos XVII e XVIII* (Lisboa: Imprensa Nacional-Casa da Moeda, 2014); Lentz, *Land, Mobility, and Belonging in West Africa*; Sarr, *Islam, Power, and Dependency*.

[49] Mariana L. R. Dantas, "Succession of Property, Sales of Meação , and the Economic Empowerment of Widows of African Descent in Colonial Minas Gerais, Brazil," *Journal of Family History* 39, no. 3 (2014): 222–38.

[50] For more on Portuguese inheritance law, see Jutta Sperling, "Women's Property Rights in Portugal under Dom João I (1385-1433): A Comparison with Renaissance Italy,"

While the law did not necessarily benefit the interests of colonial subjects, it generated possibilities for African women to accumulate property, circumventing local practices. This legal protection of inheritance and property rights had profound effects on African wives married to Portuguese men, or who had their relationships recognized by the colonial state.

By the late 1820s, individuals were renting houses, which resulted in a concentration of wealth but also in disputes over payments, land use, and properties recorded in colonial courts. Domingas Francisca de Brito, for example, demanded the payment of rent from António de Paula. Another woman, Dona Josefa Gonçalves Jardim, requested that her tenant João Dias vacate her property because she needed to move in.[51] As these cases indicate, African women could rent and sell their estates, allowing them to generate income and accumulate resources and become enriched in the process. In 1845, for example, the Black woman Micaela Ferrera de Britos sold land to Luis Pereira in the Cassoco neighborhood (see Plan 6.2). Micaela retained part of her estate, and after selling a thirty-eight-square-meter plot to Luis Pereira, they became neighbors, with their plots sharing a border.[52] Two decades later in 1864, Lucrécia Manuel announced she was renting her *arimo* along the Bengo River, nearby Luanda, indicating she did not require a male guardian or representative to conduct business.[53] Similar examples in Luanda indicate that women were quite capable of amassing and managing property that could be rented and sold. Joana Maria da Conceição, for example, sold her house on Diogo Cão road close to the infantry barracks. Dona Maria Rosa Rodrigues acquired the house that once belonged to Luis Antonio de Oliveira Machado, paying 20$000 cash for it. In Benguela, Justiano Velasco acted on behalf of Manuel Rodrigues da Silva's heirs and sold some of the deceased's houses.[54]

Portuguese Studies Review 13, no. 1–2 (2005): 59; Dantas, "Succession of Property, Sales of Meação , and the Economic Empowerment of Widows of African Descent in Colonial Minas Gerais, Brazil"; Eugénia Rodrigues, "Women, Land, and Power in the Zambezi Valley of the Eighteenth Century," *African Economic History* 43, no. 1 (2015): 19–56; Candido and Rodrigues, "African Women's Access and Rights to Property in the Portuguese Empire."

[51] ANA, Cod. 7182, "Registro de requerimentos – Benguela, 1825 a 1829," fl. 159, August 25, 1829, requerimento n. 1757; and fl. 167v, November 10, 1829, requerimento n. 1892.

[52] BPB, Termo de Terreno, fl. 6v, September 3, 1845.

[53] BOGGPA, 1864, n. 38, September 17, 1864, p. 335.

[54] BOGGPA, 1866, n. 8, February 24, 1866, p. 38. For Dona Maria Rosa Rodrigues, see BOGGPA, 1866, n. 24, June 16, 1866, p. 214. For other examples from Luanda, see Oliveira, "Donas of Luanda." For Manuel Rodrigues da Silva's properties, see BOGGPA, 1866, n. 14, April 7, 1866, p. 71.

Colonial surveyors inspected and measured landed property and estimated its value. These colonial bureaucrats ultimately developed their own ideas regarding the appropriate amount of land for Portuguese settlers and colonial subjects, differentiating that amount from the sizes of plots that African men and African women could apply for and acquire. In the colonial context, land value was influenced by ultimately outside of local conceptions of value attached to land and its use. Land was estimated, valued, and delimited by a new colonial model that privileged European notions of property and land use in the African landscape.

Most of the transactions refer to colonial sites, and it is difficult to estimate whether these practices also occurred outside of the colonial urban centers. Land commodification occurred wherever there was competition for available and productive land, including outside of the urban centers of Luanda and Benguela. In Luanda's interior, Dona Josefa Antónia Gueulete sold the estate Carlota along the Bengo River. There is no information on its size and use, but the space included a lagoon, a valuable resource for farming and herding.[55] Competition for rural land was the case with the transaction between Dona Rosa Ferreira da Mata, a single Black farmer who lived in Dombe Grande, and Pedro Ferreira de Andrade. Rosa Ferreira da Mata bought land in 1868, close to Equimina that had belonged to Pedro Ferreira de Andrade and his wife. The lawyer who registered the transfer declared that both the seller and the buyer did not know how to read or sign their names; curiously, they still valued registering the transition, attesting to the importance of ownership and the written record. To ascertain the boundaries of Mata's property, the judge of Benguela requested the presence of a local resident, Francisco Ferreira Gurgel, and the *sekulo* (elder), Cacinda, who was familiar with the area. The size of the plot is unclear, but it shared a border with the road connecting Dombe Grande to Quiera and the *sekulo* Cacinda's compound.[56] The knowledge of a local elder was crucial in determining the limits of a private property and that the colonial state recognized it, although not explicitly, that West Central Africans knew more about the territory than the occupier force. In most colonial records, local knowledge about space and geographical features are omitted, leading to the simplification of a complex process of land occupation and use.

---

[55] BOGGPA, 1869, n. 33, August 14, 1869, p. 397.
[56] ANA, cx. 1373, Dombe Grande, "Processo pedido posse de terreno arrematado em hasta publica de Benguela por Rosa Ferreira Mata," Dombe Grande," May 2, 1868; and "Processo referido de autos civis de transferência de posse de um terreno na Equimina," May 6, 1868.

Colonial laws and written records were important to the production of knowledge that consolidated rights, legitimated land apprehension and conquest, and perpetuated the notion that Africans were strangers in their own territory. The colonial appropriation of communal land and its commodification transformed how indigenous people related to and valued the landscape during the nineteenth century. It also brought about new forms of inequality between landholders and landless people and provoked profound social changes, including the association between natural resources, private ownership, and monetary value. Land acquired commercial value and became a commodity that could be bought, sold, enclosed, and transferred. This shift in practices of land ownership created a framework through which groups and individuals could assert and contest rights to land. The introduction of certificates, land registers, titles, and bills of sale were part of the colonial efforts to create colonial knowledge and insert a new order. The written standard altered oral formulas that had prevailed before the 1820s. Under colonialism, landed property was recognized through the presentation of written documents, which became an intrinsic and powerful feature of colonial policies and generated new forms of knowledge and legitimacy. Written evidence prevailed and superseded oral testimony. The cases recorded, however, reveal that colonial law was not only a written code imposed to dominate, but also a space where African women contested and asserted rights.[57]

The transmission of land and property after death reveals how notions of inheritance and land rights were altered during the nineteenth century. Late nineteenth-century and early twentieth-century ethnology reports as well as jurists' studies indicate that male nephews, sons of sisters, enjoyed inheritance rights. Among the Ndombe and other Bantu populations in the interior adjacent to Benguela, wives did not inherit property, particularly land. Their children inherited from their uncle, who enjoyed great

---

[57] Mann, "African and European Initiatives"; Kristin Mann, "Women's Right in Law and Practice: Marriage and Dispute Settlement in Colonial Lagos," in *African Women & the Law: Historical Perspectives*, ed. Margaret Jean Hay and Marcia Wright (Boston, MA: Boston University Press, 1982), 151–71; Rachel Jean-Baptiste, *Conjugal Rights: Marriage, Sexuality, and Urban Life in Colonial Libreville, Gabon* (Athens: Ohio University Press, 2014), 114–21; Sackeyfio-Lenoch, *Politics of Chieftaincy*, 46–48. For the consolidation of written evidence, see Sean Hawkins, *Writing and Colonialism in Northern Ghana: The Encounter Between the LoDagaa and "the World on Paper"* (Toronto: University of Toronto Press, 2002); Bhavani Raman, "The Duplicity of Paper: Counterfeit, Discretion, and Bureaucratic Authority in Early Colonial Madras," *Comparative Studies in Society & History* 54, no. 2 (2012): 229–50; Saliha Belmessous, "Introduction: The Problem of Indigenous Claim Making in Colonial History," in *Native Claims: Indigenous Law against Empire, 1500-1920*, ed. Saliha Belmessous (New York: Oxford University Press, 2012), 3–18; Sarr, "Land, Power, and Dependency."

power and control over nephews and nieces.[58] However, probate lists and land registers reveal that many African women took advantage of changes in land tenure in the nineteenth century to acquire land and make sure that their descendants, in many cases biological children, inherited property. For example, Dona Florencia José do Cadaval left her property to her daughter, Dona Antónia José Coelho de Souza, when she died in 1854.[59] Two decades later, Dona Maria Lucas Pinheiro, also born in Caconda, dictated her will while on her deathbed. She identified her parents as Lucas Luis Pinheiro and Bernarda, a Black woman, but was unable to remember her date of birth. She was estimated to be twenty-five years old in 1877 and had a son, Carlos José Galdinho da Rocha, who was probably seven years old. She left most of her belongings, including her *arimo* in Catumbela, to her son, while her mother, Bernarda, inherited all her textiles and clothes.[60] Inheritance practices had changed, with women leaving property to their biological children.

Legal guardians of heirs ensured that landed ownership was recognized and protected. Sometime before 1863, Teresa Jesus Maria passed away and left a plot to her son. The land was in Quicuxi and had been surveyed and demarcated. However, realizing the opportunity in Teresa Jesus's death, neighbors began relocating close to the limits of her plot and building houses there, probably to eventually claim rights of occupation. The legal guardian demanded that the colonial administration remove all trespassers and protect the rights of the legitimate owners, invoking the power of the bureaucracy and written documents. It is not clear who these so-called trespassers were or if they had historic claims to the land.[61]

Judicial delays also prevented people from enjoying their plots. Rita, a Black woman, was manumitted after her owner's death. In his will, Manuel da Costa e Souza freed Rita, identified her as Rita da Costa e Souza, and bequeathed her an *arimo* in Dombe Grande as well as three enslaved people, Mariana, Quicombo, and Antonio. Although Rita was able to take possession of the plot, she was never able to put her newly

---

[58] António Gil, *Considerações sobre alguns pontos mais importantes da moral religiosa e sistema de jurisprudência dos pretos do continente da África Ocidental Portuguesa além do Equador* (Lisbon: Tipografia da Academia, 1854), 11; Augusto Bastos, "Traços geraes sobre a ethnographia do districto de Benguella," *Boletim da Sociedade de Geografia de Lisboa* 26, no. 1 (1908): 87–88; Gladwyn Murray Childs, *Kinship & Character of the Ovimbundu: Being a Description of the Social Structure and Individual Development of the Ovimbundu of Angola, with Observations Concerning the Bearing on the Enterprise of Christian Missions of Certain Phases of the Life and Culture Described.* (London: Witwatersrand University Press, 1969), 44–45.

[59] TCB, "Autos Civis do Inventário de Florência Jose do Cadaval," 1854, fl. 7–14v.

[60] TCB, "Auto cíveis de translado de testamento de d. Maria Lucas Pinheiro," January 21, 1877.

[61] BOGGPA 1864, n. 38, September 17, 1864, p. 334.

acquired three enslaved people to work. She died one year after receiving the inheritance. The colonial state seized the land and the enslaved people due to the fact Rita did not leave a will or have natural heirs.[62]

It is not clear when African unwillingness to work for low pay and in abusive conditions began to be described as laziness, but such moral justifications became central in advocating for the use of slave labor in the Americas and in Africa, as well as to expel people from their land in West Central Africa. Land was perceived as productive for the colonial economy as long as it was in the hands of Portuguese settlers and the indigenous population was put to work. Such was the case of Manuel António Vieira Martins who received 8.4 kilometers of territory to establish a cotton plantation in the region of Duri in Dombe Grande.[63] Land grants became private property and could later be sold, leased, or used as collateral. This was the case for António José Brochado, whose heirs, after Brochado's death in 1865, put his farm Ascenção up for sale. Located in the Capangombe at Bumbo, it was twenty square kilometers.[64] Local chiefs were displaced from their roles of distributor of land access, and they faced a decline of their legal and arbitration powers, in the sum of their jurisdiction over their territories and subjects.

The changes in the civil code in Portugal in 1869 reinforced the differences between Portuguese citizens and colonial subjects. Non-Catholic indigenous overseas populations were excluded from the protection of the Portuguese legislation and were subject to customary law (*usos e costumes*). The existence of multiple jurisdictions, a practice dating back to the fifteenth-century expansion, prevented non-Catholic subjects from benefiting from protective aspects of colonial law, such as the ability of wives to inherit and administer property. In Angola, legislation in 1855 recognized that colonial administrators in the inland colonial centers acted as judges, a practice that dated to the late seventeenth century. It emphasized that Catholics were protected by and subject to Portuguese law, but when convenient, particularly in questions related to property and family rights,

---

[62] ANA, cx. 3340, Dombe Grande, doc. 53, "Letter from Chefe do Dombe Grande [Francisco José Brito] to the Governor of Benguela," fl. 33v-34v, April 20, 1865.

[63] ANA, cx. 3340, Dombe Grande, doc. 31," Letter Exchange between administrator of Dombe Grande [Ermenegildo Martins da Conceição] and the Benguela secretary," fl. 12, February 4, 1864. For more on this, see Nogueira da Silva, *Constitucionalismo e império*, 188–212; Freudenthal, *Arimos e fazendas*, 140–45; Rodrigues, "As donas de prazos do Zambeze. Políticas imperiais e estratégias locais," 17–20; Sackeyfio-Lenoch, *Politics of Chieftaincy*, 43–45.

[64] BOGGPA, 1866, n. 3, January 20, 1866, p. 15.

customary law was the legal space available for non-Catholic subjects.[65] Jurists argued that Portuguese law was incompatible with non-Catholic subjects' notions of family and property, creating the legal space for not recognizing the rights of indigenous people and their resulting dispossession and subjugation under colonialism.

African actors, particularly women, realized the importance of writing down details of their landholdings and their desires for their bequests in front of colonial officers to guarantee that loved ones received property. In cases available in different archives in Angola, locally born women, most of them with Portuguese names and living within colonial urban areas, managed to participate in a land market, buying and transmitting private property. African women exercised these rights, which allowed them to assert their financial independence and provide for their families after their death. These cases also reveal strategies to protect land ownership. In a short period of time, land became commodified, and women secured access to it, challenged claims of local chiefs, listed their newly secured plots in their wills, and leased them to individuals.

Farms and Civilization

As long as the transatlantic slave trade generated state revenue, colonial officers were not overly concerned with maximizing food production and occupying uncultivated land. With British pressure to bring the trafficking of human beings to an end, the Portuguese Empire eventually searched for new economic ventures that could replace, or at least minimize, the impact of the loss of income associated with slave exports. The idea that farming was a sign of civilization or progress dates back to the early colonial presence in the region in the late sixteenth century. By the mid-eighteenth century, besides the changes associated with governance, the Enlightenment movement also altered the relationship between farmers, land, and productivity. Across Europe, scientists influenced how bureaucrats and states dealt with crop productivity and animal husbandry. Ideals of productivity and agrarian efficiency arrived in West Central Africa with colonial officers advocating for the introduction of more "advanced" tools, such as the use of the European plow instead of the hoe, that would result in larger agricultural output. Colonial

---

[65] Gil, *Considerações sobre alguns pontos*, 24; Silva, *Constitucionalismo e império*, 216–19; Catarina Madeira Santos, "Esclavage africain et traite atlantique confrontés: transactions langagières et juridiques (à propos du tribunal de mucanos dans l'Angola des xviie et xviiie siècles)," *Brésil (s). Sciences Humaines et Sociales* 1 (2012): 127–48; Roquinaldo Ferreira, *Cross-Cultural Exchange in the Atlantic World: Angola and Brazil during the Era of the Slave Trade* (New York: Cambridge University Press, 2012), 100–04.

222   The Erasure of Communal Rights

administrators embraced liberal ideals, including the belief in the free trade, marketization, and individual property, that transformed the pace and organization of labor and land use.[66]

In urban colonial centers, crops introduced from the Americas, such as manioc and corn, were cultivated alongside sorghum, millet, beans, yams, and okra and other staples. New areas were cleared to increase production, such as the floodplains of the Bengo and Catumbela rivers.[67] By the 1830s, the colonial administration aimed at harvesting natural resources such as orchil to generate resources and profits. The risk was competition from foreign traders, as happened with the slave trade.[68] The potential of producing crops such as sugarcane or coffee in West Central Africa at lower or more-competitive rates than in Brazil or the Caribbean became a central colonial aspiration.[69] With the closure of the Brazilian market and the growing pressure to end the slave trade, colonial administrators focused on agrarian changes presented as progress, which privileged European settlers, expanded into new territories away from Luanda and Benguela, and required importing machinery to increase productivity.[70] The intention was that the local population would provide the necessary cheap labor and vacate their lands in the name of progress.[71] The indigenous population resisted, yet in Portuguese agents' accounts, they were portrayed as lazy and unwilling to work. The trader Silva Porto in Bihé filled his diaries with notations of how

[66] Felner, *Angola. Apontamentos sobre a colonização dos planaltos...*, vol. I, pp. 171–73, "Carta de Francisco Inocêncio de Sousa Coutinho para José Vieira de Araújo, capitão-mor de Benguela, 12 de Outubro de 1769; and "Instrução porque se há-de governar o capitão-mor de Caconda, João Baptista da Silva e da qual se não afastará um só ponto, 15 de Dezembro de 1769. See also Patrick Manning, *Slavery and African Life: Occidental, Oriental, and African Slave Trades* (New York: Cambridge University Press, 1990), 33–34.

[67] Vanessa S. Oliveira, "The Gendered Dimension of Trade: Female Traders in Nineteenth Century Luanda," *Portuguese Studies Review* 23, no. 2 (2015): 93–121; Esteban Salas, "Women and Food Production. Agriculture, Demography and Acess to Land in Late Eighteenth-Century Catumbela," in *African Women in the Atlantic World. Property, Vulnerability and Mobility, 1660-1880*, ed. Mariana P. Candido and Adam Jones (Woodbridge: James Currey, 2019), 55?69..

[68] ANA, Cod. 7183, fl. 71–72, August 14, 1835; and fl. 77, June 21, 1836.

[69] AHU, SEMU, DGU, Angola, 477, 1840–1843, "Registro de Correspondência Expedida," fl. 6. For more on this see Jelmer Vos, *Kongo in the Age of Empire, 1860–1913: The Breakdown of a Moral Order* (Madison, WI: University of Wisconsin Press, 2015); Roquinaldo Amaral Ferreira, "Agricultural Enterprise and Unfree Labour in Nineteenth Century Angola," in *Commercial Agriculture, the Slave Trade and Slavery in Atlantic Africa*, ed. Robin Law, Suzanne Schwarz, and Silke Strickrodt (Woodbridge: James Currey, 2013), 225–42.

[70] AHU, SEMU, DGU, Angola, 477, 1840–1843, "Registro de Correspondência Expedida," fl. 17v.

[71] ANA, Cod. 326, fl. 75, March 30, 1849.

people loitered and saw no value in working. It is important to note that he expected Bienos to feel excited about working in his fields for his own profit, while neglecting their families' needs.[72]

In the 1860s, João Duarte de Almeida, who already owned two farms in Mossamedes, requested another fifty square kilometers of land to set up a cotton, sugarcane, and coffee plantation. Authorities in Lisbon asked for evidence that the two previous land concessions were productive before granting more landed property. Eventually, Duarte de Almeida secured the land grant, which inevitably affected the populations who had until then lived in those territories.[73] Economic inequality increased during the second half of the nineteenth century as opportunities for accumulation through cultivation and trade grew, particularly for those who controlled labor and land, and could produce crops demanded in external markets such as cotton and sugar. Property disputes became increasingly contentious and conflicts over inheritance were brought to the colonial court. Once again, the paper culture prevailed, with colonial judges replacing *sobas* and other forms of authority, and the local population's role was relegated to forced laborers for the prosperity of plantations and the colonial export economy.[74]

Colonial officers and ecclesiastical personnel praised farm administrators and owners for their ability to extract labor and produce cotton, sugar, and *aguardente* (firewater) for export. Domingos Soares Rodrigues Coutinho, who managed the Santa Teresa farm along the São Francisco River in Luacho, Dombe Grande, was portrayed as a great success in achieving the civilizing goals of colonialism. The owner, Teresa Barruncho, is not mentioned in the priest's report, which can be read as an effort to silence African women's ownership, or simply a gendered perspective related to business administration. On a single visit in 1866, the priest of Benguela baptized over 300 people who worked in the farm, mostly enslaved.[75] On Dona Teresa Barruncho's farms, cotton and sugarcane production expanded alongside the production of food staples such as cassava, corn, and beans. As a result, this African woman was

---

[72] BSGL, Res 2-C 6, "Silva Porto, apontamentos de um portuense em África. Vol 2, fl. 131, June 1, 1861.

[73] AHU, SEMU, DGU, Consultas do Conselho Ultramarino, cx. 46, doc. 2160, "Consulta do conselho ultramarino ao rei D. Luis I. Requerimento do proprietário de duas fazendas em Moçamedes, João Duarte de Almeida, a pedir 5 mil hectares de terrenos baldios em Moçamedes," March 13, 1866. For other reports, see BOGGPA, 1869, n. 5, February 3, 1869, pp. 24–25, and n. 6, February 6, 1869, p. 61; n. 29, July 17, 1869, p. 345; n. 36, September 4, 1869, p. 425; and 1870, n. 15, April 9, 1870, p. 250.

[74] BOGGPA 1869, n. 29, July 17, 1869, p. 345–46.

[75] BOGGPA, 1866, n. 5, February 3, 1866, p. 25.

able to accumulate dependents but also to employ foreign agents, some of them Portuguese outlaws as in the case of José dos Santos, to control the labor force. The Rio de Janeiro trader Tomé Ribeiro Antunes accumulated debts with Dona Barruncho during his stay in Benguela. He died in her house in 1867, unable to repay a cash advance. As a result, after a two-year legal case, Teresa Barruncho acquired Antunes's farm. She had already appropriated his slaves as collateral and now had more land on which they could be put to work.[76] Antunes was not the only foreign trader to die at her house. In 1875 Luis Bernardo de Carvalho from Braga, Portugal, also died at her place.[77] By then, Dona Teresa, married to the former governor of Benguela, Vicente Barruncho, had relocated to Lisbon, where she spent the last decades of her life.

African women hosted, entertained, and nursed travelers while they were in Benguela, and Dona Barruncho combined those activities with controlling labor and land, which increased her wealth, even while residing in Lisbon. Barruncho's agricultural wealth allowed her to establish a commercial enterprise, the *Sociedade Teresa Barruncho*. The work connected with that company led her to travel regularly between Benguela, Dombe Grande, and Lisbon.[78] In 1863 alone, the *Sociedade* exported over 1,354 *arrobas* of cotton, and Barruncho became a major cotton supplier to the colonial state.[79] The transportation of the cotton from Dombe Grande to the port of Benguela was done on the backs of free and enslaved people. Although some of them were paid for their role as porters, the bulk of the profit stayed in the hands of the estate owner.[80] In the early twentieth century, the *Sociedade Teresa Barruncho*, later renamed *Sociedade Santa Teresa*, continued to export more than 84,000 kilos of cotton to Portugal yearly.[81] Barruncho's natural heirs inherited

---

[76] BOGGPA, 1870, n. 17, April 23, 1870, p. 278; and ANA, cx. 3340, Dombe Grande, maço 1, doc. S/N, "Relatório do Concelho de Dombe Grande com referência ao mês de junho de 1871," July 1, 1871. For *degredados* at Barruncho' farms, see ANA, cx. 3340, Dombe Grande, maço 1, doc. 3, "Concelho do Dombe Grande – Relação de degredados existentes neste concelho durante o mês de junho de 1871," July 1, 1871. For Antunes, see BL, Óbito, Benguela, 1858–68, July 2, 1867, fl. 77V. For Carvalho's reference, see BOGGPA, 1869, n. 33, August 14, 1869, fl. 395. Vanessa Oliveira who shared her copy of this document with me and I am thankful for her help.

[77] BL, Óbito, Benguela, 1874–76, fl. 21, July 13, 1876.

[78] BL, Dombe Grande, Batismo, 1874-75 fl. 5–6, November 11, 1874.

[79] BOGGPA, n. 6, 1864, February 6, 1864, p. 55–56, ofício 2 de fevereiro de 1864. Sá da Bandeira, *Synopse dos trabalhos do Conselho Ultramarino* (Lisbon: Imprensa Nacional, 1857), 62.

[80] AHU, Angola, Correspondência dos Governadores, Pasta 38, December 21, 1868, "Relatório do Governo de Benguela referente a 1864-1868."

[81] ANA, cx. 3340, Dombe Grande, Maço 2 – Dombe Grande governo 1863 a 1915, "Letter from lawyer Amilcar Barcar Martins da Cruz," February 10, 1913.

her assets after her death in 1881. Her assets were divided into three parts: the first two parts were given to her daughter, Teresa de Jesus da Silva Viana Costa, and her son, João Luis da Silva Viana, and the third part was divided equally among her grandchildren and placed under the management of two of her executors while the children were minors.[82] Unfortunately, I have been unable to locate an inventory listing her property and belongings in archives in Angola and Portugal. The fact that her grandchildren were not named also make it difficult to trace the family's wealth and particularly her properties in Angola after her death.

These personal stories of wealth and prosperity emphasizing individual accomplishments obscure the social costs for the majority of West Central Africans. To protect the interests of individuals, aligned with the colonial economic goals, the administration displaced local populations in the name of progress and to control the illegal slave trade. People who lived and cultivated the area from Benguela beach up to Dombe Grande were slowly removed from their land as they were accused of collaborating with non-Portuguese subjects in the business of the slave trade. In a move similar to what happened elsewhere, the colonial government blamed the Ndombe and other African people for the continuing existence of trade in human beings and slave exports, as if Europeans never engaged in the slave trade and had no responsibility for the continuing operation of slavery and its commerce in Africa and elsewhere. The governor of Benguela, Francisco João da Costa e Silva, linked the end of the slave trade with the removal of the local population and their replacement with colonial soldiers patrolling the coast.[83] Lisbon, Luanda, and Benguela authorities painted the expansion of agriculture, on the so-called legitimate trade in natural resources, as the viable solution to tackle contraband and illegal trade in human beings.

---

[82] ANTT, Feitos Findos, Registro Geral de Testamentos, Belém, L. 31, cx. 95, April 23, 1881.

[83] ANA, Cod. 326, fl. 56 v, October 10, 1848, "To the Governador of Benguela [Francisco João da Costa e Silva,] from the Secretary." For more on how Europeans portrayed Africans as responsible for the continuation of the slave trade, see Felicitas Becker, "Common Themes, Individual Voices: Memories of Slavery around a Former Slave Plantation in Mingoyo, Tanzania," ed. Alice Bellagamba, Sandra E. Greene, and Martin A. Klein (New York: Cambridge University Press, 2013), 71–87; Benedetta Rossi, "Without History? Interrogating 'Slave' Memories in Ader (Niger)," ed. Alice Bellagamba, Sandra E. Greene, and Martin A. Klein (New York: Cambridge University Press, 2013), 536–54; Richard Roberts, "The End of Slavery, Colonial Courts, and Social Conflict in Gumbu, 1908-1911," *Canadian Journal of African Studies* 34, no. 3 (2000): 684–713; Marie Rodet, "Escaping Slavery and Building Diasporic Communities in French Soudan and Senegal, ca. 1880-1940," *International Journal of African Historical Studies* 48, no. 2 (2015): 363–86.

In the 1860s and 1870s, the *Ministério dos Negócios da Marinha e Ultramar* (MNMU) allocated funds to transport any Portuguese subject interested in establishing productive farms and willing to live in the African colonies for at least five years. Portuguese emigrants received financial support, and legislation was approved to protect their interests as free people and owners (*proprietários*) who would advance the civilizing agenda. The colonial state had to enact policies to seize fertile lands so as to advance the MNMU policies and recommendations.[84] This colonial policy also aimed to prevent the rise of more powerful African women, such as Dona Teresa Barruncho. By bringing white European settlers, inevitably, locally born mixed-race and Black wealthy planters could be excluded from land ownership.

By passing laws and policies that were published as documents, bureaucrats in Lisbon and Luanda used that paper legality to portray colonial conquest as bloodless and as advancing civilization and progress. Colonial archives, however, reveal the numerous advantages provided to Portuguese settlers at the expense of the local African population. *Sobas*, the local chiefs, were viewed as dispensable, which coincided with the local judicial system being replaced by colonial law. They lost their ability to distribute land and arbitrate on disputes, which undermined their power.

Land alienation in the interior increased in the 1880s, similar to what was taking place in other European settler colonies in the African continent, such as South Africa. The licenses are silent on how the indigenous population used the land, whether for hunting, cultivation, mining, grazing, or simply building their own houses and villages. The petitions, licenses, and sale records ignore the violence and the process of dispossession that West Central African groups faced. However, they emphasize the colonial perspective of subjugation and control, which reinforces the notion that the land was empty and available for cash-crop production. These documents also normalized the privatization of land and natural resources, as something that had always existed, rather than a historical invention associated with the consolidation of liberal ideas. Along the left shore of the River Nene in Huila, Mossamedes district, Joaquim Afonso Lage controlled 0.15 kilometers, preventing any other individual from feeding their cattle along the river or using the water resources.[85] Also in Huila, Carlos Maria expanded land he

---

[84] BOGGPA, 1881, n. 42, October 15, 1881, p. 643.

[85] BGGPOA, 1881, n. 11, March 15, 1881, p. 145. For comparisons to land dispossession in South Africa, Clifton Crais, *Poverty, War, and Violence in South Africa* (New York: Cambridge University Press, 2011), 102–21; Susan Newton-King, *Masters and Servants on the Cape Eastern Frontier, 1760-1803* (Cambridge: Cambridge University Press, 1999);

already owned along the River Lupolo, while Rufina Rosa bought 20,000 meters or 0.02 square kilometers alongside her house to establish a vegetable garden. Foreigners and locally born individuals rushed to secure access to plots along rivers, with the potential to create agricultural advantages. In Caconda, Abraão Benchimol, a Benguela trader, acquired ten square kilometers to cultivate opium and indigo.[86] Aristides Urbano do Amaral secured a five-square-kilometer plot for sugarcane cultivation in Cuio, Dombe Grande.[87] As can be seen in these requests, individuals who framed their requests as an expansion of cash-crop plantations acquired larger plots. Those who were interested in expanding land they used for subsistence farming were unable to afford larger plots. Moreover, as colonial land grants to individuals expanded inland, *sobas* and local chiefs saw their control of lineage land diminish as community outsiders and nonmembers encroached on their territory, including sacred spaces. Land was increasingly recognized as the personal property of individuals who could dispose of it as they wished, regardless of local customs, which accelerated the commodification and exclusion of indigenous groups.

Land became a commodity and a political resource that contributed to Portugal's claim over territory in West Central Africa during the Berlin Conference. Empowered by imperialism and scientific racism, Portuguese settlers and merchants displaced local West Central Africans from their lands. In 1891, Francisco Maria Victor Cordon was authorized to occupy 150 kilometers of "vacant land suitable for agriculture" between Caconda and Benguela, a vast territory that included several sobas and their subjects. Despite the lack of any reference to the existing communities in this territory, the colonial administration agreed to award even larger land plots to Cordon if he could successfully make two-thirds of the land productive. For six years, he would be excused from paying taxes for production and imported machinery, while the historical document is silent on the fate of the populations who lost access to their lands.[88]

In 1880, the viscount of São Januário, Januário Correia de Almeida, who had served as governor in Cape Verde, Goa, and Macau in the 1860s and 1870s, recommended that forests and woodlands be occupied in order to cut trees that could be useful for the navy and the shipping industry. If local rulers occupied the land, the instructions were to

Jill E. Kelly, *To Swim with Crocodiles. Land, Violence and Belonging in South Africa, 1800-1996* (Lansing: Michigan State University Press, 2018).

[86] BGGPOA, 1881, n. 21, May 21, p. 302.
[87] BGGPOA, 1881, n. 11, March 12, p. 146.
[88] AHU, Angola, Direção Geral do Ultramar, Consultas da Junta do Ultramar, Cx. 7, doc. 651, 1891, December 11, 1891.

negotiate an agreement for "perpetual usufruct," allowing the Portuguese Crown to benefit at a low cost.[89] Local rulers and populations became an inconvenience for Portuguese expansion and industry and needed to be overcome at any cost. The land displacement allows us to see how the histories of colonizers and colonized were imbricated and connected, with a single side taking advantage of the events. By 1885, the Berlin Conference had recognized Portuguese control of the colony of Angola. Due to conquest and colonization, the colonial government could dispose of land. As a result, in 1888, the Eastern Telegraph Company received a plot of "empty land" to build a station for submarine telecommunication cables connecting Benguela to Luanda, Mossamedes, and Cape Town.[90] The building was erected in 1889 and remained in place until March 2015, when a fire destroyed the historical building.

Conclusion

Changes in land control soon became the central focus of colonialism in West Central Africa over the course of the nineteenth century, and individual property became the model at the expense of collective access. A dual land tenure system was accepted before the 1830s, while the transatlantic slave trade was the main economic activity that enriched the Portuguese monarchy and its elite. Before the 1830s, the colonial administration occupied only limited coastal and inland territories. On the other side, the land rights of local rulers located away from the coastal colonial centers were recognized as legitimate as long as *sobas* recognized colonial authority. In the mid-nineteenth century, however, a regime of individual property emerged, influenced by liberal ideas consolidated in Europe. In the 1850s, the colonial state declared all uncultivated land as vacant and the colonial state as the sole and legitimate arbiter of rights and access. The colonial state introduced a system of land registration and private ownership to regulate colonists' access to those lands. Native land was alienated, which had profound economic, political, and social effects. Portuguese subjects were recognized as having rights as the owners of smallholders, which exacerbated conflict and economic inequality. Land-control struggles over the replacement of subsistence farming with export agriculture and shifting recognition in ownership claims were essential to strengthening colonialism. Those struggles also shaped the dismissal of the rights of the native population and reinforced

---

[89] BOGGPA, 1881, n. 6, Supplement, February 8, 1881, p. 88.
[90] BPB, Termo de Terreno, fl. 81 v, September 14, 1894.

Portuguese colonialism, which became essential to Portugal's territorial claims during the Berlin Conference.

By the late nineteenth century and early twentieth century, colonial officers and jurists wrote treatises arguing that Africans were unable to understand the meaning of private property, implying that these ideas were ahistorical in European legal culture. This erroneous idea became a trope to justify and legitimate land occupation and colonial rule. In the early twentieth century, jurists integrated land alienation into a discourse of Africans' supposedly backward lifestyle, claiming European superiority over African societies. Anthropologists and historians have failed to address the pervasive legacy of early twentieth-century colonial jurists' writings on land use, occupation, and rights. A land-tenure system that had undergone a profound transformation during the four centuries of Portuguese occupation and colonialism was dismissed as nonexistent, in part due to the influence of colonial jurists shaped by evolutionism, scientific racism, and the consolidation of the liberal ideology of monetary value and commodification. The colonial knowledge constructed in the second half of the nineteenth century and the early twentieth century reinforced ideas regarding land abundance and labor scarcity expressed in the concept of wealth in people.

Land was not sold or commodified in Angola before the 1830s, but neither was it in mainland Portugal. In fact, it was the debate about land rights and enclosure in Angola that shaped the discussion on landed properties in Portugal. The Liberal Revolution, British pressure to bring the slave trade to an end, and the independence of Brazil affected the way the Portuguese political and commercial elite imagined its African colonies and the economic possibilities. The colonizers sought more revenue and prestige as they planned to prolong Portuguese control. Colonial authorities distributed land to individuals willing to promote cultivation, with the administration providing seeds and tools and mobilizing freed labor to work for private farmers. Luanda and Benguela residents, including many women, most of them African born, rushed to petition for land. Initially, the plots of land were granted as concessions and not necessarily as sales, but very quickly individuals began transferring the land to third parties, in fact privatizing the concessions for personal gain. The colonial administration seized unoccupied lands, including those used for grazing or occupied by spirits. Officers labeled desirable territories as vacant, a problematic term that portrays West Central African territories as unused spaces that could only become productive and useful with European ingenuity and knowledge.

Local rulers were expelled from their land due to security concerns or were accused of failing to advance agricultural production. During the nineteenth century, while some members of the colonial elite, including many locally born people, managed to secure landed property, the local population, however, was displaced in the name of progress and civilization. The colonial archives reveal that colonialism undermined the power of local chiefs and sabotaged their rule and their ability to arbitrate conflicts and distribute land access, privileging privatization of land and individual ownership.

7   Global Consumers: West Central Africans and the Accumulation of Things

The dismissal of West Central African property regimes and their uneven replacement with the Portuguese one restricted the local population to the role of a coerced laborer. They pushed back, playing key roles as manufacturers and consumers of desirable goods. West Central Africans embraced liberal ideals, such as free trade, demanding French, Dutch, and British goods. Colonial law tried to control consumption and imports by preventing French, Dutch, and British merchants from bringing their cargo directly into Portuguese colonies in Africa, in contradiction to the liberalization of trade and the free circulation of goods. Manufactured goods had to be negotiated through Portuguese import sellers, and West Central Africans acted as global consumers, interesting in accumulating goods, solidifying the supremacy of private property. To understand the circulation of goods and their meanings is also to explore how West Central Africans reflected on material culture, political and economic power. It shows the link between consumption, labor, and production. The imposition and acceptance of goods related to ideas of progress, civility, or modernity, such as shoes and hats or chairs and crucifixes, also discloses that some West Central Africans resisted drinking coffee, using forks, or attending the Catholic Church, although their presence in historical documents is less visible.

Commodities linked people to the wider world, including those living miles away from the coast. The distribution of goods connected production, consumption, and commerce, which all had their roles in the organization and expansion of the Atlantic economy. Scholars have analyzed African consumption patterns during the era of the transatlantic slave trade in an effort to understand the motivations behind the decisions of merchant and political elite to engage in the Atlantic trade.[1] Yet,

---

[1] George Metcalf, "A Microcosm of Why Africans Sold Slaves: Akan Consumption Patterns in the 1770s," *The Journal of African History* 28, no. 3 (1987): 377–94; Jeremy Prestholdt, *Domesticating the World: African Consumerism and the Genealogies of Globalization* (Berkeley: University of California Press, 2008); David Richardson, "Consuming Goods, Consuming

this remains an understudied topic and, as it is examined here, the process of being part of a global economy was part and parcel also of the coming of rights associated with liberalism. The investment in material goods, particularly luxurious ones, interconnected ideas about property, including land rights, to the accumulation of personal objects.

Wealth in personal belongings, and not necessarily exclusively in wealth in people, transformed how different West Central African societies conceived value, prosperity, and consumption. It exacerbated wealth and inequality during the nineteenth century, as well as how affluence was displayed in public and private settings.

It is a fact that transportation costs and logistics limited the number and choices of available items, and merchants and markets played a significant role in determining what people could acquire. Yet people still aspired to buy and display a variety of goods, ranging from tools that could improve agriculture production such as hoes and axes, or that would allow the manufacture of shoes, to luxury items such as dishes and silk handkerchiefs. When an African woman born in Caconda around the 1850s listed five wooden chairs, two tables, an iron bed frame, and five golden necklaces as her life possessions, or when shopkeepers' advertisements in the colonial gazette announced the availability of Rotterdam tobacco, port wine, and Huntley & Palmers biscuits, it is clear that West Central Africans aspired to acquire things, contradicting Capelo and Ivens's statement that West Central Africans "had no desire to acquire things."[2] West Central African men and women consumed items such as Indian textiles, Brazilian tobacco, and *cachaça* that con-

People. Reflections on the Transatlantic Slave Trade," in *The Rise and Demise of Slavery and the Slave Trade in the Atlantic World*, ed. Philip Misevich and Kristin Mann (Rochester, NY: University of Rochester Press, 2016), 32–63; Arnold J. Bauer, *Goods, Power, History: Latin America's Material Culture* (New York: Cambridge University Press, 2001); Colleen E. Kriger, "Mapping the History of Cotton Textile Production in Precolonial West Africa," *African Economic History* 33 (2005): 87–116; Jennifer Cole, "The Love of Jesus Never Disappoints: Reconstituting Female Personhood in Urban Madagascar 1," *Journal of Religion in Africa* 42, no. 4 (2012): 384–407; David Richardson, "West African Consumption Patterns and Their Influence on the Eighteenth-Century English Slave Trade," in *Uncommon Market: Essays in the Economic History of the Atlantic Slave Trade*, ed. Henry A. Gemery and Jan S. Hogendorn (New York: Academic Press, 1979), 303–30; Daniel B. Domingues da Silva, *The Atlantic Slave Trade from West Central Africa, 1780–1867* (Cambridge: Cambridge University Press, 2017), 122–141.

[2] Hermenegildo Capelo and Roberto Ivens, *De Benguela às terras de Iaca. Descrição de uma viagem na África Central e Ocidental*, vol. 1 (Lisbon: Europa-América, 1996), 135. Tribunal da Comarca de Benguela (TCB), "Ação cível de translado do testamento de D. Maria Lucas Pinheiro," January 23, 1877; BOGGOPA, 1881, N. 8, February 19, 1880, p. 114. See also Arnold J. Bauer, *Goods, Power, History*, 1–14.

nected them to societies and markets around the world from America to Asia but mainly in the Global South.

Surprisingly, the records available at the Arquivo Nacional de Angola and the Tribunal da Comarca de Benguela provide much information on Africans' levels and patterns of acquisition and accumulation of objects. In these documents, we can see that West Central Africans were not simply producers of crops and baskets but also people who desired things, who bought goods and displayed them to increase their social standing. Looking at how people accumulated wealth in things rather than people, it is possible to explore the movement of goods, the role of commercial centers, and the changes in taste and fashion. It also challenges the supremacy of the concept of wealth in people as a paradigm for understanding West Central African economies and processes of wealth accumulation. Inevitably, the desire of African men and women in the interior and along the coast for firearms, Indian textiles, Chinese teacups, hats and shoes, and Brazilian alcohol encouraged African political elites and warlords to engage in warfare and other strategies to enslave enemies. In many ways, the history of nineteenth-century consumption in Angola continued to be linked to the slave trade and its long survival in the South Atlantic world.[3]

The probate records analyzed in this chapter disclose the items that commoners, not African rulers, acquired and retained during their lifetime. While the colonial reports and correspondence reveal that sobas in the interior of Benguela demanded gunpowder, alcohol, textiles, and manufactured clothes, postmortem inventories expose what ordinary people were able to buy. In comparison with the total population, very few West Central Africans were able to claim the inheritance of immovable goods. In many ways, those able to engage with the colonial bureaucracy were an elite who had adopted Portuguese names and habits, such as living in brick houses or attending Catholic mass. There was also a cost associated with leaving wills, which discouraged the poorest from settling inheritance in the colonial bureaucracy. Yet despite their Portuguese names, they were still colonial subjects, and many of them were locally born women. They avidly consumed imported products, spoke Portuguese and Umbundu, dressed in Western fashions, and asserted their belonging to a colonial elite, as can be seen in Illustrations 7.1 and 7.2.

---

[3] Richardson, "Consuming Goods, Consuming People. Reflections on the Transatlantic Slave Trade," 47–48; Jelmer Vos, "Coffee, Cash, and Consumption: Rethinking Commodity Production in the Global South," *Radical History Review* 2018, no. 131 (2018): 184–85.

Illustration 7.1 A group identified as civilized Blacks, including three men, three women, and three children. It is not clear whether they were related. The three men wear suits; the women wear dresses and wraps. Two have head wraps and bracelets. Two of the children wear shoes (*Source*: Arquivo Nacional de Angola, Postais, "Benguela, um grupo de pretos civilizados," P-1-41)

By buying Portuguese firearms, English woolens, and Indian textiles, West Central Africans fostered familiarity with a global market, projecting the idea that they were closer to the colonial settlers and different from their neighbors who did not dress like them or did not own the same furniture or weapons.[4] Similar to African elites elsewhere, West Central African global consumers felt European and modern, in sync with a fast-changing economic situation associated with the expansion of legitimate commerce and the transformation of European imperialism in the second half of the nineteenth century. Individual taste and style were shaped by local understandings combined with imported ideas. Nineteenth-century decisions regarding what to wear and what to buy facilitated the creation of a distinct group of Africans and reveals how people endowed objects

---

[4] For the variety of imported commodities, see Roquinaldo Ferreira, "Dinâmica do comércio intracolonial: Gerebitas, panos asiáticos e guerra no tráfico angolano de escravos, século XVIII," in *O Antigo Regime nos Trópicos: A Dinâmica imperial portuguesa, séculos XVI-XVIII*, ed. João Luís Ribe Fragoso, Maria de Fátima Gouvêa, and Maria Fernanda Bicalho (Rio de Janeiro: Civilização Brasileira, 2001), 339–78; Domingues da Silva, *Atlantic Slave Trade*, 133–35; Vos, "Coffee, Cash, and Consumption."

Illustration 7.2 Benguela woman with gold earrings, different types of necklaces, and bracelets. She wears an elaborate dress with several layers of different textiles
(*Source*: "Costumes de Benguela," Arquivo Nacional de Angola, Postais, P-1-40)

with subjective meanings that are not always clear to an early twenty-first-century historian.[5] Goods became personal property, assets that represented affluence.

African history is filled with powerful leaders, the Big Men, who prioritized accumulating people over territory. Narratives also stress the

---

[5] Jones, *The Métis of Senegal*, 90–91; Prestholdt, *Domesticating the World*, 13–15. See also Adam Jones, "Drink Deep, or Taste Not: Thoughts on the Use of Early European Records in the Study of African Material Culture," *History in Africa* 21 (1994): 349–70; Milton Guran, *Agudás. Os brasileiros do Benim* (Rio de Janeiro, RJ: Nova Fronteira, 2000).

role of powerful female rulers and merchants engaged in similar practices.[6] In the 1870s, the travelers Roberto Ivens and Hermegildo Capelo
reported that the ruler of Bihé requested shirts, pants, and hats like those
worn by Portuguese explorers. The soba was also interested in the
travelers' golden bands. Despite the fact that their travel account clearly
indicates a desire for imported goods, Capelo and Ivens's narrative
described a land that was plentiful, "provided all, and they [the people
from Bihé] did not need anything, so there was no desire to acquire
things."[7] Capelo and Iven's account and other documents reveal that
people in the interior went beyond the ability to produce food, clothing,
and shelter for their sustainment. They desired material things that
surpassed their needs, as shown by the Bihé ruler's request for imported
pants and hats. It can be read as imitation and display of Western
fashion, but also as efforts to establish internal socioeconomic differences
between those who had and the destitute masses.

The undoing of previous ownership regimes and the expansion of
commodification turned West Central Africans into consumers. The
ability of West Central Africans to buy imported goods helped them
secure and affirm status as a local elite connected to the world. It also
suggests the importance of commodities in strategies of distinction.[8]
Personal belongings had social meanings and fostered relationships.
People bequeathed dresses, furniture, and jewelry to loved ones. Slave
owners showed appreciation for loyal enslaved individuals by leaving
used shirts and pants. Purchases and gifted items brought people into
local and long-distance markets, allowing previously marginalized people
to elaborate new identities and aim for social acceptance and inclusion in
a society facing rapid economic change.

The existence of nineteenth-century wills and inventories allows us to
explore which goods local populations desired and which were worth
transmitting to loved ones. They also reveal the social and economic

---

[6] Nwando Achebe, *The Female King of Colonial Nigeria: Ahebi Ugbabe* (Bloomington: Indiana University Press, 2011); Linda M. Heywood, *Njinga of Angola: Africa's Warrior Queen* (Cambridge, MA: Harvard University Press, 2017); Colleen E. Kriger, "From Child Slave to Madam Esperance: One Woman's Career in the Anglo-African World, c. 1675-1707," in *African Women in the Atlantic World. Property, Vulnerability and Mobility, 1680-1880,* ed. Mariana P. Candido and Adam Jones (Woodbridge: James Currey, 2019), 171–89; Vanessa S. Oliveira, *Slave Trade and Abolition. Gender, Commerce and Economic Transition in Luanda* (Madison: University of Wisconsin Press, 2021).

[7] Capelo and Ivens, *De Benguela às terras de Iaca,* 1:114.

[8] Pierre Bourdieu, *Pascalian Meditations* (Stanford: Stanford University Press, 2000), 193–98; Prestholdt, *Domesticating the World*; Graubart, *With Our Labor and Sweat,* 63–65; Amy M. Porter, *Their Lives, Their Wills: Women in the Borderlands, 1750-1846* (Lubbock: Texas Tech University Press, 2015).

interactions between people of different legal statuses. By examining the routes and mechanisms that permitted the circulation of imported goods, connections between coastal and internal elites can be explored. Evidence from Angolan archives reveals the interactions between male and female traders and the regional networks. As presented in this chapter, consumer desire, and its change over time, can be seen in the cases that expose how African men and women actually participated in the global economy, not only as producers or enslaved people, but also as consumers of goods produced in distant markets. Taste, consumption, and accumulation were related. West Central Africans were concerned with consolidating wealth in the accumulation of material things, but also with their public display. More than wealth in people, by the second half of the nineteenth century, local people displayed wealth in the accumulation of personal belongings, such as furniture, dresses, paintings, and shoes. An analysis of the interests in the accumulation of objects reveals the pervasive influence of liberal ideologies, including the rise of individual property, which accelerated the dismantling of common interests and collective goods.

The Internal Circulation of Goods

Reports from the sixteenth, seventeenth, and eighteenth centuries illustrate how West Central Africans had been consuming material goods produced elsewhere for some time. Imported goods transformed patterns of consumption, desire, and trade, with clothes, salt, copper manillas, beads, and ostrich shells circulating in internal markets and exported through the ports of Luanda and Benguela. The transatlantic slave trade operated as a legal business and custom records and ship cargo data allow historians to trace the imported goods disembarked in West Central African ports. The colonial bureaucracy recorded the items imported and their value, many of which were used in the acquisition of enslaved Africans but also in the payment of colonial troops, as a tribute to local rulers, or simply consumed by the small Portuguese population.[9]

---

[9] Joseph C. Miller, "Imports at Luanda, Angola: 1785-1832," in *Figuring African Trade: Proceedings of the Symposium on the Quantification and Structure of the Imports and Export and Long-Distance Trade of Africa in the Nineteenth Century, c. 1800-1913*, ed. Gerhard Liesegang, Helma Pasch, and Adam Jones (Berlin: Dietrich Reimer Verlag, 1986), 162–244; Phyllis Martin, *The External Trade of the Loango Coast, 1576-1870; the Effects of Changing Commercial Relations on the Vili Kingdom of Loango* (Oxford: Clarendon Press, 1972); Phyllis M. Martin, "Power, Cloth and Currency on the Loango Coast," *African Economic History*, no. 15 (1986): 1–12; Ferreira, "Dinâmica do comércio intracolonial"; Stacey Sommerdyk, "Rivalry on the Loango Coast: A Re-Examination of the Dutch in the Atlantic Slave Trade," in *Trabalho Forçado Africano. O Caminho de Ida.*, ed. Arlindo

Colonial administrators in the inland fortresses and markets also had the duty of carefully recording the commerce in human beings, wax, and ivory. In 1811, a report described the organization of the internal trade, listing the amount and quality of goods exchanged, and the names of the itinerant traders responsible for organizing that market in the Benguela region. As was the norm, enslaved people are treated as a commodity in this report, similar to pounds of wax or ivory tusks.[10] The Portuguese Crown later expanded its interests to other natural resources, such as sulfur, niter or saltpeter, iron, copper, wood, rubber, leather, and indigo, and offered lower tariffs to the traders that negotiated and transported these goods to mainland Portugal.[11]

Coastal traders and their agents traveled inland, bringing imported goods. In a similar fashion to other Atlantic ports and areas of conquest, foreign men often engaged in relationships with local women who facilitated the expansion of trade networks and acted as commercial partners, translators, and brokers. These tended to be elite women and daughters of powerful rulers. This was the case with Florinda Josefa Gaspar, daughter of the soba Joanes Gaspar, who maintained a three-decade-long relationship with the Brazilian-born trader Francisco Ferreira Gomes. These women could also be the children of established traders, as was Felipa de Assunção, the daughter of the *sertanejo* José de Assunção Melo established in the Bihé *sobado*, who was considered an example of loyalty and service to the Portuguese Crown.[12] Foreign men depended on the knowledge and social capital of indigenous women, who tended to be labeled as complicit with colonialism or as pawns. Elite women had ambiguous roles, going beyond the dichotomy of vilification or victimization.

Manuel Caldeira (Porto: CEAUP, 2009), 105–18; Daniel B. Domingues da Silva, "The Supply of Slaves from Luanda, 1768–1806: Records of Anselmo Da Fonseca Coutinho," *African Economic History* 38, no. 1 (2009): 53–76. For the circulation of imported goods as tribute and salary, see Flávia Maria de Carvalho, *Sobas e homens do rei. Relações de poder e escravidão em Angola (séculos XVII e XVIII)* (Maceió, Alagoas: Edufal, 2015), 82–97; Mariana P. Candido, *An African Slaving Port and the Atlantic World: Benguela and Its Hinterland* (New York: Cambridge University Press, 2013), 52–57.

[10] Arquivo Nacional de Angola (hereinafter ANA), Cod. 323, Cota D – N-6, "Oficios para o interior de Angola," fl. 28, "Letter from Governor of Angola to Governor of Benguela," August 19, 1811.

[11] ANA, Cod. 7183, Cota 23-1-41, "Luanda, Governo Geral, Registro de correspondência recebida, 1798–1851," fl. 33v-35v, January 11, 1825.

[12] ANA, Cod. 323, fl. 66v, "Letter from the governor of Angola [José de Oliveira Barbosa] to the governor of Benguela [Alvelos Leiria], December 23, 1812; and ANA, Cod. 323, fl. 131v, "Letter from governor of Angola [José de Oliveira Barbosa] to governor of Benguela [Senhor de Alvelos Leiria], August 18, 1815. On Florinda Josefa Gaspar see, Mariana P. Candido and Monica Lima, "Dona Florinda Josefa Gaspar," *Oxford Research Encyclopedia of African History* (forthcoming).

A complex long-distance trade connected inland markets, colonial inland fortresses such as Caconda and Ambaca, and the colonial ports of Luanda and Benguela. Coastal merchants associated with transatlantic slave traders advanced commodities on credit to itinerant traders (*pumbeiros* or *sertanejos* in colonial documents), who assumed all risks of theft, attacks, and captives' mortality. Atlantic slave traders did not assume any liability for enslaved people until they were embarked and thus enjoyed advantages in a highly competitive environment.[13] *Pumbeiros* and *sertanejos* tended to be African born, assumed financial losses, and were important in the circulation of imported goods since they negotiated prices and had relative autonomy to operate in *sobados* and inland markets. Due to the bureaucracy and efforts to control the trade, commercial agents had to obtain licenses to travel inland. This was the case with José Joaquim Domingues, who requested approval to travel to Wambu carrying goods on behalf of the coastal trader Justiano José dos Reis. Manoel Pereira Tavares applied for authorization to travel to Ngalangue with Francisco Ferreira Gomes's merchandise.[14] As stated earlier, Francisco Ferreira Gomes was related to the family of *soba* Joanes Gaspar and well connected to internal markets. In the same decade, 1820s, Justiano José dos Reis also received goods to trade in Wambu on behalf of Dona Lucrécia. Wambu was an important state in the Benguela highland region, with access to wax, ivory, and enslaved people.[15]

The commercial caravan expeditions involved hundreds of free and enslaved porters, traders, and soldiers, who traveled together for several

[13] For more on this topic, see Martin, *External Trade of the Loango Coast*; Joseph C. Miller, *Way of Death: Merchant Capitalism and the Angolan Slave Trade, 1730-1830* (Madison: University of Wisconsin Press, 1988), 207–44; Beatrix Heintze, *Pioneiros Africanos: caravanas de carregadores na África Centro-Ocidental :entre 1850 e 1890* (Lisbon: Caminho, 2004); Mariana P. Candido, "Merchants and the Business of the Slave Trade at Benguela, 1750-1850," *African Economic History* 35 (2007): 1–30.

[14] For Domingue's request, see ANA, Cod. 7182, Cota 23-1-40, "Registro de requerimentos, Benguela, 1825 a 1829," fl. 4V, July 29, 1826, requerimento n. 441. For Tavares' ANA, Cod. 7182, fl. 5v, July 29, 1826, requerimento n. 452. On Ferreira Gomes and his connections, see Roquinaldo Ferreira, "Biografia como história social: O clã Ferreira Gomes e os mundos da escravização no Atlântico Sul," *Varia Historia* 29, no. 51 (2013): 679–719; Mariana P. Candido, "Women, Family, and Landed Property in Nineteenth-Century Benguela," *African Economic History* 43, no. 1 (2015): 136–61.

[15] ANA, Cod. 7182, fl. 18, August 29, 1826, n. 579. For more on Wambu, see Linda Heywood, "Production, Trade and Power. The Political Economy of Central Angola, 1850-1930" (Ph.D., New York, Columbia University, 1984), 39–42; Luisa Mastrobueno, "Ovimbundu Women and Coercive Labour Systems, 1850-1940: From Still Life to Moving Picture" (M.A., Toronto, University of Toronto, 1992); Maria da Conceição Neto, "In Town and Out of Town: A Social History of Huambo (Angola), 1902-1961" (Ph.D., London, UK, SOAS, University of London, 2012), 70–73; Candido, *An African Slaving Port and the Atlantic World*, 296–98.

months. Long-distance trade offered opportunities for commerce, access to imported goods, and social prestige. Competition generated conflicts within caravans as well as between them. In 1826, after a caravan associated with the coastal trader Joaquim da Silva Caldas arrived in Benguela, porters and traders built their camp and received food. One unnamed Black female trader reported "trickeries" from one of the young men (*molecão*) she had bought along the way and was transporting. A confrontation between the two resulted in the female trader cutting off four of the young man's fingers.[16] Violence was employed against enslaved people, but captives also resisted their enslavement. And women operated as commercial agents in long-distance caravans.

The circulation of imported and local products tells us about local tastes, as seen in the items that West Central African societies consumed in the interior of the territory. Commercialization and circulation of imported goods indicate that inland societies, or at least some individuals, participated in a globalized economy that moved commodities across different ports and markets. Internal markets were connected, and the commerce on human beings coexisted with the movement of goods as diverse as hoes, salt, hemp, and gunpowder. Commercial houses in Lisbon, Rio de Janeiro, and Bahia shipped woven, linen, and silk textiles, as well as beads, paper, and alcohol to Benguela; these commodities later reached inland markets as far as Wambu, Bihé, and Mbailundu in the central highlands (see Map 7.1). From there, these commodities were consumed locally and re-exported to further locations.[17]

---

[16] ANA, Cod. 7182, fl. 17v, August 29, 1826, requerimento n. 567. For more on caravana organization, see J. Vansina, "Long-Distance Trade-Routes in Central Africa," *The Journal of African History* 3, no. 3 (1962): 375–90; Deolinda Barrocas and Maria de Jesus Sousa, "As populações do hinterland de Benguela e a passagem das caravanas comerciais (1846-1860)," in *II Reunião Internacional de História da África* (Rio de Janeiro/ São Paulo: CEA-USP/SDG-Marinha/CAPES, 1997); Beatrix Heintze, "Long-Distance Caravans and Communication beyond the Kwango (c. 1850-1890)," in *Angola on the Move: Transport Routes, Communications, and History*, ed. Beatrix Heintze and Achim von Oppen (Frankfurt am Main: Lembeck, 2008), 144–62; Candido, "Merchants and Business," 17–21; Stephen J. Rockel, "Slavery and Freedom in Nineteenth Century East Africa: The Case of Waungwana Caravan Porters," *African Studies* 68, no. 1 (2009): 87–109.

[17] Miller, "Imports at Luanda, Angola: 1785-1832"; Ferreira, "Dinâmica do comércio intracolonial"; Mariana P. Candido, *Fronteras de esclavización: esclavitud, comercio e identidad en Benguela, 1780-1850* (Mexico City: El Colegio de Mexico Press, 2011), 37–41; Domingues da Silva, *Atlantic Slave Trade*, 128–40. Two recent studies provide rich details in the operation of inland caravans in West Central Africa. See Rogéria Cristina Alves, "No Rastro do Marfim: A circulação do marfim in natura entre Luanda, Benguela, Brasil e Lisboa (1723-1808)" (Ph.D., Belo Horizonte, Universidade Federal de Minas Gerais, 2021); Ivan Sicca Gonçalves, "Comércio, Política e Trabalho nos Sertões de Angola: sertanejos e centro-africanos nas páginas de António da Silva Porto (1840-1869)" (M.A., Campinas, SP, Unicamp, 2021).

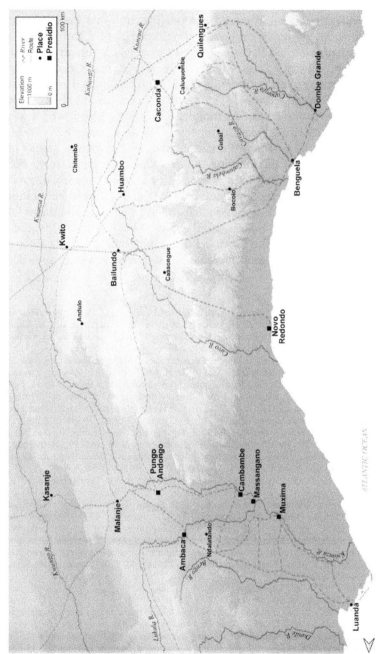

Map 7.1 Trade routes

241

African women based in Luanda and Benguela maintained strong commercial connections to inland markets, yet little has been written on women acting as agents on behalf of coastal traders.[18] In the 1820s, several women requested licenses to transport goods to inland markets. One of them, Floriana Pires Chaves, who had arrived from Rio de Janeiro, planned to travel to Caconda and Kitata, bringing an assortment of goods identified as *fazendas*.[19] These may have included blue cotton cloth, originally manufactured in India and later in England, which was considered essential for internal commerce.[20] These women traders were responsible for making decisions regarding the assortment and quality of various goods, and for determining the destination of the caravan. For example, Isabel Farias de Sousa planned to have eight porters accompany her to transport the commodities.[21] Marcelina Josefa Fernandes traveled with her slave Joaquim to Kibanda.[22] Dionísia, the agent of Pelegrino Bernardo, traveled to Ngalangue, while Veronica Joaquina Coelho traveled on behalf of Francisco Ferreira Gomes.[23] Dona Vitória Gonçalves da Silva, a Benguela merchant, had four barrels of gunpowder

---

[18] For merchant women employing agents, see Mariana P. Candido, "As comerciantes de Benguela na virada do século XVIII: o caso de dona Aguida Gonçalves," in *Laços Atlânticos: África e africanos durante a era do comércio transatlântico de escravos*, ed. Carlos Liberato et al. (Luanda: Ministério da Cultura/ Museu Nacional da Escravatura, 2017), 231–58; Mariana P. Candido, "Os agentes não europeus na comunidade mercantil de Benguela, c. 1760-1820," *Saeculum - Revista de História* 29 (2013): 97–123; Vanessa S. Oliveira, "Slavery and the Forgotten Women Slave Owners of Luanda (1846-1876)," in *Slavery, Memory and Citizenship*, ed. Paul E. Lovejoy and Vanessa S. Oliveira (Trenton, NJ: Africa World Press, 2016), 129–47; Kriger, "Madam Esperance." For women as commercial agents, or *sertanejas*, see Mariana P. Candido, "African Freedom Suits and Portuguese Vassal Status: Legal Mechanisms for Fighting Enslavement in Benguela, Angola, 1800–1830," *Slavery & Abolition* 32, no. 3 (2011): 447–59; Roquinaldo Ferreira, *Cross-Cultural Exchange in the Atlantic World: Angola and Brazil during the Era of the Slave Trade* (New York: Cambridge University Press, 2012), 33–34.

[19] ANA, Cod. 7182, fl. 19v, September 23, 1826, n. 595; and fl. 20v, September 28, 1826, n. 607.

[20] Arquivo Histórico Ultramarino (AHU), Secretaria de Estado da Marinha e Ultramar (SEMU), Direção Geral do Ultramar (DGU), Angola, 477, "Registro de Correspondência Expedida, 1840-1843," fl. 7v. For more on *zuarte* see Ferreira, "Dinâmica do comércio intracolonial"; Telma Gonçalves Santos, "Comércio de tecidos europeus e asiáticos na África centro-ocidental: Fraudes e contrabandos no terceiro quartel do século XVIII" (Lisbon, Universidade de Lisboa, 2014), 47, 110; Domingues da Silva, *Atlantic Slave Trade*, 128–32.

[21] ANA, Cod. 7182, fl. 20, September 23, 1826, n. 600.

[22] ANA, Cod. 7182, fl. 34, January 17, 1827, n. 781.

[23] ANA, Cod. 7182, fl. 21, October 3, 1826, n. 616. For more on the role of *itinerante* traders, or *sertanejo*s and *pumbeiro*s, see Heintze, *Pioneiros Africanos*; Isabel de Castro Henriques, *Percursos da modernidade em Angola: dinâmicas comerciais e transformações sociais no século XIX* (Lisbon: Instituto de Investigação Científica Tropical, 1997), 402–25.

stored at the administration warehouse and requested their delivery with the intention of selling it in inland markets.[24] Women were key commercial agents, moving goods inland. Several cases suggest that there was no impediment based on gender that prevented women from having an active role in negotiations and trade operations. They acted on behalf of major coastal and internal traders to move imported goods, natural resources, and enslaved people between markets.[25]

In some cases, women established themselves apart from male traders. In other circumstances, there was close collaboration with them. They all faced threats and could be robbed or kidnapped when traveling in the interior. *Sobas* also targeted traders, as in the case of Rosa Mística, another woman trader, whose merchandise was apprehended by soba Quibanda, and later by Carombo, a free Black man.[26] Although Mística filled out a report and complained to the colonial administration, it is not clear whether she recovered her seized goods. On other occasions, itinerant traders were kidnapped and enslaved, as in the case of Vitória Pinheiro, a free woman who operated on behalf of João Batista Benites. Despite her free status, she was enslaved, sold, and embarked on a slave ship anchored at Santo Antonio beach. It is not clear if her freedom was restored or if she joined the other 5,670 individuals shipped out of Benguela that year.[27] The female merchant Rita Pereira had similar problems when her agent was enslaved at Dombe Grande.[28] These cases

---

[24] ANA, Cod. 7182, fl. 23v, October 16, 1826, n. 644.

[25] For more examples see ANA, Cod. 7182, fl. 121, November 10, 1828, n. 1241; ANA, Cod. 7182, fl. 133, February 18, 1829, n. 1395; and ANA, Cod. 7182, fl. 151, June 23, 1829, n. 1670. For more on the operation of caravans and circulation of goods in West Central Africa, see Vansina, "Long-Distance Trade-Routes in Central Africa"; Maria Santos, *Nos caminhos de África: Serventia e posse. Angola, século XIX* (Lisbon: Ministério da Ciência e da Tecnologia/ Instituto de Investigação Científica Tropical/ Centro de Estudos de História e Cartografia Antiga, 1998); Barrocas and Sousa, "As populações do hinterland de Benguela e a passagem das caravanas comerciais (1846-1860)"; Carlos Alberto Lopes Cardoso, "A sociedade angolana do século XIX. Suas raízes, seus preconceitos, sua estrutura," *Ocidente. Revista Portuguesa Mensal* 83, no. 411–16 (1972): 146–67; Heintze, "Long-Distance Caravans and Communication."

[26] ANA, Cod. 7182, fl. 70, October 29, 1827, n. 500; ANA, Cod. 7182, fl. 73, November 26, 1827, n. 554. For more on the risks merchants faced, see Mariana P. Candido, "The Transatlantic Slave Trade and the Vulnerability of Free Blacks in Benguela, Angola, 1780-1830," in *Atlantic Biographies: Individuals and Peoples in the Atlantic World*, ed. Mark Meuwese and Jeffrey A. Fortin (Leiden: Brill, 2013), 193–210; Candido, "African Freedom Suits and Portuguese Vassal Status"; Randy J Sparks, *The Two Princes of Calabar: An Eighteenth-Century Atlantic Odyssey* (Cambridge, MA: Harvard University Press, 2004).

[27] ANA, Cod. 7182, fl. 81v, February 4, 1828, n. 709. For the volume on the slave trade in 1828, see slave voyages that identified 15 slave ships departure Benguela in that year. https://www.slavevoyages.org/voyage/database#statistics (consulted on March 17, 2021)

[28] AHA, Cod. 7182, fl. 82v, February 20, 1828, not numbered.

reveal a complex trade system, involving several small agents on the ground, moving away from the idea of an internal trade controlled by a few coastal traders.

Men and women were employed as porters in caravans that could take up to twelve months to return to their place of departure.[29] While some porters were free people and compensated for their labor, traders also used coerced labor. Free or enslaved, porters resisted and protested their labor conditions. In 1860, while leading a caravan from Benguela to Bihé, the trader António Francisco Ferreira da Silva Porto reported that a woman porter ran away with a forty-pound load of unidentified goods. Despite Silva Porto's assertions that her load was not heavy and she was well treated, she fled after her request for food and water was denied.[30] Porters engaged in petty trade, which offered personal financial opportunities. In November 1860, while en route to Mbailundu, the trader Silva Porto observed that individuals traded small pieces of textiles for bowls of *capata*, an alcoholic drink of fermented corn, and cooked chicken. This case reinforces the scholarship that claims textiles operated in the interior of Angola as a currency in the acquisition of food and were not simply a luxury item.[31] At the end of successful journeys, caravan leaders would reward porters with a shared cow and alcohol. For example, Silva Porto reported offering textiles to porters as a bonus when satisfied with the results of the commercial expedition.[32]

Caravans attracted the interest of the *sobas*, who would send emissaries to collect taxes and establish new commercial partnerships. Sometimes coastal traders offered gifts to sobas in addition to the imposed taxes in hopes of redirecting their caravan porters through new territories. However, African rulers did not always welcome caravans in their territories, and even when traders and their porters were welcomed, their actions were limited. In Kissange, for example, the sobas prohibited individuals from selling food stock to the porters of any incoming

---

[29] Biblioteca de Sociedade de Geografia de Lisboa (BSGL), Res 2-C 6, "Silva Porto, apontamentos de um portuense em África," Vol 2 "Bié 25 de outubro de 1860 a 1 de julho de 1861," fl. 105, April 16, 1861.

[30] BSGL, Res 2-C 6, Vol 2., fl. 1–2, October 27, 1860.

[31] BSGL, Res 2-C 6, fl. 7, November 10, 1860. For the meaning of *capata*, see Candido de Figueiredo, *Novo diccionário da língua portuguesa*, vol. 2 (Lisbon: Tavares Cardoso & Irmão, 1899), 772. The traveler Serpa Pinto also reported consuming capata while in Bihé. Alexandre Alberto da Rocha de Serpa Pinto, *How I Crossed Africa: From the Atlantic to the Indian Ocean, Through Unknown Countries; Discovery of the Great Zambesi Affluents, &c* (Sampson Low, Marsten, Searle, & Rivington, 1881), vol 1, 172–73. For more on textiles as currency, see Martin, "Power, Cloth, and Currency"; Ferreira, "Dinâmica do comércio intracolonial"; Santos, "Comércio de tecidos."

[32] BSGL, Res 2-C 6, fl. 8–9, November 14 and 15, 1860.

caravan. He was the only one who could initiate trade or indicate which agents could act on his behalf.[33] Caravan leaders had to offer gifts as tribute when entering new lands, usually in the form of alcohol or firearms.

Caravans were risky business, with goods stolen and porters enslaved when crossing unfriendly territories. While storing wax and rubber in his warehouse in Catumbela, a local trader had a portion of his products stolen. José António intended to hire porters to transport the goods to Benguela, but one of the local traders, Lourenço Mendes de Santana, overheard that valuable merchandise was being stored and stole the goods during the night.[34] While en route, armed groups attacked porters and seized goods in episodes of violence, such as the 1858 attack on a caravan traveling from the highlands to the colonial center of Mossamedes. Most of the ivory and wax were robbed or destroyed, sixty porters were wounded, and one *pombeiro*, an agent of a coastal merchant, was killed.[35] In other episodes, people and not only goods were seized. For example, in 1860, an entire caravan traveling from the lands of Ganguelas to Benguela was seized. The ruler Kiteke, a subordinate of Bihé's ruler, ordered their enslavement and sale and seized their cargo, which included tobacco of low quality, highly appreciated in different African markets.[36] Some caravan traders could profit by 100 percent in a

---

[33] BSGL, Res 2-C 6, fl. 2–3, October 29, 1860. For more on caravan organization and its ability to mobilize large number of people and trade, see Vansina, "Long-Distance Trade-Routes in Central Africa"; Heintze, "Long-Distance Caravans and Communication"; Heintze, *Pioneiros Africanos*; Barrocas and Sousa, "As populações do hinterland de Benguela e a passagem das caravanas comerciais (1846-1860)"; Ghislaine Lydon, *On Trans-Saharan Trails: Islamic Law, Trade Networks, and Cross-Cultural Exchange in Nineteenth-Century Western Africa* (Cambridge; New York: Cambridge University Press, 2009); Rockel, "Slavery and Freedom in Nineteenth Century East Africa."

[34] ANA, Cx. 1322, Catumbela, 1853–1935, "Correspondência Recebida," doc. Not Numbered, "De José António de S. Moranha dando parte do roubo de de gomma feito pelo Lourenço Mendes de Santana o qual remete preso." Lobito, May 11, 1853. For more on caravans in West Central Africa, see Santos, *Nos caminhos de Africa*; Heintze, *Pioneiros Africanos*; Jill R. Dias, "Mudanças nos padrões de poder no 'hinterland' de Luanda. O impacto da colonização sobre os Mbundu (c. 1845-1920)," *Penélope* 14 (1994): 43–91; Barrocas and Sousa, "As populações do hinterland de Benguela e a passagem das caravanas comerciais (1846-1860)"; Candido, "Merchants and Business."

[35] ANA, Cx. 1354, Benguela, N. 240, July 23, 1858.

[36] BSGL, Res 2-C 6, fl. 43, February 3, 1861. ANA, Cod. 455, 16.-E-4-3, "Correspondência Expedida do Governo, 21 de julho 1843 a 27 de julho 1847," fl. 13-13 v, January 19, 1843, "Letter from the Interim Governor of Benguela [João Bressame Leite], to conselho do governo [Fortunato Antônio da Libra Guimarães]". For more on tobacco and consumption in Africa, see Pierre Verger, *Fluxo e refluxo do tráfico de escravos entre o Golfo de Benin e a Bahia de Todos os Santos: dos séculos XVII a XIX* (Salvador: Corrupio, 2002); Daniel B. Domingues da Silva and David Eltis, "The Slave Trade to Pernambuco, 1561-1851," in *Extending the Frontiers: Essays on the New Transatlantic Slave Trade Database* (New

single voyage, indicating that this was a very successful business.[37] Due to its margin of profit and opportunities, the trade lasted over 300 years, well into the twentieth century. For most of this time, the internal circulation of imported goods as well as the movement of natural resources was possible due to the enslaved human beings who walked to the coast, carrying loads of ivory, beeswax, or rubber. The desire to consume imported goods clearly had a human cost for porters and the markets that witnessed attacks and raids, as well as for the societies that were pillaged and raided to provide captives of war to fill Atlantic demand for enslaved Africans.

Beginning in the early eighteenth century, coastal traders advanced imported products on credit to itinerant traders, who later repaid that debt in local products or war captives. This system was based on trust yet resulted in a series of conflicts between coastal and inland traders in which each complained about the trade conditions. In the mid-nineteenth century, the credit system continued to operate although trade in human beings was illegal. Imported goods circulated in the same trade routes that connected inland and coastal markets (see Map 7.1).[38] The arrival of large caravans from Zanzibar in 1852 created anxiety among Benguela residents regarding the expansion of the long-distance trade but also the fear that Muslim merchants would dominate Benguela and compete for markets and lands with the local population and Portuguese occupiers.[39] While coastal traders directed the trade and mobilized credit and imported merchandise, African rulers controlled internal routes and markets and could direct caravans from the East African coast to the Atlantic shores if they wished. However, this possibility generated anxiety that credit would not be honored. Credit was also

---

Haven, CT: Yale University Press, 2008), 122; Mariana P. Candido, "Negociantes Baianos no Porto de Benguela: Redes comerciais unindo o Atlântico setencentista," in *África. Brasileiros e Portugueses, Séculos XVI-XIX*, ed. Roberto Guedes (Rio de Janeiro: Maud, 2013), 67–91; Roquinaldo Ferreira, "Abolicionismo versus colonialismo: Rupturas e continuidades em Angola (século XIX)," in *África. Brasileiros e Portugueses, séculos XVI-XIX*, ed. Roberto Guedes (Rio de Janeiro: Mauad, 2013), 95–112.

[37] BSGL, Res 2-C 6," fl. 37, January 19, 1861.
[38] AHU, SEMU, Conselho Ultramarino (CU), Processos das Consultas, Cx. 22, doc. 757, 1 repartição, "Processo referente a participação pela qual o governador geral de Angola da conta dos excessos e abusos praticados pelo juiz de direito de Benguela, Luis Jose Mendes Afonso," L. 2, n. 103, Ofício de February 19, 1855. For more on the credit system, see Miller, *Way of Death*, 186–94; Candido, "Merchants and Business"; Heintze, "Long-Distance Caravans and Communication."
[39] Sebestyen, "Sociedade Ovimbundu," 86–87. The merchants Silva Porto and Magyar also register the arrival of the Zanzibar caravan in Benguela.

an important mechanism of trade, allowing middlemen to efficiently transfer goods across long distances without assuming all risks. Goats, pigs, beads, pieces of cloth, and enslaved individuals operated as bills of exchange, and anyone who received goods on credit had a set amount of time to deliver the merchandise or the enslaved individual. Failure to do so resulted in punishment via local tribunal and could include pawnship or enslavement.[40]

The internal *presídios*, the colonial centers that operated as administrative and commercial centers, were established in the important markets that predated the arrival of the Portuguese. Colonial administrators of the *presídios*, such as Caconda and Quilengues in the interior of Benguela, and Ambaca and Pungo Angongo in Luanda's interior, had a mandate to control the caravan trade, collect taxes, and impose security to protect the circulation of goods and merchants. The most profitable and important markets, however, were outside Portuguese control, which clearly indicates the limits and fragility of the colonial presence, despite its destructive force. In the mid-nineteenth century, the state of Bihé controlled its own market where local and foreign traders could acquire locally manufactured hoes, among other iron objects. Baskets and carpentry items were also commercialized, with neighboring populations, such as the Nganguela, providing high-quality salt in exchange for Bihé products. Bihé traders also sold locally produced beeswax, foodstuff, and leather products, as well as tobacco and hemp plants (*cânhamo*) to coastal traders in exchange for cloth, weapons, gunpowder, and alcohol.[41] Interior African rulers sent letters to colonial authorities requesting certain items and offering commercial advantages if coastal traders sent their agents to their controlled markets, advertising the products they had available and stating their interests in specific imported commodities. By the 1860s, the ruler of Bihé showed interest in textiles of specific qualities, including those manufactured in West Central Africa, probably referring to the wine palm and fan palm cloths from Loango that circulated as currency but also as a luxurious

---

[40] BSGL, Res 2-C 6, fl. 53, February 19, 1861; and BSGL, Res 2-C 6, fl. 58, March 2, 1861. For more on enslaved people as currency, see Green, *Fistful of Shells*, 50–52. For more on *tribunal dos mucanos*, see Roquinaldo Ferreira, "Slaving and Resistance to Slaving in West Central Africa," in *The Cambridge World History of Slavery*, ed. David Eltis and Stanley L. Engerman, vol. 3 (Cambridge: Cambridge University Press, 2011), 128–29; Ferreira, *Cross-Cultural Exchange*, 88–125; Catarina Madeira Santos, "Esclavage africain et traite atlantique confrontés: Transactions langagières et juridiques (à propos du tribunal de mucanos dans l'Angola des XVIIe et XVIIIe siècles)," *Brésil (s). Sciences Humaines et Sociales* 1 (2012): 127–48; Candido, *An African Slaving Port and the Atlantic World*, 214–15.

[41] BSGL, Res – 2-C-7, fl. 28-30, "caráter do povo Bieno," April 1, 1866.

good.[42] The elite were always in search of new items, demanding that traders introduce textiles of various colors, patterns, quality, and textures. Raffia and bark cloths lost importance as items of prestige and were quickly replaced by Indian textiles of different quality. Textiles were also offered to sobas as tribute or payment to cover any infraction.[43] People along the coast and on the interior accumulated personal objects, with symbolic and use values, which drove long-distance trade routes. Consumption and accumulation of personal wealth is an important part of West Central African history.

Consumers' Growing Desire for Imported Commodities

West Central Africans were interested in material goods produced elsewhere and had a sophisticated taste for exotic commodities.[44] David Richardson shows how firms and merchants in Liverpool struggled to meet the requirements of West African elites for particular kinds of iron bars and beads.[45] The same was true for Portuguese importers who needed to adapt their goods to the tastes and requirements of inland markets. Local demand for specific textiles altered consumer tastes and clothing markets, as occurred in other parts of the continent. Access to Asian textiles was vital for successful slave trade operations in Luanda and Benguela. Besides different qualities of cloth, coastal merchants also

---

[42] BOGGPA, 1864, N. 36, September 3, 1864, p. 304 and BOGGPA, 1864, N. 37, September 10, 1864, p. 316; and BSGL, Res – 2-C-7, "Silva Porto, notas para retocar a minha obra logo que as circunstâncias permitam," fl. 73-79, "Indústria desse povo," April 1, 1866. For more on the correspondence of rulers and colonial authorities, see Ana Paula Tavares and Catarina Madeira Santos, "Fontes escritas africanas para a história de Angola," in *Africae Monumenta. A apropriação da escrita pelos africanos*, vol. 1 (Lisbon: Instituto de Investigação Científica Tropical, 2002), 471–509; Beatrix Heintze, "A Lusofonia no interior da África Central na era pré-colonial. Um contributo para a sua história e compreensão na actualidade," *Cadernos de Estudos Africanos* 6/7 (2005): 179–207; Éve Sebestyén, "Legitimation through Landcharters in Ambundo Villages, Angola," *Perspektiven Afrikanistischer Forschung*, 1994, 363–78. For the widespread consumption of Loango textiles, see Martin, "Power, Cloth, and Currency"; Phyllis M. Martin, "The Kingdom of Loango," in *Kongo Power and Majesty*, ed. Alisa Lagamma (New York and New Haven: The Metropolitan Museum of Art and Yale University Press, 2015), 56–65.

[43] Traveler Silva Porto refers to this on several occasions. See, for example, BSGL, Res 2-C 6, fl. 44-45, February 8, 1861; pp. 49–50. See also Martin, *The External Trade of the Loango Coast*, 105–08; Miller, *Way of Death*, 82–83.

[44] Domingues da Silva, *The Atlantic Slave Trade*, pp. 122–141.

[45] See David Richardson, 'West African Consumption Patterns and Their Influence on the Eighteenth-Century English Slave Trade', *Uncommon Market: Essays in the Economic History of the Atlantic Slave Trade*, ed. Henry A. Gemery and Jan S. Hogendorn (New York: Academic Press, 1979), pp. 303–30.

provided cheap alcohol produced in Brazil in exchange for human captives, but also to acquire natural resources.[46]

In West Central Africa, material goods became visible markers for social differentiation, shaping peoples' public image and expressing social and economic hierarchies through housing and clothing styles. This was a similar process as in other coastal societies, such as Saint Louis, as detailed by Hilary Jones.[47] Customs records list Portuguese manufactured goods, such as wool textiles, beads, paper, and miscellaneous other items, that were imported into Luanda or Benguela. By the early nineteenth century, Brazil replaced Portugal as the main source of goods, which included manioc flour produced in the interior of Rio de Janeiro and shipped to two main ports of West Central Africa.[48] The availability of imports affected local industries and the quality of cloth desired by African consumers.[49] It also altered the commercialization and carving of ivory, as well as iron smelting technology and the importance of local techniques in the production of iron bars and tools. It is difficult to quantify Central African exports of natural resources and products, but their existence reveals that trade between Europeans and Africans was not simply a matter of providing alcohol, guns, and textiles for enslaved bodies. From the earliest contacts, these goods operated as currency in different markets and the Portuguese Crown hoped to acquire metals such as copper from the Ndombe people, but also seized ivory, leather, wax, and gum arabica.[50]

---

[46] Luiz Felipe de Alencastro, *O trato dos viventes. A formação do Brasil no Atlântico Sul, séculos XVI e XVII* (São Paulo: Companhia das Letras, 2000); Ferreira, 'Dinâmica do comércio intracolonial', 339–78.

[47] Jones, *The Métis of Senegal*, 89–95; Kriger, 'Making the History of Cotton Textile,' 98–105. For more on this history, see Nielson Rosa Bezerra, *Escravidão, farinha e tráfico Atlântico: um novo olhar sobre as relações entre o Rio de Janeiro e Benguela (1790-1830)* (Rio de Janeiro: Fundação Biblioteca Nacional - Minc, 2010); and Gustavo Acioli Lopes and Maximiliano Mac Menz, 'Resgate e Mercadorias: uma análise comparada do tráfico luso-brasileiro de escravos em Angola e na Costa da Mina (Século XVIII)' *Afro-Ásia* 37 (2008), 43–72.

[48] Mariana P. Candido, *Fronteras de esclavización. Esclavitud, comercio e identidade em Benguela, 1780-1850* (Mexico: Colegio de Mexico, 2011), pp. 39–40.

[49] Martin, 'Power, Cloth and Currency', 1–12. John K. Thornton, 'Precolonial African Industry and the Atlantic Trade, 1500-1800', *African Economic History* 19 (1990-1991), 1–19. See also John K. Thornton, *Africa and Africans in the Making of the Atlantic World, 1400-1800* (New York: Cambridge University Press, 1998), pp. 7–45; and Miller, *Way of Death*, 78–81.

[50] Rogéria Cristina Alves, 'Marfins africanos em trânsito: apontamentos sobre o comércio numa perspectiva atlântica (Angola, Benguela, Lisboa e Brasil), séculos XVIII-XIX', *Faces da História* 3, no. 2 (2016), 8–21; Crislayne Alfagali, *Ferreiros e fundidores da Ilamba: Uma história social da fabricação do ferro e da Real Fábrica de Nova Oeiras (Angola, segunda metade do século XVIII)* (Luanda: Fundação Agostinho Neto, 2018); and Thornton, *A Cultural History*, 63–65. For more on the role of different objects as currencies, see Santos, "Comércio de tecidos"; Paul E. Lovejoy, *Salt of the Desert Sun: A History of Salt*

During the nineteenth century, shopkeepers in Luanda and Benguela offered a variety of imported goods in their stores, the listings of such offer some insights into the types of merchandise foreign firms and traders delivered to West Central African markets. It is important to stress the role of local traders in shaping what objects were considered valuable and desired, and the fact that West Central African markets affected production and trade elsewhere evidences that global markets were connected in the nineteenth century and African consumers were not marginal actors. French merchants opened shops in Benguela that offered imported goods. One such merchant, Jean Baptiste Ytier, also employed *quitandeiras* (female street vendors) who sold the merchandise in Benguela's market stalls, reaching a wider public outside his shop, as can be seen in Illustrations 7.3 and 7.4. [51]

More and more West Central Africans were electing to buy imported goods. Advertisements in local newspapers and gazettes provide tantalizing evidence of local tastes and the variety of products coming from different markets. While some were for individual consumption, many could be sold wholesale and transported inland. The shopkeeper Dona Justina Luiza dos Santos had a shop in Luanda's Santa Efigénia square where customers could access Russian-manufactured leather shoes, children's shoes, perfumes, face powder, creams, and aromatic oils. She also sold necklaces, soap, toothpaste, cigars, and cigarettes. Other shops sold Sevillian olives, and English plates, thread, paint, and castor oil were also on display side by side with tobacco and almonds.[52] Foreign and coastal traders tried to supply what West Central Africans desired in a timely fashion, which could be sweets imported from France, embroidered linen towels, and sheets.[53]

Residents of Luanda and Benguela who had access to products coming from different markets were aware of goods produced not only in Portugal but also in Spain, France, Great Britain, and Russia.[54] José Tavares Veiga announced several items for sale in his shop in 1864, including a set of porcelain dishes, jugs of different sizes and colors,

Production and Trade in the Central Sudan (Cambridge: Cambridge University Press, 1986); Colleen E. Kriger, *Making Money: Life, Death, and Early Modern Trade on Africa's Guinea Coast* (Athens: Ohio University Press, 2017).

[51] ANA, Cod. 326, fl. 40, April 17, 1848, "To Governor of Benguela from Secretary of Angola Adminstration [Francisco Joaquim da Costa e Silva]."

[52] BOGGPA, 1869, n. 4, January 23, 1869, p. 44, and BOGGPA, 1870, n. 4, 22 January 1870, p. 43

[53] BOGGPA, 1870, n. 12, March 19, 1870, p. 211.

[54] BOGGPA,1865, n. 1, January 1, 1865, p. 41; "Annúncios de meias para senhoras"; and "Anúncio de Grinaldas para senhoras a 6$500 reis," and BOGGPA, n. 1, January 1, 1865, p. 75, "Annúncio recebidos da França."

Illustration 7.3 Women selling fruit and vegetables in Benguela, 1855
(*Source*: "Market Women, 1855," House of Commons Parliamentary Papers
HMS Linnett, 1855)

snuffboxes, neckties and tie clasps, binoculars, hairbrushes, tooth-
brushes, watches, and pipes.[55] While colonial administrators and the
coastal trade probably consumed most of these items, a portion of these
imported goods traveled inland to meet the desires of consumers living in
the presídios and sobados. Many Brazilian-manufactured products were
available, such as bottles or *pipas* (435 liters or 115 U.S. gallons) of
cachaça, and cigars made in Rio de Janeiro and Bahia. Traders also
offered the option of paying in installments for such goods as sugar, rice,
olive oil, soap, candles, green and black tea, wines, as well as tobacco
rolls, and beads.[56] At the J. C. Carvalho Bastos shop in Luanda,

---

[55] BOGGPA, 1864, n. 35, August 27, 1864, p. 301; and BOGGPA, 1864, n. 39,
September 24, 1864, pp. 342–43.
[56] BOGGPA, 1864, n. 49, December 3, 1864, p. 462.

Illustration 7.4 Street vendors with different types of baskets and
vegetables in the streets of Benguela in the early nineteenth century
(*Source*: "Quitandeiras, end of 19th century," Arquivo Nacional de Angola,
Postais, P-1-113)

consumers could buy small flagons of eau de cologne, bottles of champagne, thread, combs and straightening combs, and nailbrushes at mod-
erate prices. The shop owner only accepted cash.[57] In Luanda, dried fish
exported from Benguela was also available.[58] The possession and display
of material things were powerful tools of identity, and customers would
buy on installment when they did not have sufficient cash. The selection
of objects reveals local tastes and efforts to create new communities in
which access to ties, suits, purses, and shoes represented status and
connection to a wider world. The quality, color, and size of objects
mattered to those who described and acquired them. West Central
Africans' tastes and desires shaped the types and qualities of products
Portuguese and Brazilian traders imported and offered in the ports and
shops. West Central African consumption along the coast and in the
interior was not marginal to global commerce, and it affected textile
manufacture and trade in Europe, Asia, and the Americas.

    In inland states, local expertise in cloth manufacture existed, with
tailors (*Omesele yokutonga* in Umbundu) or sewing masters making
clothes for local consumers. It is not clear whether the establishment of

[57] BOGGPA, 1866, n. 1, January 6, 1866, p. 4.
[58] BOGGPA, 1864, n. 49, December 3, 1864, p. 463.

these professionals was a nineteenth-century phenomenon, but their presence clearly indicates a concern with owning clothes in the latest fashion. Other experts were blacksmiths who produced saws and axes and repaired and modified shotguns. In inland states, there were also shoemakers and chest makers (*Ombruaca* in Umbundu), as well as carpenters who manufactured beds, chairs, tables, and doors and sold them in exchange for pieces of cloth. Women specialized in basket making and the manufacture of palm cloth (*Messeve ye Oluhumba*). Women also worked in grinding and sifting grains and cereals and in pottery making.[59] Despite the existence of such local expertise and manufacturing, African societies imported commodities because there was a local demand for those alternative goods. The baskets, cloth, and furniture that were manufactured locally were not enough or did not fulfill the local tastes of inland societies. Local production was impacted by long-distance trade and the aspirations of commercial and political elites, forming a political economy that relied on imports to meet consumers' needs and which was connected to distant markets – Bihé to Luanda, Rio de Janeiro, Lisbon, Nantes, Macau, and Gujarat.[60]

Traders also commercialized food products, including cassava flour, which was both produced locally and imported from Brazil. Imported goods from Lisbon, in the 1860s, included tea, rice, butter, thirty-seven *pipas* or 15,540 liters of *aguardente*, cellarets with gin, twelve boxes of cognac bottles, 120 boxes of beer bottles, 202 boxes of sugar, six boxes of champagne, fifty kegs of olives, and six barrels of flour. Other non-food imports included 100 boxes of soap, one box of needles, one box of mirrors, two boxes of books, two boxes of hats, fifteen boxes of weapons, thirty caskets of oil tar, one box of decks of cards, one box of harmonicas, 600 barrels of gunpowder, fifty-six boxes of china, four brass faucets, two boxes of perfumes, seven boxes of smoking pipes, two boxes of watches, one cotton gin, iron chains, and two ox carts, among other miscellaneous items.[61]

This new consumer base was made possible by the expansion of trade circuits under the guise of free trade. By the 1860s, coastal shopkeepers maintained contact with merchants based in the United States, indicating that markets far outside of the Portuguese Empire's scope participated in supplying goods that were in demand in local West Central African

---

[59] BSGL, Res – 2-C-7, fl. 73–79, April 1866, "Industria desse povo." For more on blacksmith knowledge and industry in the region, see Colleen E. Kriger, *Pride of Men: Ironworking in Nineteenth Century West Central Africa, Social History of Africa* (Portsmouth, NH: Heinemann, 1999); Alfagali, *Ferreiros e fundidores da Ilamba*.

[60] Prestholdt, *Domesticating the World*, 62–84; Richardson, "Consuming Goods, Consuming People. Reflections on the Transatlantic Slave Trade"; Santos, "Comércio de tecidos"; Domingues da Silva, *Atlantic Slave Trade*, 128–32.

[61] BOGGPA, 1866, n. 31, August 4, 1866, p. 298.

societies, including wheat flour.[62] The U.S. ship *Jonia* unloaded 400 *pipas* of American brandy, 150 barrels of wheat flour, 100 barrels of crackers, 200 boxes of soap, 1,000 pounds of tobacco, 50 barrels of oil tar, 100 cans of paraffin oil, twelve scales, several chairs, twelve cotton gins, and twenty cans of solvent.[63] The products imported from the United States were a combination of materials for farmers engaging in legitimate commerce and the production of cotton, as well as products that could be commercialized in internal markets such as alcohol or soap. The goods from Portugal were mainly gunpowder, *aguardente*, tobacco, and smoking pipes, indicating that by the 1860s Portuguese industries were unable to supply the items in demand, and other commercial agents stepped up to sell manufactured products.[64] Coastal merchants imported goods desired by the colonial urban population as well as the inland and surrounding societies.

Caravans brought ivory, rubber, and beeswax to the coast and moved the newly imported products inland. Traders from inland states exchanged natural resources and captives of war for goods. In 1869, two large caravans (*ambacas*) from Bihé arrived in Benguela, creating excitement and opportunities for administrators and traders.[65] Some groups preferred to trade in smaller markets such as Catumbela rather than moving their products into Benguela.[66] Sobas also traded goods through their own agents, such as the case of the ruler of Ganda who sent wax and acquired alcohol.[67] For most of the nineteenth century, colonial authorities embraced the practice of advancing imported goods on credit to protect the risk of captives' death and financial losses. By 1873, however, there were efforts to restrain coastal merchants from advancing merchandise since, according to the governor of Benguela, it put extreme pressure on local traders to offer goods even when it was not financially convenient for them.[68]

---

[62] BOGGPA, 1864, n. 39, September 24, 1864, p. 343. For the trade in cassava flour between Rio de Janeiro and Benguela, see Nielson Rosa Bezerra, *Escravidão, farinha e tráfico Atlântico: um novo olhar sobre as relações entre o Rio de Janeiro e Benguela (1790-1830)* (Rio de Janeiro: Fundação Biblioteca Nacional – Minc, 2010).

[63] BOGGPA, 1866, n. 32, August 11, 1866, p. 316.

[64] BOGGPA, 1864, n. 39, September 24, 1864, p. 343; and n. 39, 29 September 1866, p. 309. See also Vos, "Coffee, Cash, and Consumption," 184–85.

[65] BOGGPA, 1870, n. 14, April 2, 1866, p. 236.

[66] BOGGPA, 1870, n. 15, April 9, 1870, p. 251.

[67] BOGGPA, 1870, n. 15, April 9, p. 250. For more on Ganda's market see Tuca Manuel, *Terra, a tradição e o poder. Contribuição ao estudo etno-histórico da Ganda* (Benguela: KAT - Aguedense, 2005).

[68] ANA, Cx. 1322, doc. 39, "From governor de Benguela to chefe do concelho da Catumbela [José Abreu Silvano], January 27, 1873. For more on the importance of credit, see Miller, *Way of Death*, 185–87; Domingues da Silva, *Atlantic Slave Trade*, 51–67.

The end of commerce in enslaved human beings did not end the interest in imported commodities along the coast or in the interior. The material objects listed in probate records, which are analyzed in the next section, disclose that people living in Benguela, Catumbela, and Caconda continued to consume gunpowder, imported textiles, and alcohol in the second half of the nineteenth century. The colonial shift to exporting raw materials and natural resources during that timeframe is evident in the custom records. Benguela merchants exported beans and dried fish to Ambriz. They also shipped *aguardente*, sugarcane alcohol produced in the Dombe Grande farms and mills, as well as maize flour, beans, and calves, to the São Tomé archipelago. Ships departing to Lisbon carried *aguardente*, raw cotton and cottonseed, palm oil, rubber, wax, yellow gum, and orchil. Only ivory pieces heavier than 15 kilos each were recorded, indicating that smaller pieces of ivory were neither registered nor taxed.[69] Production and consumption of material culture was not static, and it was affected by the geography of production and commercialization. Although both coastal and inland merchants affected the choices available for West Central African societies, the local populations of Ndombe, Bihenos, Mbailundus, and others continued to produce, export, and consume goods that they needed and desired. They were interested in material control and display, and they participated actively in the global economy.[70]

A Persistence of Taste, Accumulation, and Consumerism amid Privation

The majority of West Central Africans could not afford imported goods, but a minority were integrated into a global economy. The evidence from Angolan archives reveals that people valued their material possessions, including goods for immediate use. Furniture pieces, for example, were

---

[69] BOGGPA, 1881, n. 1, January 1, 1881, p. 7; BOGGPA, 1881, n. 4, January 22, 1881, p. 45; BOGGPA, 1881, n. 7, February 12, 1881, p. 98–99; and BOGGPA, 1881, n. 21, May 21, 1881, p. 309. For more on the economic shift toward natural resources, see W. G. Clarence-Smith, "Slavery in Coastal Southern Angola, 1875-1913," *Journal of Southern African Studies* 2, no. 2 (April 1, 1976): 214–23; Neto, "In Town and out of Town: A Social History of Huambo (Angola), 1902-1961"; Roquinaldo Amaral Ferreira, "Agricultural Enterprise and Unfree Labour in Nineteenth Century Angola," in *Commercial Agriculture, the Slave Trade and Slavery in Atlantic Africa*, ed. Robin Law, Suzanne Schwarz, and Silke Strickrodt (Woodbridge: James Currey, 2013), 225–42; Jelmer Vos, *Kongo in the Age of Empire, 1860–1913: The Breakdown of a Moral Order* (University of Wisconsin Press, 2015).

[70] Richardson, "West African Consumption Patterns"; Prestholdt, *Domesticating the World*, 62–65.

important assets. In 1815 Dona Madalena de Carvalho Menezes lent three tables to António José Carneiro when he acted as the sergeant-mor of Novo Redondo fortress. Carneiro died, and his successor, Manuel Francisco Pacheco, continued to use the tables despite de Carvalho e Menezes's repeated requests to have them returned. The governor of Benguela had to intervene to protect her ownership rights, arguing that "no one should use another person's property without the owner's agreement and that residents had no obligation to provide furniture or other household items to administrators."[71] It is not clear whether the three tables were produced locally or imported, or even the sociocultural context in which the tables were used. There is always the risk of projecting ahistorical use of objects, yet the need to assert ownership and recuperate possessions demonstrates that people acquired individual goods.

Goods listed in inventories were carefully described and identified based on their material, their use, their state of conservation, and their place of origin. In most instances, the use and social value of the objects were not specified, which could lead to anachronistic interpretations. However, the descriptions of material culture demonstrate local tastes and the expansion of consumerism, as expressed in dress or in the objects that people collected and used to decorate their homes. Wills and inventories also listed the items that were socially perceived as valuable and that local people cherished enough to bequeath to loved ones. For estates, colonial officers placed a monetary value on the land, enslaved people, and objects that demonstrated sometimes substantial material wealth. In the 1860s, Teresa de Jesus Barros e Cunha owned three Chinese paintings, and Narciso José Pacheco Lages, who lived in Catumbela, also had two Chinese paintings on display in his home.[72] Their themes or the scene represented in those images are not specified, yet their presence suggests that local traders were connected to sea routes linking Benguela to Macau. That trade network may explain the appearance of these luxury items as well as silk in the inventories of Benguela residents. For example, the trader Carlos Caldeira stopped in Benguela on his return trip from China. Other traders may have done the same, which would explain how luxury items from Asia, including pottery and tea sets, were sold and consumed by residents of Luanda, Benguela, and their interiors.[73]

[71] ANA, Cod. 323, fl. 122, "Letter from the governor of Angola [José de Oliveira Barbosa] to capitão mor de Novo Redondo [Manoel Francisco Pacheco]," March 13, 1815.

[72] TCB, "Autos Civis do Testamento e Inventário de Dona Maria Lucas Pinheiro," January 23, 1877; and TCB, "Inventário de Narciso José Pacheco Lages," October 19, 1863, fl. 10v.

[73] Carlos José Caldeira, *Apontamentos de uma viagem de Lisbon a China*, 2 vols (Lisbon: Castro & Irmão, 1853), vol. 2, pp. 177–79. I am thankful for Vanessa Oliveira bringing

Luxury items were not restricted to Asian goods. Dona Maria Lucas Pinheiro had a valuable box for imported almonds, and António Joaquim Monteiro owned a wooden wall clock with golden details.[74] Jewelry, religious images, and dresses, socks, and shoes were also costly items listed in probate records and richly described by colonial officers and travelers. George Tams, who visited Benguela in the mid-nineteenth century, described the town as a "beautiful town with attractive women" who decorated and held their hair back with locally manufactured sticks made of wood or animal bones, probably referring to ivory.[75] However, these items were not easily identified in inventories. Carved and decorated hairpins were sold in shops in Luanda and Benguela and purchased by the local elite.[76] Men and women flaunted imported items that indicated their wealth, thus reinforcing the prestige and social distinction related to their prominent economic position. Wealth was publicly displayed in clothes and jewelry of varying material and quality.

For over 300 years, West Central African societies had been involved in long-distance trade in imported textiles. People accumulated goods, such as pants, hats, shoes, socks, and gloves, which became assets, viewed as powerful objects that increased individual and family power and enhanced the public reputation and social and economic standing of elite individuals. The Portuguese Empire had legislated restrictions on clothes and social hierarchies since the *Reconquista* in the fifteenth century, insisting that Jews and Muslims wear clothing that made them easily identifiable. According to the *Pragmática do Senhor D. João V* issued on May 24, 1749, free or enslaved Blacks who lived in Portuguese possessions were forbidden from wearing silk clothing or gold jewelry. Anyone who disobeyed this law was subject to fines or corporal punishment.[77] The mid-eighteenth-century law regulating the clothing and appearance of Black people who lived in the Portuguese colonies reveals anxieties about "proper" social position, and it was challenged by wealthy Black

---

to my attention Caldeira's travel accounts. For more on this trade connections, see A. J. R Russell-Wood, *A World on the Move: The Portuguese in Africa, Asia, and America, 1415-1808* (Manchester: Carcanet, 1992), 30–32.

[74] TCB, "Translado de testamento e inventário de D. Maria Lucas Pinheiro," 23 January 1877, fl. 7; and "Inventário cívil de António Joaquim Monteiro," September 2, 1857."

[75] Georg Tams, *Visita às possessões portuguezas na costa occidental d'Africa: Com uma introducção e annotações* (Typographia da Revista, 1850), vols. 1, 105 and 128.

[76] BOGGPA, 1864, n. 35, August 27, 1864, p. 301; and BOGGPA, 1864, n. 39, September 24, 1864, p. 342–43; and TCB, "Autos Civis do Inventário de Josefa Manoel Pereira da Silva", April 18, 1865, fl. 8-9v.

[77] *Pragmática do Senhor Rey D. João V do ano de 1749* (Lisbon: Oficina de Antonio Rodrigues Galhardo, 1771), chapter IX. For more on this, see Silvia Hunold Lara, *Fragmentos setecentistas: Escravidão, cultura e poder na América portuguesa* (São Paulo: Companhia das Letras, 2007).

Africans who sought to subvert colonial expectations and rules. The law, which was dismissed two years later, suggested that "luxury is an attribute exclusive to whites" and that the "blacks and mulattoes" of the *Conquista* could not dress extravagantly without causing "inconveniences."[78] In 1751, Dom João V modified the 1749 law, "having been recently brought to my attention some considerations of equal weight to those which were available to me when I determined the said prohibition regarding the blacks and mulattoes who live in the *Conquistas*."[79] The failure of the state to control what free Black Africans wore and consumed allowed elite residents to invest in valuable furniture, clothing, and textiles.

Even people who could not afford to buy jewelry went to great lengths to display objects they had borrowed from others, creating eventual conflicts over ownership. The wife of Diniz Vieira de Sousa requested from Josefa Manoel Joaquim a pair of golden earrings. Josefa lent Sousa's wife the earrings, which she failed to return. The owner of the gold earrings filed a complaint with the colonial authorities to reclaim her jewelry.[80] Colonial courts became the space to settle disputes over objects' ownership, as seen in Chapter 3. The trader Maria Leal reported, in 1828, that Dona Juliana had seized her textiles and small objects in a commercial dispute. Dona Juliana refused to return the items despite judicial orders to do so, and she was subsequently arrested. While in prison she accused another woman, Andreza Leal do Sacramento, of stealing a pair of golden earrings and a comb made of turtle shell that belonged to her. Sacramento had asked to borrow both items but failed to return them.[81] These are perhaps trivial disputes, but African women purposefully invested in items that could evoke status and wealth. Wearing a pair of golden earrings signified public standing as belonging to the colonial elite.

West Central Africans who left wills and colonial officers who collected inventories paid careful attention to clothing and jewelry, describing the items in rich detail. Men valued their shirts, socks, uniforms, and coats, distributing some of these items to their heirs. Women invested in Western-style dresses, shoes, shawls, and shirts that differed in textile quality but also wore textiles wrapped around their waists, as can be seen

[78] Silvia Hunold Lara, "The Signs of Color: Women's Dress and Racial Relations in Salvador and Rio de Janeiro, ca. 1750–1815," *Colonial Latin American Review* 6, no. 2 (1997), 208.

[79] Quoted in Lara, "Signs of Color," 208.

[80] ANA, Cod. 7182, fl.76, December 18, 1827, n. 601.

[81] ANA, Cod. 7182, fl. 86, April 1, 1828, n. 808; and fl. 86v., April 6, 1828, n. 811; fl. 87, April 16, 1828, n. 827; and n. 831, April 19, 1828.

in Illustrations 7.1 and 7.2.[82] Clothes were markers of identity and status and in some cases were the most valuable property people owned. Officials noted if the items had been used, if they were well maintained, and their material, whether cotton, wool, or silk.[83] However, even people who lived kilometers away from the coast aspired to acquire imported textiles, demonstrating that tastes and consumption reached areas far from the Atlantic shore. In the 1860s, emissaries of the ruler Kambala, from Mbailundu state, arrived at Silva Porto's house in Bihé with the intention of purchasing fabrics for the ruler, and of buying a dog to protect his compound from animal attacks. The textiles were acquired in Benguela and sent to the ruler.[84] Edward Bowdich, who visited Benguela in the early nineteenth century, reported local rulers dressed in Westernized clothes. This practice is not surprising, considering the letters and emissaries sent to Benguela from different *sobados* with the purpose of buying pants, shirts, and shoes.[85] Photographs from the late nineteenth century and early twentieth century also portray rulers dressed in military jackets and hats (see Illustration 1.1). Unfortunately, I have not been able to locate probate records of any local ruler, but those available for other West Central Africans reveal globalized tastes and insertion into wider webs of consumption.

Florência José do Cadaval lived in Caconda, a village 220 kilometers from the coast. She died in 1854 before having a chance to dictate her will, yet her assets indicate that she was probably a commercial broker in one of the most important inland slave markets. Cadaval owned a significant number of textiles and garments at the time of her death. When she died on May 21, 1854, her personal clothing items included four used colored dresses, twenty-two used printed calico dresses, six printed calico dresses of good quality, six used woolen shawls, ten used shirts, twelve shirts of good quality made from unidentified textiles, fifteen silk handkerchiefs in different colors, six pairs of used shoes, a coat made of a light textile, and twenty pairs of silk socks.[86] Cadaval might have made her own clothes or employed one of her twenty-two enslaved men and

---

[82] This is not exclusive to West Central Africa; other scholars have noted the same patterns along the western coast. For more on African fashion, see George E. Brooks, *Eurafricans in Western Africa* (Athens: Ohio University Press, 2003), 122–60; Jones, *The Métis of Senegal*; Pernille Ipsen, *Daughters of the Trade: Atlantic Slavers and Interracial Marriage on the Gold Coast* (Philadelphia: University of Pennsylvania Press, 2015).

[83] This is similar to other contexts in Africa but also elsewhere. See, for example, Bauer, *Goods, Power, History*, 69–70; Porter, *Their Lives, Their Wills*, 27–48.

[84] BSGL, Res 2-C 6, fl. 253, March 17, 1862.

[85] Thomas Edward Bowdich, *An Account of the Discoveries of the Portuguese in the Interior of Angola and Mozambique* (London: John Booth, 1824), 30.

[86] TCB, "Autos civis do inventário de Florência José do Cadaval," June 15, 1854.

thirty-one enslaved women as tailors and seamstresses. She may have bought the items in one of the few shops available in Benguela or even from long-distance traders carrying imported goods in their caravans. Cadaval also owned three pairs of gold earrings, six gold necklaces of varying quality and purity, four gold rings with different precious stones, a golden brooch, and 209$880 in silver, equivalent to £944 pounds sterling in the 1850s. Today this amount would be equivalent to £75,695.[87] The historical evidence does not reveal her motivation behind the accumulation of these goods.

The circulation of and investment in imported objects show that dress and social presentation were important. As a result, local women offered their services as seamstresses to meet the demands of clients who aspired to wear imported fabrics. Catarina Simão Gonçalves da Silva was one of them. In the 1820s, she made several shirts for Simão Dias dos Santos, who failed to pay for her services. Simão was given twenty-four hours to pay the seamstress or risk going to jail.[88] In Luanda, Dona Maria do Carmo offered her services as a modiste specializing in dresses. She also offered cambric dresses, hats, lace shawls, and silk and woolen capes and coats for sale.[89] With the determination to dress in new styles and assert social and economic power, opportunities emerged for skilled tailors and seamstresses who could produce the items in demand and help shape local fashion.

The new fashions were not simply a process of local tastes Westernizing, but of integrating Western and local styles. Joana Mendes de Moraes from Libolo in the interior of Benguela owned nine pairs of socks, four women's shirts, six jackets, and 112 pieces of textiles that she wrapped around her waist or torso. She appears to have combined shirts and jackets with wrapped skirts and finished with head covers and head ties. Also listed in de Moraes's inventory were five new silk handkerchiefs, eight cotton handkerchiefs, two cotton belts, and five handkerchiefs of undetermined textile and quality.[90] Some might have been sewn into new dresses or worn as waistcloths or head wraps, as can be seen in Illustrations 7.1, 7.2, and 7.5. No dresses or shoes were listed in de Moreas's inventory, although wooden shoe forms were among her possessions, indicating she had the ability to produce footwear. Although de Moraes was from Libolo in the interior north of

---

[87] TCB, "Autos civis do inventário de Florência José do Cadaval," fl. 12-12v.
[88] ANA, Cod. 7182, fl. 104v, September 10, 1828, n. 1078.
[89] BOGGPA, 1866, n. 9, March 3, 1866, p. 42.
[90] TCB, "Autos cívis do inventário de Joana Mendes de Moraes," fl. 20v-24 July 3, 1861. For the importance of trade in textiles and their use, see Miller, *Way of Death*, 81–83; Santos, "Comércio de tecidos europeus e asiáticos na África centro-ocidental".

Illustration 7.5 Unidentified Umbundu woman wearing a blue cotton dress with a long white belt and a black-and-white scarf covering her shoulders. She wears red earrings and a white-and-blue bead necklace. She is barefoot and displays carefully designed braids
(*Source*: "Preta Quimbunda, de Além do Quanza," aquarela de Alberto Diniz, Arquivo Histórico Ultramarino, 1851)

the Kwanza River, she lived in a coastal town. Her belongings suggest she was not as concerned about accumulating Western-style clothing as Florinda José do Cadaval. Although imported clothing was an essential sign of status and economic distinction, de Moraes chose instead to invest her wealth in real estate, slaves, and jewelry, which could be sold if circumstances required.[91] Individuals invested in goods and real estate, but also in the labor of enslaved individuals.

In the 1860s, the trader Francisco Pacheco de Sousa Silva appears to have run a shop or other business in Benguela where he catered to consumers' demands for imported goods. His inventory included a variety of women's dresses, probably sewn by some of his seventy-six slaves. Among his enslaved individuals were Jacinto, a tailor, and Maria Quilombo, a seamstress who also ironed clothes.[92] Among de Sousa e Silva's possessions were five dozen wool reels, ten thousand sewing needles of different sizes, seven scissors, and large quantities of cotton, Indian blue cotton cloth, and *pano das costa*, all items that indicate he had a tailoring business. In addition, he apparently sold gold rings and earrings since his probate records list seventeen new boxes of pairs of earrings. But his primary business was in clothing, as the retail items in his inventory included the following items: fifteen dresses in cotton, silk, and camlet; twenty-nine women's shirts; forty-five belt buckles for women; thirty-seven women's belts; three women's silk capes; and eight skirts, in addition to dozens of gloves and thirty-two pairs of women's shoes. His business targeted Benguela residents who were eager to buy clothes associated with westernization and inclusion in a colonial society.

While the majority of Benguela's population could not afford to purchase imported goods, a small elite had access to high-quality clothes and other luxury items that differentiated them from the rest of the population. Strangers could perceive the economic power and social prestige of African women through a language of hierarchy expressed through clothing and access to imported commodities.[93] Traders and shopkeepers like Francisco Pacheco de Sousa e Silva capitalized on local demand for valuable commodities coming from distant markets. In addition to the clothing and jewelry, his 1865 probate records mentioned such consumer items as 145 decks of cards, twenty-two books on learning

---

[91] For more on this, see Heintze, *Angola nos séculos XVI e XVII*, 576–92.
[92] TCB, "Autos civis do inventário de Francisco Pacheco de Sousa e Silva," August 3, 1865, fl. 8 and 8v.
[93] Lara, "Signs of Color," 205. For the importance of clothing in differentiating people, see Sheryl McCurdy, "Fashioning Sexuality: Desire, Manyema Ethnicity, and the Creation of the *Kanga*, ca. 1880-1900," *International Journal of African Historical Studies* 39, no. 3 (2006): 441–69.

how to read and write, seventy-one hoes, and fifty dozen knives, all likely destined for the urban elite market.[94]

West Central African women invested in jewelry and other adornments such as necklaces and hairpins made of gold or silver. By the nineteenth century, African women who lived in coastal centers as well as in the interior appeared to have enjoyed more wealth and global connections than women living in other borderland regions around the world.[95] In the 1860s, the previously mentioned Joana Mendes de Moraes owned three pairs of gold earrings, one of which had diamonds. The two simpler gold earrings were estimated at 1$250 *réis*; the one with diamonds was worth 27$000 or 27,000 réis, around £121 pounds sterling in 1860, worth approximately £7,095 in 2017. She also owned gold bowls of varying quality and value, a gold ring with topaz stones (4$800 *réis*), a necklace with a gold crucifix (52$000, corresponding to £234 and £13,836 purchasing power in 1860 and 2017, respectively), and a copper crucifix with no monetary value.[96] Her jewelry included five pairs of silver earrings (4$300) and a copper necklace (1$000). While the copper items were probably manufactured locally due to the presence of copper mines in the interior of Central Africa, the origin of the gold and silver jewelry is not clear. They probably came from Brazil due to the strong connection between Brazilian and Benguela-based traders or might have been mined locally.[97] Inland societies also made extensive use of jewelry, such as the ankle bracelets portrayed in Illustration 7.6.

People also accumulated furniture during their lifetime. Probate records reveal that African men and women owned tables, chests, rocking chairs, wardrobes, and long-case clocks brought from Portugal, Brazil, or China. The Benguela resident Josefa Manoel Pereira da Silva had a chest with drawers and a mirror worth 2$000 *réis*, a pinewood table in good condition, another pinewood table with four drawers, an old chest, and a small wooden bed frame with copper details estimated at

---

[94] TCB, "Autos civis do inventário de Francisco Pacheco de Sousa e Silva."

[95] Amy Porter notes that very few women had jewelry in the Mexican borderlands at the turn of the nineteenth century. See Porter, *Their Lives, Their Wills*, 44–45.

[96] TCB, "Autos civis do inventário de Joana Mendes de Moraes," fl. 25v-27. For more on the methodology of the currency conversion and value see "A Note on Currency." For more on the equivalence of *mil réis* and pound sterling see W. G. Clarence-Smith, *The Third Portuguese Empire, 1825-1975: A Study in Economic Imperialism* (Manchester University Press, 1985), 227.

[97] Eugenia W. Herbert, *Red Gold of Africa: Copper in Precolonial History and Culture* (Madison: University of Wisconsin Press, 1984); Kriger, *Pride of Men*. Crislayne Alfagali is examining labor and local knowledges related to silver and gold mining in West Central Africa. For more on her work, see Crislayne Alfagali, "Labor in Southern African gold mines during the seventeenth and eighteenth centuries," unpublished paper.

Illustration 7.6 A woman from Cassange wearing a palm skirt with a cotton belt, golden anklets, a palm-weaved wrap, and a red bead choker. Her hair is braided with metal decorations, and she carries a pipe (*Source*: "Preta do Cassange," Aquarela de Alberto Diniz, Arquivo Histórico Ultramarino, 1851)

16$000.[98] Other residents had larger furniture collections, such as the case of Teresa Jesus de Barros e Cunha, who died in 1861 two weeks after giving birth to her son, Manoel de Barros e Cunha Vandunen. Although she was not legally married to Guilherme Van Dunen, they lived together, he recognized Manoel as their child, and he identified her belongings after her premature death. It is important to stress that all the items belonged to her, not to Guilherme Van Dunen or her deceased first husband. Her furniture included a well-maintained set of a sofa, eight chairs, and two small benches, all handmade with woven straw seats, and all imported from Porto in Portugal, estimated at 21$700 *réis*. She also owned a large mirror estimated at 4$000; four chairs in good condition made of "American wood"; a used rocking chair; an iron bed frame; three Chinese paintings; a dining table with four rounded, wooden legs and five drawers; a bedside table; a washing basin made of iron with a broken leg; a French-style writing desk; and a jacaranda-wood table with two drawers. She also had a variety of chests used to store her clothing and other valuables.[99] The emphasis on the material, carving, and style suggests the furniture was uncommon. Barros e Cunha's furniture stands out when compared to that of other residents, suggesting she was wealthy.

Dona Maria Lucas Pinheiro, born in Caconda, died in Benguela 1877. Among her possessions were an iron bed, a washing basin, two tables, and five wooden chairs. These items, which can be labeled as ordinary from today's perspective, were financially and socially valuable to Lucas Pinheiro since she left them to her son.[100] The probate documents do not reveal if the cast iron, for example, was elaborated, and important work has been done indicating that beds of various types were among some of the most valuable possessions in different European societies. More research is needed on West Central Africa. Curiously enough, the carpenter João Manoel, identified as a Black man, had no piece of furniture identified in his inventory. Colonial officers listed carpenter's tools, clothes, real estate, and enslaved people, but no chairs, tables, or bed frames such as local women had among their possessions.[101] Probate records suggest that West Central African men and women owned both locally produced and imported furniture. Pine trees and jacaranda wood were not common in Angola, so furniture made of this wood was

---

[98] TCB, "Autos civis do inventário de Josefa Manoel Pereira da Silva," April 18, 1865.
[99] TCB, "Autos civis do inventário de Teresa de Jesus Barros e Cunha," October 14, 1861, fl. 16v-17v.
[100] TCB, "Autos civis do testamento e inventário de Dona Maria Lucas Pinheiro," January 23, 1877.
[101] TCB, "Autos civis do inventário de João Preto Carpinteiro," February 3, 1870.

probably imported from Portugal and Brazil. Additionally, it should be noted that Barros e Cunha owned a writing desk in a town with no permanent school until the mid-1860s.[102]

Imported goods were also commercialized to generate even more profit, and such was the case with textiles known as "*dinheiro da terra*," or money of the land, which were used as currency in West Central Africa.[103] José Roberto Amaral Lapa, Roquinaldo Ferreira, and Telma Santos show the importance of Indian textiles which were exchanged for enslaved people in Luanda and Benguela, stressing the role of Brazilian-based traders in these commercial operations.[104] Joseph Miller argues that "Africans sold people for imported goods,"[105] and the postmortem inventories from the 1850s and 1860s suggest that cloth continued to be important as a commodity after the end of the slave trade. Benguela residents accumulated large quantities of textiles from different parts of the world. Indian blue cotton cloth (*zuarte*), baize, a kind of woolen textile (*baeta*), wool, cotton, West African cloth (*pano da costa*), and printed calico (*chita*) circulated in Benguela and its interior in different sizes and assortments. For example, *covados* were sixty-eight centimeters in length, or three-quarters of a yard. *Palmos* were one-quarter of a *vara*.[106]

The inventories of residents include textiles from India, Europe, and West Africa, demonstrating not only the internal demand for cloth but also the participation of Benguela residents in global markets. These textiles traveled miles before reaching Benguela, Caconda, or Catumbela and were carefully stored in local homes, indicating the association of cloth and power. The postmortem inventory of the goods of Joana Rodrigues da Costa of Caconda included a piece of Indian blue cotton cloth (*zuarte*) estimated at 6$000, thirteen pieces of printed calico (2$109), four blue handkerchiefs (1$500), assorted cloths (*panos de garras*, 1$092), six *cavados* of baize, and white cloth ($640).[107] Dona Florência José do Cadaval's inventory lists a variety of textiles among her goods, including seventy-one

[102] Carlos Pacheco, "Leituras e bibliotecas em Angola na primeira metade do século XIX," *Locus (Juiz de Fora)* 6, no. 2 (2000): 30.

[103] Adriano Parreira, *Economia e sociedade em Angola na época da Rainha Jinga (Século XVII)* (Lisbon: Editorial Estampa, 1997), 115–16; Martin, "Power, Cloth and Currency on the Loango Coast."

[104] Ferreira, "Dinâmica do comércio intracolonial"; Martin, "Power, Cloth and Currency on the Loango Coast"; Gonçalves Santos, "Comércio de tecidos europeus e asiáticos na África centro-ocidental."

[105] Miller, *Way of Death*, 82.

[106] For more on the fabric and size of textiles, see the glossary available in Linda A. Newson and Susie Minchin, *From Capture to Sale: The Portuguese Slave Trade to Spanish South America in the Early Seventeenth Century* (Leiden: Brill, 2007).

[107] TCB, "Autos civis do inventário de Joana Rodrigues de Costa," March 2, 1850, fl. 13-14v. For more on cloth and prestige, see Colleen E. Kriger, "Mapping the History of

pieces of Indian blue cotton cloth (390$500), thirty-one blue handker-chiefs (72$600), thirty blue handkerchiefs of lower quality (54$000), seven pieces of West African cloth (105$000), nineteen pieces of American cotton (104$500), 160 yards of American cotton (28$000), a piece of printed calico (5$000), one piece of red calico (4$500), forty-six pieces of white cloth (101$200), and one spool of sewing thread (1$800), among other items.[108] Her belongings included textiles from West Africa, India, and the Americas. Joana Mendes de Moraes collected bundles of printed and white cotton cloth, handkerchiefs of silk, cloth from West Africa, and striped calico cloth.[109] West Central Africans had become global consumers.

Probate records also refer to large amounts of natural resources, particularly for foreign-born merchants. This is not surprising and reinforces the idea that Benguela residents were part of long-distance trade connecting internal markets to the Atlantic world.[110] Wax, orchil, ivory, gum arabica, and peanut oil are some of the items listed in inventories, and although most of it was destined to the external market, it generated important local commerce. For example, in 1846, 495 kilos of orchil were seized in a warehouse in the Baía Farta where more than 400 people were held in captivity. The location of enslaved people and orchil in the same warehouse indicates how the illegal slave trade and legitimate commerce operated side by side, rather than in different moments, as in West Africa.[111]

Cotton Textile Production in Precolonial West Africa," *African Economic History* 33, no. 205: 105–07; Martin, "Power, Cloth and Currency on the Loango Coast," 5–7; Kazuo Kobayashi, "Indian Textiles and Gum Arabic in the Lower Senegal River: Global Significance of Local Trade and Consumers in the Early Nineteenth Century," *African Economic History* 45, no. 2 (2017): 27–53.

[108] TCB, "Autos civis do inventário de Dona Florência do Cadaval," June 15, 1854, fl. 7-8v.

[109] TCB, "Autos civis do inventário de Joana Mendes de Moraes," fl. 20v-22.

[110] José C. Curto, *Álcool e escravos: o comércio Luso-Brasileiro do álcool em Mpinda, Luanda e Benguela durante o tráfico atlântico de escravos (c. 1480-1830) e o seu impacto nas sociedades da África Central Ocidental* (Lisbon: Vulgata, 2002); Aida Freudenthal, "Benguela – da feitoria à cidade colonial," *Fontes & Estudos* 6–7 (2011): 197–229; Mariana P. Candido, "Trade Networks in Benguela, 1700-1850," in *Networks and Trans-Cultural Exchange Slave Trading in the South Atlantic, 1590-1867*, ed. David Richardson and Filipa Ribeiro da Silva (Leiden: Brill, 2014); Candido, "As comerciantes de Benguela na virada do século XVIII: O caso de dona Aguida Gonçalves."

[111] ANA, Cod. 326, fl. 8, December 12, 1846, "Letter to the Governor of Benguela [João do Roboredo,] from the province secretary." For the link between legitimate trade and illegal slave trading, see Ferreira, "Agricultural Enterprise"; Aida Freudenthal, *Arimos e fazendas: a transição agrária em Angola, 1850-1880* (Luanda: Chá de Caxinde, 2005); Freudenthal, "Benguela." For West Africa see, for example, Susan M. Martin, *Palm Oil and Protest: An Economic History of the Ngwa Region, South-Eastern Nigeria, 1800-1980* (New York: Cambridge University Press, 2006).

With exports of enslaved people banned in 1836, the Portuguese administration encouraged the diversification of the economy, favoring the export of local staples such as wax and orchil. The trader António Francisco da Silva Porto stated that the interior of Benguela was the land of wax, and the trade in this natural resource along with the commercialization of honey was very profitable.[112] Traders diversified their investments in search of new profits that were less risky than the illegal slave trade. Manuel Vida Cesar, a trader from Rio de Janeiro, died while on a business trip in Benguela. His death appears to have been sudden. Among other things, he had in his possession a cask of peanut oil (estimated at 30$000 *réis*), thirteen *canada* (1.5 liters) of the same (6 $500), sixty-four pounds of wax, nine pounds of ivory, and seventy pounds of orchil, items that he seemed to have recently acquired.[113]

Residents of Benguela had large quantities of items associated with legitimate commerce in their homes. Francisco Pacheco de Sousa e Silva had 1,010 pounds of wax.[114] João Batista da Silva had 640 pounds of wax (128$000), 1,134 pounds of yellow rubber, and two tips of ivory tusks (1 $500).[115] Along the West Central African coast, ivory had been an important item of trade beginning in the fifteenth century. By the nineteenth century, merchants were sending agents to the interior where they acquired ivory tusks in inland markets such as Ganguela, demonstrating the rush to secure access to new markets and acquire natural resources.[116] As seen in earlier chapters, the end of slave exports and the expansion of the cash-crop economy did not necessarily represent a rupture with the past and the start of a new economic model.[117] Probate records reveal that women owned a smaller quantity of natural resources than their male counterparts: Joana Mendes de Moraes had forty-seven

---

[112] BSGL, Res 2-C 6, fl. 57, February 27, 1861.

[113] TCB, "Autos civis do inventário Manoel Vidal Cesar," January 24, 1858, fl. 11-13v.

[114] TCB, "Autos civis do inventário de Francisco Pacheco de Sousa e Silva," August 7, 1865.

[115] TCB, "Autos civis do inventário de João Batista da Silva," July 13, 1863, 10v.

[116] BSGL, Res 2-C 6, fl. 163, August 19, 1861. For the importance of the ivory trade, see Vansina, "Long-Distance Trade-Routes in Central Africa," 377–78; Alpers, *Ivory and Slaves*; Guyer, "Wealth in People and Self-Realization in Equatorial Africa," 243–65; Mariza de Carvalho Soares, "'Por conto e peso': O comércio de marfim no Congo e Loango, séculos XV–XVII," *Anais do Museu Paulista: História e Cultura Material* 25, no. 1 (2017): 59–86. See also the contributions to Vaniciéia Silva Santos, ed., *O comércio de marfim no mundo Atlântico: Circulação e produção (séculos XV a XIX)* (Belo Horizonte: Prisma, 2017); Rogéria Cristina Alves, "Marfins africanos em trânsito: apontamentos sobre o comércio numa perspectiva atlântica (Angola, Benguela, Lisboa, e Brasil), séculos XVIII-XIX," *Faces da História* 3, no. 2 (2016): 8–21; Gonçalves, "Comércio, política e trabalho nos Sertões de Angola."

[117] Martin, *Palm Oil and Protest*; Kristin Mann, *Slavery and the Birth of an African City: Lagos, 1760-1900* (Bloomington: Indiana University Press, 2010).

pounds of wax (12$250) and a special container for melting wax.[118] The inventories of African women who died in Benguela indicate that they did not necessarily accumulate these products in their homes, nor were they listed among their probate records. The inventories of male merchants, however, offered detailed descriptions and values of raw materials, as seen in the case of Francisco Pacheco de Sousa e Silva and João Batista da Silva.

Crops, vegetable oils, oilseeds, ivory, and rubber continued to be exported from Benguela in the 1860s and 1870s. In 1866, more than 16,000 pounds of wax, 20,986 pounds of cotton, 16,031 pounds of rubber, and eleven barrels of palm oil were exported on a single ship to Lisbon.[119] Demand for raw materials in Europe and North America created a pressure that offered a chance for prosperity for landowners in Angola, who exported a variety of items such as fish oil, peanuts, ostrich eggs, leather, a variety of unidentified animal skins, ivory, copper manilla, and seahorses.[120] While some of these products supplied nascent industries in search of new sources of oil, others were displayed in museums and palaces, where they reinforced the exoticization of African societies.

Probate records reveal that locally born women owned and placed more value on kitchen utensils than men, although these items were also listed in male postmortem inventories. Some of the inventory items, such as pots, basins, barrels, and knives, were manufactured goods and mostly imported. Unlike some other parts of the African coast, Benguela residents were interested in purchasing manufactured goods.[121] Iron bars, copper rods, and other unworked metals are absent from the inventories, in part because this region had served as an exporter rather than an importer of metal since the seventeenth century. Gold jewelry is the exception, as seen in the gold rings and earrings listed in the inventories and wills.[122]

Food was also listed among kitchen items in the inventories, although it may have been destined for household use or for trade. In the case of the inventory of João Batista da Silva from Guimarães in Portugal, the

---

[118] TCB, "Autos civis do inventário de Joana Mendes de Moraes," fl. 19v -23.

[119] BOGGPA, 1866, n.39, September 29, 1866, p. 309

[120] BOGGPA, 1869, n. 6, February 6, 1869, p. 63. See also Clarence-Smith, *The Third Portuguese Empire, 1825-1975*, 65–72; Vos, "Coffee, Cash, and Consumption."

[121] For the consumption of unworked metals elsewhere, see George Metcalf, "A Microcosm of Why Africans Sold Slaves: Akan Consumption Patterns in the 1770s," *Journal of African History* 28, no. 3 (1987): 381–394; Herbert, *Red Gold of Africa*, 11; Paul E. Lovejoy, *Transformations in Slavery* (New York: Cambridge University Press, 2000), 104–05; Harvey M. Feinberg, *Africans and Europeans in West Africa: Elminans and Dutchmen on the Gold Coast during the Eighteenth Century* (Philadelphia, PA: American Philosophical Society, 1989), 51–52.

[122] Miller, *Way of Death*, 85; Candido, *An African Slaving Port*, 40–41.

kitchen and food items included knives, a butter dish, a sugar bowl, bottles, and silverware. He also owned a vinegar barrel, two pounds of tea leaves, sixty kilos of bacon, 234 *cazungueis* of beans, and sixteen *cazungueis* of corn.[123] Women's inventories do not list food items. After enslaved people, furniture, and dresses, kitchen utensils from different parts of the world were the most valuable items in women's inventories. These items were not described in the same detail as were furniture and clothing. In Joana Rodrigues da Costa's house in Caconda, for example, the number of kitchen utensils was sparse: eight dishes, a soup tureen, a bowl, three cups with matching saucers, a butter dish, a coffee pot, two old earthenware water jars, three glass bottles, and fifteen small bottles. Her more-valuable items were silverware: a set of six forks, six spoons, and six knives, made of silver; three silver candleholders; three silver teaspoons; one sugar spoon; and an old fork made of ivory.[124]

Another Caconda inventory from four years later demonstrates the international sources of items found in the kitchens of African women. At the time of her death, Florência José do Cadaval, a wealthier woman than Joana Rodrigues da Costa, had two dozen knives, eight drinking glasses, eighteen bottles, five small bottles, ten teacups from India, sixty-one soup dishes made of stone dust (*pratos de pó de pedra*), forty-three stone-dust dinner dishes, a used stone-dust soup tureen, nine serving trays, a stone basin, two stone-dust bowls, nine teacups, a sugar bowl, and two *palmatórias*, a flat piece of wood used for corporal punishment.[125] Some of these items suggest entertaining guests or parties as a way of demonstrating status, although the *palmatórias* remind us that opulence coexisted with violence. Some women had no kitchen utensils or tools listed in their inventories; others had a single item. This was the case with Maria José Martins, whose only kitchen item listed in her inventory was a copper pot.[126] Absent from the inventories in Benguela are local items such as mortars and pestles for pounding grain, baskets, or earthen pottery.[127] Kitchenware items were not identified in wills, but their presence in inventories makes it clear they had value, even if their

---

[123] TCB, "Autos civis do inventário de João Batista da Silva," July 13, 1863, fl. 12–15v. *Cazunguel* was a weight measure used in Angola that corresponded to one Portuguese *alqueire*. José Joaquim Lopes de Lima, *Ensaios sobre a statistica das possessões portuguezas na África occidental e oriental; Na Asia occidental; na China, e na Oceania*, vol. 3 (Lisbon: Imprensa nacional, 1844), 45.

[124] TCB, "Autos civis dos inventários de Joana Rodrigues da Costa," April 12, 1850, 12v–14v.

[125] TCB, "Autos civis dos inventários de Florência José do Cadaval."

[126] TCB, "Autos civis do inventário de Maria José Martins," 1861, fl. 6.

[127] In other contexts, kitchen items were valuable and the most common items in inventories. See Karen Graubart, *With Our Labor and Sweat: Indigenous Women and*

origin is not clearly identified. Perhaps the kitchen was not perceived socially as a prestigious space for free African women, which may explain so much detail regarding the silverware and chinaware compared to the cooking pots. Once again, the image projected to strangers, such as the ability to serve coffee and tea in china sets and on a silver tray, may have made these items more valuable than the tools for pounding grains or producing food.

Probate records are silent on foodstuff produced in local garden and nearby farms, which street vendors offered in the streets. Travelers commented on and portrayed women as *quitandeiras* (see Illustrations 7.3 and 7.4). These illustrations were made at least thirty years apart, but in both images, women are shown selling fruit, fish, and vegetables. Profits from marketing allowed producers, intermediaries, and sellers to increase their production or consumption of imported goods, which reinforced the desire and tastes for these goods. By 1881, for example, corn flour, cassava flour, and beans were widely available in Benguela, allowing street vendors to supply the local demand for food items and in the process capitalize on the profits, reinforcing their social and economic status.[128] The expansion of consumption and production relied on the labor of enslaved or freed individuals. Elite members became global consumers because others were impoverished and dispossessed. Consumption and wealth accumulation depend on privation.

Conclusion

Access to global markets relied on the dismantling of earlier forms of communal rights and protections. The same liberal wave that reached West Central Africa in the nineteenth century and transformed markets, land use and access, and slavery led to new values and aspirations. Desire and taste levels for imported goods operated parallel to the operation of the trade in human beings. Efforts to bring the slave exports to an end did not diminish interest in imported commodities. Examining the circulation of imported and local products allows us to understand what West Central Africans produced, consumed, and desired during the nineteenth century. The movement of goods and merchants connecting

the Formation of Colonial Society in Peru, 1550-1700, 1st ed. (Stanford, CA: Stanford University Press, 2007), 73–75; Porter, *Their Lives, Their Wills*, 34–37.
[128] BOGGPA, 1881, n. 3, January 15, 1881, p. 28. Vanessa S. Oliveira, "The Gendered Dimension of Trade: Female Traders in Nineteenth Century Luanda," *Portuguese Studies Review* 23, no. 2 (2015): 93–121; Vanessa S. Oliveira, "Gender, Foodstuff Production and Trade in Late-Eighteenth Century Luanda," *African Economic History* 43, no. 1 (2015): 57–81.

inland and coastal markets demonstrates that inland societies, or at least some individuals, participated in a globalized economy. Inhabitants of Caconda, Bihé, Wambu, and Catumbela aspired to own material things in addition to the accumulation of dependents who could provide labor, prestige, and wealth in people.

In many ways, the commerce in human beings coexisted with the movement of goods as diverse as hats, hoes, wax, hemp plants, copper, pottery, and gunpowder. Coastal and inland markets became spaces in which traders and consumers interacted and learned about new tastes, fashions, and desires. West Central Africans acquired these commodities not necessarily because they were nonexistent in their societies. Ndombe, Mbailundu, and others acquired tea sets, tobacco, and pants because they aspired to own items that differentiated them from their neighbors. Local societies responded by manufacturing cloth, tables, and shoes locally, creating products for different consumers and responding to local demands. Yet local production alone was not able to supply all the demand, and coastal merchants quickly provided imported goods that could compete for or simply complement local tastes for clothes, baskets, tables, and religious images.

The expansion of farms and plantations and coerced labor favored consumerism. Legitimate trade continued to rely on unfree labor, which generated accumulation in the hands of political and economic elites. Probate records reveal the tastes and desires of the West Central African elite. Coastal and inland societies were linked to markets elsewhere, acquiring French perfume, port wine, Brazilian cachaça, and British biscuits, as well as Indian textiles and Chinese tea sets and paintings, showing that industries elsewhere relied on West Central African consumption to keep laborers employed and traders profiting. Imported goods had symbolic value and were socially perceived as valuable, yet local societies also manufactured furniture, clothes, and kitchenware. Inventories and wills are relatively silent on the uses of objects and rarely mentioned items used in daily tasks such as grinding crops or local religious rites. While Catholic images were listed among valuable possessions, there is a silence on divination baskets, power figures, and other objects that could provide some clues on how West Central Africans expressed their faith and connected to the immaterial world. Also absent from the lists is information about weaving, although local shops sold thread and needles. It is not clear how these items circulated inland.

The systematic undone of earlier tenure systems, the dismissal of communal rights, the rise of individualism, and the imposition of new property rights profoundly transformed West Central Africans. The growth of imported goods and the accumulation of assets did not happen in a vacuum. It was part of a transformation that privileged the market and the individual, weakening communal goals and collective actions.

Historical evidence provides insights into the objects women and men collected during their lifetimes. Women are not underrepresented despite patriarchal values and colonialism. Many women managed to claim property and transmit it to loved ones, despite local customs that privileged men's ownership claims. Although they were not often present in official reports and travelers' accounts, local women exercised legal rights and recorded their wishes and desires. They seemed to have understood the power of recordkeeping and the empowerment and states written records gave to them and their progeny. During the nineteenth century, elite African men and women established themselves as property holders who valued control of material things and people and participated actively in a global economy as producers, merchants, and consumers. Consumerism reinforced dispossession, and it exacerbated violence and competition among peers.

Conclusion

Since the 1600s, West Central African populations had clear ideas about land rights and exercised ownership over people and objects, and individuals valued their possessions. Land was not empty and widely available, as European colonialists claimed and defended. Communities lived there, cultivated their food, and buried their dead, and land had more than a productive meaning for its inhabitants. This does not mean that access and allocation were devoid of conflicts. Land rights were tied to first-settler occupation and production, and its use was negotiable. Access was an important aspect of political and economic power and competition. The implementation and registration of land titles in the second half of the nineteenth century were related to the end of slave exports and the shift of the colonial economy toward crop production and raw material exploitation. That historical moment and process also promoted the idea that West Central Africans were inferior and not sophisticated enough to have a land regime and notions of ownership, which allowed Europeans to seize land and privatize it in the name of progress. As we have seen, West Central African actors debated the legitimacy of land claims and land use, and eventually written evidence was used as a mechanism to prove rights. Landlord chiefs and their subjects were evicted and displaced to allow more "developed" ideas regarding production and land use. Yet the colonial regime of property ownership was not absolute and had not existed from time immemorial. It emerged in the nineteenth century to benefit the colonial elite at the expense of the local population.

The history of wealth accumulation and dispossession in Angola has been intertwined with the consolidation of liberal notions of progress, private property rights, land enclosure, and civilization. This is not a history of progress, but an account of dismantling – dismantling of communal rights and values that ordered societies. West Central African societies did not move progressively from one type of wealth, in people, to private property. In fact, West Central African communities valued both: territory and kinship. Wealth in people cannot exist in isolation from land control. An alternative interpretation of the past is necessary, moving away from earlier arguments that placed West Central Africans as backward and reifying colonialism and land grabbing. This is an effort to problematize recent interpretations of the Angolan past that understood territorial occupation, population removals, and dispossession as inevitable. As it is clear in local archives, West Central Africans valued land since 1600 – perhaps even earlier.

European notions of property were not stable nor well defined by the early nineteenth century, as jurists and colonial offers stated. It was in the process of implementing them at home and in their colonies that a range of ideas regarding property systems emerged and were formalized. West Central Africans were exposed to ideas that rendered them inferior to the Portuguese because of their way of life, a lack of individual property rights that was clear and legible to Europeans. With the end of slave exports and the expansion of the plantation economy and legitimate trade in raw materials, Portuguese administrators measured and quantified populations, cultivation, labor, cultural practices, and ways of life, creating a language of science and materiality to justify colonialism, seizure, violence, and racism. The ideology of progress, individual rights, and improvement was based on the science of governance, which was an integral part of conquest and colonialism. Maps, population enumeration, and ethnographic reports were part of the technology of rule that normalized enslavement, forced labor, land seizure, and conquest. The colonial state mobilized bureaucracy and writing techniques to better understand and control occupied territories and their populations, and in the process elaborated ideas such as the absence of property rights in African societies that justified the colonial presence to "civilize and uplift Africans." Counting and classification led to the solidification of fixed categories, but also to the idea that everything could be measured and controlled. Liberalism intellectuals convinced administrators, jurists, and scholars that everything could be bought and sold. Land could only be productive if it generated output. Its social and religious roles have been erased.

The consolidation of violent systems of property acquisition and the structures of colonization produced problematic and simplified interpretations of the African past, which have ongoing consequences. Property rights are so ubiquitous that it is a challenge to see beyond the liberal economic model or imagine alternative pasts beyond the globalization of capitalism. Colonial officers, missionaries, anthropologists, jurists, and historians perpetuated images of African societies as isolated, profoundly different, and alienated from global processes. The result is the inability to recognize the fact that African societies have been adapting to change for a long period of time. Despite the evidence, colonial bureaucrats and jurists in Lisbon, Luanda, and Benguela insisted that West Central Africans did not have property rights, arguing that they lacked proof of ownership and dismissing local forms of knowledge and alternative ways of exercising control. When arguing that African societies privileged wealth in people due to their lack of notions of individual ownership, scholars reproduce the late nineteenth- and early twentieth-century jurists' legal arguments that supported colonialism. Colonialism and its ideology became legitimate, and the long history of West Central African forms of ownership and rights was obscured despite its clear existence in historical records. European occupation, displacement, and inequalities were normalized, giving space and logic to the stereotyped image of societies' lack of organization and institutions. West Central Africans were described as primitive, and colonialism and settler occupation took precedence in African history.

Regimes of property, whether held by African rulers or European administrators, were not transhistorical or total. The written regime of property in Angola emerged in specific contexts, articulated with imperialism, expansion of capitalism, and consolidation of the liberal notion of individual rights at the expense of collective ones. While Portuguese agents enforced a single model of property rights, local chiefs contested this model. However, by the mid-nineteenth century, the only way to exercise rights was through the legal recognition of ownership in colonial courts. Colonial property regimes altered the social order and allowed women, formerly enslaved people, and immigrants, often marginalized groups, to enjoy rights and subvert the economic and social order. The violence that exiled occupants from their own land also justified kidnapping and enslavement. However, this violence is almost erased in the colonial archives and scholarship that traces linear progress from slave trade to legitimate trade and imperialism. Nonetheless, violence and appropriation pervade the histories of slavery, property, rights, consumption, and claims.

This book is a history of wealth accumulation and imposition of new property regimes in the nineteenth century as much as it is about occupation, dispossession, displacement, enslavement, and erasure since the 1600s. The topics of land access and occupation rights are central to this study, yet locals and foreigners also clashed over ownership rights to people and material objects. All of these actors – Ndombe, *sobas*, Mbailundu porters, enslaved people, *donas* living in inland *presídos* – were part of the global economy and affected and were influenced by events and societies located far away. Therefore, this book is a history of people who experienced land alienation, forced labor, and exclusion as well as the story of an economic and political elite that profited from the imposition of a new regime of property. Rather than encountering silences in the archives, the amount of information about women, local actors, enslaved individuals, and disposed populations overwhelmed me. These are not hard to get microhistories, but narratives that historians have actively refused to acknowledge. In every box, every codex book, every legal case or ecclesiastical record, I located common people who refused to remain silent when challenged. Angolan archives are filled with individual stories overlooked or neglected.

A small number of West Central Africans profited from these nineteenth-century changes with personal connections and their ability to navigate and negotiate rights. However, their gains did not necessarily bring about long-lasting benefits under the new political order imposed during the twentieth century. Colonial records detail the repertoire of legal techniques that West Central Africans, including local rulers, their subjects, and free and unfree inhabitants living in the colonial centers, employed to exercise control over people and land. Among those able to claim rights and accumulate things, land, and people were West Central African women, demonstrating that women need to be included in analysis about land grabbing and wealth concentration. Property and dispossession were gendered, since men and woman had distinctive opportunities and employed different strategies to maintain their rights. While anthropologists and missionaries have stressed how local notions of property may have excluded women from claiming rights, historic evidence shows that women understood their colonial legal rights and used various avenues to acquire land, people, and material goods. Women are everywhere in the Angolan archives, and it is a real challenge not to see and include them in analyses of the West Central African past.

West Central Africans had land regimes and exercised ownership rights over people, land, and things before the late nineteenth century. Emphasis on wealth on people led to an overemphasis on kinship and the subsequent dismissal of the centrality of territory to political, economic, and social organization. West Central African societies had a concept of ownership, but they lacked the written documents that Europeans would use to legitimize private property claims, as well as the judicial apparatus to defend the oral rights. The regime of property that was established in the second half of the nineteenth century continues to shape the lives of Angolans as they struggle to prove land titles and are subject to displacement. This study rejects the history of our present that insists on making Black lives disposable, African economies subordinate, and accumulation of things as a goal in and of itself.

Bibliography

Archival References

Angola

Arquivo Nacional de Angola (ANA)
Códices (Cód.) 166, 220, 221, 277, 323, 326, 442, 444, 445, 452, 455, 463, 469, 471, 509, 3159, 3160, 7182, 7183
Caixas (cx.) 151, 1322, 1338, 1354, 1373, 1376, 1338, 3340, 5251, 5568

Biblioteca Província de Benguela (BPB)
Livro Termo de Terreno, 1843–1894

Bispado de Luanda (BL)
Benguela, Livro de Batismo, 1794–1806; 1846–1849, 1849–1850; 1851–1853
Benguela, Livro de Casamento, 1806–1853
Benguela, Livro de Óbito, 1770–1796 and 1797–1831, 1858–1868, 1874–1876
Dombe Grande, Livro de Batismo, 1874–1875

Tribunal da Comarca de Benguela (TCB)
"Inventário de Joana Rodrigues da Costa," 1850
"Fragmento de códice, Cartas de Liberdade," 1852–1866
"Inventário de Florência Jose do Cadaval," 1854
"Processo crime, Ministério Público, vs Francisco Luciano dos Santos Moura," 1855
"Ação commercial Autor Manuel Ribeiro Alves Réu Ana Teixeira de Sousa," 1856
"Autos cíveis de libelo Manoel Ribeiro Alves vs Ana Teixeira de Sousa," 1856
"Autos cíveis de execução Joaquim Luis Bastos vs D. Ana Teixeira de Sousa," 1856
"Inventário cívil de António Joaquim Monteiro," September 2, 1857

278

"Processo crime, Ministério Público vs Miguel Gonçalves da Cruz," 1857

"Crime tentativa de escravizar, Ministério Público vs Miguel Gonçalves da Cruz," 1857

"Inventário de Manuel Vidal Cesar," 1858

"Crime João da Silva Pereira vs Canique, Quiopa, Quipanga, and Naquibuacura," 1859

"Autos cíveis de reinvindicação da liberdade da preta Julia," 1860

"Inventário de Joana Mendes de Moraes," 1861

"Inventário de Maria José Martins," 1861

"Inventário de Teresa de Jesus Barros e Cunha," 1861

"Inventário de João Batista da Silva," 1863

"Inventário de Narciso José Pacheco Lages," 1863

"Inventário de Joana Martinho Lopes," 1864

"Autos civis do inventário de Josefa Manoel Pereira da Silva," 1865

"Inventário de Josefa Manoel Pereira da Silva," 1865

"Inventário de Francisco Pacheco de Sousa e Silva," 1865

"Deposito de duas libertas a requerimento do curador dos escravos e libertos," 1866

"Embargo de quatro libertas. Ministério Público vs Constância de Jesus," 1866

"Ação comercial Tomé Ribeiro Antunes vs João Rodrigues Teixeira," 1867

"Autos cíveis de habilitação, preta Josefina Rodrigues," 1867

"Inventário de João Preto Carpinteiro," 1870

"Libelo. Catarina Barros de Araújo vs Luis Augusto de Brito," 1872

"Auto cíveis de translado de testamento de d. Maria Lucas Pinheiro," 1877

"Testamento de d. Maria Lucas Pinheiro," 1877

"Execução: Banco de Portugal; Espólio de Eugenio Coichoix," 1879

"Execução: Agente do banco Nacional Ultramarino e Eugenio Caichoix," 1879

"Traslado de parte das peças constantes do processado na execução," 1882

Brazil

Biblioteca Nacional do Rio de Janeiro (BNRJ)
doc. I-28, 28, 29, "Notícias de São Filipe de Benguela e costumes dos gentios habitantes naquele sertão," November 10, 1797

Instituto Histórico Geográfico Brasileiro (IHGB)
DL32,02.01, "Relação dos sobas potentados, souvetas seus vassalos e sobas agregados pelos nomes das suas terras, que tem na capitania de Benguela. Dividindo em sete partes e províncias para melhor conhecimento da capitania: 1°. província da cidade de Benguela; 2°.

província de Quilengues; 3°. província do Presídio de Caconda; 4°. província do Ambo; 5°. província de Galangue; 6°. província de Bailundo; 7°. província do Bié," 1798

DL32,02.02, "Relação de Manuel José de Silveira Teixeira sobre os moradores da cidade de São Felipe de Benguela separados por raça, idade, emprego, título de habitação, oficios mecânicos e quantos mestres e aprendizes existem," 1789

DL32,02.03, "Relação de José Caetano Carneiro, primeiro tenente, da metade dos moradores da parte do norte da cidade de São Felipe de Benguela, de ambos os sexos, cor, escravos sem nomes, empregos e estados. Relação de senzalas às quais pertencem," November 29, 1797

DL32,02.10, "Relação de moradores do Distrito das Vilas de Icau, Muquiama e Quilengues contendo nome, idade, estado, emprego, gados, petrechos de sua majestade, órfãos, sobas e seu território que reconhecem e tributam vassalagem," 1789

DL81,02.19, "Inventario dos Sovas, Quilambas e Quimbares do Destrito do Calumbo que servem no serviço das Fabricas de Ferro de Novo Belém e Nova Oeiras donde se mandarão anexar todos por ordem do Ilm.o e Exm.o Snr. General, sobre os Dízimos que pagavam antes de serem isentos, e pelo que Regularão na Regulação que se fez, e o número de Filhos capazes, que cada um tem, e os que dão por Mês," 1750

DL81,02.31, "Comunicação para o Rei de Portugal sobre a possessão das terras dos Sobas do Humbo, e as disputas com outros povos," 1798

Portugal

Arquivo Histórico Diplomático (AHD)

Ministério das Colônias – Gabinete do Ministério, May 18, 1936, C. P. Garcia, "Conforme sugeri a V Excia em parecer do conselho do Império de que fui relatos"

Ministério do Ultramar, Arquivo Histórico Ultramarino, U. I. 14446, AHD/3/MU-GM/GNP-RNP/S167/UI014446, processo 26/3. "Inquérito sobre a existência da escravatura nas colônias," Luanda, 20 de dezembro de 1940

Serviço da República. Repartição dos Negócios políticos e de administração civil. Entrada n. 22, Antônio Lopes Mateus, "Informações prestadas pelas colônias sobre usos e costumes que podem ser interpretados como sobrevivência da escravatura, nos termos do artigo 7 da convenção de 1926," February 13, 1936

Arquivo Histórico Militar (AHM)

2-2-1-36, "Requerimento dos negociantes da Praça de Benguela." 1821

Arquivo Histórico Ultramarino (AHU)
Conselho Ultramarino, Angola
Códice: 542, 544, 452
Caixas (old Primeira Sessão): AHU, cx. 46 - 176
Livro 661
Miscelânea, Maço 771
Pastas (old Correspondência dos Governadores): 2, 2C, 12, 23 (1), 29,
    35, 38, 45, 47, 48

SEMU_DGU_Angola *(new organization)*
648, 661, 477, 771, 1112
Estatísticas: caixa (cx.) 2, 1854–1866
Processo das Consultas: caixas (cx.): 5, 12, 13, 22, 27, 31, 34, 36, 39,
    40, 46, 67, 69, 70

Arquivo Nacional da Torre do Tombo (ANTT)
Condes de Linhares
Maço (mç) 44, documento (doc.) 2 "Memórias do Reino de Angola e
    suas conquistas escritas por D. Francisco Inocêncio de Sousa
    Coutinho, governador e capitão general do Reino de Angola,"
    1773–1775.

Feitos Findos
Justificações Ultramarinas, África, mc. 14, doc. 1, 1805

Ministério do Reino
Maço (mç.) 499, caixa (cx.) 622, Correspondência recebida de Índia,
    Moçambique, Angola, Guiné, "Memoria do Bispo de Angola enviada
    a Rainha sobre o estado da Igreja e pede a sua demissão," 1822.

Biblioteca Nacional de Lisboa (BN)
Res. Cód. 8744

Biblioteca da Sociedade de Geografia de Lisboa (BSGL)
Res 1- Pasta D – 14 "Memória sobre o estado actual d'Africa
    Occidental seu comercio com Portugal e medidas que convinha
    adoptar em 1841," January 1841.
Res 1, pasta E, 2, António da Silva Porto, "Memorial de Mucanos,
    1841–1885,"
Res 2-C 6, "Silva Porto, apontamentos de um portuense em África,"
    Vol 2. Bié 25 de outubro de 1860 a 1 de julho de 1861,"
Res – 2-C-7 – Silva Porto, "Notas para retocar a minha obra logo que as
    circunstancias permitam," 1866

Published Primary Sources

Almada, José de. *Apontamentos históricos sobre a escravatura e o trabalho indígena nas colónias portuguesas*. Lisbon: Imprensa Nacional, 1932.

Almanak statistico da Provincia d'Angola e suas dependencias para o anno de 1852. Luanda: Imprensa do Governo, 1851.

Bastos, Augusto. "Traços geraes sobre a ethnographia do districto de Benguella." *Boletim da Sociedade de Geografia de Lisboa* 26, no. 1 (1908): 5–15; 44–56.

Boletim Oficial do Governo Geral da Província de Angola (BOGGPA), 1845-84.

Bowdich, Thomas Edward. *An Account of the Discoveries of the Portuguese in the Interior of Angola and Mozambique*. London: John Booth, 1824.

Caldeira, Carlos José. *Apontamentos d'uma viagem de Lisboa a China e da China a Lisboa*. Lisbon: G.M. Martins, 1852.

Capelo, Hermenegildo and Roberto Ivens. *De Benguela às terras de Iaca. Descrição de uma viagem na África Central e Ocidental*. Lisbon: Europa- América, 1996. 2 vols.

Carneiro, Manuel Borges. *Direito civil de Portugal*. Vol. 1. 3 vols. Lisbon: Impressão Régia, 1826.

Carpo, Arsênio P. P. de. *Projecto de uma companhia para o melhoramento do Commércio, Agricultura e Indústria na Província de Angola*. Lisbon: Typografia da Revolução de setembro, 1848.

Chatelain, Héli. *Folk-Tales of Angola Fifty Tales, with Ki-Mbundu Text, Literal English Translation, Introduction, and Notes*. Boston: The American Folklore Society by Houghton Mifflin, 1894.

Código Philippino, ou Ordenações e Leis do Reino de Portugal, Coimbra: Imprensa da Universidade, 1850-51, Livro 1

Collecção da legislação novíssima do ultramar. Lisbon: Imprensa Nacional, 1901,

Collecção de legislação relativa às colonias portuguezas em Africa. Lisbon: Companhia Nacional Editora, 1899.

Cordeiro, Luciano. "1593-1631 - terras e minas africanas." In *Viagens, explorações e conquistas dos portuguezes. Coleção de documentos*. Lisbon: Imprensa Nacional, 1881

Correspondence with the British Commissioners at Sierra Leone, Havava, the Cape of Good Hopes, Loanda, and New York Relates with the Slave Trade. Vol. 75. London: Harrison and Sons, 1865.

Costa, Alberto da Costa Abreu e. *Carta dirigidao ao Illmo Exmo Sr. João de Andrade Corvo sobre a questão do trabalho em África Ocidental*. Lisbon: Typographia Universal, 1875.

Felner, Alfredo de *Angola. Apontamentos sobre a colonização dos planaltos e litoral do Sul de Angola. Extraídos de documentos históricos*. Lisboa: Agência-Geral do Ultramar, 1940, 3 vols.

Figueiredo, Candido de. *Novo diccionário da língua portuguesa*. 2 vols. Lisbon: Tavares Cardoso & Irmão, 1899.

Gil, António. *Considerações sobre alguns pontos mais importantes da moral religiosa e sistema de jurisprudência dos pretos do continente da África Ocidental Portuguesa além do Equador*. Lisbon: Tipografia da Academia, 1854.

Gonçalves, Caetano. "O regime das terras e as reservas indígenas na colonização portuguesa." *Boletim Geral das Colônias* 2, no. 13 (1926): 26–45.

Índice Alfabéticos do Boletim Oficial da Província de Angola. Luanda: Imprensa do Governo, 1864.

Índice do Boletim Oficial da Província de Angola comprehendendo os anos que decorrem desde 13 de setembro de 1845, em que foi publicado o N. 1 até 1862 inclusive. Luanda: Imprensa do Governo, 1864.

Lacerda, Paulo Martins Pinheiro de. "Notícias da cidade de S. Felipe de Benguela e dos costumes dos gentios habitantes daquele sertão." *Annaes Maritimos e Coloniaes, Quinta Série* 12 (1845): 486–91.

Lima, José Joaquim Lopes de. *Ensaios sobre a statistica das possessões portuguezas na África occidental e oriental; na Ásia occidental; na China, e na Oceania.* Lisbon: Imprensa Nacional, 1844.

Magyar, László. *Reisen in Süd-Afrika in den Jahren 1849 bis 1857.* Leipzig: Lauffer & Stolp, 1859.

Melo, Lopo Vaz de Sampaio e. *Política indígena.* Porto: Magalhães & Moniz, 1910.

Regime da propriedade indígena, separata da "Revista Portugueza Colonial e Marítima." Lisbon: Ferin Editora, 1910.

Menezes, Joaquim Antonio de Carvalho e. *Memória geografica, e política das possessões portuguezas n'Affrica occidental, que diz respeito aos reinos de Angola, Benguela, e suas dependencias...* Lisbon: Typografia Carvalhense, 1834.

Monteiro, Joachim John. *Angola and the River Congo.* New York: Macmillan, 1876.

Monteiro, José Maria de Souza. *Os Portuguezes em Africa, Asia, America, e Occeania: Obra classica.* Lisbon: Typ. de Borges, 1850.

Pragmática do Senhor Rey D. João V do ano de 1749. Lisbon: Oficina de Antonio Rodrigues Galhardo, 1771

O Panorama. Jornal Literario e Instructivo, 1858.

Quarenta e cinco dias em Angola: apontamentos de viagem. Porto: Typ. Sebastião José Pereira, 1862.

Pinto, Alexandre Alberto da Rocha de Serpa. *How I Crossed Africa: From the Atlantic to the Indian Ocean, Through Unknown Countries; Discovery of the Great Zambesi Affluents, &c.* Sampson Low, Marsten, Searle, & Rivington, 1881.

Proudhon, Pierre Joseph. *What Is Property? An Inquiry into the Principle of Right and of Government.* Princeton, MA: B. R. Tucker, 1876.

"Regimento do Governo deste Reyno de Angolla, 12 de fevereiro de 1676" *Arquivos de Angola,* vol. I (nº 5–6) (1936), Chapter 4, no page number.

Sá da Bandeira, Marquês de. *A emancipação dos libertos. Carta dirigida ao excelentíssimo senhor Joaquim Guedes de Carvalho Menezes, presidente da relação de Loanda.* Lisbon: Imprensa Nacional, 1874.

Saldanha da Gama, António de. *Memória sobre as colônias de Portugal: situadas na costa occidental d'Africa.* Paris: Casimir, 1839.

Serpa Pinto, Alexandre Alberto da Rocha de. *Como eu atravessei a África.* Lisbon: Europa-América, 1980. 2 vols.

Silva Corrêa, Elias Aledandre. *História de Angola*. Lisbon: Ática, 1937, 2 vols.
Tams, Georg. *Visita às possessões portuguezas na costa occidental d'Africa: Com uma introducção e annotações*. Lisbon: Typographia da Revista, 1850.

Books and Articles

Abreu, Cesaltina. "'Xé, minina, não fala política!', cidadania no feminino: sine die?" In *Angola e as angolanas*. *Memória, sociedade e cultura*, edited by Selma Pantoja, Edvaldo Bergamo, and Ana Claudia da Silva, 167–86. São Paulo, SP: Intermeios, 2016.
Achebe, Nwando. *The Female King of Colonial Nigeria: Ahebi Ugbabe*. Bloomington: Indiana University Press, 2011.
Adelusi-Adeluyi, Ademide. "To Be Female & Free. Mapping Mobility & Emancipation in Lagos, Badagry & Abeokuta 1853-1865." In *African Women in the Atlantic World. Property, Vulnerability and Mobility, 1680–1880*, edited by Mariana P. Candido and Adam Jones, 131–47. Woodbridge: James Currey, 2019.
Alexandre, Valentim. "O liberalismo português e as colónias de África (1820-1839)." *Análise Social* 16, no. 61–62 (1980): 319–40
Alexandre, Valentim and Jill Dias. *O Império africano*. Lisbon: Estampa, 1998.
Alfagali, Crislayne. *Ferreiros e fundidores da Ilamba: uma história social da fabricação do ferro e da Real Fábrica de Nova Oeiras (Angola, segunda metade do século XVIII)*. Luanda: Fundação Agostinho Neto, 2018.
Alpers, Edward A. *Ivory and Slaves: Changing Pattern of International Trade in East Central Africa to the Later Nineteenth Century*. Berkeley: University of California Press, 1975.
Alveal, Carmen Margarida Oliveira. "Senhores de pequenos mundos: disputas por terras e os limites do poder local na América portuguesa." *Saeculum - Revista de História* 26 (2012): 63–77.
Alves, Rogéria Cristina. "Marfins africanos em trânsito: apontamentos sobre o comércio numa perspectiva atlântica (Angola, Benguela, Lisboa e Brasil), séculos XVIII-XIX." *Faces da História* 3, no. 2 (2016): 8–21.
Amadiume, Ifi. *Male Daughters, Female Husbands: Gender and Sex in an African Society*. London: Zed Books, 1987.
Amaral, Ilídio do. *O consulado de Paulo Dias de Novais: Angola no último quartel do século XVI e primeiro do século XVII*. Lisbon: Ministério da Ciências e da Tecnologia/ Instituto de Investigação Científica Tropical, 2000.
    O Reino do Congo, os Mbundu (ou Ambundos), o Reino dos "Ngola" (ou de Angola) e a presença portuguesa de finais do século XV a meados do século XVI. Lisbon: Ministério da Ciência e da Tecnologia/ Instituto de Investigação Científica Tropical, 1996.
Amorim, Maria Adelina. "A Real Fábrica de Ferro de Nova Oeiras. Angola, séc. XVIII." *CLIO – Revista do Centro de História da Universidade de Lisboa*, 9 (2003): 189–216
Anderson, Richard and Henry B. Lovejoy, eds. *Liberated Africans and the Abolition of the Slave Trade, 1807-1896*. Melton: Boydell & Brewer, 2020

Antunes, Cátia. "Free Agents and Formal Institutions in the Portuguese Empire: Towards a Framework of Analysis." *Portuguese Studies* 28, no. 2 (2012): 173–85.

Appadurai, Arjun. "Archive and Aspiration." In *Information Is Alive*, edited by Joke Brouwer, Arjen Mulder, and Susan Charlton, 14–25. Rotterdam: V2/ NAi Publishers, 2003.

"Number in the Colonial Imagination." In *Orientalism and the Postcolonial Predicament: Perspectives on South Asia*, edited by Carol A. Breckenridge and Peter van der Veer, 314–40. Philadelphia: University of Pennsylvania Press, 1993.

Appadurai, Arjun, ed. *The Social Life of Things: Commodities in Cultural Perspective*. New York: Cambridge University Press, 1988.

Araujo, Ana Lucia. *Reparations for Slavery and the Slave Trade. A Transnational and Comparative History*. New York, NY: Bloomsbury, 2017

"Black Purgatory: Enslaved Women's Resistance in Nineteenth-Century Rio Grande Do Sul, Brazil." *Slavery & Abolition* 36, no. 4 (2015): 568–85.

Austin, Gareth. *Labour, Land, and Capital in Ghana: From Slavery to Free Labour in Asante, 1807-1956*. Rochester, NY: University of Rochester Press, 2005.

Ball, Jeremy. *Angola's Colossal Lie: Forced Labor on a Sugar Plantation, 1913-1977*. Leiden; Boston: Brill, 2015.

Basu, Paul and Ferdinand De Jong. "Utopian Archives, Decolonial Affordances." *Social Anthropology* 24, no. 1 (2016): 5–19.

Bauer, Arnold J *Goods, Power, History: Latin America's Material Culture*. New York: Cambridge University Press, 2001.

Barrocas, Deolinda and Maria de Jesus Sousa. "As populações do hinterland de Benguela e a passagem das caravanas comerciais (1846-1860)." In *II Reunião Internacional de História da África*. Rio de Janeiro/ São Paulo, SP: CEA-USP/SDG-Marinha/CAPES, 1997.

Barry, Boubacar. *Senegambia and the Atlantic Slave Trade*. New York: Cambridge University Press, 1998.

Bay, Edna G. *Wives of the Leopard Gender, Politics, and Culture in the Kingdom of Dahomey*. Charlottesville: University of Virginia Press, 1998.

Becker, Felicitas. "Common Themes, Individual Voices: Memories of Slavery around a Former Slave Plantation in Mingoyo, Tanzania." edited by Alice Bellagamba, Sandra E. Greene, and Martin A. Klein, 71–87. New York: Cambridge University Press, 2013.

Bellagamba, Alice, Sandra E. Greene, and Martin A. Klein, eds. *African Voices on Slavery and the Slave Trade*. New York: Cambridge University Press, 2013.

Belmessous, Saliha. "Introduction: The Problem of Indigenous Claim Making in Colonial History." In *Native Claims: Indigenous Law against Empire, 1500-1920*, edited by Saliha Belmessous, 3–18. New York: Oxford University Press, 2012.

Belmessous, Saliha ed. *Native Claims: Indigenous Law against Empire, 1500-1920*. Oxford; New York: Oxford University Press, 2012.

Bennett, Herman Lee. *Africans In Colonial Mexico: Absolutism, Christianity, and Afro-Creole Consciousness, 1570-1640*. Bloomington: Indiana University Press, 2005.

Benton, Lauren. "Possessing Empire. Iberian Claims and Interpolity Law." In *Native Claims: Indigenous Law against Empire, 1500-1920*, edited by Saliha Belmessous, 19–40. New York: Oxford University Press, 2012.

A Search for Sovereignty. Law and Geography in European Empires, 1400-1900. New York: Cambridge University Press, 2010.

Law and Colonial Cultures Legal Regimes in World History, 1400-1900. New York: Cambridge University Press, 2002.

"The Legal Regime of the South Atlantic World, 1400-1750: Jurisdictional Complexity as Institutional Order." *Journal of World History* 11, no. 1 (2000): 27–56.

Berry, Sara. "Debating the Land Question in Africa." *Comparative Studies in Society and History* 44, no. 4 (2002): 638–68.

Chiefs Know Their Boundaries: Essays on Property, Power, and the Past in Asante, 1896-1996. Portsmouth, NH: Heinemann, 2001.

No Condition Is Permanent. The Social Dynamics of Agrarian Change in Sub-Saharan Africa. Madison: University of Wisconsin Press, 1993.

Bezerra, Nielson Rosa. *Escravidão, farinha e tráfico Atlântico: um novo olhar sobre as relações entre o Rio de Janeiro e Benguela (1790-1830)*. Rio de Janeiro: Fundação Biblioteca Nacional - Minc, 2010.

Bhandar, Brenna. *Colonial Lives of Property: Law, Land, and Racial Regimes of Ownership*. Durham: Duke University Press Books, 2018.

Birmingham, David. "A Question of Coffee: Black Enterprise in Angola." *Canadian Journal of African Studies* 16, no. 2 (1982): 343–46.

"The Coffee Barons of Cazengo." *Journal of African History* 19, no. 4 (1978): 523–38.

Boserup, Ester. *Woman's Role in Economic Development*. London: Allen & Unwin, 1970.

Bourdieu, Pierre. *Distinction: A Social Critique of the Judgement of Taste*. Cambridge, MA: Harvard University Press, 1984.

Bourdieu, Pierre and Abdelmalek Sayad. "Colonial Rule and Cultural Sabir." *Ethnography* 5, no. 4 (2004): 445–86.

Brito, Luciana da Cruz. *Temores da África: Segurança, legislação e população africana na Bahia oitocentista*. Salvador: UFBA, 2016.

Brizuela-Garcia, Esperanza. "Towards a Critical Interdisciplinarity? African History and the Reconstruction of Universal Narratives." *Rethinking History* 12, no. 3 (2008): 299–316.

Broadhead, Susan Herlin "Slave Wives, Free Sisters: Bakongo Women and Slavery C. 1700-1850," in *Women and Slavery in Africa*, ed. Claire C. Robertson and Martin A. Klein. Madison: University of Wisconsin Press, 1983.

Brooks, George E. "A Nhara of Guine-Bissau Region: Mãe Aurélia Correia." In *Women and Slavery in Africa*, edited by Claire C. Robertson and Martin A. Klein, 295–317. Madison: University of Wisconsin Press, 1983.

"The Signares of Saint-Louis and Gorée: Women Entrepreneur in Eighteenth Century Senegal." In *Women in Africa. Studies in Social and Economic Change*, edited by Nancy Hafkin and Edna Bay, 19–44. Stanford: Stanford University Press, 1976.

Bryant, Sherwin K. *Rivers of Gold, Lives of Bondage: Governing through Slavery in Colonial Quito*. Chapel Hill: University of North Carolina Press, 2013.

Burnard. Trevor G. *Mastery, Tyranny, and Desire: Thomas Thistlewood and His Slaves in the Anglo-Jamaican World*. Chapel Hill: University of North Carolina Press, 2004.

Byfield, Judith. "Women, Marriage, Divorce, and the Emerging Colonial State in Abeokuta (Nigeria), 1892-1904." In *"Wicked" Women and the Reconfiguration of Gender in Africa*, edited by Dorothy L. Hodgson and Sheryl A. McCurdy, 27–46. Portsmouth, NH: Heinemann, 2001.

Caldeira, Arlindo Manuel. *Escravos em Portugal. Das origens ao século XIX*. Lisbon: A Esfera dos Livros, 2017.

Escravos e traficantes no império português: O comércio negreiro português no Atlântico durante os séculos XV a XIX. Lisbon: Esfera do Livro, 2013.

Campbell, Gwyn, Suzanne Miers, and Joseph C. Miller, eds. *Child Slaves in the Modern World*. Athens: Ohio University Press, 2011.

Candido, Mariana P. "African Businesswomen in the Age of Second Slavery in Angola," In *The Atlantic and Africa: The Second Slavery and Beyond*, edited by Paul E. Lovejoy and Dale W. Tomich, 179–201. Albany: State University of New York Press, 2021.

"Des passeports pour la liberté? Conceptions raciales et déplacements de populations vers São Tomé (XIXe siècle)." In *Libres aprés les abolitions? Statuts et identités aux Amériques et en Afrique*, 71–92. Paris: Khartala, 2018.

"As comerciantes de Benguela na virada do século XVIII: o caso de dona Aguida Gonçalves." In *Laços Atlânticos: África e africanos durante a era do comércio transatlântico de escravos*, edited by Carlos Liberato, Mariana P. Candido, Paul E. Lovejoy, and Renée Soulodre-LaFrance, 231–58. Luanda: Ministério da Cultura/ Museu Nacional da Escravatura, 2017.

"Las donas y la trata de esclavos," In *Mujeres Africanas y Afrodescendientes em el Mundo Atlántico, siglos XVII al XIX*, edited by Maria Elisa Velázquez and Carolina González, 243–78. México City: DEAS-INAH, 2016.

"Women, Family, and Landed Property in Nineteenth-Century Benguela." *African Economic History* 43, no. 1 (2015): 136–61.

"Engendering West Central African History: The Role of Urban Women in Benguela in the Nineteenth Century." *History in Africa* 42 (2015): 7–36.

"Jagas e sobas no 'Reino de Benguela': Vassalagem e criação de novas categorias políticas e sociais no contexto de expansão portuguesa na África durante os séculos XVI e XVII." In *África. Históricas conectadas*, edited by Alexandre Vieira Ribeiro, Alexsander Lemos de Almeida Gebara, and Marina Berther, 39–76. Niterói: PPGHISTÓRIA - UFF, 2014.

"Conquest, Occupation, Colonialism and Exclusion: Land Disputes in Angola." In *Property Rights, Land and Territory in the European Overseas Empires*, edited by José Vicente Serrão, Bárbara Direito, Eugénia Rodrigues, and Susana Münch Miranda, 223–33. Lisbon: CEHC-IUL, 2014. http://hdl.handle.net/10071/2718.

"Trade Networks in Benguela, 1700-1850." In *Networks and Trans-Cultural Exchange Slave Trading in the South Atlantic, 1590-1867*, edited by David Richardson and Filipa Ribeiro da Silva, 143–63. Leiden: Brill, 2014.

An African Slaving Port and the Atlantic World: Benguela and Its Hinterland. New York: Cambridge University Press, 2013.

"O limite tênue entre a liberdade e escravidão em Benguela durante a era do comércio transatlântico." *Afro-Ásia* 47 (2013): 239–68.

"The Transatlantic Slave Trade and the Vulnerability of Free Blacks in Benguela, Angola, 1780-1830." In *Atlantic Biographies: Individuals and Peoples in the Atlantic World,* edited by Mark Meuwese and Jeffrey A. Fortin, 193–210. Leiden: Brill, 2013.

"Os agentes não europeus na comunidade mercantil de Benguela, c. 1760-1820." *Saeculum - Revista de História* 29 (2013): 97–123.

"Negociantes baianos no porto de Benguela: Redes comerciais unindo o Atlântico setencentista." In *África. Brasileiros e Portugueses, séculos XVI-XIX,* edited by Roberto Guedes, 67–91. Rio de Janeiro: Maud, 2013.

"Aguida Gonçalves da Silva, une dona à Benguela à fin du XVIIIe siècle." *Brésil(s). Sciences Humaines et Sociales* 1 (2012): 33–54.

"Concubinage and Slavery in Benguela, c. 1750-1850." In *Slavery in Africa and the Caribbean: A History of Enslavement and Identity since the Eighteenth Century,* edited by Olatunji Ojo and Nadine Hunt, 65–84. London: I.B. Tauris, 2012.

"African Freedom Suits and Portuguese Vassal Status: Legal Mechanisms for Fighting Enslavement in Benguela, Angola, 1800–1830." *Slavery & Abolition* 32, no. 3 (2011): 447–59.

Fronteras de esclavización: esclavitud, comercio e identidad en Benguela, 1780-1850. Mexico City: El Colegio de Mexico Press, 2011.

"Merchants and the Business of the Slave Trade at Benguela, 1750-1850." *African Economic History* 35 (2007): 1–30.

Candido, Mariana P. and Eugénia Rodrigues. "African Women's Access and Rights to Property in the Portuguese Empire." *African Economic History* 43, no. 1 (2015): 1–18.

Candido, Mariana P. and Vanessa S. Oliveira. "The Status of Enslaved Women in West Central Africa, 1800–1830." African Economic History 49, no. 1 (2021): 127–53.

Candido, Mariana P. and Vanessa Oliveira. "Slavery in Luanda and Benguela." *Oxford Research Encyclopedia in Africa History.* Oxford University Press, 2022. https://doi.org/10.1093/acrefore/9780190277734.013.869.

Candido, Mariana P. and Monica Lima, "Dona Florinda Joanes Gaspar." *Oxford Research Encyclopedia in Africa History.* Forthcoming.

Cardoso, Carlos Alberto Lopes. "A sociedade angolana do século XIX. Suas raízes, seus preconceitos, sua estrutura." *Ocidente. Revista Portuguesa Mensal* 83, no. 411–416 (1972): 146–67.

Carvalho, Flávia Maria de. *Sobas e homens do rei. Relações de poder e escravidão em Angola (séculos XVII e XVIII).* Maceió, Alagoas: Edufal, 2015.

Chalhoub, Sidney. *A força da escravidão.* São Paulo, SP: Companhia das Letras, 2012.

Visões da liberdade: Uma história das últimas décadas da escravidão na Corte. São Paulo, SP: Companhia das Letras, 2011.

Chambouleyron, Rafael. "Plantações, sesmarias e vilas. Uma reflexão sobre a ocupação da Amazônia seiscentista." *Nuevo Mundo Mundos Nuevos* (2006). https://doi.org/10.4000/nuevomundo.2260

Chanock, Martin. "A Peculiar Sharpness: An Essay on Property in the History of Customary Law in Colonial Africa." *The Journal of African History* 32, no. 01 (1991): 65–88.

"Paradigms, Policies and Property: A Review of the Customary Law of Land Tenure." In *Law in Colonial Africa*, edited by Kristin Mann and Richard L. Roberts, 61–84. Portsmouth, NH: Heinemann, 1991.

Law, Custom, and Social Order: The Colonial Experience in Malawi and Zambia. New York: Cambridge University Press, 1985.

Chaudhuri, Nupur, Sherry J Katz, and Mary Elizabeth Perry. *Contesting Archives: Finding Women in the Sources.* Urbana: University of Illinois Press, 2010.

Childs, Gladwyn Murray. *Kinship & Character of the Ovimbundu: Being a Description of the Social Structure and Individual Development of the Ovimbundu of Angola, with Observations Concerning the Bearing on the Enterprise of Christian Missions of Certain Phases of the Life and Culture Described.* London: Witwatersrand University Press, 1969.

Clarence-Smith, W. G. "Capitalist Penetration among the Nyaneka of Southern Angola, 1760 to 1920s." *African Studies* 37, no. 2 (1978).

"Runaway Slaves and Social Bandits in Southern Angola, 1875–1913." *Slavery & Abolition* 6, no. 3 (1985): 23–33.

The Third Portuguese Empire, 1825-1975: A Study in Economic Imperialism. Manchester: Manchester University Press, 1985.

Slaves, Peasants, and Capitalists in Southern Angola, 1840-1926. New York: Cambridge University Press, 1979.

Coghe, Samuël. "Reordering Colonial Society: Model Villages and Social Planning in Rural Angola, 1920–1945." *Journal of Contemporary History* 52, no. 1 (2017): 16–44.

"The Problem of Freedom in a Mid-Nineteenth-Century Atlantic Slave Society: The Liberated Africans of the Anglo-Portuguese Mixed Commission in Luanda (1844–1870)." *Slavery & Abolition* 33, no. 3 (2012): 479–500.

Cole, Jennifer. "The Love of Jesus Never Disappoints: Reconstituting Female Personhood in Urban Madagascar 1." *Journal of Religion in Africa* 42, no. 4 (2012): 384–407.

Comaroff, Jean and John L. Comaroff. "Goodly Beasts, Beastly Goods: Cattle and Commodities in a South African Context." *American Ethnologist* 17, no. 2 (1990): 195–216.

Congost, Rosa. "Property Rights and Historical Analysis: What Rights? What History?" *Past & Present* 181, no. 1 (2003): 73–106.

Cooper, Frederick and Ann Laura Stoler, eds. "Between Metrople and Colony. Rethinking a Research Agenda." In *Tensions of Empire. Colonial Cultures in a Bourgeois World*, 1–56. Berkeley, CA: University of California Press, 1997.

Cooper, Frederick, Thomas C. Holt, and Rebecca J Scott, eds. *Beyond Slavery: Explorations of Race, Labor, and Citizenship in Postemancipation Societies.* Chapel Hill, NC: University of North Carolina Press, 2000.

Corrado, Jacopo. "The Fall of a Creole Elite? Angola at the Turn of the Twentieth Century: The Decline of the Euro-African Urban Community." *Luso-Brazilian Review* 47, no. 2 (2010): 100–119.

Couto, Carlos. *Os capitães-mores em Angola no século XVIII.* Luanda: Instituto de Investigação Científica de Angola, 1972.

Craavens, Mary Caroline. "Manumission and the Life Cycle of a Contained Population: The VOC Lodge Slaves at the Cape of Good Hope, 1680-1730." In *Paths to Freedom: Manumission in the Atlantic World,* edited by Rosemary Brana-Shute and Randy J. Sparks, 99–119. Columbia: University of South Carolina Press, 2009.

Crais, Clifton. *Poverty, War, and Violence in South Africa.* New York: Cambridge University Press, 2011.

"Custom and the Politics of Sovereignty in South Africa." *Journal of Social History* 39, no. 3 (2006): 721–40.

"Chiefs and Bureaucrats in the Making of Empire: A Drama from the Transkei, South Africa, October 1880." *American Historical Review* 108, no. 4 (2003): 1034–56.

Crais, Clifton and Pamela Scully. *Sara Baartman and the Hottentot Venus: A Ghost Story and a Biography.* Princeton, NJ: Princeton University Press, 2010.

Cruz e Silva, Rosa. "The Saga of Kakonda and Kilengues: Relations between Benguela and Its Interior, 1791-1796." In *Enslaving Connections: Changing Cultures of Africa and Brazil during the Era of the Slavery,* edited by José C. Curto and Paul E. Lovejoy, 245–59. Amherst: Humanity Books, 2004.

Cunha, Anabela. "Degredo para Angola: Sentença de morte lenta." *Locus (Juiz de Fora)* 18, no. 2 (2013): 87–104.

Cunha, J.M. da Silva. *O trabalho indígena: estudo de direito colonial.* Lisbon: Agência Geral das Colónias, 1956.

Cunha, Mônica Maria da Pádua Souto da, Marcus Joaquim Carvalho, and Mateus Samico Simon. "Liberdade partida em 1/4: Alforria e pecúlio em Pernambuco sob a Lei do Ventre-Livre." *Documentação e Memória/ TJPE* 2, no. 4 (2011): 11–28.

Curtin, Patricia Romero. "Laboratory for the Oral History of Slavery: The Island of Lamu on the Kenya Coast." *The American Historical Review* 88, no. 4 (1983): 858–82.

Curto, José C. "Experiences of Enslavement in West Central Africa." *Histoire Sociale/Social History* 41, no. 82 (2008): 381–415.

"Struggling against Enslavement: The Case of José Manuel in Benguela, 1816–1820." *Canadian Journal of African Studies* 39, no. 1 (2005): 96–122.

"Resistência à escravidão na África: O caso dos escravos fugitivos recapturados em Angola, 1846-1876." *Afro-Ásia,* 33 (2005): 67–86.

Álcool e escravos: o comércio Luso-Brasileiro do álcool em Mpinda, Luanda e Benguela durante o tráfico atlântico de escravos (c. 1480-1830) e o seu impacto nas sociedades da África Central Ocidental. Lisbon: Vulgata, 2002.

"Un butin illégitime: Razzias d'esclaves et relations luso-africaines dans la région des fleuves Kwanza et Kwango en 1805." In *Déraison, Esclavage et Droit: Les fondements idéologiques et juridiques de la traite négrière et de l'esclavage*, edited by Isabel de Castro Henriques and Louis Sala-Molins, 315–27. Paris: Unesco, 2002.

Daddi Addoun, Yacine. "'So That God Frees the Former Masters from Hell Fire:' Salvation through Manumission in Ottoman Algeria." In *Crossing Memories. Slavery and African Diaspora*, edited by Ana Lucia Araujo, Mariana P. Candido, and Paul E. Lovejoy, 237–59. Trenton, NJ: Africa World Press, 2011.

Dantas, Mariana L. R. "Miners, Farmers, and Market People: Women of African Descent and the Colonial Economy in Minas Gerais." *African Economic History* 43 (2015): 82–108.

"Succession of Property, Sales of Meação, and the Economic Empowerment of Widows of African Descent in Colonial Minas Gerais, Brazil." *Journal of Family History* 39, no. 3 (2014): 222–38.

Davidson, Basil. "Slaves or Captives? Some Notes on Fantasy and Fact." In *Slavery and Muslim Society in Africa: The Institution in Saharan and Sudanic Africa, and the Trans-Saharan Trade*, edited by Allan George Barnard Fisher, 54–73. London: C. Hurst, 1970.

De Luna, Kathryn M. *Collecting Food, Cultivating People: Subsistence and Society in Central Africa*. New Haven, CT: Yale University Press, 2016.

De Luna, Kathryn M. and Jeffrey B. Fleisher. *Speaking with Substance. Methods of Language and Materials in African History*. Cham, Switzerland: Springer, 2019.

Delgado, Ralph. *A Famosa e Histórica Benguela: Catálogo dos Governadores, 1779-1940*. Lisbon: Edição Cosmos, 1940.

Dery, David. "'Papereality' and Learning in Bureaucratic Organizations." *Administration & Society* 29, no. 6 (1998): 677–89.

Dias, Jill R. "Mudanças nos padrões de poder no 'hinterland' de Luanda. O impacto da colonização sobre os Mbundu (c. 1845-1920)." *Penélope* 14 (1994): 43–91.

Dias Paes, Mariana Armond. "Shared Atlantic Legal Culture: The Case of a Freedom Suit in Benguela." *Atlantic Studies* 17, no. 3 (2020): 419–440.

Escravidão e direito. O estatuto jurídico dos escravos no Brasil oitocentista (1860-1888). São Paulo, SP: Alameda, 2019.

"Terras em contenda: Circulação e produção de normatividades em conflitos agrários no Brasil império." *Revista da Faculdade de Direito UFMG* 74 (2019): 379–406.

"Legal Files and Empires: Form and Materiality of the Benguela District Court Documents." *Administory* 4 (2019): 53–70

Diptee, Audra. *From Africa to Jamaica: The Making of an Atlantic Slave Society, 1775-1807*. Gainsville: University Press of Florida, 2012.

Direito, Bárbara. "African Access to Land in Early Twentieth Century Portuguese Colonial Thought." In *Property Rights, Land and Territory in the European Overseas Empires*, edited by José Vicente Serrão, Bárbara Direito, Eugénia Rodrigues, and Susana Münch Miranda, 256–63. Lisbon: CEHC-IUL, 2014.

Domingues da Silva, Daniel B. *The Atlantic Slave Trade from West Central Africa, 1780–1867*. Cambridge: Cambridge University Press, 2017.

The Supply of Slaves from Luanda, 1768–1806: Records of Anselmo Da Fonseca Coutinho." *African Economic History* 38, no. 1 (2009): 53–76.

Domingues da Silva, Daniel B., and David Eltis. "The Slave Trade to Pernambuco, 1561-1851." In *Extending the Frontiers: Essays on the New Transatlantic Slave Trade Database*. New Haven, CT: Yale University Press, 2008.

Doss, Cheryl, Ruth Meinzen-Dick, and Allan Bomuhangi. "Who Owns the Land? Perspectives from Rural Ugandans and Implications for Large-Scale Land Acquisitions." *Feminist Economics* 20, no. 1 (2014): 76–100.

Drescher, Seymour. *Abolition: A History of Slavery and Antislavery*. New York: Cambridge University Press, 2009.

Estermann, R. P. Ch. "Quelques observations sur les Bochimans !Kung de l'Angola Méridionale." *Anthropos* 41/44, no. 4/6 (1946): 711–22.

Everts, Natalie. "A Motley Company: Differing Identities among Euro-Africans in Eighteenth-Century Elmina." In *Brokers of Change: Atlantic Commerce and Cultures in Precolonial Western Africa*, edited by Toby Green, 53–69. Oxford: The British Academy/ Oxford Universty Press, 2012.

Fage, J. D. "Slaves and Society in Western Africa, c. 1445- c.1700." *Journal of African History* 21, no. 3 (1980): 289–310.

Farias, Juliana Barreto. "'Diz a preta mina...': cores e categorias sociais nos processos de divórcio abertos por africanas ocidentais, Rio de Janeiro, século XIX." *Estudos Ibero-Americanos* 44, no. 3 (2018): 470–83.

Feinberg, Harvey M. *Africans and Europeans in West Africa: Elminans and Dutchmen on the Gold Coast during the Eighteenth Century*. Philadelphia, PA: American Philosophical Society, 1989.

Felner, Alfredo de. Angola. *Apontamentos sobre a colonização dos planaltos e litoral do Sul de Angola. Extraídos de documentos históricos*. 3 vols. Lisboa: Agência-Geral do Ultramar, 1940.

Ferreira, Roquinaldo. *The Cost of Freedom: Central Africa in the Age of Global Abolition (c. 1820-1870)*. Princeton, NJ: Princeton University Press, forthcoming.

"Slave Flights and Runaway Communities in Angola (Seventeenth to Nineteenth Centuries)." *Anos 90* 21, no. 40 (2014): 65–90

"Abolicionismo versus colonialismo: Rupturas e continuidades em Angola (século XIX)." In *África. Brasileiros e Portugueses, séculos XVI-XIX*, edited by Roberto Guedes, 95–112. Rio de Janeiro: Mauad, 2013.

"Biografia como história social: O clã Ferreira Gomes e os mundos da escravização no Atlântico Sul." *Varia História* 29, no. 51 (2013): 679–719.

"Slavery and the Social and Cultural Landscape of Luanda." In *The Black Urban Atlantic in the Age of the Slave Trade*, edited by Jorge Cañizares-Esguerra, Matt Childs, and James Sidbury, 185–205. Philadelphia: University of Pennsylvania Press, 2013.

"Echoes of the Atlantic: Benguela (Angola) and Brazilian Independence." In *Biography and the Black Atlantic*, edited by Lisa A. Lindsay and John Wood Sweet, 224–47. Philadelphia: University of Pennsylvania Press, 2013.

"Agricultural Enterprise and Unfree Labour in Nineteenth Century Angola." In *Commercial Agriculture, the Slave Trade and Slavery in Atlantic Africa*, edited by Robin Law, Suzanne Schwarz, and Silke Strickrodt, 225–42. Woodbridge: James Currey, 2013.

Cross-Cultural Exchange in the Atlantic World: Angola and Brazil during the Era of the Slave Trade. New York: Cambridge University Press, 2012.

Dos sertões ao Atlântico: tráfico ilegal de escravos e comércio lícito em Angola 1830-1860. Luanda: Kilombelombe, 2012.

"Slaving and Resistance to Slaving in West Central Africa." In *The Cambridge World History of Slavery*, edited by David Eltis and Stanley L. Engerman, 3:111–31. Cambridge: Cambridge University Press, 2011.

"A supressão do tráfico de escravos em Angola (ca. 1830-ca. 1860)." *História Unisinos* 15, no. 1 (2011): 3–13.

"The Suppression of the Slave Trade and Slave Departures from Angola, 1830-1860s." In *Extending the Frontiers: Essays on the New Transatlantic Slave Trade Database*, edited by David Eltis and David Richardson, 313–34. New Haven, CT: Yale University Press, 2008.

"Atlantic Microhistories: Mobility, Personal Ties, and Slaving in the Black Atlantic World (Angola and Brazil)." In *Cultures of the Lusophone Black Atlantic*, edited by Nancy Prisci Naro, Ro Sansi-Roca, and D. Treece, 1st ed., 99–127. New York: Palgrave Macmillan, 2007.

"Dinâmica do comércio intracolonial: gerebitas, panos asiáticos e guerra no tráfico angolano de escravos, século XVIII." In *O Antigo Regime nos Trópicos: A Dinâmica imperial portuguesa, séculos XVI-XVIII*, edited by João Luís Ribe Fragoso, Maria de Fátima Gouvêa, and Maria Fernanda Bicalho, 339–78. Rio de Janeiro: Civilização Brasileira, 2001.

"Escravidão e revoltas de escravos em Angola (1830-1860)." *Afro-Ásia* 21–22 (1998): 9–44.

Ferreira, Roquinaldo and Roberto Guedes. "Apagando a nota que diz escrava: Efigênia da Silva, os batismos, os compadrios, os nomes, as cabeças, as crias, o tráfico, a escravidão e a liberdade (Luanda, c. 1770-c. 1811)." *Almanak* 26 (2020), 1–57.

Ferreira, Aurora da Fonseca. *A Kisama em Angola do século XVI ao início do século XX. Autonimia, ocupação e resistência.* 2 vols. Luanda: Kilombelombe, 2012.

Figueiroa-Rêgo, João and Fernanda Olival. "'Cor da pele, distinções e cargos: Portugal e espaços atlânticos portugueses (séculos XVI a XVIII).'" *Tempo* 16, no. 30 (2011): 115–45.

Fonseca Ferreira, Aurora da. "Ocupação de terras: Problemas de ontem e hoje." *Cadernos de Estudos Sociais* 1 (2005): 35–99.

Freudenthal, Aida. *Arimos e fazendas: A transição agrária em Angola, 1850-1880.* Luanda: Chá de Caxinde, 2005.

"A questão da terra em Angola. Ontem e Hoje." *Cadernos de Estudos Sociais* 1 (2005): 15–33.

"Os quilombos de Angola no século XIX: a recusa da escravidão." *Estudos Afro-Asiáticos* 32 (1997): 109–34.

Fromont, Cécile. *The Art of Conversion: Christian Visual Culture in the Kingdom of Kongo.* Chapel Hill: University of North Carolina Press, 2014.

Fuentes, Marisa J. *Dispossessed Lives: Enslaved Women, Violence, and the Archive.* Philadelphia: University of Pennsylvania Press, 2016.

Garnsey, Peter. *Thinking about Property: From Antiquity to the Age of Revolution.* New York, Cambridge: Cambridge University Press, 2007.

Gluckman, Max. *The Ideas in Barotse Jurisprudence.* New Haven, CT: Yale University Press, 1965.

Glymph, Thavolia. *Out of the House of Bondage: The Transformation of the Plantation Household.* New York: Cambridge University Press, 2008.

Goheen, Miriam. *Men Own the Fields, Women Own the Crops: Gender and Power in the Cameroon Grassfields.* Madison: University of Wisconsin Press, 1996.

Gomes, Armindo Jaime. *As civilizações lacustres das margens do Kupololo.* Benguela: KAT, 2007.

Goody, Jack. *Technology, Tradition, and the State in Africa.* London: Oxford University Press, 1971.

Death, Property and the Ancestors. Stanford: Stanford University Press, 1962.

Gordon, David M. *Invisible Agents : Spirits in a Central African History.* Athens: Ohio University Press, 2012.

Grant, Kevin. *A Civilised Savagery: Britain And The New Slaveries In Africa, 1884-1926.* Routledge Chapman & Hall, 2005.

Grassi, Aharon. "Changing Paths and Histories. Mapping Precolonial Connections in Africa". *Radical History Review* 131 (2018): 169–75

Grassi, Aharon and Jesse Salah Ovadia. "Trajectories of Large-Scale Land Acquisition Dynamics in Angola: Diversity, Histories, and Implications for the Political Economy of Development in Africa." *Land Use Policy* 67 (2017): 115–25.

Graubart, Karen B. "Shifting Landscape. Heterogenous Conceptions of Land Use and Tenure in the Lima Valley." *Colonial Latin American Review* 26, no. 1 (2017): 62–84.

"Learning from the Qadi: The Jurisdiction of Local Rule in the Early Colonial Andes." *Hispanic American Historical Review* 95, no. 2 (2015): 195–228.

"The Limits of Gender Domination. Women, the Law, and Political Crisis in Quito, 1765–1830." *Colonial Latin American Review* 24, no. 1 (2015): 114–16.

With Our Labor and Sweat: Indigenous Women and the Formation of Colonial Society in Peru, 1550-1700. Stanford: Stanford University Press, 2007.

Green, Toby. *A Fistful of Shells: West Africa from the Rise of the Slave Trade to the Age of Revolution.* Chicago: Chicago University Press, 2019.

"Baculamento or Encomienda? Legal Pluralisms and the Contestation of Power in the Pan-Atlantic World of the Sixteen and Seventeenth Centuries." *Journal of Global Slavery* 2 (2017): 310–36.

Brokers of Change: Atlantic Commerce and Cultures in Precolonial Western Africa. Oxford: The British Academy/ Oxford Universty Press, 2012.

The Rise of the Trans-Atlantic Slave Trade in Western Africa, 1300-1589. New York: Cambridge University Press, 2012.

Greene, Sandra E. "Family Concerns: Gender and Ethnicity in Pre-Colonial West Africa." *International Review of Social History* 44 (1999): 15–31.

Slave Owners of West Africa: Decision Making in the Age of Abolition.
Bloomington, IN: Indiana University Press, 2017.

Grinberg, Keila. "Re-escravização, direitos e justiças no Brasil do século XIX."
In *Direitos e Justiças - ensaios de história social*, edited by Silvia Hunold Lara
and Joseli Maria Nunes Mendonça, 101–28. Campinas, SP: Editora da
Unicamp, 2006.

Guran, Milton. *Agudás. Os brasileiros do Benim.* Rio de Janeiro, RJ: Nova Fronteira,
2000.

Guyer, Jane I. "Wealth in People, Wealth in Things – Introduction." *The Journal
of African History* 36, no. 01 (2009): 83–90.

"Wealth in People and Self-Realization in Equatorial Africa." *Man* 28, no. 2
(1993): 243–65

"Female Farming in Anthropology and African History." In *Gender at the
Crossroads of Knowledge: Feminist Anthropology in the Postmodern Era*, edited
by Micaela di Leonardo, 257–77. Berkeley: University of California Press,
1991.

Guyer, Jane I., and Samuel M. Eno Belinga. "Wealth in People as Wealth in
Knowledge: *Accumulation and Composition in Equatorial Africa.*" *Journal of
African History* 36, no. 1 (1995): 91–120.

Hambly, Wilfrid Dyson. *Ovimbundu of Angola.* Chicago: Field Museum of
Natural History, 1934.

Hanger, Kimberly S. "Landlords, Shopkeepers, Farmers, and Slave-Owners:
Free Black Female Property-Holders in Colonial New Orleans." In *Beyond
Bondage: Free Women of Color in the Americas*, 219–36. Urbana: University of
Illinois Press, 2004.

Hanretta, Sean. "Women, Marginality and the Zulu State: Women's Institutions
and Power in the Early Nineteenth Century." *The Journal of African History*
39, no. 3 (1998): 389–415.

Hanson, Holly Elisabeth. *Landed Obligation: The Practice of Power in Buganda.*
Portsmouth, NH: Heinemann, 2003.

Harms, Robert. *Games Against Nature: An Eco-Cultural History of the Nunu of
Equatorial Africa.* New York, NY: Cambridge University Press, 1999.

Hartman, Saidiya. "Venus in Two Acts." *Small Axe* 12, no. 2 (2008): 1–14.

Havik, Philip J. "Gender, Land, and Trade: Women's Agency and Colonial
Change in Portuguese Guinea (West Africa)." *African Economic History* 43,
no. 1 (2016): 162–95.

*Silences and Soundbites: The Gendered Dynamics of Trade and Brokerage in the Pre-
Colonial Guinea Bissau Region.* Munster: LIT Verlag Münster, 2004.

Hawkins, Sean. *Writing and Colonialism in Northern Ghana: The Encounter Between
the LoDagaa and "the World on Paper."* Toronto, ON: University of Toronto
Press, 2002.

Hay, Margaret Jean and Marcia Wright, eds. *African Women & the Law: Historical
Perspectives.* Boston, MA: Boston University Press, 1982.

Heintze, Beatrix. "Hidden Transfers: Luso-Africans as European Explorers'
Experts in Nineteenth-Century West-Central Africa." In *The Power of
Doubt: Essays in Honor of David Henige*, edited by Paul Landau, 19–40.
Madison: Parallel Press, 2011.

"Long-Distance Caravans and Communication beyond the Kwango (c. 1850-1890)." In *Angola on the Move: Transport Routes, Communications, and History*, edited by Beatrix Heintze and Achim von Oppen, 144–62. Frankfurt am Main: Lembeck, 2008.

Angola nos séculos XVI e XVII. Estudo sobre fontes, métodos e história. Luanda: Kilombelombe, 2007.

"A Lusofonia no interior da África Central na era pré-colonial. Um contributo para a sua história e compreensão na actualidade." *Cadernos de Estudos Africanos* 6/7 (2005): 179–207.

Pioneiros Africanos: caravanas de carregadores na África Centro-Ocidental: entre 1850 e 1890. Lisbon: Caminho, 2004.

"Angola under Portuguese Rule: How It All Began." In *Africae Monumenta. A apropriação da escrita pelos Africanos*, edited by Ana Paula Tavares and Catarina Madeira Santos, 1:535–59. Lisbon: IICT, 2002.

Asilo ameaçado: Oportunidades e consequências da fuga de escravos em Angola no século XVII. Museu Nacional da Escravatura, Instituto Nacional do Património Cultural, Ministério da Cultura, 1995.

"Ngonga a Mwiza: Um sobado angolano sob domino português no século XVII." *Revista Internacional de Estudos Africanos* 8–9 (1988): 221–34.

"Luso-African Feudalism in Angola? The Vassal Treaties of the Sixteenth to the Eighteenth Century." *Separata da Revista Portuguesa de História* 18 (1980): 111–31.

"The Angolan Vassal Tributes of the 17th Century." *Revista de História Económica e Social* 6 (1980): 57–78.

Henderson, Carol. "AKA: Sarah Baartman, The Hottentot Venus, and Black Women's Identity." *Women's Studies* 43, no. 7 (2014): 946–59.

Henriques, Isabel de Castro. *Percursos da modernidade em Angola: dinâmicas comerciais e transformações sociais no século XIX*. Lisbon: Instituto de Investigação Científica Tropical, 1997.

Herbert, Eugenia W. *Red Gold of Africa: Copper in Precolonial History and Culture*. Madison: University of Wisconsin Press, 2003.

Herzog, Tamar. *A Short History of European Law: The Last Two and a Half Millennia*. Cambridge, MA: Harvard University Press, 2018.

Frontiers of Possession. Spain, Portugal in Europe and the Americas. Cambridge, MA: Harvard University Press, 2015.

"Colonial Law and 'Native Customs': Indigenous Land Rights in Colonial Spanish America." *The Americas* 69, no. 3 (2013): 303–21.

Hespanha, António Manuel. "Luís de Molina e a escravização dos negros." *Análise Social* 35, no. 157 (2001): 937–60.

Hespanha, António Manuel and Catarina Madeira Santos. "Os poderes num Império Oceânico." In *História de Portugal, O Antigo Regime*, edited by António Manuel Hespanha, Vol. 4. Lisbon: Estampa, 1997.

Heywood, Linda M. *Njinga of Angola: Africa's Warrior Queen*. Cambridge, MA: Harvard University Press, 2017.

"Slavery and Its Transformation in the Kingdom of Kongo: 1491–1800." *The Journal of African History* 50, no. 01 (2009): 1–22.

"Portuguese into African: The Eighteenth Century Central African Background to Atlantic Creole Culture." In *Central Africans and Cultural Transformations in the American Diaspora*, edited by Linda Heywood, 91–114. New York, NY: Cambridge University Press, 2002.

"Slavery and Forced Labor in the Changing Political Economy of Central Angola, 1850-1949." In *The End of Slavery in Africa*, edited by Suzanne Miers and Richard Roberts, 415–35. Madison: Wisconsin University Press, 1988.

"The Growth and Decline of African Agriculture in Central Angola, 1890-1950." *Journal of Southern African Studies* 13, no. 3 (1987): 355–71.

Heywood, Linda M. and John K. Thornton. *Central Africans, Atlantic Creoles, and the Making of the Foundation of the Americas, 1585-1660*. New York, NY: Cambridge University Press, 2007.

Higgs, Catherine. *Chocolate Islands. Cocoa, Slavery, and Colonial Africa*. Athens: Ohio University Press, 2012.

Hilse Dwyer, Daisy. "Outside the Courts: Extra-Legal Strategies for the Subordination of Women." In *African Women & the Law: Historical Perspectives*, edited by Margaret Jean Hay and Marcia Wright, 90–109. Boston, MA: Boston University Press, 1982.

Hilton, Anne. *The Kingdom of Kongo*. Oxford; New York: Oxford University Press, 1985.

Hiribarren, Vincent. *A History of Borno: Trans-Saharan African Empire to Failing Nigerian State*. New York: Oxford University Press, 2017.

Hoehler-Fatton, Cynthia. *Women of Fire and Spirit. History, Faith, and Gender in Roho Religion in Western Kenya*. New York: Oxford University Press, 1996.

Holt, Thomas C. *The Problem of Freedom: Race, Labor, and Politics in Jamaica and Britain, 1832-1938*. Baltimore, MD: Johns Hopkins University Pres, 1992.

Honig, Lauren. "Selecting the State or Choosing the Chief? The Political Determinants of Smallholder Land Titling." *World Development* 100, no. Supplement C (2017): 94–107.

Hopkins, A. G. "The New Economic History of Africa." *The Journal of African History* 50, no. 2 (2009): 155–77.

"Property Rights and Empire Building: Britain's Annexation of Lagos, 1861." *The Journal of Economic History* 40, no. 4 (1980): 777–98

An Economic History of West Africa. New York: Columbia University Press, 1973.

Inikori, J. E. *Africans and the Industrial Revolution in England: A Study in International Trade and Economic Development*. Cambridge University Press, 2002.

Ipsen, Pernille. *Daughters of the Trade: Atlantic Slavers and Interracial Marriage on the Gold Coast*. Early Modern Americas. Philadelphia: University of Pennsylvania Press, 2015.

Jean-Baptiste, Rachel. *Conjugal Rights: Marriage, Sexuality, and Urban Life in Colonial Libreville, Gabon*. Athens: Ohio University Press, 2014.

Jerónimo, Miguel Bandeira, *Livros Brancos, and Almas Negras. A "missão civilizadora" do colonialismo português, c. 1870-1930*. Lisbon: Imprensa de Ciências Sociais, 2010.

"The 'Civilising Guild': Race and Labor in the Third Portuguese Empire, c. 1870-1930." In *Racism and Ethnic Relations in the Portuguese-Speaking World*, edited by Francisco Bethencourt and Adrian Pearce, 173–99. Oxford: Oxford University Press, 2012.

Johnson, Jessica Marie. "Markup Bodies: Black [Life] Studies and Slavery [Death] Studies at the Digital Crossroads." *Social Text* 36, no. 4 (2018): 57–79.

Jones, Adam. "Female Slave-Owners on the Gold Coast. Just a Matter of Money?" In *Slave Cultures and the Cultures of Slavery*, edited by Step Palmié, 100–111. Knoxville: University of Tennessee Press, 1995.

"Drink Deep, or Taste Not: Thoughts on the Use of Early European Records in the Study of African Material Culture." *History in Africa* 21 (1994): 349–70.

Jones, Hilary. "Women, Family & Daily Life in Senegal's Nineteenth-Century Atlantic Towns", in *African Women in the Atlantic World: Property, Vulnerability and Mobility, 1660-1880*, org. Mariana P. Candido e Adam Jones (Woodbridge: James Currey, 2019), 233–47

"Fugitive slaves and Christian evangelism in French West Africa: a protestant mission in late nineteenth-century Senegal". *Slavery & Abolition* 38, no 1 (2017): 76–94.

The Métis of Senegal: Urban Life and Politics in French West Africa. Bloomington: Indiana University Press, 2013.

Kagan Guthrie, Zachary. *Labor, Mobility, and Colonial Rule in Central Mozambique, 1940-1965*. Charlottesville: University of Virginia Press, 2018.

"Introduction: Histories of Mobility, Histories of Labor, Histories of Africa." *African Economic History* 44, no. 1 (2016): 1–17.

Keim, Curtis "Women and Slavery among the Mangbetu C. 1800-1910." In *Women and Slavery in Africa*, eds. Claire C. Robertson and Martin A. Klein (Madison, WI: University of Wisconsin Press, 1983), 144–159;

Keese, Alexander. "Forced Labour in the 'Gorgulho Years': Understanding Reform and Repression in Rural São Tomé e Príncipe, 1945–1953." *Itinerario* 38, no. 1 (2014): 103–24

Kelly, Jill E. *To Swim with Crocodiles. Land, Violence and Belonging in South Africa, 1800-1996*. Lansing: Michigan State University Press, 2018.

Kinsman, Margaret. "'Beasts of Burden': The Subordination of Southern Tswana Women, ca. 1800-1840." *Journal of Southern African Studies* 10, no. 1 (1983): 39–54.

Klein, Martin A. "African Traditions of Servitude and the Evolution of African Society." *Ab Imperio* 2014, no. 2 (2014): 27–45.

Slavery and Colonial Rule in French West Africa. New York: Cambridge University Press, 1998.

"Studying the History of Those Who Would Rather Forget: Oral History and the Experience of Slavery." *History in Africa* 16 (1989): 209–17.

Klein, Martin A., Alice Bellagamba, and Sandra E. Greene, eds. *Bitter Legacy: African Slavery Past and Present*. Princeton: Markus Wiener, 2011.

Knight, Marie-Hélène. "Gorée au XVIIIe siècle du sol." *Revue française d'histoire d'outre-mer* 64, no. 234 (1977): 33–54.

Kobayashi, Kazuo. "Indian Textiles and Gum Arabic in the Lower Senegal River: Global Significance of Local Trade and Consumers in the Early Nineteenth Century." *African Economic History* 45, no. 2 (2017): 27–53.

Kodesh, Neil. *Beyond the Royal Gaze: Clanship and Public Healing in Buganda.* Charlottesville: University of Virginia Press, 2010.

Kreike, Emmanuel. *Re-Creating Eden: Land Use, Environment, and Society in Southern Angola and Northern Namibia.* Porstmouth, NH: Heinemann, 2004.

Kriger, Colleen E. "From Child Slave to Madam Esperance: One Woman's Career in the Anglo-African World, c. 1675-1707." In *African Women in the Atlantic World. Property, Vulnerability and Mobility, 1680-1880,* edited by Mariana P. Candido and Adam Jones, 171–89. Woodbridge: James Currey, 2019.

Making Money: Life, Death, and Early Modern Trade on Africa's Guinea Coast. Athens: Ohio University Press, 2017.

Cloth in West African History. Rowman Altamira, 2006.

"Mapping the History of Cotton Textile Production in Precolonial West Africa." *African Economic History* 33 (2005): 87–116.

Kuznesof, Elizabeth Anne. "Ethnic and Gender Influences on 'Spanish' Creole Society in Colonial Spanish America." *Colonial Latin American Review* 4, no. 1 (1995): 153–76.

Landers, Jane. "Founding Mothers: Female Rebels in Colonial New Granada and Spanish Florida." *Journal of African American History* 98, no. 1 (2013): 7–23.

Lahon, Didier. *O negro no coração do império: uma memória a resgatar: Séculos XV-XIX.* Lisbon: Ministério da Educação, 1999.

Lara, Silvia Hunold. *Fragmentos setecentistas: Escravidão, cultura e poder na América portuguesa.* São Paulo, SP: Companhia das Letras, 2007.

La Rue, George Michael. "Zeinab from Darfur: An Enslaved Woman and Her Self-Presentation in Egypt and the Sudan." In *African Voices of Slavery and the Slave Trade,* edited by Alice Bellagamba, Martin A. Klein, and Sandra E. Greene. New York: Cambridge University Press, 2013.

Law, Robin, ed. *From Slave Trade to "Legitimate" Commerce: The Commercial Transition in Nineteenth-Century West Africa.* Cambridge: Cambridge University Press, 1995.

Law, Robin, Suzanne Schwarz, and Silke Strickrodt. "Introduction." In *Commercial Agriculture, the Slave Trade and Slavery in Atlantic Africa,* edited by Robin Law, Suzanne Schwarz, and Silke Strickrodt, 1–27. Woodbridge: James Currey, 2013.

Lawrance, Benjamin N. *Amistad's Orphans: An Atlantic Story of Children, Slavery, and Smuggling.* New Haven: Yale University Press, 2015.

"'En proie à la fièvre du cacao': Land and Resource Conflict on an Ewe Frontier, 1922-1939." *African Economic History* 31 (2003): 135–81.

Lentz, Carola. *Land, Mobility, and Belonging in West Africa.* Bloomington: Indiana University Press, 2013.

Liberal Fernandes, Francisco. "O direito de propriedade em Angola: Aspectos gerais da lei de terras." *Boletim de Ciências Econômicas* 57, no. 2 (2014): 1463–78.

Libby, Douglas Cole, and Clotilde Andrade Paiva. "Manumission Practices in a Late Eighteenth-century Brazilian Slave Parish: São José D'El Rey in 1795." *Slavery & Abolition* 21, no. 1 (2000): 96–127.

Lofkrantz, Jennifer. "Idealism and Pragmatism: The Related Muslim West African Discourses on Identity, Captivity and Ransoming." *African Economic History* 42, no. 1 (2015): 87–107.

Lovejoy, Paul E. *Jihād in West Africa during the Age of Revolutions*. Athens: Ohio University Press, 2016.

"'Freedom Narratives' of Transatlantic Slavery." *Slavery & Abolition* 32, no. 1 (2011): 91–107.

"Pawnship, Debts, and 'Freedom' in Atlantic Africa during the Era of the Slave Trade: *A Reassessment*" 55, no. 1 (2014): 55–78.

Transformations in Slavery. New York: Cambridge University Press, 2000.

"Concubinage and the Status of Women Slaves in Early Colonial Northern Nigeria," *The Journal of African History* 29, no. 2 (1988): 245–266.

Salt of the Desert Sun: A History of Salt Production and Trade in the Central Sudan. Cambridge: Cambridge University Press, 1986.

Lovejoy, Paul E. and Toyin Falola, eds. *Pawnship, Slavery, and Colonialism in Africa*. Trenton, NJ: Africa World Press, 2003.

Lovejoy, Paul E. and Jan S. Hogendorn. *Slow Death for Slavery: The Course of Abolition in Northern Nigeria, 1897-1936*. Cambridge: Cambridge University Press, 1993.

Lovejoy, Paul E. and David Richardson. "Trust, Pawnship, and Atlantic History: The Institutional Foundations of the Old Calabar Slave Trade." *The American Historical Review* 104, no. 2 (1999): 333–55.

Lowe, Lisa. *The Intimacies of Four Continents*. Durham, NC: Duke University Press, 2015.

Lund, Christian. *Local Politics and the Dynamics of Property in Africa*. New York: Cambridge University Press, 2008.

Lydon, Ghislaine. *On Trans-Saharan Trails: Islamic Law, Trade Networks, and Cross-Cultural Exchange in Nineteenth-Century Western Africa*. Cambridge; New York: Cambridge University Press, 2009.

MacGaffey, Wyatt. "Crossing the River. Myth and Movement in Central Africa." In *Angola on the Move. Transport Routes, Communications and History*, edited by Beatrix Heintze and Achim von Oppen, 221–38. Frankfurt am Main: Verlag Otto Lembeck, 2008.

Kongo Political Culture: The Conceptual Challenge of the Particular. Bloomington, IN: Indiana University Press, 2000.

MacQuarrie, Helen and Andrew Pearson. "Prize Possessions: Transported Material Culture of the Post-Abolition Enslaved – New Evidence from St, Helena." *Slavery & Abolition* 37, no. 1 (2016): 45–72.

Madeira Santos, Catarina. "Esclavage africain et traite atlantique confrontés: transactions langagières et juridiques (à propos du tribunal de mucanos dans l'Angola des xviie et xviiie siècles)." *Brésil (s). Sciences Humaines et Sociales* 1 (2012): 127–48.

"Administrative Knowledge in a Colonial Context: Angola in the Eighteenth Century." *The British Journal for the History of Science* 43, no. 4 (2010): 539–56

"Luanda: A Colonial City between Africa and the Atlantic, Seventeenth and Eighteenth Century." In *Portuguese Colonial Cities in the Early Modern World*, edited by Liam M. Brockey, 249–70. New York: Ashgate Publishing, 2008.

"Escrever o poder. Os autos de vassalagem e a vulgarização da escrita entre as elites africanas Ndembu." *Revista de História*, no. 155 (2006): 81–95.

Malhi, Amrita. "Making Spaces, Making Subjects: Land, Enclosure and Islam in Colonial Malaya." *The Journal of Peasant Studies* 38, no. 4 (2011): 727–46.

Mamigonian, Beatriz. "In the Name of Freedom: Slave Trade Abolition, the Law and the Brazilian Branch of the African Emigration Scheme (Brazil–British West Indies, 1830s–1850s)." *Slavery & Abolition* 30, no. 1 (2009): 41–66.

"Conflicts over the Meanings of Freedom: The Liberated Africans' Struggle for Final Emancipation in Brazil, 1840-1860." In *Paths to Freedom: Manumission in the Atlantic World*, edited by Rosemary Brana-Shute and Randy J. Sparks, 235–63. Columbia: University of South Carolina Press, 2009.

Mann, Kristin. "African and European Initiatives in the Transformation of Land Tenure in Colonial Lagos (West Africa), 1840-1920." In *Native Claims: Indigenous Law against Empire, 1500-1920*, edited by Saliha Belmessous, 223–58. Oxford; New York: Oxford University Press, 2012

Slavery and the Birth of an African City: Lagos, 1760-1900 (Bloomington: Indiana University Press, 2010).

"Women, Landed Property, and the Accumulation of Wealth in Early Colonial Lagos." *Signs* 16, no. 4 (1991): 682–706.

Marrying Well: Marriage, Status, and Social Change among the Educated Elite in Colonial Lagos. New York: Cambridge University Press, 1985.

"Women's Right in Law and Practice: Marriage and Dispute Settlement in Colonial Lagos." In *African Women & the Law: Historical Perspectives*, edited by Margaret Jean Hay and Marcia Wright, 151–71. Boston: Boston University Press, 1982.

Mann, Kristin and Richard L. Roberts, eds. *Law in Colonial Africa*. Portsmouth, NH: Heinemann, 1991.

Mann, Kristin and Richard Roberts. "Law in Colonial Africa." In *Law in Colonial Africa*, edited by Kristin Mann and Richard L. Roberts, 3–58. Portsmouth, NH: Heinemann, 1991.

Manning, Patrick. *Slavery and African Life: Occidental, Oriental, and African Slave Trades*. New York: Cambridge University Press, 1990.

Slavery, Colonialism and Economic Growth in Dahomey, 1640-1960. Cambridge, MA: Cambridge University, 1982.

Manuel, Tuca. *Terra, a tradição e o poder. Contribuição ao estudo etno-histórico da Ganda*. Benguela: KAT - Aguedense, 2005.

Marques da Silva, Elisete. *Impactos da ocupação colonial nas sociedades rurais do sul de Angola*. Lisbon: Centro de Estudos Africanos ISCTE, 2003.

Martin, Phyllis. *The External Trade of the Loango Coast, 1576-1870; the Effects of Changing Commercial Relations on the Vili Kingdom of Loango*. Oxford: Clarendon Press, 1972.

Martin, Phyllis M. "Power, Cloth and Currency on the Loango Coast." *African Economic History* 15 (1986): 1–12.

"The Kingdom of Loango." In *Kongo Power and Majesty*, edited by Alisa Lagamma, 47–85. New York and New Haven: The Metropolitan Museum of Art and Yale University Press, 2015.

The External Trade of the Loango Coast, 1576-1870; the Effects of Changing Commercial Relations on the Vili Kingdom of Loango. Oxford: Clarendon Press, 1972.

Martin, Susan M. *Palm Oil and Protest: An Economic History of the Ngwa Region, South-Eastern Nigeria, 1800-1980.* New York: Cambridge University Press, 2006.

Martino, Enrique. "Panya: Economies of Deception and the Discontinuities of Indentured Labour Recruitment and the Slave Trade, Nigeria and Fernando Pó, 1890s-1940s." *African Economic History* 44, no. 1 (2016): 91–129.

Mattos, Hebe. "'Black Troops' and Hierarchies of Color in the Portuguese Atlantic World: The Case of Henrique Dias and His Black Regiment." *Luso-Brazilian Review* 45, no. 1 (2008): 6–29.

Das cores do silêncio: Os significados da liberdade no sudeste escravista: Brasil Século XIX. Rio de Janeiro: Arquivo Nacional, 1995.

Mbembe, Achille. *Critique of Black Reason.* Durham, NC: Duke University Press, 2017.

McMahon, Elisabeth. *Slavery and Emancipation in Islamic East Africa: From Honor to Respectability.* New York: Cambridge University Press, 2013.

Mendes, António de Almeida. "Africaines esclaves au Portugal: Dynamiques d'exclusion, d'intégration et d'assimilation à l'époque moderne (XVe-XVe siècles)." *Renaissance and Reformation* 31, no. 2 (2008): 45–65.

Meneses, Maria Paula G. "O 'indígena' africano e o colono 'europeu': a construção da diferença por processos legais." *e-cadernos CES.* 07 (2010). http://eces.revues.org/403.

Mendonça, Joseli Maria Nunes. *Entre a mão e os anéis: a lei dos sexagenários e os caminhos da abolição no Brasil.* Campinas, SP: Editora da Unicamp/ CECULT/ FAPESP, 1999.

Metcalf, Alida C. "Women and Means: Women and Family Property in Colonial Brazil." *Journal of Social History* 24, no. 2 (1990): 277–98.

Metcalf, George. "A Microcosm of Why Africans Sold Slaves: Akan Consumption Patterns in the 1770s." *The Journal of African History* 28, no. 3 (1987): 377–94.

Miers, Suzanne, and Igor Kopytoff, eds. *Slavery in Africa: Historical and Anthropological Perspectives.* Madison: University of Wisconsin Press, 1977.

Miers, Suzanne, and Igor Kopytoff. "African Slavery as an Institution of Marginality," 1–78, In: *Slavery in Africa: Historical and Anthropological Perspectives.* Madison: University of Wisconsin Press, 1977.

Mignolo, Walter D. "Epistemic Disobedience, Independent Thought and Decolonial Freedom." *Theory, Culture & Society* 26, no. 7–8 (2009): 159–81.

The Darker Side of the Renaissance: Literacy, Territoriality, and Colonization. Ann Arbor: University of Michigan Press, 1995.

Miller, Joseph C. "Women as Slaves and Owners of Slaves. Experiences from Africa, the Indian Ocean World, and the Early Atlantic." In *Women and Slavery.*, edited by Gwyn Campbell, Suzanne Miers, and Joseph C. Miller, 1:1–40. Athens: Ohio University Press, 2007.

"Central Africans during the Era of the Slave Trade, c. 1490s-1850s." In *Central Africans and Cultural Transformations in the American Diaspora*. Cambridge: Cambridge University Press, 2001.

Way of Death: Merchant Capitalism and the Angolan Slave Trade, 1730-1830. Madison: University of Wisconsin Press, 1988.

"Imports at Luanda, Angola: 1785-1832." In *Figuring African Trade: Proceedings of the Symposium on the Quantification and Structure of the Importa and Export and Long-Distance Trade of Africa in the Nineteenth Century, c. 1800-1913*, edited by Gerhard Liesegang, Helma Pasch, and Adam Jones, 162–244. Berlin: Dietrich Reimer Verlag, 1986.

"Imbangala Lineage Slavery." In *Slavery in Africa: Historical and Anthropological Perspectives*, edited by Suzann Miers and Igor Kopytoff, 205–33. Madison: University of Wisconsin Press, 1977.

Kings and Kinsmen: Early Mbundu States in Angola. Oxford: Clarendon Press, 1976.

Misevich, Philip and Kristin Mann, eds. *The Rise and Demise of Slavery and the Slave Trade in the Atlantic World*. Rochester, NY: University of Rochester Press, 2016.

Moore, Henrietta L. and Megan Vaughan. *Cutting down Trees: Gender, Nutrition, and Agricultural Change in the Northern Province of Zambia, 1890-1990*. Portmouth, NH: Heinemann, 1994.

Morgan, Jennifer L. "Archives and Histories of Racial Capitalism. An Afterword." *Social Text* 33, no. 4 (2015): 153–61.

Laboring Women: Reproduction and Gender in New World Slavery. Philadelphia: University of Pennsylvania Press, 2011.

Moser, Gerald. "Héli Chatelain: Pioneer of a National Language and Literature for Angola." *Research in African Languages* 14, no. 4 (1983): 516–37.

Mota, Maria Sarita. "Sesmarias e propriedade titulada da terra: O individualismo agrário na América Portuguesa." *Sæculum – Revista de História* 26, no. 1 (2012): 29–45.

Motta, Marcia Maria M. "Das discussões sobre posse e propriedade da terra na história moderna: velha e novas ilações". In *O direito às avessas:Por uma história social da propriedade*, organizado por Marcia Maria M. Motta e María Verónica Secreto, 19–45. Niteróis, RJ: EDUFF, 2011.

Direito à terra no Brasil. A gestação de um conflito, 1795-1824. São Paulo, SP: Alameda, 2009.

Mudimbe, V. Y. *The Invention of Africa. Gnosis, Philosophy, and the Order of Knowledge*. Bloomington: Indiana University Press, 1988.

Naanen, Benedict B. B. "'Itinerant Gold Mines': Prostitution in the Cross River Basin of Nigeria, 1930-1950." *African Studies Review* 34, no. 2 (1991): 57–79.

Nafafé, José Lingna. *Lourenço da Silva Mendonça and the,Black Atlantic Abolitionist Movement in the Seventeenth Century*. Cambridge: Cambridge University Press, 2022.

Nascimento Augusto. "As fronteiras da nação e das raças em São Tomé e Príncipe: São-tomenses, Europeus e Angolas nos primeiros decênios de Novecentos." *Varia História* 29, no. 51 (2013): 721–43.

Nascimento, Augusto, and Alfredo Gomes Dias. "A Importação de libertos em São Tomé no Terceiro Quartel de Oitocentos." *Revista de História Económica e Social* 25 (1989): 1–70.

Neto, Maria da Conceição. "A República no seu estado colonial: Combater a escravatura, estabelecer o 'indigenato.'" *Ler História* 59 (2010): 205–22.

"De escravos a serviçais, de serviçais a contratados: Omissões, percepções e equívocos na história do trabalho africano na Angola colonial." *Cadernos de Estudos Africanos*, 33 (2017): 107–29.

Newton-King, Susan. *Masters and Servants on the Cape Eastern Frontier, 1760-1803*. Cambridge: Cambridge University Press, 1999.

Nogueira da Silva, Cristina. *A construção jurídica dos territórios ultramarinos portugueses no século XIX. Modelos, doutrinas e leis*. Lisbon: Imprensa da Ciências Sociais, 2017.

Constitucionalismo e império: a cidadania no ultramar português. Lisbon: Almedina, 2009.

Nogueira da Silva, Cristina, and Keila Grinberg. "Soil Free from Slaves: Slave Law in Late Eighteenth- and Early Nineteenth-Century Portugal." *Slavery & Abolition* 32, no. 3 (2011): 431–46.

Nwokeji, Ugo. *The Slave Trade and Culture in the Bight of Biafra: An African Society in the Atlantic World*. New York: Cambridge University Press, 2010.

Ojo, Olatunji. "'Èmú' (Àmúyá): The Yoruba Institution of Panyarring or Seizure for Debt." *African Economic History* 35 (2007): 31–58.

"The Atlantic Slave Trade and Local Ethics of Slavery in Yorubaland." *African Economic History* 41 (2013): 73–100.

Oliveira, Vanessa S. *Slave Trade and Abolition. Gender, Commerce and Economic Transition in Luanda*. Madison: University of Wisconsin Press, 2021.

"Spouses and Commercial Partners: Immigrant Men and Locally Born Women in Luanda (1831-1859)." In *African Women in the Atlantic World. Property, Vulnerability and Mobility, 1680-1880*, edited by Mariana P. Candido and Adam Jones, 217–32. Woodbridge: James Currey, 2019

"Donas, pretas livres e escravas em Luanda (Séc. XIX)." *Estudos Ibero-Americanos* 44, no. 3 (2018): 447–56.

"Slavery and the Forgotten Women Slave Owners of Luanda (1846-1876)." In *Slavery, Memory and Citizenship*, edited by Paul E. Lovejoy and Vanessa S. Oliveira, 129–47. Trenton, NJ: Africa World Press, 2016.

"Gender, Foodstuff Production and Trade in Late-Eighteenth Century Luanda." *African Economic History* 43, no. 1 (2015): 57–81.

"The Gendered Dimension of Trade: Female Traders in Nineteenth Century Luanda." *Portuguese Studies Review* 23, no. 2 (2015): 93–121.

"Trabalho escravo e ocupações urbanas em Luanda na segunda metade do século XIX." In *Em torno de Angola. Narrativas, identidades e conexões atlânticas*, 265–67. São Paulo, SP: Intermeios, 2014.

"Notas preliminares sobre punição de escravos em Luanda (século XIX)." In *O colonialismo português - novos rumos da historiografia dos PALOP*, edited by Ana Cristina Roque and Maria Manuel Torrão, 155–76. Porto: Húmuss, 2013.

Pacheco, C. "Leituras e bibliotecas em Angola na primeira metade do século XIX." *Locus (Juiz de Fora)* 6, no. 2 (2000): 21–41.

Arsénio Pompílio Pompeu de Carpo: uma vida de luta contra as prepotências do poder colonial em Angola, 1992.

José da Silva Ferreira: O homem e a sua época. Luanda: União dos escritores angolanos, 1990.

Pagden, Anthony. "Law, Colonization, Legitimation, and the European Background." In *The Cambridge History of Law in America*, edited by Michael Grossberg, Christopher Tomlins, Michael Grossberg, and Christopher Tomlins, 1–31. Cambridge: Cambridge University Press, 2008.

Paiva, Eduardo França. *Dar nome ao novo: Uma história lexical da Ibero-América entre os séculos XVI e XVIII (as dinâmicas de mestiçagens e o mundo do trabalho)*. Belo Horizonte: Autêntica, 2017.

Pantoja, Selma. "Gênero e comércio: As traficantes de escravos na Região de Angola." *Travessias* 4/5 (2004): 79–97.

"Donas de 'arimos': um negócio feminino no abastecimento de gêneros alimentícios em Luanda (séculos XVIII e XIX)." In *Entre Áfricas e Brasis*, edited by Selma Pantoja, 35–49. Brasilia: Paralelo, 2001.

"Quintandas e quitandeiras: História e deslocamento na nova lógica do espaço em Luanda." In *África e a Instalação do Sistema Colonial (c. 1885-c. 1935): Actas da III Reunião Internacional de História de África*, edited by Maria Emília Madeira Santos, 175–86. Lisbon: Centro de Estudos de História e Cartografia Antiga, 2000.

Parker, John. *Making the Town: Ga State and Society in Early Colonial Accra*. Portsmouth, NH: Heinemann, 2000.

Parreira, Adriano. *Economia e sociedade em Angola na época da Rainha Jinga (Século XVII)*. Lisbon: Editorial Estampa, 1997.

Pels, Peter. "The Anthropology of Colonialism: Culture, History, and the Emergence of Western Governmentality." *Annual Review of Anthropology* 26 (1997): 163–83.

Peters, Beverly L., and John E. Peters. "Women and Land Tenure Dynamics in Pre-Colonial, Colonial, and Post-Colonial Zimbabwe." *Journal of Public and International Affairs* 9, no. Spring (1998): 183–203.

Polasky, Janet L. *Revolutions without Borders: The Call to Liberty in the Atlantic World*. New Haven, CT: Yale University Press, 2015.

Portugal e o mundo nos séculos XVI e XVII: encompassing the globe (Lisbon: Instituto dos Museus e da Conservação, 2009)

Postma, Johannes. *The Dutch in the Atlantic Slave Trade*. New York: Cambridge University Press, 1990.

Pouwels, Randall Lee. *Horn and Crescent: Cultural Change and Traditional Islam on the East African Coast, 800-1900*. New York: Cambridge University Press, 1987.

Premo, Bianca. "Before the Law: Women's Petitions in the Eighteenth-Century Spanish Empire." *Comparative Studies in Society and History* 53, no. 2 (2011): 261–89.

Prestholdt, Jeremy. *Domesticating the World: African Consumerism and the Genealogies of Globalization*. Berkeley: University of California Press, 2008.

306   Bibliography

Raman, Bhavani. *Document Raj: Writing and Scribes in Early Colonial South India.* Chicago, IL: University of Chicago Press, 2012.

"The Duplicity of Paper: Counterfeit, Discretion, and Bureaucratic Authority in Early Colonial Madras." *Comparative Studies in Society & History* 54, no. 2 (2012): 229–50.

Raminelli, Ronald. "Impedimentos da cor: Mulatos no Brasil e em Portugal c. 1640-1750." *Varia Historia* 28, no. 48 (2012): 699–723.

Rau, Virgínia, and José Manuel Garcia. *Sesmarias medievais portuguesas.* Lisboa: Editorial Presença, 1982.

Ray, Carina E. *Crossing the Color Line: Race, Sex, and the Contested Politics of Colonialism in Ghana.* Athens: Ohio University Press, 2015.

Reese, Ty M. "Wives, Brokers, and Laborers: Women at Cape Coast, 1750-1807." In *Women in Port: Gendering Communities, Economies, and Social Networks in Atlantic Port Cities, 1500-1800*, edited by Douglas Catterall and Jody Campbell, 291–314. Leiden: Brill, 2012.

Reginaldo, Lucilene. "'África em Portugal': Devoções, irmandades e escravidão no Reino de Portugal, século XVIII." *História (São Paulo)* 28, no. 1 (2009): 289–319.

"André do Couto Goudinho: Homem preto, formado em Coimbra, missionário no Congo em fins do século XVIII." *Revista História* 173 (2015): 141–74.

"'Não tem informação': Mulatos, pardos e pretos na Universidade de Coimbra (1700-1771)." *Estudos Ibero-Americanos* 44, no. 3 (2018): 421–34.

Os Rosários dos Angolas: Irmandades de africanos e crioulos na Bahia setecentista. São Paulo, SP: Alameda, 2011.

Richardson, David. "Consuming Goods, Consuming People. Reflections on the Transatlantic Slave Trade." In *The Rise and Demise of Slavery and the Slave Trade in the Atlantic World*, edited by Philip Misevich and Kristin Mann, 32–63. Rochester, NY: University of Rochester Press, 2016.

"West African Consumption Patterns and Their Influence on the Eighteenth-Century English Slave Trade." In *Uncommon Market: Essays in the Economic History of the Atlantic Slave Trade*, edited by Henry A. Gemery and Jan S. Hogendorn, 303–30. New York: Academic Press, 1979.

Roberts, Richard L. *Litigants and Households: African Disputes and Colonial Courts in the French Soudan, 1895-1912.* Portsmouth, NH: Heinemann, 2005.

"The End of Slavery, Colonial Courts, and Social Conflict in Gumbu, 1908-1911," *Canadian Journal of African Studies* 34, no. 3 (2000): 684–713;

Roberston, Claire C. "We Must Overcome: Genealogy and Evolution of Female Slavery in West Africa." *Journal of West African History* 1, no. 1 (2015): 59–92.

Robertson, Claire C., and Iris Berger. *Women and Class in Africa.* New York: Africana, 1986.

Rockel, Stephen J. "Slavery and Freedom in Nineteenth Century East Africa: The Case of Waungwana Caravan Porters." *African Studies* 68, no. 1 (2009): 87–109.

Rodet, Marie. "Escaping Slavery and Building Diasporic Communities in French Soudan and Senegal, ca. 1880-1940." *International Journal of African Historical Studies* 48, no. 2 (2015): 363–86.

Rodney, Walter. *How Europe Underdeveloped Africa*. Cape Town: Pambazuka Press, 2012.

Rodrigues, Eugénia. "Women, Land, and Power in the Zambezi Valley of the Eighteenth Century." *African Economic History* 43, no. 1 (2015): 19–56.

Portugueses e africanos nos Rios de Sena. Os prazos da coroa em Moçambique nos séculos XVII e XVIII. Lisbon: Imprensa Nacional-Casa da Moeda, 2014.

"As donas de prazos do Zambeze. Políticas imperiais e estratégias locais." In *VI Jornadas Setecentistas: conferências e comunicações*, edited by Magnus Pereira and Nadalin, 15–34. Curitiba: Aos Quatro Ventos, 2006.

"Chiponda, a Senhora que tudo pisa com os pés. Estratégias de poder das donas dos prazos do Zambeze no século XVIII." *Anais de História de Além-Mar* I (2000): 101–32.

Rodrigues, Manuel. *Os Baldios*. Lisbon: Caminho, 1987.

Rose, Carol M. *Property and Persuasion: Essays on the History, Theory, and Rhetoric of Ownership*. New Perspectives on Law, Culture, and Society. Boulder, CO: Westview Press, 1994.

Rossi, Benedetta. "Without History? Interrogating 'Slave' Memories in Ader (Niger)." edited by Alice Bellagamba, Sandra E. Greene, and Martin A. Klein, 536–54. New York: Cambridge University Press, 2013.

"Slavery and Migration: Social and Physical Mobility in Ader (Niger)." In *Reconfiguring Slavery: West African Trajectories*, edited by Benedetta Rossi, 182–206. Liverpool: Liverpool University Press, 2009.

Russell-Wood, A. J. R. "Iberian Expansion and the Issue of Black Slavery: Changing Portuguese Attitudes, 1440-1770." *The American Historical Review* 83, no. 1 (1978): 16–42.

Sá, Ana Lúcia. "The Concept of 'Land' in Bioko: 'Land as Property' and 'Land as Country.'" In *Doing Conceptual History in Africa*, edited by Axel Fleisch and Rhiannon Stephens, 138–61. New York: Berghahn, 2016.

Sackeyfio-Lenoch, Naaborko. *The Politics of Chieftaincy. Authority and Property in Colonial Ghana, 1920-1950*. Rochester, NY: University of Rochester Press, 2014.

Saho, Bala. *Contours of Change: Muslim Courts, Women, and Islamic Society in Colonial Bathurst, the Gambia, 1900-1965*. Lansing: Michigan State University Press, 2018.

Salau, Mohammed Bashir. *The West African Slave Plantation: A Case Study*. New York: Palgrave Macmillan, 2011.

Salas, Esteban Alfaro. "Women and Food Production. Agriculture, Demography & Access to Land in Late Eighteenth-Century Catumbela." In *African Women in the Atlantic World: Property, Vulnerability and Mobility, 1660-1880*, edited by Mariana P. Candido and Adam Jones, 55–69. Woodbridge: James Currey, 2019.

Sampaio, Gabriela dos Reis, Lisa Earl Castillo, and Wlamyra Ribeiro de Albuquerque. *Barganhas e querelas da escravidão: tráfico, alforria e liberdade (séculos XVIII e XIX)*. Salvador: Edufba, Editora da Universidade Federal da Bahia, 2014.

Santos, Maria Emília. *Nos caminhos de África: serventia e posse. Angola, século XIX*. Lisbon: Ministério da Ciência e da Tecnologia/ Instituto de Investigação

Científica Tropical/ Centro de Estudos de História e Cartografia Antiga, 1998.

Santos, Eduardo dos. *Regime de terras no ex-Ultramar Português: Evolução da política legislativa até 1945*. Lisbon: Universidade Técnica de Lisboa/ Centro de Estudos Africanos, 2004.

Santos, Vanicléia Silva, ed. *O comércio de marfim no mundo Atlântico: Circulação e produção (séculos XV a XIX)*. Belo Horizonte: Prisma, 2017.

Sarr, Assan. *Islam, Power, and Dependency in the Gambia River Basin: The Politics of Land Control, 1790-1940*. Rochester: University of Rochester Press, 2016.

"Land, Power, and Dependency along the Gambia River, Late Eighteenth to Early Nineteenth Centuries." *African Studies Review* 57, no. 03 (2014): 101–21.

Saunders, A. C. de C. M. *A Social History of Black Slaves and Freedmen in Portugal, 1441-1555*. Cambridge: Cambridge University Press, 1982.

Schenck, Marcia and Mariana P. Candido. "Uncomfortable Pasts: Talking About Slavery in Angola." In *African Heritage and Memories of Slavery in Brazil and the South Atlantic World*, edited by Ana Lucia Araujo, 213–52. Amherst, NY: Cambria Press, 2015.

Schwarz, Suzanne "The Impact of Liberated African 'Disposal' Policies in Early Nineteenth-Century Sierra Leone." In *Liberated Africans and the Abolition of the Slave Trade, 1807-1896*, edited by Richard Anderson and Henry B. Lovejoy, 45–65. Melton: Boydell & Brewer, 2020.

"Adaptation in the Aftermath of Slavery. Women, Trade, and Property in Sierra Leone, c. 1790-1812." In *African Women in the Atlantic World: Property, Vulnerability and Mobility, 1660-1880*, edited by Mariana P. Candido and Adam Jones, 19–37. Woodbridge: James Currey, 2019.

"'A Just and Honorable Commerce.' Abolitionist Experimentation in Sierra Leone in the Late Eighteenth and Early Nineteenth Centuries." *African Economic History* 45, no. 1 (2017): 1–45.

"Reconstructing the Life Histories of Liberated Africans: Sierra Leone in the Early Nineteenth Century." *History in Africa* 39 (2012): 175–207.

Scott, James C. *Seeing like a State: How Certain Schemes to Improve the Human Condition Have Failed*. New Haven, CT: Yale University Press, 2005.

Scott, James C., John Tehranian, and Jeremy Mathias. "The Production of Legal Identities Proper to States: The Case of the Permanent Family Surname." *Comparative Studies in Society and History* 44, no. 01 (2002): 4–44.

Scott, Rebecca J. *Slave Emancipation in Cuba the Transition to Free Labor, 1860-1899*. Pittsburgh, PA: University of Pittsburgh Press, 2000.

Scott, Rebecca J. and Jean M. Hébrard. *Freedom Papers: An Atlantic Odyssey in the Age of Emancipation*. Cambridge: Harvard University Press, 2012.

Scott, Rebecca J., and Michael Zeuske. "Property in Writing, Property on the Ground: Pigs, Horses, Land, and Citizenship in the Aftermath of Slavery, Cuba, 1880-1909." *Comparative Studies in Society and History* 44, no. 4 (2002): 669–99.

Scully, Pamela. "Rape, Race, and Colonial Culture: The Sexual Politics of Identity in the Nineteenth-Century Cape Colony, South Africa." *The American Historical Review* 100, no. 2 (1995): 335–59.

"Malintzin, Pocahontas, and Krotoa: Indigenous Women and Myth Models of the Atlantic World." *Journal of Colonialism and Colonial History* 6, no. 3 (2005) doi:10.1353/cch.2006.0022.

Scully, Pamela and Diana Paton, eds. "Introduction: Gender and Slave Emancipation in Comparative Perspective." In *Gender and Slave Emancipation in the Atlantic World*, 1–33. Durham, NC: Duke University Press, 2005.

Sebestyén, Éve. "Legitimation through Landcharters in Ambundo Villages, Angola,." *Perspektiven Afrikanistischer Forschung*, 1994, 363–78.

Seibert, Gerhard. "Sugar, Cocoa, and Oil. Economic Sucess and Failure in São Tomé and Príncipe from the Sixteenth to the Twenty-First Centuries." In *African Islands: Leading Edges of Empire and Globalization*, edited by Toyin Falola, R. Joseph Parrott, and Danielle Porter Sanchez, 68–95. Rochester: University of Rochester Press, 2019.

"Colonialismo em São Tomé e Príncipe: Hierarquização, classificação e segregação da vida social." *Anuário Antropológico* 2 (2015): 99–120.

Seixas, Margarida. "Escravos e libertos no Boletim Oficial de Angola (1845-1875)." *E-Revista de Estudos Interculturais do CEI* 3 (2015).

Semley, Lorelle. "Writing the History of the Trans-African Woman in the Revolutionary French Atlantic." In *African Women in the Atlantic World. Property, Vulnerability and Mobility, 1680-1880*, edited by Mariana P. Candido and Adam Jones, 191–215. Woodbridge: James Currey, 2019.

To Be Free and French: Citizenship in France's Atlantic Empire. Cambridge: Cambridge University Press, 2017.

Serrão, José Vicente. "Property, Land and Territory in the Making of Overseas Empires." In *Property Rights, Land and Territory in the European Overseas Empires*, edited by José Vicente Serrão, Bárbara Direito, Eugénia Rodrigues, and Susana Münch Miranda, 7–17. Lisbon: CEHC-IUL, 2014. http://hdl .handle.net/10071/2718.

Silva, Filipa Ribeiro da. "Private Business in the Angolan Trade, 1590s-1780s." edited by David Richardson and Filipa Ribeiro da Silva, 71–101. Leiden: Brill, 2015.

Soares, Mariza de Carvalho. "'Por conto e peso': o comércio de marfim no Congo e Loango, séculos XV–XVII." *Anais do Museu Paulista: História e Cultura Material* 25, no. 1 (2017): 59–86.

People of Faith: Slavery and African Catholics in Eighteenth-Century Rio de Janeiro. Durham, NC: Duke University Press Books, 2011.

Sommerdyk, Stacey. "Rivalry on the Loango Coast: A Re-Examination of the Dutch in the Atlantic Slave Trade." In *Trabalho Forçado Africano. O Caminho de Ida.*, edited by Arlindo Manuel Caldeira, 105–18. Porto: CEAUP, 2009.

Sousa Santos, Boaventura de. *Epistemologies of the South: Justice Against Epistemicide*. London: Routledge, 2014.

O direito dos oprimidos. Lisbon: Almedina, 2014.

Sparks, Randy J. *Where the Negroes Are Masters: An African Port in the Era of the Slave Trade*. Cumberland, RI: Harvard University Press, 2014.

The Two Princes of Calabar: An Eighteenth-Century Atlantic Odyssey. Cambridge, MA: Harvard University Press, 2004.

Sperling, Jutta. "Women's Property Rights in Portugal under Dom João I (1385-1433): A Comparison with Renaissance Italy." *Portuguese Studies Review* 13, no. 1–2 (2005): 27–59.

Spicksley, Judith. "Contested Enslavement: The Portuguese in Angola and the Problem of Debt, c. 1600–1800." *Itinerario* 39, no. 2 (2015): 247–75.

Staller, Jared. *Converging on Cannibals: Terrors of Slaving in Atlantic Africa, 1509-1670.* Athens: Ohio University Press, 2019.

Stephens, Rhiannon. "'Wealth', 'Poverty' and the Question of Conceptual History in Oral Contexts: Uganda from c.1000 CE." In *Doing Conceptual History in Africa*, edited by Axel Fleisch and Rhiannon Stephens, 21–48. New York: Berghahn, 2016.

Stilwell, Sean Arnold. *Paradoxes of Power: The Kano "Mamluks" and Male Royal Slavery in the Sokoto Caliphate, 1804-1903.* Portsmouth, NH: Heinemann, 2004.

Stockreiter, Elke. *Islamic Law, Gender, and Social Change in Post-Abolition Zanzibar.* New York: Cambridge University Press, 2015.

Stoler, Ann Laura. "Colonial Archives and the Arts of Governance." *Archival Science* 2 (2002): 87–109.

"'In Cold Blood': Hierarchies of Credibility and the Politics of Colonial Narratives." *Representations*, 37 (1992): 151–89.

Tamale, Sylvia. "Researching and Theorising Sexualities in Africa." In *African Sexualities: A Reader*, edited by Sylvia Tamale, 11–35. Cape Town: Pambazuka Press, 2011.

Tavares, Ana Paula and Catarina Madeira Santos. "Fontes escritas africanas para a história de Angola." In *Africae Monumenta. A apropriação da escrita pelos africanos*, 1:471–509. Lisbon: Instituto de Investigação Científica Tropical, 2002.

Tavares, Ana Paula and Catarina Madeira Santos, eds. *Africæ Monumenta: Arquivo Caculo Cacahenda.* Lisbon: Instituto de Investigação Científica Tropical, 2002.

Thompson, E. P. *The Making of the English Working Class.* New York: Pantheon Books, 1964.

Thornton, John K. *A History of West Central Africa to 1850.* New York: Cambridge University Press. 2020.

Thornton, John. *A Cultural History of the Atlantic World, 1250-1820.* New York: Cambridge University Press, 2012.

"Cannibals, Witches, and Slave Traders in the Atlantic World." *The William and Mary Quarterly*, Third Series, 60, no. 2 (2003): 273–94.

Africa and Africans in the Making of the Atlantic World, 1400-1800. New York: Cambridge University Press, 1998.

"Precolonial African Industry and the Atlantic Trade, 1500-1800." *African Economic History* 19 (1990): 1–19.

"The Slave Trade in Eighteenth Century Angola: Effects on Demographic Structures." *Canadian Journal of African Studies* 14, no. 3 (1980): 417–27.

Trevor R. Getz. *Slavery and Reform in West Africa Toward Emancipation in Nineteenth-Century Senegal and the Gold Coast.* Western African Studies. Athens, OH: Ohio University Press, 2004.

Vansina, Jan. "Ambaca Society and the Slave Trade c. 1760-1845." *Journal of African History* 46, no. 1 (2005): 1–27.
How Societies Are Born: Governance in West Central Africa before 1600. Charlottesville: University of Virginia Press, 2004.
Paths in the Rainforests: Toward a History of Political Tradition in Equatorial Africa. Madison: University of Wisconsin Press, 1990.
"Memory and Oral Tradition." In *The African Past Speaks: Essays on Oral Tradition and History*, edited by Joseph Calder Miller, 262–79. Folkestone, Eng: Dawson, 1980.
"Long-Distance Trade-Routes in Central Africa." *The Journal of African History* 3, no. 03 (1962): 375–90.
Vaughan, Megan. Creating the Creole Island: Slavery in Eighteenth-Century *Mauritius*. Durham, NC: Duke University Press, 2005.
Verger, Pierre. *Fluxo e refluxo do tráfico de escravos entre o Golfo de Benin e a Bahia de Todos os Santos: dos séculos XVII a XIX.* Salvador: Corrupio, 2002.
Vos, Jelmer. "Coffee, Cash, and Consumption: Rethinking Commodity Production in the Global South." *Radical History Review*. 131 (2018): 183–88.
Kongo in the Age of Empire, 1860–1913: The Breakdown of a Moral Order. Madison: University of Wisconsin Press, 2015.
"Work in Times of Slavery, Colonialism, and Civil War: Labor Relations in Angola from 1800 to 2000." *History in Africa* 41, no. 1 (2014): 363–85.
"Child Slaves and Freemen at the Spiritan Mission in Soyo, 1880-1885." *Journal of Family History* 35, no. 1 (2010): 71–90.
Weber, Max. *The Theory of Social and Economic Organization.* New York: Oxford University Press, 1947
Wheat, David. *Atlantic Africa and the Spanish Caribbean, 1570-1640.* Chapell Hill: University of North Carolina Press, 2016.
"Garcia Mendes Castelo Branco, Fidalgo de Angola y mercaders de esclavos en Veracruz y el Caribe a principios del siglo XVII." In *Debates Históricos Contemporáneos: Africanos y Afrodescendientes en México y Centroamérica*, edited by María Elisa Velázquez, 85–107. Mexico City: INAH, 2011.
Wissenbach, Maria Cristina Cortez. "As feitorias de urzela e o tráfico de escravos: Georg Tams, José Ribeiro dos Santos e os negócios da África Centro-Ocidental na década de 1840." *Afro-Ásia*. 43 (2011): 43–90.
Wright, Marcia. "Women in Peril: A Commentary on the Life Stories of Captives in Nineteenth Century East-Central Africa," *African Social Research* 20 (1975): 800–19
Yannakakis, Yanna. *The Art of Being In-between: Native Intermediaries, Indian Identity, and Local Rule in Colonial Oaxaca.* Durham: Duke University Press, 2008
Zeleza, Paul Tiyambe. *The Study of Africa.* Dakar, Senegal: CODESRIA, 2006.

Unpublished Dissertations:

Alveal, Carmen Margarida Oliveira. "Converting Land into Property in the Portuguese Atlantic World, Sixteenth to Eighteenth Century." Ph.D., Johns Hopkins University, 2008.

Alves, Rogéria Cristina. "No Rastro do Marfim: A circulação do marfim in natura entre Luanda, Benguela, Brasil e Lisboa (1723-1808)." Ph.D., Universidade Federal de Minas Gerais, 2021.

Dias Paes, Mariana Armond. "Escravos e terras entre posses e títulos: A construção social do direito de propriedade no Brasil (1835-1889)." Ph.D., Universidade de São Paulo, 2018.

Figueiredo, João de Castro Maia Veiga de. "Política, escravatura e feitiçaria em Angola (séculos XVIII e XIX)." Ph.D., Universidade de Coimbra, 2015.

Gonçalves, Ivan Sicca. "Comércio, política e trabalho nos Sertões de Angola: sertanejos e centro-africanos nas páginas de António da Silva Porto (1840-1869)." M.A., Unicamp, 2021.

Grassi, Aharon. "Provisional Reconstructions: Geo-Histories of Infrastructure and Agrarian Configuration in Malanje, Angola". Ph.D., University of California, Berkeley, 2015.

Heywood, Linda. "Production, Trade and Power. The Political Economy of Central Angola, 1850-1930." Ph.D., Columbia University, 1984.

Mastrobueno, Luisa. "Ovimbundu Women and Coercive Labour Systems, 1850-1940: From Still Life to Moving Picture." M.A., University of Toronto, 1992.

Neto, Maria da Conceição. "In Town and out of Town: A Social History of Huambo (Angola), 1902-1961." Ph.D., SOAS, University of London, 2012.

Olympia Perry Vidal Pereira Bastos. "A colonização portuguesa no planalto de Benguela." Tese apresentada ao concurso de admissão, Escola Normal Superior, 1920.

Pimenta Pires, Carlos Manoel. "A educação dos neocolonizadores: a Escola Colonial e a investigação no ultramar no Império Português (séculos XIX e XX)." Ph.D., Universidade de Lisboa. Instituto de Educação, 2016.

Salas, Esteban Alfaro. "Making Portuguese Colonial Governance: Slavery, Forced Labor, and Racial Ideology in the Interior of Benguela, 1760–1860." Ph.D., University of Notre Dame, 2021.

Santos, Telma Gonçalves. "Comércio de tecidos europeus e asiáticos na África centro-ocidental: Fraudes e contrabandos no terceiro quartel do século XVIII." M.A. Universidade de Lisboa, 2014.

Index

African Studies Series

For EU product safety concerns, contact us at Calle de José Abascal, 56–1°,
28003 Madrid, Spain or eugpsr@cambridge.org.

www.ingramcontent.com/pod-product-compliance
Ingram Content Group UK Ltd.
Pitfield, Milton Keynes, MK11 3LW, UK
UKHW020400140625
459647UK00020B/2574